American Notes

American Notes

Selected Essays

DANIEL AARON

Northeastern
University Press
Boston

Library of Congress Cataloging-in-Publication Data
Aaron, Daniel, 1912–
American notes : selected essays / Daniel Aaron.
p.   cm.
Includes bibliographical references and index.
ISBN 1-55553-195-4 (alk. paper)
1. American literature—History and criticism.   2. United
States—Civilization.   I. Title
PS121.A23   1994
810.9—dc20   94-4526

Designed by Virginia Evans

Composed in Berkeley by Coghill Composition, Richmond,
Virginia. Printed and bound by Thomson-Shore, Inc., Dexter, Michigan.
The paper is Glatfelter Supple Opaque Recycled, an acid-free sheet.

MANUFACTURED IN THE UNITED STATES OF AMERICA
99 98 97 96 95 94   5 4 3 2 1

To Janet

If Heaven should find it useful or necessary to produce a new edition of me and my life I would like to
make a few not superfluous suggestions for this new
edition chiefly concerning the design of the frontis-
piece and the way the work is laid out.

G. F. LICHTENBERG

CONTENTS

V History and Fiction

Epilogue

INTRODUCTION

The articles and essays that compose *American Notes* were written over the past half-century. Their arrangement is topical rather than chronological, but I have tried to keep readers on the historical track and to personalize the teller and his times with interpolated asides, explanations, notes, and reminiscences.

I present myself chiefly as an observer and reporter, something of a social historian and literary critic and academic scholar and journalist. And although I have lived through strenuous decades in the USA and abroad and known or seen or barely missed meeting prominent persons,* I have been mostly a spectator looking in from the outside, comfortable in my marginality and unsystematically incorporating what I have seen, heard, and read. (See the section "Feeding on Books" on pp. xxix–xxx.)

Rather than consecrating myself to a single lifetime project, I have hopped from subject to subject and accepted assignments without quite knowing where they would take me. Yet I think anyone who had the time and patience to sift through my published and unpublished writing would discern a prevailing angle of vision or intellectual disposition or style of expression. Since I am the first and probably the last to conduct such an investigation, I offer my own analysis of the glue that binds the disparate entries of *American Notes*.

---

*On my ninth birthday, I saw Tom Mix "plain." He wasn't riding his famous horse, Tony. He was driving a slinky Locomobile, and he waved his white sombrero at me. In 1929, I almost met Herbert Hoover. The senator from Illinois said to my uncle as we stood in the lobby of the Mayflower Hotel, "Charlie, if you'd told me your nephew was coming to Washington, he could have shaken hands with the president." In 1938, at the end of the final examination of English 7 (I was a teaching assistant at Harvard College), John F. Kennedy rather loftily, I thought, slapped his blue book on my desk and passed into the future. (I marked his paper B, a rather respectable grade in those days.) In the early 1950s, carrying a letter of introduction from his niece, I called on Palmiro Togliatti at the headquarters of the Communist Party in Rome. A surly unshaven doorman told me that Comrade T had just taken off for Egypt. I spent election evening, 1948, with Norman Thomas in Easthampton, Massachusetts. (He said he was glad Dewey had lost.) I had my picture taken with Adlai Stevenson right in front of my house. Once I played horseshoes with Admiral Nimitz. And so it goes. (*American Heritage*, 40 [December 1989], 76.)

This book is mostly about Americans who wrote novels, poems, biographies, and autobiographies, who set themselves up as cultural arbiters, who took part in both shooting and ideological wars. Until my twentieth year, the America they described and objectified had little meaning for me. More compelling by far were foreign places and foreign faces, the imaginative realm of my own construction, literary England, and the "Europe" evoked by James Gibbons Huneker. Huneker, Mencken's mentor, had long been out of fashion when I first read him in 1929, my freshman year at the University of Michigan, and became his acolyte. His enthusiasm for what he called the "soul wreckers" infected me. I stuccoed my secret journal with quotations from Schopenhauer, Leopardi, Strindberg, Huysmans, Nietzsche, and Dostoevsky.

Still self-cocooned, I graduated in 1933, the pit of the Great Depression, and applied for a job on the Chicago News Bureau, then said to be the best training school for aspiring reporters; but with more than four hundred better-qualified applicants already on the waiting list, nothing came of it. An alternative was graduate school. That fall Harvard University accepted me as a doctoral candidate in the department of English.

Three years later I switched from what seemed to me then a remote and rarefied area of learning to a newly established interdepartmental program in "American Civilization." No doubt the shock of the Depression at home and the confident strides of fascism and Communism in Europe had something to do with this shift. Whatever the reason, I welcomed the chance to ransack the past in search of clues to "the situation of our time" that according to Auden's *The Double Man* surrounded us "like a baffling crime." The Harvard program pointed in the direction I wanted to go. It plotted the course for a coordinated study of American history and literature, of American religion, education, and political thought. It quickened my spirit of social mission and gave me, son of recent immigrants (and thereby in the eyes of many an "outsider"), a proprietary feeling toward my country and its institutions. It ballasted me with facts and made me, if not immune, at least resistant to windy doctrines.

During my Los Angeles childhood and Chicago adolescence, I had fitted into my local brier patch as naturally as Brer Rabbit did into his. I remember thinking, "You are Daniel Aaron, a character in the neighborhood." That sense of belonging lessened in college and graduate school, where my name stamped me as "one of them."[1] Neither then nor later did I feel shut out of any company I yearned to cultivate, but being a Jew probably affected my sensitiveness to social issues. I suspect I listened to the trans-Atlantic broadcasts of Hitler and the radio harangues of Father Coughlin less impersonally than did many of my non-Jewish friends. Nor is it accidental that so much of my writing is about rebels, reformers, and dissenters, or that I found Thorstein Veblen so congenial. I could identify with the "renegade Jew" he describes in one of his essays, "a disturber of the peace," a "wanderer in the intellectual no-man's land," one of the "aliens of the uneasy feet." I could applaud his irreverent commentary on American business enterprise.[2]

The American Studies movement got started in the late 1930s, not without the strong reservations of traditionalists who thought it diffuse and sentimental, or chauvinistic and grandiose in its expectations, or simply "unsound." For those of us enrolled in the new program, however, the prospect of cutting through the barbed wire of departmental prerequisites and fixed boundaries and of exploring American culture on a broad scale was seductive. Candidates for the American Civilization degree, as it was called at Harvard, enjoyed a licensed "extra-vagance." We had no assigned advisers to report to. If no courses existed in our chosen fields of concentration, we were expected to work up the materials ourselves.

Eventually, there were calls to rationalize the program, to buttress it with a "methodology," but at the outset, content with the latitude it promised and undaunted by its hard requirements,[3] we saw no urgent need to do so. Nor did we anticipate the day when American Studies would splinter into factions, each with its theorists, journals, newsletters, and star articulators. Everything we studied and wrote about could be classified under the conveniently vague rubric "the American experience."

ii

Harvard in the 1930s, a political decade if there ever was one, might be described as a not-so-still point in the churning world. I have written elsewhere (see the section "Cambridge in the Thirties" on pp. xxxi–xxxiv) on the Cambridge scene—the electricity produced by clashing ideological factions and my ambivalent response to the Communist Party. A journal entry of 1937 spells out my dissatisfaction with its leaders two years before the signing of the Nazi-Soviet nonaggression pact. Describing them as maladroit, priggish, and rigidly dogmatic, I sketched tentatively my political and social model. It would be America-centered, at once ethical and pragmatic, disciplined and free. It would fuse the discrete and often mutually repellent strains in American political thought. How I intended to amalgamate and reconcile the Puritan concept of stewardship, Franklin's civic spirit, Tom Paine's anticlericalism, the conservatism of Madison, Tocqueville, and James Fenimore Cooper, the social theories of communitarian experimenters, Thoreau's principled anarchism, Whitman's universalism, industrial unionism, and Vernon L. Parrington's progressivism I have no idea.

This eclectic approach to the American past suggests, if nothing else, more than a hint of my future self: an inclination to register emotional perturbations through political symbols, a readiness to entertain incompatible ideas, an often indiscriminate curiosity, and a greed for facts. I like to think that the last three attributes may have helped me to write about people and events without inordinate bias.

At Harvard I read the sermons of seventeenth- and eighteenth-century New England divines and under the tutelage of Perry Miller and Kenneth Murdock corrected my simplistic notions of the Puritan mind. To relish simultaneously, as I did, the indecorous E. E. Cummings and Nathanael West and the pungent diatribes of colonial preachers didn't strike me as incongruous. The times demanded both secular scoffing and sacred rage. Puritan denunciations of the "sordidly covetous" devoid of "Public Spirit" applied equally well to President Roosevelt's "malefactors of great wealth," no less negligent of their obligations of "Stewardship." Although unmoved by Jonathan Edwards's grand doctrine of Original Sin, I could still acknowledge "the labyrinthine deceits of the human heart" and feel, if not the charm, at least the force of the hard-featured Puritan ethic.[4] I swore by Melville, not so much the satirist of evangelical missionaries I had written about in an early article,[5] but the author who spoke of the wisdom that is woe.

iii

In the summer of 1936, Professor Howard Mumford Jones suggested a topic for my doctoral dissertation: a cultural history of the Ohio Valley in the 1830s and 1840s. It would necessarily touch on, he advised me, "the coming in of schools and lyceums, of architecture and painting, of the introduction of religion and politics in that region." Professor Jones enjoyed tackling surveys of this kind, whereas I was on the lookout for a tighter and less amorphous subject.[6] Hence, I decided to focus on antebellum Cincinnati, Ohio, a city that embodied the flux and flow of the Great Valley in microcosm. Deep in Tocqueville's *Democracy in America*, my bible for the preceding several years, it occurred to me that the values and assumptions of the Cincinnatians might be used to test not only his generalizations about the American character but also Frederick Jackson Turner's "frontier thesis," then under the close scrutiny of historians impatient with its myths and its overemphasis on American individualism.

Political considerations probably account for my historical squint when I began my investigations and concocted the prematurely "new historicist" design of my thesis. It was accepted without enthusiasm by my faculty readers, one of whom, I'm sure, regarded it as an object lesson of what can happen when disciplinary frontiers are willfully breached. For the next half-century, according to the urban historian, Carl Abbott, it remained "a sort of interlibrary loan classic for specialists in the history of American cities." It was published in 1992 after a long residence in the deposit stacks of the Harvard University Library.[7]

iv

Reading one's early writing can be a strain, especially if the reader is embarrassed by his junior self. What strikes me most about the Cincinnati dissertation and the reviews and short pieces I wrote in the mid-thirties and in the next decade is their confident and authoritative air and their moral earnestness. A glow of partisan conviction shines through a good many of them, be they about comparative revolutions, American graphic art, Southern politicians,

Yankee missionaries, Thorstein Veblen, Herman Melville, or Ayn Rand. My opinions aren't wildly heterodox, but neither are they paralyzed by qualification.

In time, for both good and ill, I grew more attentive to the reader over my shoulder and the critical eyes of my peers. A little knowledge is a dangerous thing, but so, although less demonstrably, is the caution that comes with its acquisition. "I love the acquaintances of young people," Dr. Johnson once remarked. "I love the young dogs of this age: they have more wit and humour and knowledge of life than we had; but then the dogs are not so good scholars." I think my scholarship got sounder as I aged, but in the 1940s its demands impressed me less than getting published in magazines of opinion and adding my yawp to the resounding voices of the day. To see my name in the contributors' list of the *New Republic*, *Partisan Review*, the *Antioch Review*, and *Tomorrow* gave me a lot of satisfaction, partly out of vanity, partly too, because appearing in their columns allowed me to snipe at American business and business culture.

Just when I began to formulate stereotypical images of "Business" I can't recall. The collapse in 1929 of what the historian Charles Beard called the myth of rugged American individualism had touched off a derisive reaction against the celebrators of triumphant capitalism. I went through the Depression comparatively unscathed, but it opened my mind to the subversive irony of Veblen and to works that dwelled on the deplorable social consequences of untrammeled business enterprise. To one whose professed concerns were chiefly moral and aesthetic, Big Business in most of its economic, political, and cultural incarnations signified everything hostile to justice and equality in American life: financial spoilsmen, accumulators of immense fortunes, union-busting corporations, company police and espionage, press lords like Hearst and Robert McCormick, Roosevelt haters, the Roman Catholic hierarchy, and all the creatures and clients of the Establishment. Against these enemies, I shot unlethal arrows in the hope of damaging their authority.[8]

Looking back to the years between 1940 and the mid-Fifties, it's plain to see how unfocused I was, how unstructured and unprofessional, which is another way of saying that I saw no need to stake out a piece of turf in a conventionally defined "field" of study. My territory encompassed the USA in all its historical, literary, and cultural manifestations. A hopeful seeker for the Good Society, I was alert to the signs of social and intellectual disorder and fascinated by writers who concealed cheerless messages in harshly comic wrappings.

There were ample reasons, God knows, to question the beneficent tendency of history. Reports of far-flung atrocities confirmed the dark insights of Kierkegaard and Kafka, the ironies of George Orwell and Reinhold Niebuhr—writers very much in vogue. They fired intense conversations and no doubt affected my perspective on the times; but I can't honestly claim to have been profoundly shaken by their revelations. I remember wondering later why tweedy young men who had suffered nothing more dire than the whooping cough had earned the right to discourse on "the tragic sense" and to brood over the social implications of Original Sin. Such phrases came trippingly off my tongue, thanks in part to seminars with Perry Miller and F. O. Matthiessen and an early immersion in the works of Melville, the first major American author I studied in depth. Yet for all my flirtations with the Power of Blackness, I was never a Manichean, never saw America as Tartarus or a poisoned garden, and never believed the blighted world was irredeemably evil. My response to the Puritan drama of damnation and salvation (with Jonathan Edwards principally in mind) was aesthetic, not doctrinal.

Most telling for me, a firm nonbeliever, were his opinions of religious revivals expressed in "Treatise Concerning Religious Affections." Here Edwards, while not condoning the excesses of religious frenzy that accompanied the Great Awakening, reaffirmed his faith in the religion of the heart. Passion without light ignited destructive conflagrations, yet "where there is a kind of light without heat," Edwards wrote, "a head stored with notions and speculations, with a cold and unaffected heart, there can be nothing divine in that light."[9] To this passage I gave a secular application.

v

These reflections on Edwards were in keeping with my earlier disavowal of Vernon L. Parrington's reductive anti-Puritanism and indeed of his arbitrary separation of American writers into good Jeffersonian sheep and bad Hamiltonian goats. While subscribing wholeheartedly to his political philosophy and contextualizing of literature, I ignored his mechanical dichotomies when it came to American writing and paid more attention to the social undertones of language and style. Matthiessen's complex treatment of culture and society was more to my liking than Parrington's simplifications, and I said so in a prim and rather tentative review of his *American Renaissance* (1941)[10]—one that warrants an autobiographical flashback.

While Matthiessen was at work on *American Renaissance*, Henry Nash Smith and I furiously prepared for our oral exams. As the guinea pigs of Harvard's new American Civilization Program, we spent two intense years, largely on our own, in search of ways to link American history in all its phases with American literary expression. The scope of our reading is partially conveyed in a historiographical essay we wrote at this time. Among other things, it mentioned "a wide range of materials that historians of an earlier day had neglected" and stressed the importance of F. J. Turner and Charles A. Beard in shifting the focus in American history from "the rivalries of heroic statesmen" to the study of "sectional tensions and class struggles." It also singled out Parrington's "great influence on literary studies during the past decades" and approvingly noted the "recent tendency in American literary studies to abandon an excessively esthetic emphasis in order to consider American writers in terms of the social environment in which they moved."[11]

But even as we hailed this "tendency," Matthiessen's lectures were demonstrating to us that close textual analysis of a poem or novel, the explication of a word or symbol, might also enhance the historical import of a literary work. To us, Matthiessen was something of an anomaly. An admirer of T. S. Eliot, a Christian, a man of the Left (only his conviction of Original Sin, he once told me, kept him from joining the Communist Party), he felt less at ease with Parrington, I suspect, than did his Harvard colleagues Howard M. Jones and Perry Miller. But he was a more sensitive reader than either and better able to explicate the art of writers like Poe or Hawthorne or Henry James who didn't fit comfortably in Parrington's procrustean bed.

In reviewing Matthiessen's book, I pointed out that his canonical five—Emerson, Thoreau, Hawthorne, Melville, and Whitman—wrote about banks, tariffs, and caucuses not so much as social critics and political theorists or Jeffersonians and Hamiltonians but as poets and moralists, which is to say emblematically. But I also noted how naturally his literary criticism passed into social and cultural criticism. *American Renaissance*, I said, was at once exemplary literary scholarship, a "profound reflection on 19th century American society," and a rebuke to blinkered historians who dismissed visionary romantics like Emerson as cloud-cuckoos and minimized the arts in the annals of their countrymen.

I was then deep in Emerson. I looked upon him as one of those minds (Montaigne, Lichtenberg, Johnson, Coleridge, Kenneth Burke are others) who have something arresting to say about anything they observe or think about or read. I liked his synthesizing of opposites—antinomian impulse and prudential reserve, trust and distrust of man in the aggregate, defiance of and dependence on the props of culture—and was puzzled and pleased by his contradictory messages. Far from complaining about his "artificial scholarship," as Whitman did, I found it nutritious and bracing, for he mostly wrote down what he could experientially endorse. For me Emerson was a festal rhetorician and poet, an artful quoter, a Yankee Ali Baba who unsealed caves and brought out treasures,* and spokesman for a company of men who, as he put it, "entertain a good hope."

VI

Men of Good Hope: A Story of American Progressives (1951) was an imperfect attempt to define and explicate an indigenous strain of American radical thought that, so I claimed, the liberal community had forgotten or disdained. Ostensibly a series of linked essays on nineteenth-century "prophetic agitators," the book was many things: a composite of a set of readings absorbed during an extended search for the "usable past," an exercise in the organic relation of social philosophy and literary style, and a brief for a liberal politics both pragmatic and visionary.

It won a hearing, but it might have done better had I dismantled the ideological apparatus that deflected attention from its substance

---

*Alfred Kazin and I spent the summer of 1957 reading Emerson out loud and combing his journals, essays, and letters for specimens of his incandescent prose. The outcome of that happy interlude was *Emerson: A Modern Anthology* (Boston: Houghton Mifflin, 1958), which I still think is one of the best introductions to his work. Assembling it gave us both much pleasure.

to its message, and written more detachedly about my hand-picked disturbers of the peace. Richard Hofstadter's *The American Political Tradition and the Men Who Made It* (1948), which I enthusiastically reviewed,[12] would have been an excellent model. I admired his ability to enclose the views of his ten great party leaders within a single political frame, and I approved of his implicit political slant. But I was impatient with him for not plainly declaring his political position. Where did he stand on party patronage, the dispensing of loaves and fishes? Did he think contemporary problems called for more radical policies than previous American politicians had subscribed to? Hofstadter had sensibly refrained from directly raising such questions. I was less wary, readier to commend the utopian quotient in the progressive tradition (which I believed had mitigated the harshness of laissez-faire capitalism) at precisely the moment when it was being firmly rejected by the advocates of a no-nonsense, tough-minded "new" liberalism.

To complicate matters, I half agreed with their indictment. One had only to recall the moral and intellectual bankruptcy of the American Communist Party, the disintegration of Henry Wallace's Progressive Party, and, indeed, the fiascos of more innocent social movements that failed to reckon with political realities and a perverse humanity. "Unlike more austere and pessimistic faiths," I conceded, progressivism "was peculiarly susceptible to the insipid and the sentimental." Yet I wasn't prepared to junk it because some of its leaders failed to comprehend the irrational and the brutish. "Vision must constantly outshoot technique," Randolph Bourne wrote, and I concurred, but I also strived to correct the caricature, sinister or ridiculous, of the visionary.[13]

How to account, after more than forty years, for the unresolved paradoxes and conflicts of *Men of Good Hope*? I think it's the only book I ever wrote not instigated by someone else. What really moved me to write it? My forays against Big Business had abated. Now I was trying to make the case for the Middle Way and its enlightened middle-class promulgators (an indication of how far I had traveled from the bourgeoisie-baiting days of the Thirties) who had written powerfully and wittily on capitalist enterprise.

I don't remember how I chose my cast of characters. I do know I didn't intend to write a series of mini-hagiographies; but why did I include writers—Veblen for one, but most notably Brooks Adams—

who were hardly clear-cut examples of the progressive ideal? (In fact, the latter, as I made clear in what was generally reckoned to be the best chapter in the book, was a true reactionary.) Perhaps I thought American progressives circa 1950 needed some grit in their intellectual diet and might well ponder Thoreau's remark about the stink of "goodness tainted."[14] This may be one reason that I blackballed Henry Wallace from my select club, to the disappointment of Matthiessen. He had urged me to end my book with the only presidential candidate who read and understood William James, but by this time my early enthusiasm for Wallace had chilled. I think I was less put off by his concessions to his Communist supporters than by the Progressive Party's calculated folksiness and its genuflections to the Common Man.

My own brand of progressivism so far as I could tell cut little ice with any group in the political spectrum—not the Wallace partisans on the left or the right-wingers for whom it was hogwash or even the Americans for Democratic Action (ADA), an organization of non-Communist liberals founded in 1947 to oppose the Wallace Progressive Citizens of America. I joined the ADA, voted with some hesitation for Truman, and gave serious thought to the dark sermons of the ADA's official theologian, Reinhold Niebuhr, on the Left's "persistent blindness to the obvious and tragic facts in man's social history." At the suggestion of Wystan Auden, after he had heard me talk on Randolph Bourne, I read Kierkegaard's *Fear and Trembling*, but I still bore the utopian taint, still believed in natural goodness as well as natural sinfulness, still looked more kindly on earlier radical movements than did the majority of mainstream historians and intellectuals.

Men of Good Hope was out of tune with the times and save for the chapter on Brooks Adams had small appeal for most professional historians.* Nor, although conscientiously "interdisciplinary," did it belong to the Myth and Symbol school of American Studies favored by some of my peers. Part historian, part literary critic, part political

---

*An exception was Richard Hofstadter. "Your book," he wrote me, "has this impact on my thinking: it confirms me in my liberal-conservative-elitist-ethical brand of private socialism. So far as its intended effect, I think you have done an important thing in getting the ethical-utopian element back into the center of things. God knows our progressivism needs a booster shot of that." Another was Mary McCarthy, who fancied the chapter on William Dean Howells.

theorist, an irregular in the ranks of the "non-Communist Left," I didn't fit neatly into any niche. I had little talent or taste for polemics. I opted instead for a purposeful screening of the past; I read sermons in historical stones.

vii

Throughout the war years, I taught at Smith College, my application for a commission in the U.S. Naval Reserve having been politely denied. I had expected to be drafted quickly even though my status as an over-thirty married teacher with one child put me in a special category. Twice the Draft Board advised me to prepare for induction, but the call never came. Thus, to my chagrin, I missed the key event for my generation. I expect my impatience at the war's end to get out of the United States, which I soon did, had something to do with being penned up in Fortress America while my friends were getting shot at in foreign parts.

I spent the summer of 1949 at the Salzburg Seminar in American Studies.[15] This was the first of a succession of short and extended visits abroad as a representative of the USA and expounder of its civilization. The faculty participants of this session had not come to "sell" America but to explain it. Presumably we hoped (although I am sure this wasn't uppermost in our minds) to induce sixty or so gifted young men and women of Europe to question their preconceptions about the United States, to interest them in its history and politics, and to make the best case we could for American literature, music, and art. It never occurred to us to conceal or condone our national blemishes. To do so would have seemed dishonest and stupid. I think we took a perverse pleasure in itemizing them lest the students suspect us of whitening a sepulcher. The America we presented was an evolving society more open than most to the world's inspection and (a sign of its strength and confidence) readier to display its sores.[16]

Not surprisingly, American officials didn't approve of this approach, particularly after the Cold War intensified and the international clash of ideas became serious business. In the deepening chill, a reorganized and perforce less quixotically managed Salzburg Seminar lost something of its original élan.*

Two years after my Salzburg summer, I went to Finland with my wife and children for a year's stint as the Smith-Mundt visiting professor at the University of Helsinki. Aside from the charm of voyaging to Ultima Thule and the prospect of civilizing three small sons, I had no compelling reason to go there. I knew little or nothing about Finland's history, social structure, language, or literature. Finnish culture for me boiled down to the music of Sibelius, which I didn't especially like, the architecture of the elder Saarinen, which I did, and the *Kalevala*, Finland's national epic, which I hadn't yet read. The only American Finns I had run into were hard-drinking lumberjacks in northern Wisconsin and the Finns in Fitchburg, Massachusetts.

My stay in Helsinki proved to be an "*aha! Erlebnis*," an introduction to a remarkable people and, for me, a strange and beguiling culture. It corrected my skewed notions of the recent Finnish-Russian war and the unjustly maligned General Mannerheim, designated the "White Guard butcher" by the Communist press. It strongly affected my attitude toward the USSR.

Helsinki in 1951 was one of the listening posts for Western intelligence and a stopping point for journalists and officials passing to and from the Soviet Union. The Korean War had just started, and the Finnish Communists were attacking the renegade Marshal Tito, expelled from the Cominform two years before, and accusing an imperialistic American government of conducting germ warfare against the North Koreans. As proof, one Communist newspaper carried on its first page a blurry photograph of infected insects crawling out of a shell casing.

I went to the university to teach American literature, but I soon learned that being an American representative involved me willy-nilly in the stateside commotions growing out of security anxieties.

*Unforeseen benefits from my stints at the Salzburg Seminar (I taught there three more times) and from succeeding sojourns in Europe and elsewhere (most of them brief, a few lengthy) were the connections I was able to establish with young foreign scholars and writers. A number of them who took part in a kind of floating seminar I conducted at Harvard over the years became my close friends and eventually the leading American Studies authorities in their respective countries.

I was irked at the outset to discover that some nervous functionary in Washington had removed controversial volumes from the books donated to the university library, most notably those of Matthiessen and Ezra Pound. This isn't to say that I felt pressured in any way to toe a line or bridle my tongue, quite the contrary. Called upon at the drop of a hat to discuss any phase of American life before assorted audiences, I spoke my mind freely and had no qualms about disputing official government positions on touchy subjects.[17] And yet in Helsinki's charged political atmosphere, it was hard to be simply a purveyor of facts and interpreter of American culture. The broadcasts from Leningrad, introduced with spooky music and warning listeners to beware "the dollar shadow over Europe," and the stream of slurs pouring out of the Soviet "camp" hardened my anti-Stalinist convictions.

One episode proved to be especially unsettling, an encounter with First Secretary F. A. Garanin of the Soviet Embassy, from whom I hoped to obtain a visa to visit Moscow. What troubled me most about the last and craziest of our get-togethers was his taking for granted that I, like himself, was a government agent of some sort, a charge I huffily denied. He gave me an unbelieving smile when I told him I had no "boss" to report to. Several weeks later I ran into a political officer of the American Legation and mentioned the meeting with Garanin. He was shocked. Why had I waited so long to tell him? This Garanin, he said, was an NKVD man known to be constantly sniffing around for putative defectors. So in the end, I did report my conversations as best I could and published a version of them in the spring of 1953.[18] According to a Helsinki correspondent, Garanin disappeared shortly after.

An impressionistic essay on Helsinki and the Finns I wrote when I got back fared less well.[19] My Helsinki friends, loyal as only Finns can be, gamely praised it amidst the hurt and angry responses, but even they were privately wounded by what seemed to them insensitive descriptions of a drab city and the drinking habits of its inhabitants. I, in turn, was a bit ruffled by their misreading of what to me was a tribute to Finnish integrity, courage, and endurance. I admired Finland and the Finns and thought I had clearly indicated as much; now I think I was ham-handed and too studiedly blunt. A few changes and cuts, the elimination of an inept word or phrase here and there, might have made all the difference.

I came back from Europe to a United States allegedly swarming with Red Termites. McCarthyism flourished, abetted by ancestral fears of foreign conspiracy and the senator's sensational charges of traitorous people in high places.

My only and hardly heroic part in academia's feeble counteroffensive against the McCarthy crusade was a talk I gave to a joint meeting of Northampton's Kiwanis and Rotary clubs in which I criticized the procedural methods of the congressional tribunals investigating "un-American activities." A stony-faced audience received my message in complete silence except for one man who whispered as he filed past without looking at me, "I'm glad you said that." Other than this abortive exercise, I shied away from making statements on public issues. Two quotations I copied in a 1953 journal may be pertinent to my state of mind, one from an unidentified source ("Authority has a nose of wax; it can be twisted in either direction"), the second by Sir Walter Raleigh ("Whosoever, in writing modern history, shall follow truth too near the heels, it may haply strike out his teeth").

In the spirit of Raleigh's caveat, I observed the social tumult from behind my academic bastion and preserved my teeth. Once again I turned to history and literature for clues to the present, likening McCarthyism to previous outbursts of xenophobic rage.[20] I failed to appreciate how the anti-Communist zeal of former Communist intellectuals contributed to the climate of fear and the erosion of civil liberties in the McCarthy years. Nothing I wrote at this time bore directly on loyalty oaths and blacklists, or on the "invitations" received by teachers and writers and actors to expiate their political errors and "clear" their names,[21] but I did allude to such matters in an essay best described as an attempt to separate genuine conservatism from the spurious conservatism of right-wing Republicanism.[22]

viii

In the summer of 1954, Clinton Rossiter, a Cornell University professor of government, invited me to take part in a project the New York *Times* called "an objective historical investigation of Communist influence in American life." One of the two "areas" to be explored was "Communism and American literature."

My knowledge of this "area" was skimpy, to say the least, for all of my antifascist and pro-Soviet feelings in the 1930s and desultory effects to master Marxist theory. But so far as Rossiter was concerned, my spectatorial view of the Communist movement was an advantage. He chose me in part because I had never been a member of the Communist Party, and he excluded former Communists from his team of "seasoned scholars" because they might have been "scarred" by their experiences. Presumably only outsiders were qualified to gather and weigh allegations of Communist infiltration and (as the New York *Times* put it) "portray in its actual size and without exaggeration, the purely internal Communist menace."

I didn't think there was any such thing but happily accepted my assignment, undeterred by the ire and scorn of Senator McCarthy and his spirited claque that greeted the announcement of the Fund for the Republic's "investigation." J. B. Matthews, McCarthy's one-time aide, flailed away at its president, Robert Maynard Hutchins, and his anti-anti-Communist hirelings. These included the "false conservative" Clinton Rossiter and all his handpicked "scholars," most of whom Matthews brushed aside as incompetent or hopelessly biased or both. A few passages he excerpted from *Men of Good Hope* betrayed my softheaded "political and ideological orientation,"[23] but I got off more lightly than most of my better-known colleagues.

Matthews rightly took for granted that we despised McCarthy and his crusaders; he wrongly predicted that our respective estimations of Communist influence would be fraudulent. The completed volumes, each conscientiously researched, may not have been models of icy detachment, but they separated facts from rumors and demonstrated, *pace* McCarthy, how little Communist doctrine had penetrated American history. By then, however, anti-Communist hysteria had begun to subside and McCarthy was disgraced and dead.

Initially I had no purpose in mind for my volume other than to determine how deeply Communism had "penetrated" the literary community, but from the start, I was less absorbed in the niceties of literary Communism than in the human spectacle—the mix of idealism, dedication, courage, religiosity, self-deception, vanity, and damn foolishness exhibited by the radical brotherhood. This interest grew as I pursued my inquiries and became personally involved in the ancient feuds of some of the principal actors. Still, I did my best to maintain the manner of the detached witness and cultural historian of tragicomic events whose function was to describe and explain, not to take sides and pass judgment. Friendly critics attributed this neutral stance to my forbearance or fair-mindedness or objectivity; others saw it as a cop-out, a failure of responsibility.

Subsequently I reflected in print on the difficulty of writing about one's contemporaries and agreed with some, but not all, of my fault-finders' reservations.[24] I had spent a number of years studying the American radical tradition, the last six of them devoted to writers caught up in decades of ideological conflict. I had interviewed and come to know a good many of these men and women in the process of trying to disentangle their convoluted lives, and I had plowed through reams of magazines, memoirs, biographies, and letters in search of evidence that confirmed or corrected their testimonies. What is more, I was old enough to remember the events and the occasions they wrote about—strikes, trials, elections, marches, riots, the publication of a book, the performance of a play, the disputes of literary factions. On the other hand, as Clinton Rossiter reminded me, there was always the risk of losing sight of the forest in the profusion of trees.

He urged me to generalize more boldly, a suggestion I was reluctant to follow, and especially to be on guard against the genial coercions of Joseph Freeman, then a paid consultant of the Fund for the Republic. Adviser, guide, and finally intimate friend, he had been drummed out of the Party in the late Thirties and thereafter lived in a limbo of his own making, harassed by the FBI for his refusal to testify against his old comrades. I now believe he saw in me an agent for his political and literary rehabilitation, but I think he also liked and trusted me as I did him. Only in one instance did he deflect me from taking up a controversial issue—the preponderance of Jews in the Communist literary movement—and blew up when I proposed to address it.[25] All the same, without his help I should never have gained access to a number of former Communist writers or been privy to his inside history of the Communist Left.

ix

Writers on the Left was said to be the first attempt to give a detailed and comprehensive explanation of why so many American writers in the 1920s and 1930s grew disaffected with their society and responsive to the appeal of Communism. Published at the end of McCarthy's hunting season, it anticipated a rush of memoirs, biographies, volumes of correspondence, and special studies (a number of which I reviewed) that both supported and complicated my story of the radical past. It also made me overnight an expert on the "Red Decade"[26] and in fact on every aspect of the American dissenting tradition. That I was nothing of the sort didn't stop me from writing about radicals and reformers of all periods and persuasions.

A few years later I tackled a subject of comparable scope, American writers and the Civil War—an assignment it wouldn't have occurred to me to undertake on my own hook but one I gladly threw myself into after the historian Allen Nevins invited me to contribute a volume to his series on the Civil War's "impact" on American life and culture. Much of my reading, teaching, and research had prepared me for the project. I had lectured on writers and the war at a commemorative conference in Gettysburg, Pennsylvania,[27] and debated its causes and consequences while collaborating on a history of the United States.[28]

I had no preconceived thesis in mind in 1965 when I agreed to write what eventually turned into *The Unwritten War*,[29] but I can't say I approached this task with complete disinterest. My devotion to the Union cause had never deviated. I took immense satisfaction in the defeat of the Confederacy, and although I had long discarded the hoary stereotypes about the South, I am uncertain to this day whether biases fed by fiction and current events might not have sneaked into my book. Professor Nevins had asked for "a thorough, well-rounded treatment" of Civil War literature. That is what I tried to produce. I had no wish to write a survey of this vast literature but rather to register the war's impact on the writer-combatants and civilian writers, North and South, and also on postwar writers whose imaginations were subsequently engaged by it.

At the end of a long stint of reading authors from the days of Emerson and before to William Faulkner, I felt up to hazarding a comment on Whitman's famous assertion that the "real war" would never "get in the books" and would stay "unwritten." I assumed he meant that a war so atrocious, engulfing, and psychically shattering would never be sounded and comprehended. In my view, much of the war's horror and anguish did "get in the books," including his, but it didn't get "written" for another reason: its chroniclers would not or could not confront the issue of race that kindled it and kept it burning. Without the long presence of chattel slavery and the anxieties it engendered, I argued, sectional frictions would not have blazed into a civil war, yet in recording it few writers squarely faced their racial fears and antipathies. They often presented "the Negro" sympathetically ("which ordinarily meant sentimentally and patronizingly"), but he "remained even in the midst of his literary well-wishers an object of contempt or dread, or an uncomfortable reminder of abandoned obligations, or a pestiferous shadow emblematic of guilt and retribution."[30]

Comparable racial antipathies pervaded the haunted mind of the Confederacy-obsessed Arthur Crew Inman, whose diary of some fifteen million words written without inhibition (or paragraphs) I would explore and chart for six years and pare down to less than one tenth of its original size. I took on the job (paid for by the Inman estate) because of my great fondness for diaries. Rather soon I regretted my decision, depressed by the sheer magnitude of the task and by the spoiled, prejudiced, manipulative, sadomasochistic, self-pitying author sequestered for a good part of his life in the heavily curtained room of a seedy Boston apartment hotel. Inman was hardly the man to chronicle the history of his times for posterity. Newspapers, radio, and books furnished part of his "diary fodder," but mostly he fed on the life stories of hundreds of men and women who answered his advertisements for paid "talkers" (he had plenty of money and time) and submitted to his relentless interrogations.

The diary didn't bring him the immortality he craved. Many reviewers of my two-volume abridgment were so taken up or put off by Inman's outrageous opinions and bizarre behavior that they did less than justice, I thought, to the self-defined "bastard gazatteer" and his four-decade report of the American scene "in day-to-day minuscule." The character Arthur Inman disclosed after massive cutting was the same detestable sick soul who had materialized in the early volumes of the diary. (I presented him as the hero of a kind of nonfiction novel punctuated by comic and shocking episodes and ending inexorably in his suicide.) But over the years he developed into a powerful narrator and observer, at once comic and preposterous in his unquenchable lust for fame. I felt an obligation to make him famous. And I believed that my haphazard excursions in American history and literature (not to mention the fact that Inman's diary covered a period of years in my own lifetime) made me a legitimate interpreter of the man and his moment. Editing the diary helped me to put into perspective "the long foreground," as Emerson would say, of my own career.

Since taking my degree, I had spread myself thinly in many directions, as if being an "Americanist," horrid word, entitled, indeed obliged, me to annex all things American into my province and to cut a broad swath. Now it occurred to me that all along I had been making a survey of the American literary and intellectual landscape, constantly plumping for its little known or neglected glades without palliating its bogs and arid spots. Thus I could see my part in the launching of The Library of America five years after the death in 1972 of its projector, Edmund Wilson (whom I had known well and written about extensively), as the climax of my private campaign to recover America's literary resources. The Library is Wilson's monument, but for me it also stands for what was best about the early American Studies movement.

X

Over the years I encouraged myself to believe that I wasn't without literary insight, but I could understand why one reader described *The Unwritten War* as "a series of essays on individual authors . . . presented in the context of a series of historical interpretations and generalizations," and another placed me "among contemporary critics of American literature . . . more concerned with exploring the relationships of literature to context and writers to society, rather than with analytic, formalist, mythopoeic, or psychological criticism."

If not a proper literary critic as defined by that school, was I a historian? Yes, but not an orthodox or scientific practitioner of a historical method. It would be more accurate to say that almost everything I wrote was awash in history, that despite my passion for hard facts and hard history, I believed every historian, in selecting facts and fashioning them into a narrative, necessarily strained them through a personal sieve. Some of the pieces in these American Notes are moralistic, partisan, satirical, others celebratory, even patriotic, if by that term is meant not only the love of country but also the capacity to be curious, puzzled, worried, and amused by Americans and their institutions. More than a few smack of the kind of cultural nationalism, no longer in good odor, expounded by the likes of Randolph Bourne, Van Wyck Brooks, Edmund Wilson, and Newton Arvin. These writers looked at America critically but never apologetically and although steeped in other literatures weren't ashamed of their own. America in their eyes wasn't Whitman's "greatest poem" so much as a complex place usually praised or blamed for the wrong reasons and still in need of excavation.

The selections to follow, together with the titles of articles, reviews, testimonials, and introductions listed at the back of this book constitute the pile of my own diggings. They also trace the saltatory course of a career largely spent thinking and talking about American things. Or so it seems to me as I approach the end of a long haul.

Feeding on Books

Generally speaking, the "adventures" reported in *American Notes* are bookish ones or at least connected with the business of books. I have lived in them and on them since I first began to read, as the following reminiscence suggests:

My parents were book readers, and our family library was well stocked with sets of standard authors. Not being precocious, I didn't pay much attention to my mother's and father's books until my teens. What I read was a heterogeneous mix: children's "classics" like the *Jungle Books* of Kipling; books written and illustrated by Howard Pyle; the Oz books of Frank L. Baum; the historical novels of G. P. Henty; sea stories by a wonderful writer named Charles Boardman Hawes, and many others. I spent hours with our set of *The Book of Knowledge* and volumes with "Golden" in the title about sundry heroes and heroines, and Andrew Lang's collections of fairy tales (Blue, Green, Yellow, etc.) and Greek, Roman, and Norse mythologies, and three absorbing volumes (all the words hyphenated to make for easy reading) entitled *Famous Men of Greece and Rome,*

Famous Men of the Middle Ages, and *Famous Men of Modern Times* (no famous women be it noted), and James C. Ridpath's thick, multivolumed *History of the World* (mainly for the pictures), which began with the primordial slime and ended, I think, with the Franco-Prussian war. I loved animal stories of all kinds, Ernest Thompson Seton, of course, but also the blessed and forgotten author of *The Pirate Shark*, *The Rogue Elephant*, *The King Condor of the Andes*, *The White Tiger of Nepal*, *The King Bear of Kodiak Island*. I read dozens of books about Tom Swift, the boy inventor, dozens of books about the exploits of the Boy Allies in the First World War, and, it goes without saying, baseball fiction (*Lefty Locke, Pitcher Manager, Guarding the Key-Stone Sack, Brick King, Backstop*, etc.). *Famous Cavalry Leaders* (my favorites were Genghis Khan, Tamerlane, Gustavus Adolphus, Von Zieten, Phil Sheridan) and *Famous Indian Chiefs* by the same author especially delighted me.

Then I passed through a period when I was absorbed in what my elders referred to as "trash." I soaked up the novels of Zane Grey (I still remember the opening paragraphs of *The Lone Star Ranger* introducing the hero, Buck Duane, the two-gun ace of the Nueces), and of Edgar Rice Burroughs (a careless writer on occasion but the author of the Tarzan books and tales of interplanetary adventure). I came to know very well the contributors to *The Saturday Evening Post*, *Redbook*, *Collier's*, *Cosmopolitan*, *Liberty* and extended my vocabulary in the process. From Frank L. Packard's mysteries about a gentleman safecracker ("long slim tapering fingers that seemed to sense a thousand nerves were the fingers of Jimmy Dale") I picked up words like "denizen," "purlieu," "alias"—which I pronounced "a-lī-us"; from the exotic Achmed Abdullah ("the heel of my back to you, the curve of my spine, you son of a noseless Jew and a she-hyena") the word "yashmak," along with considerable Middle-Eastern lore; from Sax Rohmer, "insidious," a term applied with complete justice to the fiendish but brilliant Dr. Fu Manchu.

Most of these writers were shameless racists, inveterate glorifiers of Anglo-Saxon blood. To them all Mexicans were "greasers," Jews invariably "little" and abominable, any persons east of Calais "niggers." But I can't say their ugly biases affected me in the slightest. I am grateful to these accomplished hacks for supplying me with grit for my literary crop and helping me to appreciate their betters when the time came to concentrate on more arresting and abiding books.

(From "Trash, Classics and the Common Reader," *The Texas Humanist*, 6 [May–June 1984], 41.)

Cambridge in the Thirties

Harvard University celebrated its tercentenary in 1936. Two events connected with that occasion stand out in my mind: a lecture by Carl Jung on the mandala and a presidential motorcade down Massachusetts Avenue.

I don't remember what Jung said, but at the end of his talk, I took a close look at him when I walked up to the platform with my companion, Charles Olson (then deep in his Melville book, *Call Me Ishmael*), and stood staring while Charlie asked Jung if he detected the mandala figure in the graphic symbolism of *Moby-Dick*. President Roosevelt's topless limousine—it might have been on the same day as Jung's lecture—passed a few yards from me, and I saw plainly the uptilted, smiling face. Impulsively I tossed my arms in the air and shouted. He was the first president I had ever seen in the flesh, and although I regarded myself then as considerably to the left of the New Deal, I still managed to square my disapproval of some of his policies with my admiration of the man.

Roosevelt's son Franklin, Jr., was an undergraduate at the time of his father's visit. I once spotted him with a group of blue-shirted Hasty Pudding boys as they tried to hoot down a radical speaker who was addressing a crowd of students from the steps of Widener Library. There were lots of such gatherings then, and all manner of factions competed for attention. I heard the Reverend Gerald L. K. Smith, ally of the recently assassinated Huey Long, talk at a meeting sponsored by Harvard's Young Conservatives, a beleaguered minority in those days. The audience was so noisily hostile that Smith ended his harangue by threatening with destruction Harvard and all it stood for. Exponents of Vilfredo Pareto's "elites" also had their moment in the university limelight, but generally speaking, what the Chicago *Tribune* and the Hearst papers referred to as Harvard's "Reds" and their fellow-traveling sympathizers made up the most determined and energetic segment of the social-minded in the Harvard community. They influenced the policies and tactics of the Harvard Teacher's Union to which I belonged. It pleased me that our union was an affiliate of the C.I.O., and although it exercised little real power, it served as a forum where its members could express their solidarity with the working class.

I'm sure I never tried to guess how many of my friends were actually Communists, and not until the McCarthy investigations did I learn that several of them who attended the Marxist study group which met weekly at my apartment on Sumner Road were attached to the local Communist Party branch. It would have made no difference to me if I had known, for in this popular front period being a Communist seemed scarcely more exotic than being a Republican or an Elk.

Thanks to its leadership in stirring up support for the Spanish Loyalists, the Party had reached the apogee of its popularity with the non-Communist intellectuals, and Harvard was aflame with fervor over Spain. Communists mingled harmoniously with other antifascist elements at the cocktail parties held to raise money for ambulances and medical supplies and at emotional gatherings like the one where the chain-smoking André Malraux, gaunt and hollow-eyed, and his American guide, the then Communist journalist Louis Fischer, held forth on the heroism of the Spanish people and the crimes of General Franco. Archibald MacLeish did too, and we savored his plangent words. The war in Spain foreshadowed greater wars to come, he told us. "How then can we refuse our help to those who fight our battles?"

Neither I nor my friends paid any attention to the stories or "lies" about the suppression of the Left opposition in Spain which were appearing in the "Trotskyite" or anti-Stalinist press (not until long after did I grasp the pejorative implication of that suffix, "ite"). But given our closed-mindedness, it is doubtful that we would have touched those renegade sheets with a pair of tongs. Nor can I remember our being particularly aroused by the "show trials" in Moscow. The image of the Soviet Union taking shape in our minds derived largely from Soviet films like *Chapayev* or accounts by enraptured visitors to the Workers' State of strolls through parks of culture and rest.* Among the so-called progressive nations, hadn't Russia alone, under the leadership of the sagacious Stalin, dared to challenge the legions of Mussolini and Hitler?

Granville Hicks, literary editor of the *New Masses*, was part of the

---

*See pp. 21.

Cambridge scene in 1938–39. He had been invited to Harvard as one of the half-dozen "counsellors" in American Civilization, and the hullabaloo in the "capitalist press" which followed the announcement of his appointment ensured Harvard's welcome to its notorious alumnus. It was appropriate that the biographer of John Reed should be around when a portrait of the revolutionary martyr was presented to Adams House. He was good friends with the hard-drinking journalists who made up the first contingent of Nieman Fellows, and he guided the ad hoc Sumner Road seminar through the mysteries of the *Marxist Handbook*. Hicks proudly wore his Party label, but it was a point of honor with him not to proselytize students, a resolution to which he had always scrupulously adhered.

I think the most memorable episode of his Cambridge stay was his debate with Father Francis Curran, editor of the *Brooklyn Tablet*, held in Boston's Mechanics' Hall. Curran, a jovial and floridly rhetorical priest and the darling of the New England "Coughlinites," had featured stories of horrific atrocities allegedly committed by the Spanish Republicans. Busloads of Coughlin's followers from a wide area poured into the hall that night, raising their arms in what looked to us like the Nazi salute and screaming and hugging each other when their idol appeared on the platform. The few of us who had accompanied Hicks to the meeting were no match for Curran's intimidating group, and their howls drowned out our tentative cheers. Hicks would never have spoken at all had not Curran silenced the crowd with a wave of his arm and permitted Hicks to deliver a short and totally unpersuasive speech. This scary experience confirmed our belief in the sinister power of the Roman Catholic hierarchy and in what John Strachey called, in a much discussed book, the "coming struggle for power."

Yet, despite my feelings about Spain and the Soviet Union, I felt no strong inclination to join a party whose programs and vocabulary made me uneasy. In retrospect, I attribute this reluctance to my sense that the Party, for all its celebration of Tom Paine, Walt Whitman, and Abraham Lincoln, was out of touch with the America whose history and culture were now my chief interest. I enjoyed the cartoons in the *New Masses*, the trips to New York to see *Waiting for Lefty* and *Awake and Sing*, and the Mercury Theater's production of *Julius Caesar*, in which black-shirted and jackbooted Romans strutted across the stage, but no more, I think, than the Ballet Russe de Monte Carlo or the Old Howard. The Harvard atmosphere, in my case at least, was not conducive to the making of revolutionists. Rather, it fostered irreverence. I memorized the poems of E. E. Cummings, read the novels of Nathanael West, made fun (as Communists often did in private) of Party jargon, and composed and sang lugubriously a campaign song for the gubernatorial candidate of the Communist Party of Massachusetts, Otis Hood, to the tune of the "Volga Boatman." ("O-tis Hood, O-tis Hood/ He's good, he should/ Win your vote.") Moreover, I realized even then, for I was studying American church history, that to join the Party was the equivalent of joining a church. I felt no doctrinal commitment and wasn't prepared to make a metaphysical leap into faith. So when Granville Hicks hesitantly suggested I do just that, I declined.

He did not press me. In fact, it seemed to me that he approved of my refusal, and I soon found out why. He himself was trembling on the edge of apostasy before the Soviet-German pact gave him the excuse he needed to resign. (From "Cambridge 1936–39," *Partisan Review: The 50th Anniversary Edition*, ed. William Phillips [New York: Stein & Day, 1985], 346–349.)

Notes

1. See "The Hyphenate Writer and American Letters," *Smith College Alumnae Quarterly* (July 1964), 213–217.

2. "Thorstein Veblen, Moralist and Rhetorician," *Antioch Review*, 7 (Fall 1947), 381–390.

3. Howard Mumford Jones, one of the architects of the American Civilization Program at Harvard, called the subject of American life and letters "one of the most difficult and demanding disciplines in the world of scholarship, for the good Americanist must know not only literature, history, music, art, architecture and folkways of the United States and Canada but also the life and culture of our European sources and of the vast stream of American life south of the Rio Grande." Few "Americanists," then or later, measured up to this exacting standard.

4. A snippy if not entirely pointless rejoinder to Santayana's *The Last Puritan* I wrote in 1936 suggests the extent to which I had incorporated a highly personal notion of "Puritanism" into my social philosophy. See *New England Quarterly*, 9 (1936), 683–686.

5. "Melville and the Missionaries," *New England Quarterly*, 8 (1935), 404–408.

6. For example, his *America and French Culture* (1927). I had already

been impressed by his learning and wide-ranging interests while working with him on a heavily footnoted article we jointly published, "Notes on the Napoleonic Legend in America," *Franco-American Review*, 2 (1937), 10–26.

7. *Cincinnati: Queen City of the West, 1819–1838* (Columbus: Ohio State University Press, 1992), xxiv–xxv.

8. For example, my review of James Truslow Adams, *Big Business in a Democracy*, in the *New Republic* (September 24, 1945), 379–381, and "A Note on the Businessman and the Historian" in the *Antioch Review*, 6 (1946–47), 575–581.

9. From my "Jonathan Edwards" in *The Northampton Book: Chapters from 300 Years in the Life of a New England Town, 1654–1954*, ed. L. E. Wikander et al. (Northampton, Mass., 1954), 15–21.

10. *Kenyon Review*, 4 (1942), 102–106.

11. "Recent Works in the Social History of the United States, 1935–1939," *International Review of Social History*, 4 (1938), 499–509.

12. *American Quarterly*, 1 (1949), 94–96.

13. Reviewing Arthur E. Bestor, Jr., *Backwoods Utopias* (1950) in *New England Quarterly*, 24 (1951), 104–106, I wrote: "It is now fashionable to debunk the early nineteenth-century communitarians as escapists and nitwits, even as the harbingers of twentieth-century totalitarianism, [whereas both religious and secular communities in the early days] were efforts to regenerate society, not to escape it. . . . Neither individualistic nor revolutionary, the communitarian wanted immediate reform without violence. Having no faith in independent efforts to meet the problems created by a newly industrialized America, he took what was for him the highly practical step of working through a collectivity. The communitarian, unlike the doctrinaire socialist, believed in social harmony rather than in class warfare, voluntary action in place of compulsion. He was experimental and pragmatic in his thinking. In his attitudes and goals, he differed little from his fellow countrymen, as Emerson noted, and his communitarianism was far more congenial to the Americans of the mid-nineteenth century than . . . scientific European socialism, with its aura of free-love and infidelity."

14. For some reason, Thoreau didn't have a chapter to himself. Possibly I then thought Thoreauvian individualism too disdainful of men, as Whitman put it, and inhumanly insistent on self-sufficiency. See my review of Joseph Wood Krutch's *Henry David Thoreau* in the *Kenyon Review*, 11 (1949), 145–148.

15. Founded in 1947 and chartered in 1950 by the Commonwealth of Massachusetts as a nonprofit educational organization, it was supported primarily by private foundations and individuals to enlarge European understanding of American political, economic, and intellectual life.

16. Or so I recalled in "The Salzburg Seminar: A Retrospective View," *International Educational and Cultural Exchange* (Winter 1966), 20–24.

17. When three State Department speakers, one of them black, de-

scribed the prosperous conditions of African Americans and their glowing prospects, I rebutted them in three public lectures on the somber history and current state of black-white relations.

18. *The Reporter*, 8 (March 31, 1953), 24–27.

19. Ibid., 7 (September 2, 1952), 24–27.

20. A decade later, Michael Rogin corrected this interpretation in *The Intellectuals and McCarthy*. I summarized his conclusions as follows: "Mc-Carthyism was never a mass movement that disrupted traditional voting patterns. It might better be described as a short-lived but intense expression of right-wing Republicanism especially strong in the middle-western branch of the party whose hard core recoiled from eastern cosmopolitanism, New Dealism, and Communism." *Commonweal* (September 8, 1967), 556–557.

21. Subsequently I addressed this issue in a review of Victor S. Navasky's *Naming Names* in the *New York Review of Books*, 17 (December 4, 1980), 6, 8.

22. "Conservatism, Old and New," *American Quarterly*, 6 (1954), 99–110.

23. Matthews's passing remark that for all of my glaring inadequacies I was "not in any sense of the word a Communist" may have blunted later suspicions or allegations that I was. Thus a USIA official in Montevideo, who defined a Communist as anyone who read C. Wright Mills, failed to block my visit to Uruguay under the sponsorship of the State Department.

24. See " 'Writers on the Left' Assessed," *Indian Journal of American Studies*, 3 (June 1973), 1–7, and "The Treachery of Recollection" in *Essays in History and Literature*, ed. Robert H. Bremner (Columbus: Ohio State University Press, 1966), 3–27.

25. I did a few years later. See "Some Reflections on Communism and the Jewish Writer" in *The Ghetto and Beyond: Essays on Jewish Life in America*, ed. Peter I. Rose (New York: Random House, 1969), 253–269.

26. In 1970 Robert Bendiner and I brought out a collection of economic, political, and cultural documents, *The Strenuous Decade: A Social and Intellectual Record of the Nineteen-Thirties* (Garden City, N.Y.: Anchor Books). By then that "record" seemed ancient and tarnished to many young radicals and certainly less "relevant" than the manifestos of the "New Left" and the "Counter-Culture." See "The Thirties—Now and Then" and the transcript of the discussion I moderated in which Kenneth Burke, Malcolm Cowley, Granville Hicks, and William Phillips reflected on the first American Writers' Conference and its historical implications. *American Scholar*, 35 (Summer 1966), 490–516.

In the spring of 1967, I presided over what was supposed to be a discussion between two veterans of the Old Left (Richard Rovere and Dwight Macdonald) and two spokesmen of the New Left (Tom Hayden and Ivanhoe Donaldson). The printed version of this encounter considerably straightened out Hayden's and Donaldson's often incoherent spoken remarks, but both spurned the questions raised by their seniors. As Rovere remarked, "the parties passed each other like ships in the night." "Confrontation: The Old Left and the New," *American Scholar*, 36 (Autumn 1967), 567–588.

27. "The Epic Is Yet to Be Written," *American Heritage*, 9 (October 1958), 112–116.

28. Richard Hofstadter, William Miller, and Daniel Aaron, *The United States: History of a Republic* (Englewood Cliffs, N.J.: Prentice-Hall, 1957).

29. *The Unwritten War: American Writers and the Civil War* (New York: Alfred A. Knopf, 1973).

30. *The Unwritten War: American Writers and the Civil War* (Madison: University of Wisconsin Press, 1987), 332, xxii.

31. *The Inman Diary: A Public and Private Confession*, 2 vols. (Cambridge, Mass.: Harvard University Press, 1985).

Writing about the Left

Writers on the Left, I've been told, helped to defuse what had long been in the United States the explosive subject of literary communism. It also encouraged friends and strangers to complain of omissions in my account, to correct and amplify it, and to pass on to me or to the public their own recollections of the radical Thirties. Some of this uninvited commentary seemed to me cranky or irrelevant—but by no means all of it. Had I paid too much attention to my cast of principals at the expense of equally or more important groups and issues? Had I relied too uncritically on the testimony of jaundiced actors and made the internecine wars of the intelligentsia more significant than they were?

The entries that follow can be read as meditations on the hazards of writing about one's contemporaries and as afterthoughts on persons and events touched upon or alluded to or unmentioned in my book.

They also address questions prompted by the spate of monographs, biographies, memoirs, letters, and articles about the "Red Decade" that appeared in the wake of my book.

What strikes me now about these pieces after a long stretch of years is not their detachment and neutrality but their skepticism and irreverence toward the Left as well as the Right. The solemnity and religiosity of the ideologues of both persuasions attracted me to their opposites: to the bleak satirist Nathanael West, whom I first wrote about in 1947; to Kenneth Burke, who counseled his fellow dissenters to adopt subtler tactics if they hoped to topple capitalism, a system neither so weak nor so rotten as its gravediggers supposed; and to the poets and fiction writers and literary critics who spoke for the Left in highly undoctrinaire ways.

The Treachery of Recollection:

The Inner and the Outer History

What I propose to do in this talk is to raise certain problems and to ask certain questions about the writing of contemporary history. More particularly, I shall refer to events which have taken place during my own lifetime and which have involved a number of people who are still alive. These men and women (to narrow the scope of my discourse even further) were or are writers and intellectuals, and the events I shall mention belong to the history of literary radicalism during the 1920s and 1930s. Since these remarks might be subtitled "Some belated conclusions about writers and political movements," and since they also might be considered a personal documentation of T. S. Eliot's unconsoling reflections on history, my approach to the subject will be necessarily autobiographical.

i

As interest in the Thirties keeps mounting, a number of special studies are appearing on the politics and culture of this period—the first trickles of an impending flood. Already some of the writers and intellectuals who came of age between two world wars have written

Originally published in *Carleton Miscellany*, 6 (Summer 1965), 3–19. This essay was delivered as a lecture at the Ohio State University, January 21, 1965, in a symposium, "History and Literature," sponsored by the Graduate School and the Department of History in honor of Professor Foster Rhea Dulles.

their memoirs in whole or in part, and the recollections of other hitherto reticent men and women will doubtless follow.

This sudden burst of reminiscence comes a little tardily. Until a short time ago, scholars and writers rather studiedly avoided the Thirties; the Depression decade, in contrast to the supposedly apolitical Twenties, became one to forget or to denigrate. Veterans of those embattled years had retired to lick their wounds or to brood over their disenchantment, publicly or privately; and writers who had once thrilled to dubious Soviet statistics or had mourned the defeats of the Spanish Republicans now dropped old political loyalties with huge relief, happy to be restored once again to the stupid but unwittingly prophetic community. Some flagellated themselves in print; some trivialized their adventures in nonconformity, dismissing their radical enthusiasms as youthful aberrations or follies and joking about episodes that once had kindled a passionate concern. All in all, the Forties and Fifties saw a good deal of soul-searching, breast-beating, and mutual recrimination.

This wholesale rejection of old convictions need not have been carried on so masochistically, but candid retrospection was discouraged after the war by a poltical and cultural assault on what came to be stigmatized as the liberal fallacies of the Thirties. Not only Marxism was attacked. All the liberal clichés fell under the postwar ban, with former Leftists presiding over the autopsy of the radical-liberal corpse. These same people and their disciples took pains to announce in literary quarterlies, in classrooms, in summer conferences for young writers, that the old formulas were hopelessly inadequate. Few had a good word to say for the popular left-wing writers of the Thirties or for the literary forms and styles these writers had used to convey their angry or hopeful messages. The new line was to dismiss them as primitives, clumsy practitioners who simplified art, advocated naive social cures, and sentimentalized corrupt human nature.

The new literary stance was conservative, formal, and noncommittal. Writers and intellectuals too young to have remembered either the exhilaration or anguish of the Thirties accepted the afterthoughts and reconsiderations of their elders, both in politics and in art. At least it seemed so to many critics in the Fifties who found the new writing disciplined and restrained and a little flat. They dubbed the postwar generation, perhaps unfairly, the "conservative," the "timid," the "anxious" generation—a far cry from the writers and intellectuals who once held powerful convictions and acted upon them.

With the deflation of McCarthyism, curiosity (especially in academic circles) about the former radicals whose names had appeared in the reports of congressional investigating committees began to manifest itself. An ostensibly apolitical "Beat" generation discovered some of its ancestors in the "Bottom Dog" writers of the Depression, and college students, perhaps surfeited with bittersweet chronicles of the "Lost Generation" era, started to ask questions about literary life during the Roosevelt years. Why did this particular writer become involved with the Left movement? And why did he or she break away? Were many writers involved? How important was the influence of Communism on writers? How many were bona fide revolutionaries and how many merely rebels, indignant about all injustices?

These were some of the questions I asked myself in the mid-Fifties when I began to study the American literary Left movement and to investigate the political activities and beliefs of writers who played a part in it. What follows will be reconsiderations of the problems and difficulties anyone faces who seeks to set down the internal as well as external history of the recent past and who wants to tell the story while many of the actors are still alive.

ii

Aldous Huxley once said that only the dead are consistent. The historian of the past confines his attentions to the "consistent" dead who are safely under the ground and therefore is spared certain embarrassments that he may not appreciate until he turns his attention to the inconsistent living. His dead subjects belong to the public domain. He can write about them with impunity, unless, of course, the manuscripts and letters are guarded by solicitous heirs or supervised by property-conscious executors who place stipulations upon their use.

Yet even with these obstacles, the historian of the past is free to probe into the lives of the departed with the comfortable feeling that they are not likely to talk back or sue him for libel. He can judge them, speculate about their motives, deal with the most intimate and delicate moments of their careers, and he can do this in the knowledge that they are beyond pain. In other words, writing about a man who "was" rather than about a man who "is" encourages candor. The historian or biographer is able to arrange his subject in a variety of poses, treat him clinically or irreverently, psychoanalyze him, or make him a text for a sermon.

This latitude is denied to historians who write about their living contemporaries, but in compensation they enjoy obvious advantages that historians of the past are necessarily deprived of, most notably the chance to see and to talk with many of the principal actors. The adage "Dead men tell no tales" is as relevant for historians, literary or otherwise, as it is for pirates, and in my own case, the prospect of talking with live authors (who have many tales to tell if they can be induced to talk) was an alluring one. All of us at one time or another have daydreamed about reversing the Time Machine: of waking up, for example, in the eighteenth century like the hero of Henry James's unfinished novel, *The Sense of the Past*; of eavesdropping on the unreported conversations between Melville and Hawthorne as they strolled in the Berkshires, or discussing "Song of Myself" with Walt Whitman while riding on a Broadway omnibus.

Now it would seem that the historian of the present has less need to resort to such fancies. He can write letters to the people he is concerned with. He can visit them, record their statements, extract information from their friends and enemies. Their books and articles are efficiently catalogued, and libraries purchase their papers well before the writers themselves have cashed their last checks. With this plethora of palpable evidence, secrets and mysteries would seem to disappear.

I say would *seem* to, and yet I suspect that anyone who has written about his contemporaries would disagree. He might not say that it was much harder to write about the living than the dead, but he might well assert that it was a different and trickier undertaking and one replete with inhibiting traps and pitfalls. The historian who writes of the past might be likened to a naturalist as he observes and analyzes specimens in a museum or perhaps animals caged in a zoo. The historian of the present resembles rather a hunter stalking his unpredictable quarry in a jungle. And to push the analogy further, in this hunting game, the quarry keeps changing shape.

What starts out looking like a rabbit may turn into a porcupine; an elephant is transmogrified into a mouse. To put it still another way: when the investigator tracks down his man (or his woman) some twenty-five to forty-five years after a particular episode, he is not seeing and talking to the same man who wrote the manifesto or who paraded in the picket line or sent a congratulatory message to the *New Masses* on its anniversary or who bit another celebrity in the leg during a drunken party. Or would it be more accurate to say that he is confronting a different man in the same body, a man not necessarily the most reliable authority on his previous self?

Granted that we err in arbitrarily chopping Time into past, present, and future, that time flows in both directions and that there can be no Now unconnected with what was or will be, nevertheless what a person was or did or thought thirty years ago is past and dead, even if that person is technically alive. The living relic is his own ancestor; and feeling a deep familial piety for his defunct historical self, he indulges in ancestor-worship, tidies up embarrassing disorders of his dead past, reverently conceals his own skeleton in a hidden closet. The astute interrogator may hear the reverberations of the telltale heart, but he is also susceptible to misdirection and perhaps deserves less trust, finally, than the unborn scholarly detective who will disinter the "truth" long after the objects of his researches have become authentic corpses.

In the meantime, the historian who writes about his contemporaries may wonder from time to time whether he has any business raking up the pasts of people who are still alive. In this age of public relations, covert investigations, and wholesale violations of privacy, should the scholar join the pack? I raise this question, because not only was I concerned with the former opinions and actions of writers still very much alive, but I was also particularly interested to learn about their involvement in a political movement retroactively condemned as subversive. What is more, I was approaching them at the close of the McCarthy period.

Some of the people I hoped to interview were still in the "Movement," that vague and elastic euphemism for the Left; some were politically homeless; and a few had moved over to the right of Senator Goldwater. The majority were liberals who had broken with the movement at various moments during the turbulent Thirties. But you will recall that in Senator McCarthy's heyday, fifteen or more years of a politically free existence cut no ice with congressional headhunters. We are still uncomfortably close to the days when writers were "invited" to testify about their former political affiliations, when prominent and forgotten people denounced old associates, and skittish employers fired or dare not hire the blacklisted. Quite obviously in 1956, my own project, no matter how detached and scholarly and scrupulous my intentions, might ultimately hurt someone. Why should these writers pour out their hearts to an outsider engaged in excavating a past they had either forgotten or had no desire to recall?

One of them,* whose faith in Communism remained strong after half a century, wrote to me in reply to my request for an interview:

> I am suspicious of young scholars who set out to make a career out of cannibalizing the history of Communism and Socialism and all social thought in this country, not engaged themselves, observers and critics only, as though they were spies or something. I mean, "who walks without sympathy and passion is walking to his own funeral in a shroud." Something like this was said by Walt Whitman.

His letter, which must have expressed the feelings of a good many other veterans of the cause, reminded me of the dialogue between the narrator and the antique owner of the Aspern papers in Henry James's story:

> "Do you think it's right to rake up the past?" [She asks.]
> "I don't feel that I know what you mean by raking it up. [He replies.] How can we get at it unless we dig a little? The present has such a rough way of treading it down."
> "Oh I like the past, but I don't like critics," my hostess declared with her hard complacency.
> "Neither do I, but I like their discoveries."
> "Aren't they mostly lies?"
> "The lies are what they sometimes discover," I said, smiling at the quiet impertinence of this. "They often lay bare the truth."
> "The truth is God's, it isn't man's; we had better leave it alone. Who can judge of it?—who can say?"

*Michael Gold.

Who indeed? The only answer I could offer my correspondent and others who shared his suspicions was to say that this "cannibalizing" had been going on for some time and that after the mountains of misinformation about the radical movement and the intellectuals, it might be a good thing to get the facts straight, or at least to convey as faithfully as possible what it was like to be alive in those days of political convictions and illusions. This is the job for the historian. If he refuses to deal with his times on the grounds that contemporary history is hardly more than vulgar journalism, then the popularizer and the sensationalist rush in where the historian fears to tread.

For some, my professed concern for "truth" was hardly an inducement to tell all, especially if this meant dredging up the memory of a youthful gesture or expression of opinion violently at odds with the popular image of the men-now-become-older. One very successful and widely known entrepreneur of letters bluntly refused me permission to quote from some "nonsense" he had written to friends in the early Thirties on the grounds that he composed this "bit of childish indignation" when he and his friends "were all off in the head, often because we were starving." Neither he nor his friends were literally starving, of course, but that was his latter-day "vision of the Thirties" and his highly improbable explanation for his radical phase.

As it turned out, most of the writers I wanted to see were not so reticent about their left-wing adventures and were prepared to talk with me and to answer questions if only, perhaps, to dispel legends about themselves and their friends. If they felt any hesitation, it was not so much because of their past or present opinions but simply because the more eminent among them had been pestered by inquirers of all ages and levels. We are living at a time when high school, college, and graduate students are encouraged to go directly to the source in preparing papers and theses on living men of letters. American writers of any reputation are constantly receiving requests from youthful strangers demanding answers to the most personal questions and even seeking permission to rummage through their private files. It is not hard to understand why these writers, both the remembered and the forgotten, regard students and scholars with mournful misgivings and concoct ingenious schemes to circumvent literary detectives.

For these reasons, and for some yet to be mentioned, writing about one's contemporaries can be as painful as it is challenging. It is bad enough to probe into a person's political or private life like one of Hawthorne's cold-hearted Paul Prys, to enjoy (no matter how deeply repressed) the thrill of digging up the forgotten and the concealed. But the guilty Private Eye may also be troubled by the very abundance of alleged "facts" that don't reveal as much as they obscure. Are proffered explanations, given in good faith, about why a writer did or did not take a particular stand to be taken at face value? Self-denigration in personal reminiscence is not uncommon, yet few people like to confess low motives for lofty ends; moreover, distance lends enchantment. One learns that squabbles of a generation ago or earlier still divide people no longer politically engaged; that old quarrels still rankle, quarrels seemingly ideological but which may very well have been prompted by professional jealousy, a bad book review, a stolen mistress; and that the autobiographer writing his memoirs in the 1960s may still be settling old scores after an interval of thirty years.

The historian attempting to record a literary war when many of the veterans are still alive exposes himself to the flying pop-bottles that threaten any umpire. He pays for his sins of omission, and he may also suffer embarrassment because he knows too much. I have listened to a perfectly rational explanation for an antipathy or a change in heart, knowing all the time that the speaker had withheld or forgotten some crucial fact I had already obtained from another. Because I was steeped in the gossip of the past and familiar with many sides of ancient scandals and debates, I was constantly fearful that I might offend a particular man or woman by telling an unfamiliar version of an episode, or hurt another by inadvertently revealing unwelcome information.

If this solicitude seems unbecoming to the historian, it is the price he pays for the confidence of those he writes about. When he is invited into a man's house, a gesture of qualified acceptance, he subjects himself to subtle pressures. It is not merely the threat of libel suits (a real one in my case) that induces restraint, that tempts him to exclude, to suppress, to be oblique. It is something quite different, something harder to define.

Let us assume that the historian comes to know his subjects after repeated letters and conversations and drinks. They cease to be merely historical figures of ideological abstractions. They become people. And when they talk to him trustfully, when they divulge past indiscretions or drop facts perhaps unimportant in themselves but quite conceivably portentous when added to the questioner's store of information, they take it for granted that the questioner does not intend to crucify them. Having obtained knowledge in such circumstances, the historian may never *intentionally* keep back any relevant fact, but he may find himself writing less sharply, perhaps, than he otherwise would if the writers were merely names or incarnations of literary abstractions.

iii

Having reached the stage where the historian has completed his research among the living repositories of the past, what follows? Has he left out some essential piece in the puzzle, neglected an important figure? Has he distorted the picture by blurring contextual relations? Has he relied too much on the testimony of one person, or a single group? These misgivings, which never left me, were intensified after a well-known man of letters* wrote to me that although a quotation from one of his letters I had fastened upon might be factually accurate, "It is no more authentic in revealing my position than a single candid camera shot which catches its subject in the midst of a grimace is in revealing his true physiognomy."

Since receiving this comment, I have thought a good deal about his phrase, the "true physiognomy," and I have wondered whether the portraits of our living or recent contemporaries can ever be more than impressionistic daubs. One would suppose that the historian-painter, with his model seated before him, ought to achieve a recognizable likeness, but the reverse is often true.

Consider the question of factual accuracy. It sometimes turns out that the profusion of historical evidence itself compounds the possibility of error. I have in my possession a long letter from a once popular writer which retells and analyzes certain episodes in his career described in the published memoirs of a former friend. He does not accuse the writer of deliberate falsifying, but he attributes the incorrect allegations and errors of fact in the book to the politi-

*Lewis Mumford.

cal point of view of the author at the time he was writing his autobiography. Whether or not my correspondent's strictures are justified, they remind us that no writer enjoys total recall, that every recollection is suspect.

Nor can newspapers always be trusted. In 1935, the New York *Times* reported that the proletarian novelists Jack Conroy and Nelson Algren had driven to Alabama with a committee of writers and had been shot at by some of the local goons. Later I learned from Conroy that Algren had reneged at the last moment and hadn't gone. This is a trivial example, but if other so-called facts, embalmed in history like flies in amber, are as unreliable, how much more questionable or unascertainable are the conversations and meetings and alcoholic parties recollected in tranquility? How true, really, are the tales from the horse's mouth? Eyewitness accounts of a murder or accident, we are told, often contradict each other. How much more untrustworthy may be the recollections of people who have conscious or unconscious motives for selective remembering or forgetting, who are themselves parties to the events described, whose view of the past is blurred by ignorance, hostility, or sentimentality? And when these murky memories are recorded by imperfect receivers, themselves deaf to finer vibrations, then written history concocted from such sources can become little more than hypotheses about what might have happened.

Would the historian of the present, then, be better advised to skip the interviews, stay aloof from the actors, and write without inhibitions from the published evidence? Might not the story of literary men and radicalism be more profitably and objectively examined twenty-five to fifty years from now when all the people concerned have vanished, all the autobiographies finished, and all the letters published?

After my long stint of gathering material about living writers—or the recently living—I am left with the uncomfortable feeling that my record of their lives, my explanations for their behavior and motives, are grounded on half-truths and partial evidence. At the same time, I don't think my mistakes or distortions or omissions could have been corrected in every instance by more rigorous methods of research, and I don't think the project was premature.

Every historian must feel occasionally that his results are questionable without entirely discounting them, and the recognition of ambiguities can often be illuminating in itself. I have listed some of the difficulties that beset the historian who seeks to explain his contemporaries. In the remainder of my talk, I should like to show how direct association with the men and women who lived through the Twenties and Thirties can enlighten as well as perplex him.

iv

A few years ago, Mr. Lewis Mumford observed in a letter to me:

> The moving idea during the thirties was not the vision of socialist transformation of our country. What made people join all sorts of movements, from technocracy to communism, from the Douglas plan to socialism, was the desire to repair the broken down machinery of our society and overcome the poverty and misery and fear that visited even the middle classes and the once-affluent professional classes. So badly had the dominant economic and political organizations failed that they were willing to try anything in order to correct injustices and restore life to our paralyzed economic limbs, as a person stricken with a fatal disease is willing to try anything, from homeopathy to surgery, provided it promises relief. The spectacle of human suffering was so widespread and inescapable that only the stupid or the hard-hearted could accept the existing order as the last word.

Other contemporaries had stated the same idea more or less eloquently. But why did particular men and women join or not join the Communist Party? Why did writers break away from the movement at one time and not at another? A person's motives may be as mysterious to himself as to others, but it would seem on closer inspection that the decision had more behind it than responsiveness to human suffering.

I should be the last to discount the real despair of the Thirties that fed upon Depression conditions or to play down any more than Mr. Mumford would the generous indignation excited by poverty and human callousness. But my interviews and reading lead me at the same time to a conclusion I cannot document, but which I nevertheless strongly believe, that some writers joined or broke from the movement because of their wives, or for careerist reasons, or because they read their own inner disturbances into the realities of social dislocation. To put it another way, the subject matter of politics (left-wing politics in this case) was often simply the vehicle for nonpolitical emotions and compulsions.

This conviction was reinforced after I had received a letter from Mr. Kenneth Burke, a writer I had read and admired for many years and whom I thought I understood pretty well. I had selected him for special scrutiny, and I had described his response to Communism as primarily rational and intellectual rather than religious or emotional. Later he wrote me that his feelings toward the Left movement had not been nearly so detached and whimsical as I had suggested, and he cited one of his poems, published in the *New Masses* (a plea to harness human passions) as an illustration:

> Try if you can [he wrote] . . . (so much gets lost between the writing and the written!) imagine it being written, or try to, in an orgy of weeping. For that's exactly how it was written. Analyzing it in later years, I realize that the principle of unification here celebrated was by no means of the political sort that the poem designates on its face. Or, more accurately, the personal, psychological motives that are not there at all, for the reader viewing the poem *ab extra* (as, of course, it should be read, for public aesthetic purposes).
>
> I could cite many other things that I wrote during that period, things involving an order of motives that I know for a fact were implicated, yet do not reveal themselves if read simply on their face.

The points he continued to explicate in this letter were the profound nonpolitical aspects of his affiliation with the Left and the impossibility of solving the mystery of political commitment. "What is the point of all this?" his letter concludes.

> Simply to state my feeling that, among every man whose ideas and antics you review, there were many for whom their political stand was interwoven with many strands not thus specifically political at all (except in the sense that one cd. reduce all human relations to politics). Yet the merging is so thorough, one would be hard put whether to say that it is or is not "deeply or religiously felt." I know it for a fact that the motives involved in my verses . . . were not reducible to the terms that show on the face of the poem. In this sense, the politics might be called a sham. Yet there was no other way to state this poem, and the political attitude was vitally necessary to their utterance. In this sense,

they might be said to "give depth" to the political dimension. For some, politics had very definite sexual tie-ups (normal or perverted); for others, it meant the alternative to such involvements. For some it meant marriage, for some it meant divorce. . . . What it all amounts to, I don't know. And I don't know how much you can trust what anybody says about it, no matter how accurate he may be at self-diagnosis and how willing to state what he finds. But I'm sure that there was a whole world of such motives operating somehow, in a tangle behind the tangle. . . .

These comments on the tangled skein of motives operating invisibly behind the show of events encourage a mistrust any historian feels towards his human subjects. Perhaps they should also awaken a kindred mistrust for his own distorting mind and eye. If the men and women he interviews are guilelessly contributing to the legend of the past, how can he be sure that he is not also the inadvertent falsifier dazzled by the mirage of the recent past and unable to divest himself of his own contemporaneity? The "objective" history shades into autobiography or merely adds another footnoted rumor to the historical romance of his times. Ideally, the historian should always be *in* history, so steeped and soaked in it that for short periods he loses his own identity. But of course he never can, or perhaps never should, for as Meinecke said, the historian "would thereby deprive himself of a source of perception." And what drives him to choose a man, a period, an event is an inner necessity of which he may very likely be unaware.

When I wrote about the events of my own lifetime and of a selected group of people who flourished during this period, was I willy-nilly closer to these events imaginatively than I was, let us say, to the American Civil War? I dare say I was and that I should have been if I had never undertaken the study of the literary Left and spent every day of my life plowing through the records of the "Great Rebellion." The sense, if not the meaning, of the recent past rubs off on a contemporary even if he has walked through the tunnel of years in pitch blackness. In my case, the tunnel was not completely dark and my eyes were half open. But in trying to resee these years through the eyes of other witnesses, the historian must cope with the tricks of memory and with unconscious falsifications and distortions—his own included. How faithful to the spoken and unspoken words are the notes for his interviews that help to determine his historical design? In the Thirties, many writers looked at the world through a grille of bias. This ordered or "angled" perspective affected accounts of personal relationships as well as history. Even during less passionate times, the astigmatic views of every recorder are corrected by built-in mechanical adjustments.

What gives the historian of contemporary events the sense that he is somehow face to face with reality is that the "facts" he purports to reveal are still close enough to their moment of birth to give him the illusion of their plasticity and liveness. *Rigor mortis* has not yet frozen them; the facts are not yet artifacts. Or to change the metaphor, recent facts retain for a time an afterglow. This is what the historian attempts to catch before the afterglow fades away. Yet it is only an afterglow, and the historian is very likely color-blind. As the contemporary ceases to be contemporary and drops into the past, compounded errors and paradoxes are discarded; blurred faces come into focus, and no eyewitness remains to say: "You're wrong. That wasn't the way they looked at all." Until these living testaments depart, the historian dares only to surmise. Depending upon people with fallible memories, trusting to the "reconsidered passion" of his informants, his attempts to reconstruct the recent past can be at best only experiments in model building.

And yet these reflections on contemporary history must inevitably proliferate doubts about all history. The "inconsistencies and contradictions" the historian of the present detects in the living witnesses, as Alan Bullock reminds us, "are frequently bewildering, but the historian who hopes to escape from such conflicts of evidence by flying to the Sixteenth and Seventeenth centuries only deceives himself. For the history of the Sixteenth and Seventeenth centuries was once contemporary history—for the witnesses on whose evidence he has often to rely." In how many instances have the keys, the essential disclosures, been lost or unrevealed? And how much history, whether written by contemporaries or by historians centuries later, has been the work of misinformed people relying upon incomplete data?

Let us concede that the attempt to record the present can only result in a reasonably accurate facsimile. The historian's clumsy probings, nevertheless, may ultimately prove to be of greater usefulness than he suspects. Thanks to his occasional insights as well as blunders, his successors—less baffled by the "supple confusions" that obsessed him—will wander with more assurance through history's "contrived corridors" and "cunning passages" and possibly find an exit. In the meantime, the historian "trying [as Eva Reichmann has put it] to pierce through the tangle of present-day happenings towards an understanding of his own place in the maze," may share Henry James's delight in what he called "a palpable imaginable *visitable* past," a past close enough to be grasped, still unprotected by the "dignity" of history, and blending at once the strange and the familiar.

American Writers in Russia:
The Three Faces of Lenin

The introductory poem in H. H. Lewis's volume of poems *Thinking of Russia* (1932) opens with the lines:

> I'm always thinking of Russia,
> I can't keep her out of my head,
> I don't give a damn for Uncle Sham,
> I am a left-wing radical Red.

Lewis, a revolutionary Missouri farmhand and author of a crude but expressive doggerel he called "Bumthoughts" or "Bolshegrams," was only one of the more colorful American proletarian poets for whom Russia in the Thirties was an ideal—almost an incantation:

> Russia, Russia, righting wrong
> Russia, Russia, Russia!
> That unified one sovereign throng
> That hundred and sixty million strong
> Russia!
> America's loud *Example-Song,*
> Russia, Russia, Russia.[1]

For the past fifteen years, a handful of American radical bards had been celebrating the USSR and its leaders in ecstatic if uneven

Originally published in *Survey*, no. 41 (April 1962), 43–57.

verse. Hymns to peasants, Moscow, the Red Army, Lenin, Trotsky, Karl Radek, and Sen Katayama and rhymed protestations of loyalty to the Russian proletariat regularly appeared in the pro-Bolshevik press. But with the advent of the Great Depression, a good many American writers and intellectuals, hitherto uninterested in the Soviet experiment or at best mildly curious about "one sixth of the globe," turned their minds eastward and sometimes traveled in that direction. If they did not exult in socialist reconstruction so buoyantly as H. H. Lewis, they nonetheless began to think that perhaps the heirs of Lenin might have discovered a radical cure for an economically and spiritually sick society. No longer satisfied with the tenuous impressions of Russia obtained from Russian literature and music, they were now ready to tap the almost inexhaustible sources of information and misinformation that had been accumulating without letup since the 1917 revolution.

From this stream of essays, memoirs, exposés, diaries, economic analyses, political treatises, and cultural surveys, the inquirer could learn that revolutions do much harm materially, socially, and spiritually—and much good; that the Bolsheviks were the architects of a viable socialism or its gravediggers; that the Soviets had been compelled to change their policies in order to win over the peasants; that Russia was moving toward capitalism; that Bolshevism was a semi-Asiatic autocracy; that the habit of autocracy in Russia was not Bolshevik at all but Russian and that Russian socialism provided the world with the only escape from capitalist wars; that Russian Communism was "still a constructive political and economic experiment, but not what you would call revolutionary"; that Soviet Russia sought to emulate the worst features of Western society—its industry, its soulless mechanism—and was simply the reverse side of Babbitt America; and that Bolsheviks were fated

> to be a tonic-purgative for an over-sophisticated, cynical, senescent, cunningly complicated world of individualistic enterprise, a world which long since solved the problem of adequately producing wealth, but falters at the task of finding satisfactory methods for controlling and justly equalizing its distribution.[2]

In general, the vociferous but hardly influential literary partisans of the Russian experiment before the Thirties belonged to the corps of political and intellectual rebels who had come of age during the two administrations of Woodrow Wilson. John Reed, author of *Ten Days That Shook the World* and already by the early Twenties a minor saint in the Soviet pantheon, was the most celebrated member of this group, but its program had been energetically pressed by such radicals as Max Eastman, Floyd Dell, Joseph Freeman, Michael Gold, V. F. Calverton, and others in the columns of the left-wing magazines. All but Dell had spent some time in the USSR before 1930; each had done his best to refute the canards of the Philistines (for whom the Soviet Union was a hideous amalgam of anarchism, free love, atheism, and despotism, worse, said the venerable labor leader Samuel Gompers, than "the most unwashed and freakish" bohemianism of Greenwich Village), and to persuade the apolitical avant-gardists and expatriates that here was a society from which there was no need to alienate themselves.

The Left intelligentsia made little impression on the American reading public who held to their image of "Red Rooshia" as a horde of boors ruled by licentious bomb-throwing scoundrels. By the late Twenties, however, they had made considerable headway with intellectuals depressed by their own institutions and culture and receptive to reports of artistic experimentation in the USSR. A dearth of translations of Soviet plays, poems, and fiction prevented much firsthand acquaintance with Soviet accomplishments, but between 1928 and 1930 a number of recent Soviet works appeared in English together with articles and books on the Russian theater. Even so, as late as 1930 no survey of Soviet art and literature existed in English, a gap that was only partially filled by *Voices of October* (1930),[3] a pioneer study by Joseph Freeman, Joshua Kunitz, and Louis Lozowick.

Had American writers taken the time to sample the literature, pro and con, about Soviet society, and had they been living in a period conducive to detached assessment, something approximating a balanced view of the noble/barbarous Russian state might have emerged. What hampered any judicious appraisal before 1930 and after were the dark associations engendered by the very words "Russia" and "Communism" and the deeply ingrained prejudices of those who elected to attack or defend them. Many Soviet apologists, for example, were first- or second-generation Eastern European Jews.

They or their parents had carried to America memories of savage pogroms and an understandable hatred of czarist oppression. Thus when Maurice Hindus, himself a Jew born in a Ukrainian village, returned to his birthplace in a Chekhovian mood and in his book *Red Bread* (1931) referred sympathetically to a little priest he talked to there, Michael Gold sardonically commented: "This little priest may have wielded an axe in chopping off Jewish heads in pogroms, or he may have been a glutton, a drunkard and Tsarist spy."[4]

Most American radicals were likely either to approach Russia through a Dostoevskian fog or to contrast Old Russia—backward, primitive, a land of besotted serfs, secret police, and Siberian penal colonies—with the New Russia crowded with clean-cut, undrunken, literate proletarians and rosy-cheeked *kolkhozniki*. The New Russians could be seen framed in the pages of *USSR in Construction*, happily driving homemade tractors, attending operas, and parading through the Red Square in gym suits. Even the street workers, according to one American poet, labored happily to the tune of an inner music:

> The workers here spill onward at their own sweet rate and
> Their rhythm is confident and the tune of their feet temperate:
> Daily out in the street the river of them moves abreast to lathes,
> To shops and furrows, each unit lifting a red flag like a sail:
> Also the poised river flows two ways around an island of street repairs
> Where muscles already move well,
> Shovels slamming the soil to finish the job by nightfall.[5]

Most of the American literary visitors to Russia lacked the knowledge and the background to determine whether the attitudes and behavior they praised or blamed were the fruits of Bolshevism or merely evidence of persisting national traits. Like all travelers, they transported their preconceptions with their luggage. Russia was a new world for them, a world whose bizarre geography they had conned from obsolete texts or unreliable promotional tracts, but it was also a mirror which reflected their own hopes and anxieties. For many of them, Russia was a way station in their spiritual itinerary, as England, France, Italy, and Germany had been for their nineteenth-century counterparts. Unlike their predecessors, however, a good many of the literary voyagers of the Thirties were leaving an

America that seemed to have lost its confidence and drive. The new Communist society served as a gauge to measure the strengths and weaknesses of their faltering though still powerful country.

Of the score or more American writers who traveled to Russia between 1920 and 1940,* three are of particular interest not only because they were and are of major importance in contemporary American literary history, but also because each represented a philosophy, an aesthetic, a kind of political and intellectual stance shared by others of their generation. One was anti-Communist and aggressively nonpolitical; two were fellow travelers at the time and predisposed to favor the Soviet regime. Each wrote an account of his experiences, but although their trips took place within a space of five years and although they saw many of the same sights and passed through the same regions, their accounts could not possibly be more unlike.

E. E. Cummings, self-defined *"peesahtel y hoodozhnik,"* left Paris for the USSR in the spring of 1931 and spent about a month in what was for him a vast and dreary "Enormous Room." He stayed in Moscow most of the time, but he had one night in Kiev and a week in Odessa before he "escaped" via a Soviet steamer to Constantinople and thence to blissful Paris. Cummings did not go to Russia as a member of any delegation nor did he choose to join any tourist party. He had no interest in "economic or sociological problems," nor did he want to go to Russia as a writer or a painter: "No," he told an official at the Soviet Embassy in Paris, "I wish to go as myself."

And (on the strength of a supporting letter from his friend John Dos Passos) that is the way he went, although he found a number of uncongenial and genial escorts to guide him on his visits to theaters, circuses, museums, pubs, nightclubs, and social gatherings. Factories, collective farms, reformatories for prostitutes, prophylactic stations, divorce courts (the usual high points for touring Americans) Cummings ignored. He did inspect a model jail, talk to Russian writers, and take in the "casual filth" and "aimless commotion" of

*In addition to those already mentioned, these included Lincoln Steffens, Theodore Dreiser, John Dos Passos, Sinclair Lewis, Joseph Wood Krutch, Babette Deutsch, Anna Louise Strong, Claude McKay, Josephine Herbst, Matthew Josephson, Maurice Hindus, Isidor Schneider, Scott Nearing, W. H. Chamberlain, Dorothy Thompson, and many others.

the Soviet capital. What made his trip bearable were the accidental as well as the sought-for meetings with the dissidents, native and foreign: impoverished gentry precariously surviving in the New Russia, cynical American correspondents, shady entrepreneurs. Interviewed in Paris on his return, Cummings said the Russians were a "marvellous people," but it was "silly to rave about Russia if you don't know anything about it." He scornfully dismissed the "generalizers" who spouted platitudes and announced he was planning to publish his travel notes, which he had smuggled out of the country.[6]

Two years later, *Eimi*, erroneously advertised as a novel, made a brief appearance and then vanished from the literary scene. Cummings wrote later that his "diary of a pilgrimage to Marxist Russia was dutifully damned by America's fellow-travelling literary gangsters," and it is certainly true that the tone and content of his travelogue went against the prevailing pro-Soviet mood. But the failure of this extraordinary work could be explained as much or more by its portmanteau words, fractured syntax, and Cummingsesque typography as by its anti-Soviet bias. Marianne Moore called *Eimi* a "large poem" composed in the author's "mental handwriting,"[7] and even Ezra Pound, no foe of verbal experimentation, observed in a congratulatory letter to Cummings that "the longer a work is [*Eimi* was 432 pages] the more and longer should be the passages that are perfectly clear and simple to read." Pound complained that he "found it difficult to read the stuff consecutively."[8] If Cummings had written his tragicomic vision of the totalitarian *Inferno* in straightforward prose, it very likely would have received a more sympathetic hearing.

Before his voyage into the dehumanized land of "was," a friend in Paris had warned him not to be duped by the Potemkin villages and to keep his eye cocked for the "Gay Pay Oo." From the moment he crossed the Polish border, Comrade "Kem-min-kz" (as the Russians called him) began to record his impressions of that "joyless experiment in force and fear," the Soviet state. Not merely the discomforts, graphically recounted, disturbed him, the long waits, the bad beer, the ugly non-men and non-women, the propaganda, the inefficiency, the "unmitigated dullness" of the theater, the "exjailbirds" and "shysters" who ran the country. More dreadful were the somber crowds mindlessly floating through the parks of culture and rest and the systematic quenching of joy:

. . . that's," comrade Kem-min-kz exploded, "what's lousy here! Trying!
everybody's never feeling; never for a moment relaxing, laughing, wondering—everybody's solemnly forever focusing upon some laughless idiotic unwonderful materially non-existent impermanence, which everybody apparently has been rabotatically instructed tovarich to welcome.
God damn undream! May the handshaking hell of the Elks and morons
bugger to a bloody frazzle everybody who spends his nonlife trying to
isn't.""

As a latter-day transcendental-anarchist, Cummings opposed not
revolution but "what has been miscalled the Russian revolution."
An idea is revolutionary, he has one of his spokesmen say, only
when it springs from the instincts, when it liberates. "What is an
idea? Idayn, a pattern. Superficial because incited. Instinct: the fundamental, the what you call Is; the inciting power, the instigating
force." By this criterion, the only living things he found in Russia
were some canvases by Picasso and Matisse in a Moscow museum
and the few real alive men and women he occasionally encountered
in the "indissoluble promiscuity" of the USSR.

Eimi has been read as a kind of dream voyage into an inferno,
and indeed the Dantean parallels are undisguisedly suggested at almost every point. K (Kem-min-kz, Cummings, Kafkaesque Everyman) passes through the infernal portal replete with smells at the
Polish border and is guided by his Virgil (Henry Wadsworth Longfellow Dana, grandson of the poet and an enthusiast for everything
Russian) through what is ostensibly heaven but is actually the lower
levels of hell. Cummings's Beatrice (reincarnated as Jack London's
daughter) usurps Virgil's place as K moves among the hopeless
specters and monstrous fabrications of the socialist state. "Factory-
fodder all," he calls them, "all machines' meat, efficiently disporting
itselfless necessarily itselfless seeking automatically finding itselfless. Directed flesh, managed vitality, conditioned purpose."
Leaving the hell of Moscow for the purgatory of Kiev and Odessa,
he at last sails to paradise and to liberty in his Communist ghost
ship.

Cummings's friendly and unfriendly Left critics tended to regard
his effort "to high hat an entire social system" with a certain indul-
gence and explained his distorted image of Russia as the self-por-
trait of a talented anachronism. Cummings, they decided, was a

vestige of a defunct lyric-Bohemia, a poet whose audience had out-grown him and who was as hostile to socialism as he was to One Hundred Per Cent Americanism. He was kin (to quote D. S. Mirsky's description of another American square peg, John Gould Fletcher) "with thousands of European intellectuals who wish to preserve the individualism that was allowed them by the liberal and competitive Capitalism of the nineteenth century, and who are equally afraid of the juggernaut of monopolistic Capitalism and the hammer and sickle of Communism."[9]

The Marxist explanation, however, missed the real significance of Cummings's undivine comedy. *Eimi* was not the book of a fright-ened or a desperate man. For all its self-indulgence, perverseness, and egocentricity, it took its cue from the ironic discomfitures of Mark Twain abroad and the individualism of Emerson and Thoreau. As Paul Rosenfeld observed in a brilliant essay on *Eimi*, the "main symbol is a grotesque personal accident, the absurd contradiction of an expectation by an event."[10] This is also the main symbol of *Innocents Abroad*. Cummings, the wise innocent, comically con-trasts the chimera of the propagandists—a gleaming, modern, joy-ous Russia—with its dingy gloomy reality. Russia inflates the Yan-kee in him, enhances his Cambridge, Mass., parochialism, just as Italy made Mark Twain think fondly of his spick-and-span America. Like Mark Twain again, who professes astonishment at his fellow tourists' ecstatic response to Leonardo's "Last Supper" when he can barely discern its faded outlines on the battered wall, so Cummings expresses his own amazement that the American tourists he meets have transmogrified an *inferno* into a *paradiso*. The values with which he measures Soviet success and failure are the values of the American Transcendentalists who judged all institutions by the amount of life or death they contained.

Unlike *Innocents Abroad*, unfortunately, *Eimi* is not a good-na-tured book, for all its gaiety and beauty. Too often the comic mood subsides into sour sarcasm. He tells his Virgil that he doesn't hate socialism: "so far as I can feel, I don't hate anything except hate." Yet his shrill contempt, his tiresome jokes about vulgar Jews, his obsession with dirt and stench clash with his affirmations of hope, Is, Instinct. His book is not anti-Russian; Cummings responded to goodness and manhood wherever he met them. Nevertheless his hatred for tyrannical abstractions extended to the people who embodied them.* If his sharp-eyed honesty kept him from substituting the ideal Russia for the New Russia ("in all its slavic unfinishedness," as Ezra Pound put it), his romantic disregard for time and history and his unremitting devotion to the private self removed a large part of the indispensable social context from his candid gaze.

Waldo Frank—novelist, critic, traveler—also went to Russia in 1931. His book *Dawn in Russia* came out a year later, and although it is inferior to *Eimi* as literature, it reflects a point of view more in keeping with the pro-Soviet mood. Not that Frank was uncritical of what he saw or less dedicated than Cummings to the cult of the flowering self, but he was more critical of America's spiritual and cultural inadequacies and had much greater confidence in the future of Soviet collectivism.

Although Frank was only five years older than Cummings, he seemed positively venerable in comparison to the "bad boy" of Cambridge; aesthetically and politically, they were worlds apart. In the Twenties, Cummings and his friends spurned the notion of literature as a branch of morality and delighted in verbal experimentation, the lively arts, and the pleasures of pure sensation. Frank, who had been part of a circle that included such serious-minded and almost priestlike intellectuals as Randolph Bourne and Van Wyck Brooks before the First World War, retained the social concern of the Wilsonian era throughout the so-called jazz age.

Between 1917 and 1931, Frank published a number of volumes, fictional and nonfictional, in which he laid bare the inner poverty of an America that had squandered its "spiritual substance." Trips to Spain and Latin America brought him into contact with societies materially impoverished but organic and integrated. He called upon his countrymen to consider the possibility of a culture which would unite "the world of fact in which we suffer all together with the world of dream in which we are alone," a society of separate persons whose individual natures would be liberated and extended through their harmonious identification with the Whole. He had not yet

*His response to Soviet bureaucracy constitutes some of the most mordant satire of his book. See, for example, his happy recognition of art *sans* politics and his feelings toward the killing weed of dogma which destroys it (p. 58) and his amusing and savage résumé of the "materialist dialectic" dispensed to visiting nonpolitical Americans like himself (pp. 83–87).

been to Russia, but one gathers from his random references to the Soviet Union that it shared with "all the peasant and proletarian peoples of Europe" the "deep potential energy," religious and aesthetic, that America lacked. He did not pretend to know what was actually happening in Russia, but he believed in "the universal value of the Soviet experiment." In professing to free men "from servitude to wealth," the Russians were engaged in "holy work."[11]

As far back as 1917 Frank had published a prose poem, "Holy Russia," in which he announced that his generation "knew" Russia even before the Revolution. They had seen the unborn Russia foreshadowed in its tortured youth who had sought asylum in America, in its "terrible" books, its songs and music. Out of Russia's agony, the poet declares, came life: "the gladness in the gloom of her tales, the prayer within her angry symphonies, the hunger and sorrow of her prophets—all of the love of hating Russia is made manifest!"[12] Apparently Frank had never renounced this messianic conception of Holy Russia, although he recognized that the beleaguered Soviets, "straining all forces toward that industrial reorganization which alone can save the Revolution," and feeling impelled "to overcome the self-indulgent 'dreaminess' which was a vice in repressed Tsarist Russia," were deliberately suppressing the mystical predilections of the masses.[13]

Frank got his first look at Russia in 1931. He did not go as a convert, a pilgrim, or a detached observer, but as God's spy who would look at the USSR "with the lazy eye of intuition." Russia did not disappoint him nor did it totally allay his apprehensions. Communist society, he believed, inevitably inherited the evils of bourgeois society; it was constantly threatened by "a dogmatic rationalist creed (by no means discoverable in Marx) whose inadequate depth and breadth would ultimately exclude the creative energies of mankind." But Frank was pretty well convinced even before he went to Russia that Marx's "organic rationale" of revolution together with the spiritual resources of the Russian people would assure a just and creative social order.

Coming from Stockholm and Helsinki to the drabness of Leningrad did not seem to him a descent into unlife. The miserably clad, homely crowds moving along the Nevsky Prospekt, far from resembling Cummings's dreamlike undone shades, seemed transfigured by an electric current. The Russian physiognomy spoke to him of "confineless promise . . . intelligence, emotional complexity of the spirit, making the face of the average North American or Frenchman by contrast a mere smart grimace."

He determined to familiarize himself with the "dark root" of the Russian past before hastening in tourist fashion to the factories, workers' clubs, hospitals, and schools. To the dismay of his guide, he explored Dostoevsky's St. Petersburg, which now abounded in rotten buildings and the human detritus of the Revolution. Its ugliness did not depress him, for he saw it as "the bleak root from which burst the red flowers—1905 and 1917"! Throughout the rest of the trip, he contrasted the almost ubiquitous squalor (the "dismal heritage" of the past) with the transfiguring look of the proud citizens "still forced to live in the husk of the days of their enslavement."

There is something a little irritating in Frank's seerlike stare at the Soviet scene, his eye that penetrates the flux of appearance to the substratum of Reality, the ear attuned to the faintest reverberations of unspoken thought. The toilers in a communal dining room, he notes, "have eyes that rest tenderly upon me." A tiresome wait for a Volga steamboat enables him to become "a fragment of living Russia," to immerse himself "in this plasma of the Russian folk." A Russian village beats with "the pulse of earth and beast and man together." Nowhere in Russia can one discover the money-making look. Russian factory workers (unlike the proletariat in many parts of the world) are happy

> because here are whole men and women. Although their individual job be a single motion endlessly repeated, although they stand enslaved for hours to the turn of a wheel which they must feed and feed—yet in these dismal halls there is a whole humanity. Dream, thought, love, collaborate in the tedious business of making electric parts, since these toilers are not working for a boss—not even for a living: the least of them knows that he is making a Worker's union, that he is creating a world.

Comments like these help to explain Evelyn Waugh's annoyance with Frank's "pseudo-intimate personal emotions" and another reviewer's remark about the "moral self-indulgence" common to most travelers to the USSR.

Of course Frank does not always write so seraphically. He can be blunt in his fault-finding or reporting, whether he notes the poor food, the uncomfortable accommodation, the reluctance of all but the solidly entrenched Communist to criticize the government, or a "sugar-water" talk by the saintly Gorki. Clouds of doubt occasionally obscure his radiant vision of Russia's destiny. He understands why the regime carries on its war against the churches, but the crude antireligious propaganda offends him. To employ a falsehood in order to emancipate a people enslaved by a falsehood is perhaps "a need made acute by Russia's state of siege," but isn't there a danger, he asks, "that the Communist truth take an accessible form that is half-truth? that the half-truth harden into a lie? that a new formal falsehood stifle Russia?" He considers the possibility as well that Russia might lose "the spirit of Communism," settle into "an industrialized, collectivist order, regimented by a new ruling caste." Then it would "become a menace: an engine of irresistible might (mechanized and well fuelled) which its rulers could direct in conquest against Orient and Europe."

Frank refused to dwell upon these doleful speculations. The human nature of the Russians made such a course unlikely. The next phase in Soviet history would be the emergence from the economic to the cultural stage of Communism after the USSR had made itself immune from the threats of the capitalists. In the meantime, every person of good will owed his loyalty to Russia, "to its social aims . . . to the soldiers in the revolutionary ranks," but not to its methods and dogmas. Americans in particular, Frank concluded, had to eschew the "false emulation" which betrayed the spirit of Russian innovation and to remain true to their "own needs and intuitions."

When Edmund Wilson journeyed to Russia in 1935, events had occurred since the visits of Cummings and Frank which tempered the optimism of hitherto faithful travelers: inside Russia, forced collectivization, the mass deportation of the kulaks and the "socially dangerous," and the sinister aftermath of the Kirov assassination; outside Russia, the successes of Mussolini and the German Communist Party's role in the rise of National Socialism.

Since the mid-Twenties, Wilson's interest in Russia had gradually extended from its art to its politics, from Russian films to Marxism-

Leninism, and by 1932 he was backing the Communist Party with the other "cool-headed revolutionists" who looked to Russia. "I, too, admire the Russian Communist leaders," he acknowledged, "because they are men of superior brains who have triumphed over the ignorance, the stupidity, and the short-sighted selfishness of the mass. . . . As a writer I have a special interest in the success of the 'intellectual' kind of brains as opposed to the acquisitive kind."[14] The American Communists were delighted with what they chose to regard as his confession of faith although they were somewhat put off by his thorny individualism. As his friend Malcolm Cowley noticed, Wilson "sheered away from all sorts of political groups even when their ideas appeared to be similar to his own." This skepticism and open-mindedness made him receptive to ideological heresies tabooed by the American CP. For example, he approved of Trotsky's condemnation of the Party line on "social fascism," criticized the repression of intellectual freedom in the USSR, and even listened to the "slanderous vileness" of the "degenerate" Russian émigrés. On the eve of his two-month visit to the USSR, it would have been hard to predict just what kind of report on Soviet society he would write.[15]

It appeared in book form as *Travels in Two Democracies* (1936),[16] the first section of which was composed of articles on Depression America written between 1932 and 1934. Presumably the reader was invited to contrast a riven, angry, and hopeless society with a slovenly, confident one, but his vignettes of Soviet life interlaced with his own reflections on politics, history, and culture did not satisfy the partisans or the foes of the USSR. Wilson possessed no cosmic truth, as Waldo Frank did, which might have illuminated the inner meaning of the Russian experiment. He distrusted, and with good reason, the kind of instantaneous understanding displayed by Cummings. Each of the two "democracies" had its special distinctions—America its durable republican values, Soviet Russia its place on the "moral top of the world"—yet he did not give the nod to either. The people in both societies allowed "obsolete authorities" to decide their destinies, invoked the same "invisible forces" whether in the name of God or the masses. Rather than rely upon these "mythologies," Wilson preferred to fall back on "accuracy of insight" and "courage of judgment" (p. 325).

Wilson's Russian impressions must be tested by these standards.

He describes first and then reflects, bringing into his explanations a wide and apposite learning, a sense of history, and a relish for the actual. He is not indulgent toward the Russians as Frank was or self-indulgent as Cummings was. Leningrad strikes him as shabby and drab, yet the "dingy and mute monotonous hordes" who "move like slow floods of water" along "the straight interminable streets" are neither electrically charged nor ghostlike. They aren't noisy but neither are they "straining" or "anxious" like the American crowds. The city belongs to them; they are "not pitted against an alien environment."

Although Wilson accommodated himself quite easily to that mixture of severity and slackness he found in the Russia of 1935, he had none of Frank's capacity for attuning his soul to the collective spirit of the Soviet toilers. The Park of Rest and Culture—"neutral, enormous, bare, colorless" (which Cummings had rendered as one of hell's lower precincts)—Wilson designated as a "limbo." Had these dumb expressionless crowds, he asked, lost all capacity for enjoyment? And yet they moved freely, unvexed by the harassments of petty officials.

Always alert and hawk-eyed, sensitive to the concretely typical and the implications of the seemingly trivial, inhaling nuances, Wilson made an admirable reporter. Few travelers to the USSR so adroitly avoided the temptations of over- and under-praising. "People invariably come here," he wrote, "whether they think they are for or against, in such an inflamed state of mind; and even those who are least inflammable are subject to those strange alternations of enthusiasm and disappointment." A lost suitcase might signify to one traveler a breakdown of the Soviet system; a helpful official might enforce a conclusion "that the Russian peasants are the happiest in the world." Wilson refused to "gush" about the Soviet Union or do anything more than observe and think. He sniffed the smell of fear and said so. He asserted that Soviet patriotism could impel officials to justify the bad. He questioned Soviet claims that neuroses common to the West were unknown in the USSR. He deplored the persecution of political deviationists, the glorification of Stalin, and the Stalinist distortion of history. Emotionally and temperamentally, he seemed closer to the nineteenth-century Russian intelligentsia—the uneasy and alienated Dostoevskians and the Goncharov Hamlets who had "come back as we had done at home to a straggling provincial civilization"—than he was to the practical single-minded Communists.

The unattractive features of Russia, it must be emphasized, did not distract him from the accomplishments of the Revolution. Fresh from observing the blights of his own country, he reminded his readers that some Americans also had to put up with snooping police.[17] He told his friend Mirsky that Ford's plant in Dearborn, "completely walled off from the rest of Detroit," was subject to an industrial discipline and company espionage—not, he couldn't resist adding, unlike Russia's. At bottom, he genuinely liked Russians, approved of their program, respected their leaders. The Russian masses endured a great deal, he thought, and yet appeared to be resigned to the hardships in store for them. As he passed through Poland, Germany, and France on his return to the United States, it seemed—especially to one who had recently traveled through America and the USSR—that these former "immense entities" resembled "a pack of little quarrelsome states maintaining artificial barriers and suffering from morbid distempers."

In his final reflections, Wilson's mind flashed back to Lenin's tomb and to the man whose statue with its "peering and genial" eyes he had first glimpsed in Leningrad. Cummings had also taken a long look at the embalmed Lenin and so had Waldo Frank. The faces of Lenin as they are described in their respective books serve as a kind of Rorschach test for the three observers.

Cummings sees Lenin's mausoleum as

a rigid pyramidal composition of blocks; an impurely mathematical game of edges: not quite cruelly a cubic cerebration—equally glamourless and emphatic, withal childish . . . perhaps the architectural equivalent for "boo!—I scared you that time!"

and its sainted inmate as little more than a "trivial idol throned in stink." His descent into the tomb "(toward death's deification moving)" parallels Dante's descent into the lowest circles of hell, the furthermost remove from light and life. Cummings files slowly downward with the line of un-men, unmovingly moving "toward the grave of themselves, all toward the grave of Self," and reaches the guarded "prismshaped transparency" where he beholds "a small-not-intense head and a face-without-wrinkles and a reddish beard." The historical Lenin never appears. The Lenin of the crypt is a wax-work, less alive than the "mightier deeper puppets" of Coney Island. He is "silly unking of Un-," the Negation of negations, who merely says: "I Am Mortal. So Are You. Hello," in short, an appropriate icon for the country of the dead. Lenin, the dark necromancer, has become for Cummings the symbol of the mystagogue who animated an abstraction and thereby deprived of life the masses he ostensibly liberated.

Like Wilson, Frank was also struck by the "huge iron 'ikon'" of Lenin in the Finland Station, and like Cummings he stood in line to enter Lenin's tomb, thrust "deep into earth to hold the body of the new earth savior." Frank approached the holy sepulcher as a reverent pilgrim in rapport with the rest of the pious company, and he saw in the face of Lenin the history and meaning of the Revolution:

> He lies in a soldier's simple uniform with his hands clasped on his chest. The hands are delicate and pale and long: they bespeak precision, the exquisite capacity for pain is in them and the equal power to respond to pain with exquisite method. The head is bald, its roundness bulges forward at the brow, giving the dynamic quality of motion. All thought and feeling seem here perfectly conjoined, and the sure harmony has a single rhythm of the march, of indefeasible direction. I look on Lenin's face. The beard is cropped short and the mouth shows. The upper lip is long and hard, the lower pushes forward in the same indefeasible direction. The features have the Tatar glint that I have seen in Volga towns. The eyes are shut, but were they open they would still be hidden. The face gleams with an intricate emotion. There is resentment in it, cold and terrible. There is pain, tender as a child's. There is intelligence, the response to both the pain and the resentment: it quickens the face, not with fire but light. And there is a terrible hilarity, the laughter of a storm ready to burst and overwhelm the world. The varying emotions merge in a calm integer: the pain has fused in the intelligence as understanding, the resentment has fused in it as will. The face is an intellectual engine fuelled by feeling. Death dims the brightness of the face, and shrinks the body. But death has made perfect the man's impersonal beauty. In Lenin's suffering, his will to overcome the cause of suffering, in the pure methodology of mind that his will fathered, in this body of a man cleansed of the personal, I feel the embodied spirit of the Revolution.

Wilson's finely modeled and resonant portrait of the face in Lenin's tomb dwells upon some of the features mentioned by Frank, "the aggressive intellect of the box like skull," the "slightly slanting eyes," the "exquisite fineness" of the features. But Wilson detected nothing of the suffering Christ in Lenin's aristocratic lineaments:

> yet if this is an aristocrat, it is an aristocrat who has not specialized as one: and it is a poet who has not specialized as a poet, a scientist who has not specialized as a scientist. Nor is it in the least the face of a saint. Except for the slightly slanting eyes, it seems today hardly even the face of a Russian. For here has humanity bred, independent of all the old disciplines, the scientist whose study is humanity, the poet whose material is not images but the water and salt of human beings—the superior man who has burst out of the classes and claimed all that is superior which man has done for the refinement of mankind as a whole.

The entombed face which moved him so profoundly was the face of a poet-innovator who had summoned the Russian masses "from their sluggish plasm." It was the face of Marxism, as Wilson conceived of it in 1935—logical, naturalistic, anti-traditional—as well as the face of a hero who had forced the world "to extend its conception of what man, as man alone, can accomplish."

Wilson's left-wing critics praised the set piece on Lenin but worried about its implications. Wasn't he developing a cult of genius? Didn't his concern for the superior person imply an almost libelous denigration of the masses? Perhaps *Travels in Two Democracies* reflected more than Wilson realized his feeling that democracy in both Russia and the United States tended "to lower cultural standards." Hence his attraction to the unterrified social engineer of Bolshevism who had energized a people and set them on the right path.

Looking back at himself twenty years later, Wilson declared that like "other inheritors of the eighteenth-century tradition," he had overlooked the place of myth, ritual, and symbol in the USSR, and, more significant, that he had failed to recognize behind his studied rejection of supernatural religion the "yearning for 'Holy Places' " that emanates from his passage on Lenin's face. Moreover, he had not yet perceived Marxism's "disguised utopianism" even as his "atavistic Protestantism" made him susceptible to Marxian morality. When he finally saw the mythical and dogmatic elements in Marxism, he abandoned them as dangerous ingredients in an otherwise plausible system of social analysis. Unlike Cummings and Frank, Wilson never made pronouncements on the sacredness of Personality or on the meaning of history, but neither did he relinquish a qualified trust in the power of the "human will" and "moral force" in mankind's struggle toward order in an impersonal universe.

Wilson had read the proceedings of the first Zinoviev-Kamenev trials while floating down the Volga and had concluded even before his return that they were faked. Not long after, he was writing his angry but controlled reflections on the crimes of Soviet officialdom. Waldo Frank agonized over the first trial, called upon the Soviet Union "as a loyal defender of your great cause" to explain itself to the world, concluded several years later that the trials were probably valid, and—still agonizing over the 1937 trial—recommended an impartial inquiry to reassure the demoralized "young liberals and radicals" that all was well. In 1940, he stigmatized Stalin's "methods of blood and guile" while reaffirming his faith in "the Russian future."[18] As for Cummings, he shifted his attack on the "kumrads" from prose to poetry:

> every kumrad is a bit
> of quite unmitigated hate
> (travelling in a futile groove
> god knows why)
> and so do i
> (because they are afraid to love).

The "red youthful giant" who had awakened the "deepest hopes" of American radicals in the Twenties and early Thirties had suddenly transformed himself into an ogre, a devourer of his own children. And blotting out the faces of Lenin—the aristocrat, the engineer, the philosopher-king, the savior—were the masks of his dissimulating successor.

Notes

1. Here the repetition of the word "Russia," as William Carlos Williams noted in the *New Masses*, could be likened to Louis Aragon's onomatopoetic use of the letters SSSR in his poem "Le Front Rouge." "It goes to his head, as he says repeatedly, it maddens him with hope, with conviction,

with certainty, with belief, the belief that sets him singing. His songs are songs, as good as he can make them, of triumph, realization. A poet's view of a real future." Aragon's poem was translated brilliantly, although reluctantly, by his friend E. E. Cummings during his visit to the USSR in 1931. See *The Red Front* (Chapel Hill, N.C.: Contempo Publishers, 1933).

2. *Dial*, 85 (1928), 245.

3. Particularly valuable sections in this book are Kunitz's "Men and Women in Soviet Literature," based on a firsthand knowledge of Soviet poetry and fiction and illustrated by many quotations, and Joseph Freeman's essay on the Russian film. The parts dealing with music and the arts are sketchy, but *Voices of October* is probably the last book written by Americans close to the Party which contains a sympathetic account of the Russian Constructivists, Futurists, and Suprematists.

4. *New Republic*, 67 (October 7, 1931), 211.

5. Charles B. Strauss, "Moscow Street," *New Masses*, 14 (January 8, 1935), 15.

6. See Charles Norman, *The Magic Maker: E. E. Cummings* (New York: Macmillan, 1958), 277ff.

7. *Poetry* (August 1933), 278.

8. Norman, *The Magic Maker*, 299–300.

9. *Criterion* (April 1931), 535.

10. *Wake*, no. 5 (Spring 1946), 31.

11. Waldo Frank, *Our America* (1919), 231; *The Re-Discovery of America* (1929), 264–265.

12. *Seven Arts* (May 1917), 60–61.

13. *America-Hispana* (1931), 175.

14. "What I Believe," *Nation* (27 January 1932), 98.

15. See the *New Republic* (January 10, 1936; December 28, 1932); *New Masses* (September 1, 1936). That Wilson had doubts about his decision to use his Guggenheim Fellowship to visit Russia is borne out in a letter to his friend and mentor, Professor Christian Gauss of Princeton University: "The recent events in Russia have inspired me with certain misgivings about my trip. The Comrades over here consider me attainted with Trotskyism; and I see that a number of people were expelled from the Marx-Engels Institute lately for 'ideological perversion,' a sin of which I'm as likely as not guilty." *The Papers of Christian Gauss*, ed. K. G. Jackson (1957), 304–305.

16. The Russian section was republished in *Red, Black, Blond and Olive, Studies in Four Civilizations: Zuni, Haiti, Russia, Israel* (1956). In this version, Wilson added the notations he had omitted in 1936 together with retrospective comments. The revised edition, however, loses part of its force by being detached from its American half.

17. An attitude which he still retains. The two "democracies" mirror each other's defects. Thus, the United States is also "used to mediocrity," has its own cult of the common man. "Our recent security purges and

political heresy-hunts," he asserts, "must have been inspired by the Russian trials." Like the Russians, Americans have alternated between cycles of xenophobia and xenophilia. See *A Piece of My Mind* (1958), 65–80.

18. See the *New Republic* (February 27, 1935, May 12, 1937), 19–20; *New Masses*, May 18, 1937; Waldo Frank, *Chart for Rough Waters* (1940), 75.

The American Left:

Some Ruins and Monuments

The recently reported upsurge of the New Left, it is being said, has helped to rekindle interest in the 1930s. But in spite of the alleged similarities between the old radicals of that much written-about and much misunderstood decade and the new, most commentators have thus far discovered very little that links the Marxian socialists of the Great Depression with the loosely confederated Party of Dissent whose sit-ins and teach-ins and marches are featured in today's press. Unlike the Old Left, the New Left seems to be confined pretty much to the generation under thirty and to be concentrated largely in the academies. Although it contains Marxist elements and plumps for some kind of noncapitalist society, a humane and untotalitarian socialism, its primary concerns at the moment are civil rights and peace, not the overthrow of international capitalism.

A movement so amorphous is difficult to assess, as the new radicals themselves concede. Apparently a portion of its membership is satisfied with verbal intransigence, moral pronouncements, and utopian projections, while its leading spirits and a committed minority believe in hard work and organization, distrust theory, and preach action. Taking the New Left as a whole, it would seem that its radicalism is as personal and subjective as it is ad hoc and eclectic. It offers no blueprints, no sacred writ, no leader, no model coun-

Originally published in *Denver Quarterly*, 1, no. 2 (Summer 1966), 5–23.

try; its antipathies are plainer than its goals. It might almost be said that the New Left is as opposed to the "style" or "image" of the Establishment or Power Structure (those all-encompassing and sinister designations for the Enemy) as it is to the Establishment's political and economic policies. Finally, like other youth movements before it, the New Left is imbued with idealism, even a kind of religiosity, but its style is "cool" and its tactics pragmatic; it dreams of no lost Eden or New Jerusalem. It lives only in the existential "now."

In making these generalizations, I realize that I am describing the New Left as a much more definable and cohesive movement than it is, but I offer this imperfect description—for what it is worth—as a point of departure. Like their conservative counterparts, the New Left has written off the Thirties as irrelevant to our times, if not as a historical blunder. It dismisses the radical veterans either as capitulators to the American consensus or as perpetrators of old obsessions: "tedious, tired of themselves, full of self-hate, and chained to an idealism so abstract that it precludes all love of life." Sometimes sorrowfully, more often impatiently, it lectures to the Reds of the Thirties. "You may have aspired to our goals," it says in effect, "but you fatally compromised yourselves by turning means into ends and by yielding to ideology. You placed your hopes in the future while we keep ours in the present. You were sectarian, suspicious, exclusive, and you made a fetish of reason. We are open-minded, flexible, down-to-earth, and we abominate pompous intellectuality. You appealed to authorities and equivocated when you felt it to be necessary. We don't try to escape our moral dilemmas via the dialectic; for us there are no 'good' wars and 'bad' wars. You were Marxists with a creed, sacred texts, a Holy Land, and a party hagiology; we are existentialists. You were solemn 'Squares' who never had any fun; we are irreverent and uninhibited."

Thus far, no sustained dialogue has taken place between the Old Left and the New, largely, I suspect, because the relics of the former, when they speak at all, have not set themselves up as mentors for the radical Sixties. It is not my purpose here to reverse the judgment of the New Left on the Old, but to resurrect, momentarily and sketchily, the decade which the New radicals with their disregard for history have seldom bothered to investigate. In doing so, I must examine some of the clichés about the Thirties that have been accumulating over the years, particularly the notion still stubbornly clung to that artists and intellectuals sold their cultural birthright for a mess of red pottage, and I must attempt a brief survey of those times from which little or nothing of importance seems to have been salvaged.

Some months ago, a critic, presumably under forty and writing (as Carl Becker once said of another historian) "without fear and without research," asserted that "No decade of American culture has been so thoroughly and frequently repudiated as a cultural entity, as the nineteenth-thirties. . . . In retrospect, the thirties seems a decade that has not only espoused fallacious thoughts but also killed budding talents." I cite this mortuary judgment, so sweeping and so unqualified, not because I think it is true or false, but because it exemplifies a widely held belief that the Thirties were dismal and lethal, that the decade left few monuments and a vast pile of ruins.

Apart from the fact that decades have the annoying habit of running into each other and that generations, fed by the same ideals and sharing similar goals, inconveniently straddle time spans wider than ten years, it is still too early to make any final statements about the richness or barrenness of the Thirties. If they were violent, anxious, exciting, and confused, if they were befogged by "fallacious thoughts" and hostile to "budding talents," so, very likely, were less publicized decades. What we discover about the past after closer inspection often depends on our private preconceptions and on the assumptions of the age in which we live—assumptions that unconsciously affect the evaluations of even the most alert and professional observer. It is not surprising, therefore, that the published recollections of artists and intellectuals and men of affairs who flourished between the two world wars not only illuminate the period they lived through but also assist in the process by which public and private history is transmogrified into legend.

In attempting to answer the question "What was it like to live in the Thirties?" the chronicler is free to consult the growing number of histories, monographs, and anthologies on the age of the Great Depression, to leaf through files of newspapers and magazines, to examine the pertinent memoirs and autobiographies now appearing in such profusion, and perhaps to talk with some of the survivors.

He must always bear in mind, however, the warning issued by one of the most articulate interpreters of the decade, Joseph Freeman, in his novel *Never Call Retreat*:

> Everyone falsifies history, even if it is his own personal history. Sometimes the falsification is deliberate, sometimes unconscious; but always the past is altered to suit the needs of the present. The best we can say of any account is not that it is the real truth at last, but that this is how the story appears to us now.

But let us concede that the past, if recaptured at all, will be mutilated, that events, as F. M. Cornford once observed, are being transformed "from the moment of their occurrence." It is still possible to draw a roughly accurate picture of a comparatively recent decade before, to quote Cornford once more, "fact shifts into legend, and legend into myth."

One irrefragable fact dominated the years between 1929 and 1939: the worldwide Depression. This economic convulsion spawned the wars and the revolutions abroad and confronted the United States with its most threatening crisis since the Civil War. It not only colored the economic and political life of the country; it also stamped its mark on literature and the arts, on sports events, on religion, on education, crime, entertainment, and popular culture. The country mobilized, to borrow President Roosevelt's metaphor, as if it were repelling a foreign invasion, and although huge expenditures of time and money were made in efforts to escape from Depression realities, the unchallengeable evidence of poverty, unemployment, and social war hung over the diversions of the people as much as they did their workaday activities. By 1935, the prospects of disaster had considerably diminished, but mounting confidence never entirely expelled national anxiety until the medicine of war finally restored the ailing economy.

In what fashion people met these pressures, of course, depended on how prepared they were financially, socially, and temperamentally to face up to their everyday problems. We can only guess at the response of the amorphous and many-faced poor, the clientele of soup kitchens and breadlines. Many of them had lived on the ragged edge even during the days of the Coolidge and Hoover prosperity and were not strangers to economic insecurity. Largely inarticulate, not particularly aggressive, their feelings are probably most success-fully captured in the photographs of such documenters as Dorothea Lange and Walker Evans—photographs which record the expressions of shock, bewilderment, and frustration of the urban and rural poor. Perhaps the best gauge of their collective dissidence was the millions of ballots cast for F.D.R. in the elections of 1932 and 1936.

The stock market crash and the ensuing Depression came as a nasty jolt to the well-to-do but for most of them (excepting the well-publicized suicides) it meant curtailment of expenditures, not deprivation. A look at the fashion magazines in the early years of the decade is instructive. *Vogue* and *Harper's Bazaar* filled their pages with hints on how to cut corners by substituting beer for champagne, serving simpler supper parties, and offering hints on how "to administer First Aid to crippled incomes to help build sound and smart wardrobes from shattered budgets." *Vogue* advised the debutante to dress casually:

> if a line of economy must be drawn, there are certain places in her wardrobe where it is easiest, or at least less painful to draw it. The evening coat is one. Although four evening dresses are the very mini-mum (six are better), the wrap she wears . . . need not be very grand or very expensive. . . . Another field for economy is her choice of street clothes. She hardly ever needs them. . . . Her only need for street clothes is on those days when she must go at the very crack of dawn . . . to the Junior League and yawn through lectures on the slums and social service.

It was a different story for many Americans in the middle-income bracket, especially the elderly business and professional men who lost their jobs or who found their standard of living cut to the bone. Such people found it less easy to adjust to the economic crisis than those who had always lived close to poverty and were accustomed to accept relief from charitable agencies. Unprepared for physical hardship and hagridden by guilt over personal failure, they were especially susceptible to the Depression malaise and broke down more quickly than those cushioned by money or experience. "First indifference; next, reassuring faith; third, galling bitterness; fourth, morbidity." So wrote the author of an article, "Broke at Fifty-Five," in a 1931 issue of the *Nation*. What frightened him most was his loss of nerve, not the physical courage it takes to risk one's life but "the nerve it takes to ask a stranger for a job, when you've turned down thousands of men yourself without batting an eye; to tell a friend how good you are, and watch his face continue blank." You reach the point of no return, he decided, when you begin "to feel toward yourself as you imagine other folks are feeling toward you," when people pass you by "as one no longer interesting or useful to them," when your shoulders droop and the look in your eye becomes "furtive, expectant, resentful."

The young of both sexes, particularly those in their late teens and early twenties, were just as "expectant" and "resentful." Hundreds of thousands of them who normally would have been absorbed into farms, factories, stores, offices found all doors closed. Added to the uncertainty that a young person is likely to feel even in relatively stable times about his chosen vocation was the uncertainty of whether he could find a job or hold it, go into business and survive, or be sure of a roof over his head and enough to eat. As late as 1933, the jungle camps and boxcars were filled with young hoboes making joyless peregrinations from one end of the country to another. They slept in shanty towns, in haystacks, on the floors of missions or jails.

Here is the testimony of one of the articulate ones published at the bottom of the Depression:

> I wrote letters, I tramped hundreds of blocks to answer ads, I tried for jobs as teamster, clothing model, wringer man, floor-walker, garbage collector, truck driver. I wrote a Civil Service examination. I made ten dollars painting the ceiling of a barber shop. I managed an interview with my former superintendent, but he didn't remember me very well. I lived on a loaf of bread for ten days and then my money was all gone.

After sleeping on cornhusks, living on bread and soup (usually eaten standing up), frequenting flophouses, borrowing from relatives, panhandling, and learning how to wash the lice out of his shabby clothes, he was ready to consider crime:

> If it were necessary—if there were a famine, if I were a genius, an explorer, a martyr—I could endure cold and hunger, even degradation and insults, without a murmur. . . . But it is all so unnecessary, there is so little for me to look forward to, that I am beginning to think that it isn't so worthwhile to keep straight. The best I could look for, as a

reward for going through another winter, or three, or five, like the last two, would be a job somewhere, sometime. And then could I feel secure? Another depression might catch me with no more resources than I had this time.

Such litanies of misery were not uncommon before the relief operations of the New Deal began to take effect and even afterward.

Of course the Communists made propaganda out of Depression conditions and agitated for the day when, as the *New Masses* put it, "we'll spit on our hands and dig into the job of cleaning up this fine land of ours of all its fat lice and bedbugs." But the Communists did not have to invent these stories from the abyss. Slum babies had been bitten by rats, and families evicted and strikers clubbed and Negroes lynched for over a half-century at least in the United States. This was the first time in American history, however, when such symptoms of economic and social demoralization were so widespread and so extensively publicized. As might be expected, the liberal and radical press (usually of small circulation but nonetheless influential) did most to focus public attention on national blemishes, but newspapers and magazines representing all political persuasions carried accounts of the Depression's ravages. Perhaps no other decade produced so many denunciations, exposés, mass demonstrations, leagues, committees—the paraphernalia of organized dissent.

The conception of the "Angry Thirties" which is now so thoroughly ingrained in the history of that period derives very largely, it would seem, from the memories of this collective protest, so that some writers have pictured the decade as a huge WPA mural painted in the style of socialist realism. Fat-assed sheriffs are flogging Negroes; company police shoot down Chicago steelworkers on Memorial Day; Fritz Kuhn's Nazis, dressed in the uniforms of their Brownshirted brothers abroad, clash with American Legion veterans in Yorkville; gaunt farm women with their grimy children pose in front of sagging cabins; Steinbeckian jalopies rattle slowly westward; workers sit by their machines in Flint, Michigan, while National Guardsmen wearing gas masks and carrying rifles patrol the company grounds; the rabble-rousers, Father Charles Coughlin and Huey Long or the eloquent Gerald L. K. Smith ("distending the superficial blood-vessels of his temples and neck," writes H. L.

Mencken, "as if they were biceps"), conduct their sweaty revivals. Already the facts, authentic enough in their separateness, conglomerate into myth.

Had such scenes, featured in proletarian fiction and revolutionary reportage, been as prevailing and as ubiquitous as they were alleged to have been at the time, the republic might well have collapsed. It didn't because the crisis abated under the leadership of the New Deal, and because the only movement strong enough to make a revolution—organized and unorganized labor—had no inclination to do so. The crisis, furthermore, had its invigorating and liberating aspects, one result of which was a camaraderie of deprivation. "We pooled our troubles," John Steinbeck recollected, "our money when we had some, our inventiveness and our pleasures." He remembers the Depression "as a time of mutual caring. If one of us got hurt or ill or in trouble, the others rallied with what they had. Everyone shared bad fortune as well as good."

Perhaps not everyone. But if it be kept in mind that common anxieties can unite a people as well as divide them, that threats from the outside or inside—whether ideological or economic—temporarily override social animosities, and that distractions of all kinds—entertainment, fads, natural catastrophes—tend to divert people from self-preoccupation, then it can be understood why such adjectives as "desperate," "terrible," "angry," "tragic," "hopeless," and "Red" are inadequate designations for the Thirties. The misery of the miners in Harlan County, Kentucky, and the ordeal of the Scottsboro boys in Alabama, the Bank holiday, the Townsend Plan, the expulsion of the Bonus Army from Washington, Detroit's Black Legion, National Socialism, the Hoovervilles, and hunger marches—all characterize the decade; but so do the exploits of John Dillinger, the Joe Louis–Max Schmeling encounters, the great New England hurricane of 1938 and the Martian invasion in 1939, Amos n' Andy, Benny Goodman's swing band, and Joe DiMaggio and Dizzy Dean.

Even if the American Left had been well-coordinated, better financed, and less divided, it is doubtful, given the realities of American life, that it could have made a greater impact than it did. Strong in many cities and finding pockets of support in scattered areas of the country, it never made contact with vast segments of the population, because the rank and file had no interest in economic theory and felt a deep distrust for political "isms." Coughlin's followers may have believed in his neo-populistic explanations for the Depression, and thousands of people had faith in Mr. Townsend's primitive panacea, but neither left- nor right-wing propagandists ever diagnosed or ministered to the collective ailment of the American people, the symptoms of which were shock, bitterness, frustration, pessimism, and emptiness. The stunned casualties of the Depression believed they had been shortchanged by a hitherto beneficent Providence, that the "promise of American life" had been broken, but this conviction did not make them receptive to the message of revolution.

Not that the influence of the Left was negligible. The Communists' role in the councils of the trade union movement was substantial; in publishing and the arts, in education and organized religion, in federal agencies like the WPA, left-wing ideas and ideals left their mark. But the country as a whole remained immune to Communist suggestion despite the attempts of the Party to quicken social resentments among "the toiling masses" and to make them more aware of their exploitation and their power. How, a *New Masses* contributor asked, could "the millions of working class and lower middle-class citizens" be weaned away from "the politely-dressed filth" of the pulps? The Party press exposed the reactionary propaganda of the cheap fiction magazines but offered no Marxist replacements for such "fascist" fantasies as "The Red Invader" or "Invasion of the Dark Legions" that flourished in magazines like *Spider* or *Operation No. 5* during the mid-Thirties.

After the inauguration of the Popular Front in 1935 and the Party announcement that Communism was twentieth-century Americanism, the *Daily Worker* began to pay attention to a potential readership unconcerned with Left-sectarian heresies. It introduced a comic strip, "Little Lefty," featuring a class-conscious urchin whose politics were considerably to the left of Little Orphan Annie and a sports page replete with box scores and special stories about prominent teams and athletes. Ordinarily the editors purveyed sports news untendentiously, although one of their popular columnists, Mike Gold, detected capitalist skullduggery in professional baseball, and the paper's boxing expert could not resist some ideological hosannas after Joe Louis regained his heavyweight title:

Give me a night in June beneath the moon at the Yankee Stadium [he exulted] with Joe Louis slipping off his bathrobe, stepping to the middle of the ring and blasting Max Schmeling to the canvas in 2 minutes and 4 seconds of the first round as the spontaneous cry of "Back to Hitler, Bum!" spreads like wildfire through the 90,000 fans and I'll give you the big moment of the 1938 sports season.

There was something at once poignant and comic in the Party's unsuccessful wooing of the masses, in its efforts to awaken the American people to their revolutionary tradition. The new policy, with its conscientious celebration of Jefferson, Paine, Whitman, and Lincoln, seemed as contrived as it was belated and simply confirmed the skepticism of writers and intellectuals—whose connection with the orthodox Left had never been more than marginal—that the Party was politicizing culture, writing *at* the people rather than *of* or *from* them.

By 1939 many of these intellectuals who had belonged in some fashion to the Left vanguard, or whose works and public activities helped to fix the popular stereotypes of the decade, repudiated the Party lock, stock, and barrel. Their denigrations not only set the tone for the subsequent exposés of the Party's moral and cultural bankruptcy but also influenced the repudiation of the Thirties in the postwar years. Communist spokesmen, on the other hand, who stuck to the Party even after the Nazi-Soviet pact and later embarrassing disclosures, defended the decade as a time of moral and cultural regeneration,

one that marked the coming of age of our literature, and burned out much shoddiness, opportunism, adolescent fear, and hesitation. It taught American writers to be proud of their craft, because through it they could lead the people toward great goals. It taught them to act and write like men and citizens, not like perpetual Harvard schoolboys or entertainers or mystic outcasts from national life. No longer was the honest writer an alien; he had rooted himself in the soil of the American people.

This was a Party "myth," if you will, but in correcting its simplicities, the middle-class apostates and disenchanted fellow travelers inadvertently set up a Thirties myth of their own. This myth, a composite, like other myths, of overextended "truths" and unqualified "facts," might be summarized in the following little scenario.

Leading writers and intellectuals, partly out of mental fuzziness, emotional need, personal inadequacy, unfocused idealism, or soft-headed sentimentalism, permitted themselves to become the tools of a ruthless political apparatus, to take refuge in a "closed system of belief," and to commit creative suicide. Whether they actually belonged to the inner cadres of the Party organization or whether they served as literary window dressing for the cultural "front" groups, they wittingly or unwittingly carried out the Party's political and aesthetic dictates. They exhibited "an almost psychological hatred and distrust of 'pure' writing," insisted that writers and intellectuals must present their observations from the "class angle," and, generally speaking, compliantly accepted the policies handed down to them by the Party commissars. This meant in the days of the Popular Front that writers were expected to cultivate a new patriotic brand of Communism (the cult of the "usable past") and to practice what Wallace Stevens called "a factitious Americanism" even as they continued their slavish adherence to Moscow. Under such conditions it was no wonder that leftist criticism consisted mainly of ill-tempered polemics on extraliterary issues and that the so-called creative writing of the Left in large measure was crude propaganda. Finally the Party succeeded in placing its henchmen in the centers of cultural power and dominated publishing houses, Broadway and Hollywood, and the colleges; its impact on American culture was disastrous.

I should be the last to discount the high costs paid by writers and intellectuals who sacrificed their honesty and their talents for the sake of Party unity and who allowed themselves to become hatchet men for a cause blindly adhered to. But it is simply not true that most of the American intelligentsia betrayed themselves and others or that nothing fruitful emerged from the Thirties.

Virtually every writer of any importance was affected in one way or another by the social and intellectual climate—by the Depression itself, by the expansion of fascism, by the powerful impact of the USSR; but the majority of those who were politically engaged did not feel bound by Party fiat. If every intellectual who distrusted America's business leaders, raged against abuses, backed organized labor, signed petitions against some act or policy of the government had been a Communist, then the Party would have indeed been a power in the land. But there was by no means the degree of consensus among the friends and supporters of the Left that has sometimes been suggested. And the writers in particular were a nonconformist breed.

Dreiser, for example, remained illogical, fumbling, cynical, outspoken—as he always had been. The Party used him, but it never knew when the old man might commit some ideological indiscretion, and neither the Depression nor Communism lifted his flagging talents. Sherwood Anderson published *Puzzled America*, his impressions of the economic collapse, and contributed occasionally to the radical magazines, but he studiously held himself aloof from the Party. Sinclair Lewis alternately pleased and infuriated the Left with attacks against fascism at one moment and lyrical celebrations of the middle class at another. The letters of Thomas Wolfe are filled with grim and indignant passages about the suffering and human degradation he observed, yet Communism never attracted him; he kept his provincial prejudices and above all his overweening absorption in himself. F. Scott Fitzgerald, chastened by his own crisis as well as the nation's, caught the mood of the Thirties in his backward glance at the jazz age, first in his dark examination of the corrupt high-bourgeoisie in *Tender is the Night* and later in *The Crack-Up*, but he was hardly "political." Nor was William Faulkner, like Fitzgerald in disrepute among the vociferous liberals in the 1930s who tended to regard him as a glorified pulpwriter, "the Sax Rohmer of the intelligentsia." Faulkner hardly fits into the stereotype of the Thirties, and yet a half-dozen volumes of his best fiction appeared between 1929 and 1939, and his evocations of violence (dismissed as irrelevant and merely Poe-esque) anticipated the coming horrors more vividly than did any other fiction of the times.

I could go on naming other typically untypical writers, each of whose response to the Thirties was idiosyncratic and not inspired by any Party directives. What I am saying, in short, is that the literature of the 1930s, the work of writers as different as Erskine Caldwell, Thornton Wilder, Henry Roth, Nathanael West, John Steinbeck, Ernest Hemingway, John Dos Passos, James T. Farrell, Richard Wright, John Marquand, Edward Dahlberg, is too diverse, reflective of too many points of view and conflicting literary traditions, to lend itself to easy formulation. Their collective output may have contained few if any "monuments" (although *Death in the Afternoon, Absalom! Absalom!*, and *U.S.A.* would dignify any decade), but it strikes me as impertinent, considering the variety and power of this writing, to say that the Thirties crippled artistic talent.

On the contrary, it is not arguable that the turmoil of the Thirties provided new subjects and new perspectives? Did not some writers at least—I'm thinking now of James T. Farrell, John Steinbeck, and John Dos Passos—reach their apogee in this difficult but exciting period? Anyone who looks through the little magazines that flourished briefly and withered in the opening years of the Thirties (there were hundreds of them) will see immediately how the times affected the subject matter and style of the contributors. Certainly, as one of them observed recently, writers were not "in any important way crippled or frustrated by the Thirties. The times were enormously liberating, and destroyed (or at least banished for a few years) a great many petty and fruitless illusions. . . . The Thirties supplied writers with an interest in theory and in history. . . . Minds moved more freely in time and space. Vision was larger and more social."

Granted that a number of works appearing in these fugitive publications were hardly more than proletarian fairy stories or the crudest documentaries. Poems, plays, and fiction, written by literary amateurs whose desire to communicate their experiences and feelings far exceeded their talents, often turned out to be dreadful stuff and are deservedly forgotten. Yet these same magazines sometimes discovered a Eudora Welty or a Tennessee Williams. What is more, they provided an outlet through which the galled and the exacerbated, with plenty of time on their hands for brooding, could discharge their outraged emotions.

Two points should be kept in mind as we scan the prolet-art and agitprop art in the ephemeral radical press.

First, the subject matter was ready-made. Workers and farmers did suffer from terrible poverty on occasion; employers often did have the police, the military, and the courts on their side; industry did hire gangsters to break strikes; the Nazis were already torturing and exterminating their victims; General Franco, with Fascist assistance, was crushing a popular revolution in Spain.

Second, what is usually overlooked by those who identify vulgar Marxist aesthetics with the spirit of the Thirties is that simplistic and clumsy protest writing was roughly handled from the start by the majority of critics, Left as well as Right. Their review-lectures carried the same refrain: don't overemphasize the grimy side of working-class life; don't brand as escapist and evasive all literature that deals with an idyllic past; don't write as if techniques and sincerity are antithetical; don't make the capitalist world more rotten and moribund than it really is; don't assume that James, Proust, and Joyce must be condemned in the name of the revolution. Such injunctions more nearly approximated critical consensus in the Thirties than did crude Marxist apologetics.

Actually, only writers possessed by the proletarian *mystique* required these admonitions. A good deal of the most vigorous Depression literature took the form of "reportage," eyewitness accounts of tension spots selected with the intention of extracting the maximum amount of social implication. A trial, a strike, a congressional investigation, conversations with factory workers or farmers, a slum scene, the inside of a miner's shack—each served as a metaphor for a social comment. Frequently angry and bitter, this writing was at the same time personal and random, the response to politics rather than party, and quite similar to some of the current reportage of the new radicalism.

The activists of the New Left have not paid much attention to the still uncharted and unclassified literature of dissent written during the Thirties. It seems almost axiomatic in our history that every rebellious generation must begin afresh, as if the trials and errors and accomplishments of the past can have no bearing on the present.

The crucial difference between the Thirties and the Sixties, of course, is the economic one: the former was depressed, the latter is affluent. Thus the nay-sayers of today are willy-nilly the beneficiaries of this prosperity, and even the poor and the jobless, however miserable their lot, are guaranteed a margin of security denied to their counterparts of thirty years ago. Clearly, dissent in an age of full employment and unprecedented prosperity would appear to have little in common with dissent in a period of extreme social discontent and economic dislocation.

And yet this fundamental difference does not negate every other meaningful link between the age of Roosevelt and the age of Johnson. Almost every kind of issue or crisis that exists today (excepting the threat of worldwide nuclear holocaust) faced the Left in the

Thirties. That is why the experiences of the old radicals, no matter how naive, silly, or iniquitous they appear to us now, can be seen as prefigurings of our own dilemmas. They faced the Birchers of their own day, found themselves involved in the fight against racial discrimination, risked their lives in the South, took sides in foreign revolutions and civil wars, spent their quota of time in jails, charted the landscape of the American wasteland, and found their deepest satisfaction in the company of true believers. They also prevaricated, rationalized their motivations, deluded themselves, allowed their craving for belief to blur their judgments and their moral vision.

Given the urgencies of the times, their failures are understandable. One often hears that we are immeasurably closer to annihilation in this nuclear age than ever before; certainly the atomic bomb has become the *primum mobile* for the New Left's platform and philosophy. But few of us really *live* as if we believed in this Damoclean symbol. In the Thirties, however, the premonitions of Armageddon vibrated in the minds of millions and were justified by the daily headlines. The more intensely a person felt the imminence of the cataclysm, the readier he was to sacrifice his freedom and intellectual flexibility for the sake of a disciplined resistance against an Enemy terribly incarnate. This conviction was at times the source of the committed man's effectiveness as well as a trap. It explains why some people submitted too trustfully to the commands of the Party.

The New Left is making no such demands upon its followers at the moment and could not if it would; options are still possible and the dangers for most are still distant. The New Radicals, nevertheless, cannot afford to evade the moral and intellectual problems that bedeviled their seniors either by neglecting them or by purposeful forgetting. A few years ago, a man who had spent most of his life in the Left movement observed in a letter to me that "changes in political nomenclature and institutions cannot by themselves change the mind, the heart, and the will of man and therefore his conduct." He saw the old disputes of the Thirties being revived in the Sixties "without the necessary awareness that these are old problems, and that the experience of the past thirty years has amply confirmed how absurd it is—and how fatal—to treat politics as if it were literature and literature as if it were politics." The New Radicalism, he concluded, could "avoid many mistakes, and make much greater progress, if it learned how the 'old' radicalism dealt with the problems of politics and poetry, what it did on this score that was right and what it did that was wrong. But to profit by the mistakes and creative achievements of the past we must have a true account of the past."

I have very strong doubts that history teaches the kind of lesson that my friend had in mind, but I agree with Professor E. H. Carr that "history deals with a line or procession of events, half of which lies in the past and half in the future, and you cannot have an intelligent appreciation of one half unless you also concern yourself with the other half." The current myths of the Thirties, it seems to me, suggest an inability or an unwillingness to study that decade with curiosity and imagination. It was not so heroic as it is sometimes made out to be. No radical cause is immune from the social contagion it seeks to eliminate. Nor was it so contemptible as many would have us believe. Men were no better or worse at that time than they ever were or will be. We cannot and ought not to look back to the Depression decade for precedents or directives, but by examining it attentively, we might conceivably come to a better understanding of ourselves and our present concerns.

Late Thoughts on Nathanael West

West and His Contemporaries

The revival of interest in Nathanael West, now of some fifteen years' duration, continues to mount. In the reappraisal of the literary Thirties, West has caught up with and overtaken most of the triple-decked naturalists whose solemn and often infelicitous documentations no longer are devoured with relish. Over thirty years ago, West decided that

> Lyric novels can be written according to Poe's definition of a lyric poem. The short novel is a distinct form especially fitted for use in this country. . . . Forget the epic, the master work. In America fortunes do not accumulate, the soil does not grow, families have no history. Leave slow growth to the book reviewers, you have only time to explode. Remember William Carlos Williams' description of the pioneer women who shot their children against the wilderness like cannonballs. Do the same with your novels.

West wrote these words when, as Angel Flores observed about the same time, "the current vanguard taste" insisted "on directing literature towards the casehistory, gravymashpotatoe tradition," and only a few mavericks like F. Scott Fitzgerald (an admirer of *Miss Lonelyhearts*) shared West's dislike for the long-winded Scandinavian novel.

To see West, however, as a misunderstood and neglected "taker-

Originally published in *Massachusetts Review*, 6, no. 2 (1965), 307–317.

outer" shouldered into obscurity by the more celebrated "putter-inners" is to exaggerate his singularity. Besides doing an injustice to a number of discerning critics who read his books with delight and appreciation,[1] such a view detaches him from a small but distinct group of literary kinsmen. Being a radical in the 1930s (and West was a faithful subscriber to Party manifestos) did not necessarily mean that one had to write ritualistic proletarian novels or Whitmanesque exhortations to revolt. There was another kind of writing; Edward Dahlberg called it "implication literature," tinged with "just as deep a radical dye." West belonged to that select company of socially committed writers in the Depression decade who drew revolutionary conclusions in highly idiosyncratic and undoctrinaire ways: in the eerie episodes of Dahlberg's *Bottom Dogs* and *From Flushing to Calvary*, in the nightmarish poems of Kenneth Fearing, and in the pointed buffoonery of S. J. Perelman. Like these writers, West supported the objectives of the Left while retaining the verbal exuberance, the unplayful irony, the nocturnal surrealist fancies associated with a certain school of expatriate writing in the Twenties.

Had West (and the same might be said of Fearing) been merely an unaffiliated rebel, an inveterate non-joiner suspicious of causes and unburdened by any social philosophy, his satire and humor would hardly have been condoned by the Communists. The 1930s was not a good time for antinomians, as the career of the brilliant E. E. Cummings attests. Orthodox Party intellectuals detected no ideological heresies in the fiction of West or the poetry of Fearing, and they never attacked them as they did a number of other literary deviationists, but neither did they regard these masters of the grotesque and the macabre as the proper models for the proletarian literature of the future. Their dark vision of society, their twisted wry comedy, their recognition of an ineradicable evil denser and more durable than the capitalist blight violated the spirit of socialist realism. It was all well and good to depict the hells of bourgeois capitalism, imperialism, and fascism, but in the last reel, the glow of the Heavenly City ought to be revealed.

Literary experimentation in Left circles came more and more to be identified with cultism and individual self-indulgence. The whole point of radical satire might be lost if the writer subordinated social purpose to literary effect. When James Agee, writing in the *New Masses* in 1937, asserted that Left artists and surrealists were both revolutionaries and "that there are no valid reasons why they should be kept apart," he was told by a Communist critic that he stood on very dangerous ground:

> Certainly the proletarian movement has made use of much that was in the early part of the century regarded as experimental. But it is the strength of proletarian art that it can take to itself only that which it can use. Under the mandate of its approach to life and the necessity to communicate, it cannot lose itself in blind alleys. It has learned from experimental art when that experimentation actually devised effective modes of expression or rediscovered what was fine and effective in the art of remoter times. But when experimentation lapsed into cultism, the health was gone out of it.
>
> Just what has Gertrude Stein to offer? Is not her whole attempt to divorce language from meaning a cul-de-sac? And just how will a living art, based upon realities so pressing that even former Dadaists have been forced to face them, gain from the mumbo-jumbo of the latter day transitionists?
>
> Revolution is not made in the hazy caverns of the subconscious, not by any mystic upsurge of the human spirit. This is not to deny that the dream life of man is real; but to contemplate dream states for their own sake and isolated from the rest of reality is a sickness which we cannot afford.
>
> All who rebel are by no means revolutionary in our sense of the word. If the proletarian movement took to its bosom all who call themselves revolutionary, there would be no disciplined movement either in politics or the arts—only confusion and betrayal.

Now, West could not be accused of divorcing dreams from reality, but the literary and artistic streams that fed his bizarre imagination—the French school of the *fin de siècle*, Dostoevsky, squalid pulp fiction, the comic strip, the cinema—set him apart from the proletarians who saw no revolutionary significance in myths and dreams. For this reason, despite such discerning readers as Josephine Herbst, Edmund Wilson, Fitzgerald, William Carlos Williams, Angel Flores, and others, the movement never took West to its bosom. In misconstruing his humor and failing to explore his baleful Wasteland, it committed both a political and an aesthetic blunder.

Miss Lonelyhearts: Variety of Religious Experience

In "Some Notes on Miss L.," Nathanael West disclosed that his novel could be considered as a classical case history "of a priest of our time who has a religious experience." The portrait of Miss Lonely-hearts was

> built on all the cases in James' *Varieties of Religious Experience* and Star-buck's *Psychology of Religion*. The psychology is theirs not mine.[2] Chapt. I—maladjustment. Chapt. III—the need for taking symbols liter-ally is described through a dream in which a symbol is actually fleshed. Chapt. IV—deadness and disorder: see Lives of Bunyan and Tolstoy. Chapt. VI—self-torture by conscious sinning; see life of any saint. And so on."

It would be handy if West had left an annotated copy of his Wil-liam James for his biographers, and yet anyone who reads *Miss Lonelyhearts* in the light of the *Varieties* will understand what West meant when he declared that if the novelist is no longer the psychol-ogist, psychology has provided him with a vast quantity of case histories which "can be used in the way the ancient writers used their myths. Freud is your Bullfinch; you can learn from him." Un-doubtedly Freud helps as an interpreter of Miss Lonelyhearts' sub-liminal self, but William James, as he acknowledged, supplied the structure of the novel. West, I think, drew most heavily from two chapters, "The Religion of Healthy-Mindedness" and "The Sick Soul," but his hero displays all of the classical symptoms of the conversion experience described throughout James's book.

According to James,

> There are people for whom evil means only a maladjustment with *things*, a wrong correspondence of one's life with the environment. Such evil as this is curable, on principle at least, upon the natural plane, for merely by modifying either the self or the things, or both at once, the two terms may be made to fit, and all go merry as a marriage bell again. But there are others for whom evil is no mere relation of the subject to particular outer things, but something more radical and general, a wrongness or vice in his essential nature, which no alteration of the environment, or any significant rearrangement of the inner self, can cure, and which requires a supernatural remedy.

James hazarded the generalization (which Santayana was to elaborate in his novel *The Last Puritan*) that it was the "Germanic races" rather than the Latin who capitalized the S in sin and conceived of it as "something ineradicably ingrained in our natural subjectivity, and never to be removed by any superficial piecemeal operation."

Miss Lonelyhearts, it will be remembered, is the son of a Baptist minister, "the New England puritan" with a high forehead, long fleshless nose, and bony chin. He can find no consolation in the faith of the "healthy-minded" for whom evil is merely a disease and a preoccupation with evil an additional manifestation of the sickness. His "healthy-minded" sweetheart, Betty, attributes his "anhedonia" (dreariness, discouragement, dejection, disgust) to some physical ailment. "What's the matter?" she asks him. "Are you sick?" And Miss Lonelyhearts lashes back: "What a kind bitch you are. As soon as anyone acts viciously, you say he's sick. Wife torturers, rapers of small children, according to you they're all sick. No morality, only medicine. Well, I'm not sick. I don't need any of your damned aspirin. I've got a Christ complex, etc."

The conversion process is already under way. Before the unregenerate man can attain saintliness, he must go through the stages of "depression, morbid introspection, and sense of sin." Preparatory to the bliss of grace is "the pitch of unhappiness so great that all the goods of nature may be entirely forgotten," and when the sufferer happens to be a neurotic with a very low threshold of pain, his agony is almost unbearable. His anguish takes the forms of self-loathing, extreme exasperation, self-mistrust, self-despair. Miss Lonelyhearts' despair is patterned on the melancholia of Tolstoy overwhelmed by a heightened awareness of objective evil. And just as John Bunyan was sickened by the depths of his own iniquity, so Miss Lonelyhearts writhes in the presence of his own corruption and his inability to control it.

Miss Lonelyhearts' conversion during a bout of fever is quite similar to many of those recorded by William James, and although his brief interlude of ecstasy and his ridiculous death are presented almost farcically, there is no reason to conclude that West was denying the value of saintliness in his modern *Pilgrim's Progress*. The torments of the misfits and the grotesques in *Miss Lonelyhearts* may be exacerbated by sordid social conditions—it is, in a technical sense, a Depression novel—but is West really saying that the plight

of Sick-of-it-all, Broken-hearted, Broad-shoulders, and Disillu-
sioned-with-tubercular-husband could have been solved by the ex-
propriation of the expropriators? To the healthy-minded Communist, West's lonely madman could only be judged as a dupe
ministering to the duped. But the novel, as I read it, implicitly en-
forces rather the conclusion of William James than that of Karl
Marx.

The healthy-minded, James remarks at the end of his chapter
"The Sick Soul," reject as "unmanly and diseased" the "children of
wrath and cravers of a second birth." But James predicts that if the
days of killing and torture ever return, "the healthy-minded would
at present show themselves the less indulgent of the two." Healthy-
mindedness, however adequate it is for certain cheery temperaments, fails "as a philosophical doctrine, because the evil facts
which it refuses positively to account for are a genuine portion of
reality, and they may after all be the best key to life's significance,
and possibly the only openers of our eyes to the deepest levels of
truth." *Miss Lonelyhearts* is a profane assertion of this idea.

West and Political Satire

The Horatio Alger hero in West's third novel, *A Cool Million* (1934),
comes of age during the Great Depression, and after a slapstick
sequence of nasty and brutal misadventures (he loses his scalp, one
eye, a leg, all of his teeth, and finally his life) he winds up as a
fascist martyr. Some of West's admirers have detected Dostoevskian
profundities in his "Tattered Tom" parody, but *A Cool Million* is the
most dated and the most tiresome of his novels, a sour joke that the
author cannot sustain. What redeems it (besides its flashes of lurid
comedy) is West's initial conception; the ruthlessly innocent American Boy, one of Norman Rockwell's wholesome caricatures, who
moves dreamily through a Hieronymus Bosch landscape, survives
one outrage after another, and dies still loyal to his benighted code.
Here is a text on the perversion of healthy-mindedness in "the days
of killing and torture."*

*West had remarked in the October 1932 issue of *Contact*, of which he was one of the
editors, that every manuscript sent to the magazine had "violence for its core." The
editors, he said, "did not start with the idea of printing tales of violence. We now feel
that we would be doing violence by suppressing them."

A Cool Million made even less stir among the literary radicals than Miss Lonelyhearts did, and the reasons were not entirely aesthetic. Party intellectuals and their literary supporters tended to be as doctrinaire about the right and wrong uses of humor as they were about a good many other matters, and A Cool Million, through Marxist glasses, was as ideologically unfocused as its predecessor. To Kyle Crichton, "humorist" and columnist in the New Masses who wrote under the pen name of Robert Forsythe, merely to have a sense of humor was not enough—especially when the working class was being slaughtered by fascists, betrayed by Trotskyites, and deceived by the hirelings of Hearst and Morgan. Satire of the Perelman–Benchley–Donald Ogden Stewart variety favored by the New Yorker magazine merely diverted a segment of the society that was beyond redemption. "It is the old dada stuff," Forsythe complained, "the irrelevant incongruous type of humor; you start with one thing and end up with something utterly different and silly." The purpose behind his own humor, he went on to say, was to make the working classes "realize that they had nothing to fear from their so-called betters." To Perelman, whose New Yorker pieces (Strictly from Hunger, 1937) provoked these remarks, Forsythe concluded:

> if you really want to do something with that great talent in humor, learn at what point it is necessary to stick the stiletto in and twist it around! If there is a loud scream of anguish, you will know you've written something. If it's hilarious to the people it helps, it's humor.

Forsythe's commentary makes it easier to understand why West's humor and satire were not highly esteemed in the New Masses. He knew how to twist the stiletto all right, but his writing also smacked of that "crazy" humor Forsythe disliked.

West had dedicated A Cool Million to his brother-in-law, a gesture both fraternal and literary, for Perelman, the author of "Dawn Ginsburg's Revenge" and creator of Ming Toy Epstein, was himself a master of the Victor "Tom Swift" Appleton style. Both possessed a talent for blending the esoteric, the technical, and the commonplace into absurd and brilliant combinations, and neither was at his best (despite their left-wing affiliations) when he was being studiedly political and dealing with what the Party would call "real issues." In a zany mood, Perelman could paint a dadaist portrait of the author of *Miss Lonelyhearts* that is a masterpiece of nonsense.[3] His pieces in the *New Masses*, however, lacked the spontaneity and outrageousness of his best work, perhaps because the policies of the magazine checked his usual extravagance. They point up the dilemma of the humorist who is required to be funny about unfunny things, in this case anti-Semitism, xenophobia, and lynchings.

Mr. Kenneth Burke, who has at one time or another managed to say something important about almost every literary problem, touched on this matter in one of his reviews. In 1935 Burke was serving as a superior if unappreciated aesthetician for the Marxists, and in a discussion of Kyle Crichton's humor, he extracted some significant principles from Crichton's topical and jejune commentaries.[5]

Burke defined three kinds of humorist: the "comic exorcist," the "universal satirist," and the "satiric propagandist." The first, and most acceptable to the Establishment, diverts society's attentions from the portentous to the inconsequential by changing "the scale of things, turning major terrors into minor annoyances." The "comic exorcist" is much sought after by magazines like the *New Yorker*, he says, because "with the help of such magazines, the Vague Shapes of Historical Calamity are whisked away, to be displaced by odd discomforts, reassuring in their tininess." The "universal satirist" is unselectively critical, sees all mankind as foolish or swinish or worse, and is engaged in a general and universal denigration. Unlike the first two types, the "satiric propagandist" is not allowed to swivel his guns in all directions. If the "comic exorcist" hates no one and the "universal satirist" hates everyone, the "satiric propagandist" has "a clear alignment of friends and foes" and exempts the former from his wrath. He wishes neither to reduce grave problems to triviality nor to magnify them to such a degree that no solution seems possible. Selecting his targets according to a particular social platform, he sees capitalism as a system that organizes "the anti-social, giving it efficiency, voice, and authority, and consolidating it with the help of the educative, legislative, and constabulary forces."

This very selectivity, as Burke realizes, presents a danger, because the man engaged in "political excoriation," especially the self-righteous moralist, hesitates to trust his wit and humor alone. He becomes in effect an editorialist for a party and feels obligated to keep wigwagging his message to readers whose response is partly determined by their familiarity with the ephemeral events and personalities he deals with. He dare not stray beyond the fences of their prejudices or play games with their gods, and his shuttling back and forth "between the serious and the mock serious" is both politically and aesthetically disquieting.

Into which of the Burkean categories does Nathanael West fall? Plainly he is an exorcist of a kind, for all comedy is cathartic; and clearly he tried to become on occasion a "satiric propagandist." *A Cool Million* is an anticapitalist satire, its well-defined targets obvious in 1934 to any Communist, fellow traveler, or even liberal. It is hardly an example, however, of the socially conscious fiction the Left was calling for, and it displays the Westian idiosyncracies that kept him from becoming an acceptable political marksman for the Party: pessimism, an impatience with codes, and an inability to accommodate revolutionary parables to his gothic imagination.

At his most authentic, West is the "universal satirist." His humor is savage and sad, in contrast to Perelman's brash spoofing, and it springs, I think, from his tragicomic view of the world, from his wry awareness of the disparity between secular facts and his suppressed religious ideals. His slapstick ends in a scream; the self-hatred of his characters, their efforts—sometimes grotesque and always painful—to find answers or relief, only curdles his pity. In *A Cool Million*, as in his other novels, the real culprit is not capitalism but humanity.

Notes

1. "The entire jumble of modern society, bankrupt not only in cash but more tragically in emotion, is depicted here like a life sized engraving narrowed down to the head of a pin." Josephine Herbst, *Contempo*, 3 (July 25, 1933), 4.

2. Stanley Edgar Hyman, *Nathanael West* (University of Minnesota Pamphlets no. 21, p. 16), is skeptical of this claim: "some or all of this may be Westian leg-pull."

3. It is entitled "Nathanael West: A Portrait," and I cannot refrain from reprinting it in its entirety below, as an appendix to these notes.

4. "Thunder Over Alma Mater: The Rover Boys and the Young Radicals" (*New Masses*, 17 [December 17, 1935], 32) tells how Tom and Dick Rover and their cronies united to save old Effluvia College from "certain weak-minded members of the faculty" who were "preparing to seize power, set up a soviet in the Administration Building, and nationalize the girls of

Sweetbread Hall." Masterminding this coup is Dan Baxter (really Dan Baxtrovich), "a notorious single-taxer, anarchist and firebrand." The "alert and clear-eyed" vigilantes raid the college library, where they discover works "of a number of inflammatory and un-American writers of the crazy so-called 'modern' school." Another squad surprises a group of the younger English professors and forces "the cowardly 'intelligentsia' " to recant after "some innocent horseplay involving castor-oil and a rubber-hose." Meanwhile Tom's sweetheart, Eunice Haverstraw, has been kidnapped by Baxtrovich. She is rescued just in time from his non-Aryan embraces by her husky lover who wins her hand and a managership in her father's plant. The promised sequel is "The Rover Boys and Their Young Finks."

5. "Protective Coloration," *New Republic*, 83 (July 10, 1935), 255–256, a review of *Redder Than the Rose* by Robert Forsythe (pseudonym for Kyle Crichton).

NATHANAEL WEST: A PORTRAIT

Picture to yourself a ruddy-cheeked, stocky sort of chap, dressed in loose tweeds, a stubby briar in his teeth, with a firm yet humorous mouth, generous to a fault, everready for a flagon of nut-brown ale with his cronies, possessing the courage of a lion and the tenderness of a woman, an intellectual vagabond, a connoisseur of first editions, fine wines, and beautiful women, well above six feet in height and distinguished for his pallor, a dweller in the world of books, his keen grey eyes belying the sensual lip, equally at home browsing through the bookstalls along the Paris quais and rubbing elbows in the smart literary salons of the Faubourg St. Honoré, a rigid abstainer and non-smoker, living entirely on dehydrated fruits, cereals, and nuts, rarely leaving his monastic cell, an intimate of Cocteau, Picasso, Joyce and Lincoln Kirstein, a dead shot, a past master of the foils, dictating his novels, plays, poems, short stories, epigrams, aphorisms, and sayings to a corps of secretaries at lightning speed, an expert judge of horseflesh, the owner of a model farm equipped with the latest dairy devices—a man as sharp as a razor, as dull as a hoe, as clean as a whistle, as tough as nails, as white as snow, as black as the raven's wing, and as poor as Job. A man kind and captious, sweet and sour, fat and thin, tall and short, racked with fever, plagued by the locust, beset by witches, hag-ridden, cross-grained, a fun-loving, serious-minded dreamer, visionary and slippered pantaloon. Picture to yourself such a man, I say, and you won't have the faintest idea of Nathanael West.

To begin with, the author of *Miss Lonelyhearts* is only eighteen inches high. He is very sensitive about his stature and only goes out after dark, and then armed with a tiny umbrella with which he beats off cats who try to attack him. Being unable to climb into his bed, which is at least two feet taller than himself, he has been forced to sleep in the lower drawer of a bureau since childhood, and is somewhat savage in consequence. He is meticulously dressed, however, and never goes abroad without his green cloth gloves and neat nankeen breeches. His age is a matter of speculation. He claims to remember the Battle of the Boyne and on a fine night his piping voice may be heard in the glen lifted in the strains of "For She's my Molly-O." Of one thing we can be sure; he was seen by unimpeachable witnesses at Austerlitz, Jena, and Wagram, where he made personal appearances through the courtesy of Milton Fink of Fink & Biesemyer, his agents. What I like about him most is his mouth, a jagged scarlet wound etched against the unforgettable blankness of his face. I love his sudden impish smile, the twinkle of those alert green eyes, and the print of his cloven foot in the shrubbery. I love the curly brown locks cascading down his receding forehead; I love the wind in the willows, the boy in the bush, and the seven against Thebes. I love coffee, I love tea, I love the girls and the girls love me. And I'm going to be a civil engineer when I grow up, no matter WHAT Mamma says."—S. J. Perelman (*Contempo*, 3 [July 25, 1933], 1, 4).

Outsiders

In the early days of the American Studies movement, I assumed, or wanted to believe, that despite their differences in class, race, ethnic origin, sex, politics, and religion, Americans opted for a United States at once heterogeneous and solidified. Like Randolph Bourne, I looked forward to the day when a "cooperation of cultures" would gradually erode narrow parochialism and at the same time prevent American society from "being swept into a premature and nebulous cohesion."

No such miracle happened. I grew increasingly alert to the more blatant signs of coercive consensus and obdurate prejudice but only belatedly to the discrimination against women (which as a good liberal I opposed in principle but seldom in print) and against the homosexual community, about which I knew only by hearsay. The trial and conviction in 1960 of my friend and intellectual mentor, Newton

Arvin, charged with possessing "pornographic materials," brought home to me as nothing had before the vulnerability of homosexuals to publicly sanctioned harassment.

The articles in this section, written from the point of view of a not-so-detached observer, focus on the excluders and the excluded, on black and Jewish self-hatred, on the process by which some minority writers moved out of their physical and mental enclosures into the national mainstream. Each touches upon a pervasive theme in my work: social and cultural conflict and the outsider's hunger for acceptance.

The Hyphenate Writer and
American Letters

The adjective "hyphenate" is an Americanism no longer found in most up-to-date dictionaries, but its origins go back as far as the late nineteenth century. During the period of the First World War, it referred specifically to American citizens of foreign birth or descent (as German-American or Irish-American) whose complete loyalty to their adopted country was suspect. The hyphen or short line that separated the word "American" from the words "Polish" or "Italo" or "Mexican" or "Japanese" symbolized the reluctance of "other" or older North Americans to grant complete acceptance to the latecomer. It signified their intention to hold him at "hyphen's length," so to speak, from the established community—at least until the heat of the melting pot had burned away old loyalties. Thus Hawthorne was thinking "hyphenatically" when he wrote in his journal during his consulship in Liverpool: "Nothing is so absolutely abominable as the sense of freedom and equality, pertaining to an American, grafted on the mind of a native of any other country in the world. I do hate a naturalized citizen; nobody has a right to our ideas, unless born to them." For a century after Hawthorne's journal entry, the hyphenate American kept reappearing as the "alien in our midst," as the indigestible spewings of Europe and Asia, and not infrequently as the "un-American."

Originally published in *Smith College Alumnae Quarterly* (July 1964), 213–217.

Today, historians and social scientists use the hyphen descriptively rather than pejoratively. They will speak, for example, of Italo-American or Polish-American voting blocs—less frequently of Jewish or Afro-Americans, because the hyphen is supposed to indicate national origin, not religion or race. But I shall use the adjective "hyphenate" in a metaphorical rather than in a literal sense. The hyphen that separates two words is also mentally disjunctive. It signifies a tentative but unmistakable withdrawal on the part of the user; it means that mere geographical proximity does not entitle the newcomer or outsider to full and unqualified national membership despite his legal qualifications and despite official disclaimers to the contrary. How else can we account for the dictionaries of ugly or contemptuous epithets that usually, if not necessarily, imply overt or concealed antipathy: mick, kike, nigger, wop, frog, spic, kraut, and the like.

I am less concerned with the colorful nomenclature of rejection, however, than I am with the intellectual or (for want of a better term) the spiritual consequences of hyphenation, the feeling of "outsidedness" and its effect on the literary imagination. It is a commonplace to say, I know, that all true artists, including the literary ones, are spiritual hyphenates, "Isolatoes," bearing the stigma of genius that separates them from the pigheaded majority. But on a less exalted level, the writers I shall be principally concerned with—Negro writers and writers of recent ethnic origin—have been keenly conscious of their social separation from the "American" Americans, and the same might be said about those writers affiliated by design or by accident with any minority group. The writer of Jewish or Negro or Asiatic extraction may feel the twinge of hyphenation even when it is not ascribed to him or when the critic distinguishes him from his white Anglo-Saxon counterparts with no ostensible malice. He is sometimes told that he represents (or should represent) a culture, a tradition, a style, an attitude that is somehow not native to this country.

Given the fact that a significant portion of the most interesting literature produced in the United States during the past twenty-five years has been written by men and women who are connected in some way with minorities—racial, ethnic, and cultural—it can no longer be argued that a foreign-sounding name or a colored skin is a professional handicap. A recent collection of criticism lists twenty of the more notable contemporary fiction writers. Of these, James Baldwin and Ralph Ellison are the Negro representatives; Truman Capote, Flannery O'Connor, Carson McCullers, and William Styron make up the Southern contingent; seven writers of Jewish origin are included (Nelson Algren, Saul Bellow, Herbert Gold, Bernard Malamud, Philip Roth, J. D. Salinger, Norman Mailer); Vance Bourjaily and Jack Kerouac add Lebanese and French-Canadian ingredients; and four writers (Paul Bowles, Wright Morris, James Purdy, and John Updike) compose an unaffiliated and unsouthern WASP minority.

It may be that I am stretching a point by mentioning the Southern-American group as if they were hyphenates of a sort, but I think it can be demonstrated that the so-called Southern Renaissance of recent years was the work of writers who were simultaneously the products and articulators of a society outside the main currents of American industrial life, a society almost as alien and as remote to the average Northern reader as China. If this sounds mildly preposterous, I ask you to consider for a moment some analogies that have been drawn between the Southern writers, as representatives of one kind of minority, and the contemporary Jewish writers, as representatives of another.

I don't mean merely that they constitute two of the most vigorous and fertile strains in our current writing, but that each speaks in the name of a defeated and humiliated people, each writes out of a peculiar inheritance that compels it to approach the past at once critically and emotionally. For both the Southern and the Jewish writer, the family and family traditions and memories are a tremendously important source of inspiration, and each is given to reporting the personal and social history in a "mode of discourse" (I am borrowing Allen Tate's phrase) that is both voluble and self-conscious. Finally, I think, what Robert Penn Warren says of the Southern writer—that he is historical-minded, and that if he touches up, distorts, or glamorizes the past, he nonetheless treats it as a "repository of values"—can also be said of a Saul Bellow or a Bernard Malamud. The spokesmen for these in many ways disparate minorities, self-conscious about themselves and their past, seem closer to tradition and ritual, to the common experiences of their relatively homogeneous cousinship, than do writers living outside the minority enclaves.

After the emergence of what I have perhaps too neatly designated as the "Southern" and the "Jewish" school, the twin antagonisms—Southern vs. Yankee, Jew vs. Gentile—slackened to the point that permitted the Jewish writer to break out of his literal and metaphorical ghetto, and the Southern writer to range beyond his literary Confederacy, to move, in other words, from a parochial and provincial world into a larger America and into a still larger and more universal mythic world. The Jewish writer has remained, for the most part, inveterately urban even during the peregrinations of Augie March and the African adventures of Henderson the Rain King, just as the Southern writer still lives, mentally at least, in a preindustrial republic; but in our time we are discovering a new territory, as yet uncharted, where the minority Huckleberry Finns, no longer "hyphenates," are beginning to congregate.

The process by which the "minority" writer has passed from what I have called "hyphenation" to "dehyphenation" might be divided very roughly into three stages.

In stage number one, the pioneer spokesman for a hitherto unspoken-for minority—ethnic, racial, or cultural—writes about his Negro or Jewish compatriots in an effort to overcome—or better, to blur—the antiminority stereotype already stamped in the minds of the old-stock Americans. For example, old-stock Americans ascribed to each ethnic minority in the 1890s some unflattering or undignified attribute. Irishmen were drunken and shiftless, Jews clannish and grasping, Negroes childlike or primitive, Germans stupid and cloddish—all cartoon types speaking outlandish dialects and ridiculed, not always ill-humoredly, in the comic magazines and in the music halls. The hyphenate writer, at first a kind of local colorist, often exploited the strangeness and uniqueness of his human material not only for the purpose of winning the sympathies of the unhyphenated but also in the hope of humanizing the stereotyped minority and dissipating prejudice. It was as if he were saying to his suspicious and opinionated audience: "Look, we have customs and manners that may seem bizarre and uncouth, but we are respectable people nevertheless and our presence adds flavor and variety to American life. Let me convince you that our oddities—no matter how quaint and amusing you find them—do not disqualify us from membership in the national family." In their efforts to placate the suspicions of the majority, the minority writer may even have indulged the cherished preconceptions of his readers by incorporating into his characters some of the recognizable features of the stage Irishman or Jew or Negro or German.

In stage number two, the hyphenate writer tends to be less conciliatory, less willing to please. The minority he writes about has begun to sink roots into the native soil. Their children have passed through the primary and secondary schools; a few have gone even further. Now he knows enough to detect and to protest against the disparity between the American creed and practice. A James T. Farrell, for example, or a Michael Gold or Richard Wright lashes out at the restrictions—political, social, economic—which place his hyphenate associates and himself at a disadvantage. As he personalizes the consequences of discrimination and exploitation, he incurs the risk of a double criticism: from the official voices of the status quo, who resent his unflattering or even "un-American" image of American life, and from his own ethnic or racial fellows who would prefer a genteel and uncantankerous spokesman and who accuse him of misrepresenting his own people.

Finally, in the third stage, the minority writer passes from the periphery to the center of his society, viewing it no less critically, perhaps, but more knowingly. He no longer feels hyphenated, because he has appropriated its culture and linked himself with his illustrious literary predecessors to the degree that he can now speak out uninhibitedly as an American, as a deserving beneficiary of his country's intellectual heritage. Yet the dropping of the hyphen does not completely eliminate his marginal perspective. He has detached himself, to be sure, from one cultural environment without becoming a completely naturalized member of the official environment. It is not so much that he retains a divided allegiance but that as a writer (if not necessarily as a private citizen) he has transcended a mere parochial allegiance and can now operate freely in the republic of the spirit. Without renouncing his ethnic or racial past, he has translated his own and his minority's personal experiences (what for the local colorist and the militant protestor comprised the very stuff of their literary material) into the province of the imagination. He has acquired, in short, the "double vision," as F. Scott Fitzgerald used this phrase.

•

I have been described what may be nothing more than a tendency as if it were a chronological process with each of the three stages clearly demarcated from the others. Of course literary periods and groupings and developments never work out so patly in actuality as they appear to do in the summaries of literary historians. And within a single minority group may be found examples of contemporaries who fit into one of the three stages I've been talking about. But in a general way, I think, this course of dehyphenization can be documented. James T. Farrell's treatment of the Chicago Irish is quite clearly different from Edwin O'Connor's treatment of the Irish Bostonians, and James P. Donleavy has nothing in common with either. Abraham Cahan's fine novel, *The Rise of David Levinsky* (1917), Michael Gold's *Jews Without Money* (1930), Saul Bellow's *The Victim* (1947), and Bernard Malamud's *The Assistant* (1957) all deal with Jews, but the last two books are by writers who feel more at home in their country than did their ghetto-bred forerunners. Their characters are people who also happen to be Jews, just as O'Connor's characters (I don't mean the intentionally stagey ones) are people who happen to be Irish. To put it another way, it is not the subject matter of the minority writer that changes; he may continue to deal with the ethnic or racial locale. Rather it is his attitude, his mental stance, his way of looking at his friends and relatives, at himself and the world—that changes. He no longer peers out from behind the minority barricade. In fact, he is no longer the *conscious* "representative" of a national or racial group, but a writer, a disaffiliate. Race and religion and ethnic origin are merely so many colors for his writer's palette.

Can we say that any of the so-called minority writers I have been alluding to have reached that point of sublime disinterestedness or quintessential dehyphenation? Probably not, although the process, it seems to me, has long been underway and may ultimately complete itself.

But a more troublesome question still remains: assuming that the white minority writer breaks out of his self-determined or enforced segregation into a larger United States, and from there into a universal republic, can the Negro-hyphenate, the Afro-American, win even the *right* of passage? Of all the minority groups, the Negroes (for obvious if not good reasons) have had the most difficult task of coming to terms with their society. The Negro voyager, bearing the badge of color, is constantly being detained at the frontiers, rejected or accepted for extraliterary considerations, exposed to the discriminations of his friends as well as his enemies. And yet a handful of Negro writers, the legatees (as they would be the first to admit) of the Negro-hyphenates who cleared a path for them, now find themselves in the last stages of a journey during which the Negro pilgrim—ambushed periodically by the native tribesmen (some of them disguised as friends)—has passed from subservience to angry aggressiveness. Now he approaches the most tortuous stage of all, one that demands neither docility nor berserker rage but critical understanding.

James Baldwin has described this experience in two brilliant collections of autobiographical essays, *Notes of a Native Son* and *Nobody Knows My Name*. A persistent theme in these books, as well as in his last novel, *Another Country*, is the theme dear to Negro writers for the past sixty years at least—the theme of the invisibility of the Negro. The white majority can't *see* him, Baldwin thinks, because for the past two centuries, it has nourished a monstrous stereotype of Negro-ness or blackness that prevents the discovery of Negro identity. Partly because too much time has elapsed between his violent uprooting and the present to enable him to reestablish connections with African culture, and partly, too, because he has come to accept the white man's view of blackness, the Negro has reinforced the stereotype of blackness by hiding from himself. Before the Negro writer could recognize his own complicity in this deception, he had first to see it and study it within the context of the entire American experience (history, traditions, moral assumptions, and the like) in which he and his fellow Negroes have participated, and to see it (as one Negro poet observed a few months ago) "from the point of view of his own emotional history in this country—as its victim and chronicler, a man existing outside the boundaries of commercial diversion or artificial social pretense." It was only after reseeing his personal experiences in that context that Baldwin could write: "I love America more than any other country in the world, and exactly for that reason, I insist on the right to criticize her perpetually." In making this statement, Baldwin automatically dehyphenated himself by arbitrarily allying himself with such earlier "perpetual critics" as Emerson, Thoreau, Melville, and Whitman. By identifying the Negro predicament with the American predicament, a handful of Negro writers—Baldwin and Ellison—have discovered their own moral center.

Now, all writers, as I have suggested, are "outsiders" in a sense, and the majority of us, who are so immured in the density of trees that we never see the forest, must depend upon their detachment if we are to get a proper perspective on ourselves. What is true of writers in general has been even truer of the more distantly removed minority writer; and at the moment, it may be that the gifted Negro writer is in a position to make the most penetrating and decisive comments on certain little-discussed aspects of our national life and character, to disclose to the white majority truths about itself that this white majority has heretofore refused to entertain. For today it is the marginal Negro intellectual or artist who has usurped the role that Thorstein Veblen once assigned to the renegade Jew. It is the Negro who now destroys "the peace of mind that is the birthright of the safe and sane quietist." It is the Negro writer who has become "a disturber of the intellectual peace," the wanderer, the uncomplacent discontented alien of "the uneasy feet." And finally it is the Negro writer who feels most directly the contradictions between our national precept and practice. That is why Baldwin and Ralph Ellison and Lorraine Hansberry are perceptive critics of both white and black America.

Ellison inadvertently described his own role very imaginatively in his speech accepting the National Book Award for his novel *Invisible Man*. He invoked the myth of Proteus, a symbol, he suggested, "for both America and the inheritance of illusion through which all men must fight to achieve reality." The task of the novelist, he said, is to challenge Proteus—that is to say, to challenge the ever-changing face of America until "it surrenders its insights, its truth."

> We are fortunate as American writers [he continued] in that with our variety of racial and national traditions, idioms and manners, we are as yet one. On its profoundest level, American experience is of a whole. Its truth lies in its diversity and swiftness of change. Through forging forms of the novel worthy of it, we achieve not only the promise of our lives, but we anticipate the resolution of those world problems of humanity which for a moment seem to those who are in awe of statistics, completely insoluble.

Ellison in this instance spoke as an American novelist, not as a Negro novelist, but certainly for the Negro the process of reaching that point where he can honestly say, "American experience is of a whole," is a triumph of courage and understanding.

The outsider is by definition a kind of voyeur or eavesdropper, but the Negro, because of his invisibility, has heard and seen things denied to the most sensitive of the white writers. His reports, I might say, while heartening in some respects, are very disheartening in others. We can learn from Negro writers what the daily warfare between white and black is really like, how the interracial hand-shake or the interracial marriage (as Baldwin says) can be as "cruci-fying as the public hanging or the secret rape." They remind us that the sociologizing of life—the reduction of unpleasant realities to categories and statistics (a particularly American penchant, it seems to me)—can be a cruel evasion. They show how the "oppressed and the oppressors are bound together within the same society" in a dreadful symbiosis; they demonstrate that when a minority (by de-sign or accident) is treated as subhuman, it may accept that image of itself on occasion and dramatize the terrible estrangement by acts of violence.

This racial estrangement, Baldwin would say, measures the depth of the white man's estrangement from himself. His dark image of the Negro is a projection of his private shadows he dare not contem-plate directly. Hence his habit of objectifying the Negro in a succes-sion of spurious guises—as Uncle Tom or Aunt Jemima or as their "uppity" and demonic opposites. Thus the white man, Baldwin thinks, avoids the confrontation with himself, evades all genuine experience, in fact; and he will never learn to assess the experiences of others or achieve an imaginative identification with others until he has come to a proper assessment of himself. When that time comes, if it ever does, he may begin to question the melting-pot ideal that everyone should be as much alike as possible.

The self-emancipated Negro (like any emancipated victim of op-pression who by some miracle has managed to heal himself of crip-pling psychological wounds, or at least to live with them) has learned to assess the experience of others in the process of discover-ing his own identity. In the case of Baldwin, I suspect this healing process or self-acceptance has been assisted by sojourns abroad. Most of our writers have profited from similar experiences, crossing the ocean for purposes of contemplation or escape, but living abroad for the Negro writer has been of particular importance because his short or lengthy expatriation was prompted in part, if not solely, by racial considerations. In Europe, he could be a writer without having constantly to brace himself against gratuitous slurs and stupid insults. Richard Wright, a courageous militant, lived out his last years in Paris for this reason and remained a hyphenate, or a renegade in the Veblenian sense, cut off from the white America and from the new Africa in which during his few visits he had felt even less at home.

Ellison and Baldwin, his younger friends, were encouraged by his generous assistance (he proved once again that a Negro could be a writer and a good one), but they could not follow him into exile. Even if they lived uncomfortably in the United States, it was the only place they could do their work. When *Time* magazine listed Ellison among the expatriate writers on the strength of a two-year fellowship in Italy, he wrote to the editors that although he could "sympathize with those Negro Americans whose disgust with the racial absurdities of American life" lead "them to live elsewhere, my own needs—both as a citizen and as an artist, make the gesture of exile seem mere petulance." Some writers wrote their best work in Europe, like James and Hemingway; some, like Richard Wright, did not. "Personally," Ellison said, "I am too vindictively American, too full of hate for the hateful aspects of this country, and too possessed by the things I love here to be too long away."

Not Europe, then, and not Africa beckoned to Ellison. Before Baldwin, he discovered that he had more in common with white Americans than with Africans.

> To the question, *what am I?* [Ellison told an interviewer], I answer that I am a Negro American. That means far more than something racial. It does not mean race, it means something cultural, that I am a man who shares a dual culture. For me, the Negro is a member of an America-bound cultural group with its own idiom, its own psychology, growing out of all its history. The American Negro stock is *here*, a synthesis of various African cultures, then of slavery, and of all the experiences of Negroes since.

Until several years ago, Ellison's friend James Baldwin was saying almost the same thing, although he had arrived at this point only after serving his time as an expatriate abroad. He had decided to follow Richard Wright's example in 1948 when he was twenty-four years old. He returned a decade later, convinced by this time that only in America could the Negro writer discover his birthright and that "even the most incorrigible maverick," as he put it, "had to be born somewhere. He may leave the group which produced him—or he may be forced to—but nothing will efface his origins, the marks which he carries with him everywhere. I think it is important to know this and even find it a matter of rejoicing, as the strongest people do, regardless of their station. On this acceptance, literally, the life of a writer depends." When the same person who interviewed Ellison asked Baldwin how he would reply to a man from Mars who posed the question "What are you?," he answered that in 1948, he would have said: " 'I am a writer'—with an edge in my voice while thinking: 'I am a nigger, you green bastard.' Now I think I'd say to him: 'I am a writer with a lot of work to do and wondering if I can do it.' "

This was in 1960. Since then Baldwin has taken an increasingly militant stand in the Negro civil rights movement and appears to have reverted to a position closer to Richard Wright's than to Ralph Ellison's. Certainly, the moderation and hopefulness that marked Baldwin's first two volumes of essays are absent in his passionate warning to the whites, *The Fire Next Time*, and particularly in his recent play in which the rage and protest and hatred seemed to be aimed against "whiteness" itself. This fierce partisanship of Baldwin's has been noted approvingly by a fine and justly respected literary critic, Irving Howe. Howe has argued that the Negro writer can't be really true to himself, or true to his experience as a Negro, if he wills to move into what I have been calling "the third stage" and tries to transcend his Negro-ness. His argument might be summed up in some such fashion as this:

1) The Negro writer, because he is a Negro, may try to separate his social and artistic responsibilities, but his writing will suffer as a consequence.

2) Try as he might, no Negro can entirely erase his hate and ferocity against the white race. (Howe quotes with approval Baldwin's remark: "No American Negro exists who does not have his private Bigger Thomas living in the skull.")

3) Since "violence is central to the life of the American Negro,"

the Negro writer who sounds the note of "willed affirmation," who declares that he will accept his burden, is only whistling in the dark. What is more, Howe implies, it is capitulation, for which the Negro writer pays a price.

4) The price is the failure of conviction. When he writes about the white world, the Negro writer fails. Furthermore, it is a "moral and psychological impossibility" for the Negro writer to achieve aesthetic detachment in dealing with Negro experience, for "plight and protest are inseparable from that experience." The "unqualified assertion of self-liberation" that ends *Invisible Man* simply doesn't ring true. It violates the realities of Negro life.

5) Thus, the Negro writer, if he is to "assert his humanity," must write in protest and rage, even though he may have to discard the "suave" and the "elegant" (presumably derived from his white peers) for the "harsh, clumsy, heavy-breathing" prose that is the appropriate vehicle for "the pant of suppressed bitterness."

Howe's essay provoked a reply from Ralph Ellison, the sharpness of which seems to have shocked him. Howe had praised Ellison's literary gifts and pronounced his novel *Invisible Man* "a brilliant though flawed achievement, standing with *Native Son* as the major fiction thus far composed by American Negroes." Why then did Ellison turn almost savagely against Howe and then follow up his first attack with a vehement denunciation of Howe's views together with an eloquent justification for his own refusal to make " 'Negroness' a metaphysical condition"?

I suspect Ellison especially resented Howe's implication that the Negro, at least for the moment, could and ought not to drop the hyphen, and that by thinking of himself as a writer first and a Negro second, he was somehow attempting to escape from his Negritude. Even the well-wishers of the Negro, it seemed, were imprisoned by their liberal stereotypes, asserting unequivocally that all Negroes had identical experiences, bore the same psychic wounds, suffered the same slights and irritations. By the same logic, the Jew was somehow betraying himself and Jewry in the act of transcending his Jewishness. Ellison insisted that he was not denying his race by designating Eliot, Malraux, Dostoevsky, and Faulkner as his literary ancestors rather than Richard Wright—a generous friend, a "relative" of sorts, but a writer who had less to teach him than Hemingway did. I think that Ellison, in his open letters to Howe, was accusing him in effect of wanting to confine the Negro writer to a kind of literary Harlem and to draft him into the civil rights army.

The irony of a white critic telling a Negro writer what he must do to be saved, both as a man and as an artist, is not lost on any reader of the Howe-Ellison exchange. Ellison, an ex-Communist, was not unfamiliar with this argument. Once he had accepted it. But in 1964, he believes that a "protest" need "not necessarily take the form of speaking for a political or a social program."

> If *Invisible Man* [he says] is even "apparently" free from "the ideological and emotional penalties suffered by Negroes in this country," it is because I tried to the best of my ability to transform these elements into art. My goal was not to escape, or hold back, but to work through; to transcend, as the Blues transcend the painful conditions with which they deal. The protest is there, not because I was helpless before my radical condition, but because I *put* it there. If there is anything "miraculous" about the book it is the result of hard work undertaken in the belief that the work of art is important in itself, that it is a social action in itself.

One final problem remains—and then I am finished. Can the minority writer will his "personal realization"—determine of his own free will that he can be the kind of writer he wants to be, affiliate with the company of artists whom *he* selects as his literary ancestors? Or must he attach himself to his respective minority, fight for it, glorify it, and articulate its grievances, until it has won complete freedom?

This is a question that many minority writers are not allowed to forget—even when they have stopped thinking "hyphenatically" themselves. When they present realistically a segment of Jewish or Irish-Catholic or Italian or Negro experience from what I have been calling a "third stage" perspective, the still unassimilated or hyphenated Jews or Negroes or Irish or Southerners may be hurt and offended by the unflattering "image" of the particular minority.

Some months ago, Philip Roth was taken to task by a number of Jewish readers who were outraged by his picture of middle-class Jewish life and who charged that Roth—a Jew himself—had corroborated the anti-Semitic canards. Why, these critics asked, could he not have written about the great "saga" of Jewish history, the hardships Jews had overcome, the honors they had achieved? Why must he write about adulterers and weaklings and opportunists? Why, at the very least, couldn't he have presented a more balanced view of his co-religionists?

In his reply, Roth claimed for the minority writer the same freedom that all writers of fiction are entitled to. "Fiction," he said, "is not written to affirm the principles and beliefs that everybody seems to hold." Nor is fiction public relations. A serious writer does not ask himself, "What *will* people say?" but "What *do* people think?" He is less concerned with the breadth and range of presentation than he is with the depth of his representation, and he quite properly refuses to be inhibited by the possibility that weak and malicious people might misinterpret his work. The public relations attitude toward literature perpetuates the hyphenate psychology by counseling "invisibility." It divides America into the camps of "we" and "they." It creates an atmosphere of timidity and paranoia. In contrast, the minority writer who boldly exposes the sensitive issues which the "safe and sane quietist" abominates, who explores the caves of fantasy, is the true liberator. "A book like . . . *Invisible Man*," Roth writes, ". . . seems to me to have helped many whites who are not anti-Negro, but who do have Negro stereotypes, to surrender simple-minded notions of Negro life." And again: "The writer must speak to, not speak for—people."

What Mr. Howe would say to this, I can't say. But what he demands—perhaps "expects" is the better word—of the Negro writer has never been demanded of writers belonging to any other minority ethnic or racial group, and runs counter to the American literary experience as I understand it. Some minority writers may never feel comfortable with the assimilated, and some can never return to the fold. At what juncture a minority writer drops his hyphen will depend upon a variety of circumstances—social, cultural, and political—upon his parents and family experiences, upon his geographical location, his education, and his personal luck. The signs of dehyphenation are not revealed in a writer's subject matter (for he may well continue to write about the marginal people of his origins, to transport his heritage, so to speak, into new provinces of the imagination). But they are revealed in his attitude toward his old world and toward the larger world into which he has moved. He will not write as a "race-man," or a "minority man" who has kept the faith, but as a writer who has extracted something pertinent and valuable from his life.

"Dehyphenation," as I use the term, is thus not hostile to the democratic dream of diversity, or to the foreign bodies in national life that have invigorated American language and literature and helped to prevent our culture from becoming more bland and homogenized than it is. Nor is the dehyphenated writer necessarily conciliatory and apolitical. His protest or revolt, however, is made as a man and as a writer—not as a self-appointed spokesman for a minority, a class, a race. It is the human condition and the human predicament, finally, that engage him and that evoke his love, his concern, his hate, and his hope.

Out of a Dark Wood:

Edward Dahlberg

Since the publication in 1930 of his underground novel *Bottom Dogs*, Edward Dahlberg has been negotiating angrily and publicly with a spotted world and with himself. *Because I Was Flesh*, his latest book, is subtitled an "autobiography," but it might better have been called an exercise in self-exorcism. A very self-conscious and studiedly selective account of his boyhood and early life, it is as revealing for what it leaves unrevealed as for what it unshrinkingly and remarkably reports. Not unlike Rousseau in his *Confessions*, like Henry Adams in his *Education*, and perhaps most of all like Sherwood Anderson in his half-fabricated or tinted reminiscences, Dahlberg has daringly exposed a portion of himself without resorting to the cluttering detail or the amplitude of statement that could have blurred the line of his story about a loving-hating son and his mother.

She first appeared in *Bottom Dogs* and in its sequel, *From Flushing to Calvary*, as Lizzie Lewis; and although now Dahlberg presents her as Lizzie Dalberg (he added the "h" to his own name) and in a baroque oracular style so different from the naturalistic pavement prose of his earlier work, he has left her character and her physical appearance unaltered. She emerges after more than thirty years as the same incontinent, vulgar, gullible, ridiculous, suspicious, generous, hopeful, and indomitable creature who drifted through the

Originally published as a review of *Because I Was Flesh: The Autobiography of Edward Dahlberg* (1963) in the *Hudson Review*, 17, no. 2 (1964), 312–315.

chapters of his earlier rancid novels. Her marriages and abortive liaisons, her comi-tragic sojourns in Dallas, Memphis, Kansas City, and New York are retold and reseen. Once again we are in a Dahlbergian ambiance of lady barbershops, cuspidors, roaches, varicose veins, and greasy plates. His adolescent years in a Cleveland Jewish orphan asylum are relentlessly exhumed, and the foulness and stench and drabness that suffused the atmosphere of *Bottom Dogs* like the stink of a sewer are if anything more pervasive in the autobiography. Dahlberg, it would seem, is obsessed with the abominations of the flesh and ingeniously various in depicting the sordid. His youth is grubby, louse-infested; his father is "some baleful seminal drop of a depraved rotting forefather"; the whores and demireps he observes in his mother's "sanitary" barbershop have sour mouths and prolapsed wombs; he is haunted by sweating undergarments and hair and the sound of flushing toilets; the children retch and vomit over their unspeakable meals; his mother carries "her truss of grief" and the buzzing flies are "lecherous." Even reading is at best "a squalid pleasure" for the ugly graceless narrator; the discovery of Plato brings no rapture but leaves him "still covered with the vermin of ignorance."

And yet *Because I Was Flesh* in its way is a beautiful book in addition to being an extraordinary one, whereas *Bottom Dogs*, although powerful and disturbing, is not. What differentiates one from the other, I think, is not merely that Dahlberg is now looking at his mother and his environment from the inside out, but that he is also trying to understand his Ishmaelitish wanderings, to salvage some meaning from them, and to make tardy oblations to the Hagar toward whom he felt such shame and horror and love. Given the rhapsodic and often postured writing, his "impostumed" prose (to borrow one of the archaic or obsolescent words he seems fond of), one might be tempted to suspect the genuineness of Dahlberg's feelings. Yet to yield to such a temptation would be wrong. What keeps the confessional narration from becoming overripe and merely mannered is the distance he manages to place between his boyhood and his present self. His emotions are invariably tempered by reflection, the personal transmuted to the archetypal.

Interpolated throughout his autobiography are meditations, often brilliantly shaped, on the tidal fluctuations of luck, or observations on the fatality of casual experience. Dahlberg, looking back at his unappetizing life, decides that a man rather perfects than corrects his vices, "for we die with all our sins entire, and every wrong, thought or dream or vision in the child matures in the man." He is possessed by the gross desires of adolescence, the yearning for "jocular rumps" and "dimpled thighs," and the poignancy of postcopulative despair. "Each man's past is his Nemesis," he concludes, but he must hug his cockroachy memories even though he swoons with nausea at their recollection. To suppress them would be the ultimate impiety.

The self-revulsion so notable in *Bottom Dogs* has in *Because I Was Flesh* by no means disappeared, but in the autobiography it is distilled into a self-mockery that can turn the grotesque antics of orphan inmates into a sort of comedy. Their exploits and fiascoes are related in a mock-heroic vein as if they were Greek heroes, Socratic dialecticians, or Hebrew prophets. The lofty language he employs, however, is not intended as pure irony. If Melville (and this is a very Melvillean book) can borrow the accents of Shakespeare and Sir Thomas Browne to dignify his whalers, so can Dahlberg call upon seventeenth-century prose writers as well as Homer, Tourneur, Lucian, St. Augustine, Pascal, Rabelais, and the Talmud to mythologize his "jillflirts," "poltfoots," "gullyguts," "hunkers," "wittols," and "noddies." Only in this way, perhaps, could "the bastard issue of a lady barber with dyed grizzled hair" give dimension and meaning to his maggoty life.

The events, spiritual and intellectual, that changed Dahlberg from a regular contributor to the *New Masses*, a writer of what he once called "implication literature," into a celebrator of pagan rites and a composer of sensual hymns "of flesh and sweat" are precisely those about which he is silent. Only his violent repudiation of socialist and sociological writing in *Can These Bones Live* and his disgusted comments about the "cloacal revulsions" of Caldwell, Farrell, and Dos Passos measure the distance he had traveled between 1930 and 1941.

Because I Was Flesh alludes to some of the literary and philosophical midwives who delivered him from Communism's "cankered, miserable skin," but it contains no homage to D. H. Lawrence, his first discerning reader and the man whose condemnations of the fecundless modern wasteland Dahlberg seems to have taken to heart after a brief Marxist interlude.

In his introduction to *Bottom Dogs*, Lawrence had nothing particularly good to say about Dahlberg the writer except that he had succeeded in capturing "the under-dog mind," a "strange, external superficial mind" detached from "the affective and effective self. His will-to-persist is intellectual also. Beyond this, nothing." Lawrence confessed he was glad to have read this "genuine" and "objectionable" novel, so "perfectly sane" and yet so close to "criminal insanity," because it disclosed "the last word in repulsive consciousness, consciousness in a state of repulsion." But he did not want "to read any more books like this."

By far the largest part of Lawrence's essay had to do with Dahlberg's book as an emblem of a sick and savage society. Lawrence believed that the western continent invariably broke the hearts if not the will of its colonizers: "The flow from the heart, the warmth of fellow-feeling which has animated Europe and been the best of her humanity, individual, spontaneous, flowing in thousands of little passionate currents often conflicting, this seems unable to persist in the American soul." *Bottom Dogs* documented the mutual repulsiveness Americans felt for one another, a hostility masked by the cant of social benevolence. The breakdown of "blood-sympathy," the sensing of others "by their sweat and their kitchens," accounted for the perfection of American "plumbing," the horror of "halitosis," the "American nausea at coughing, spitting." Tolerant of "tin cans and paper and broken rubbish," American townships went "crazy at the sight of human excrement," a fact which signified for Lawrence the exhaustion of "the transcendental bodiless brotherliness" of the last hundred years, thought but never felt, and the deepening of an inward and physical revulsion of man for man.

The cry of self-revulsion and the accusatory refrain "They stink! My God, they stink!" that Lawrence heard in *Bottom Dogs* resounds even louder in *From Flushing to Calvary* and in Dahlberg's next book, *Those Who Perish*, a deservedly forgotten hysterical antifascist novel published in 1934 in which the New York Jews come off almost as badly as their oppressors. Seven years later, however, in *Can These Bones Live* (interpretations of, among others, Tolstoy, Cervantes, Melville, Shakespeare, and Dostoevsky), Dahlberg was not only drawing Lawrencian conclusions about the American mind and literature but also diagnosing the source of its bloodlessness. The "classic hieroglyphical scriptures" of our great writers, he said, were all refusals of the flesh, symptoms of the American's "revulsion against one's own blood flow, the anathema of the covert bowels, the unholy dread of the sub rosa Unclean Man."

Because I Was Flesh might be read as Dahlberg's belated recognition of certain truths (confirmed by his own life and by the sages): that the denial of man, "the defecating, eating and copulating animal," ends in the nightmare of the body, that man casts off his humanity at his own peril, and that the only way back to life is "through the continuous memory of his own egoism and organs." If Lorry Lewis, the autobiographical hero of *Bottom Dogs*, despises himself, thrilling to his own repulsiveness, as Lawrence notes, "in a terrified, perverted way," the "I" of the autobiography has learned to accept his own stench and is saved, as he says of Tolstoy's Ivan Ilytch in *Can These Bones Live*, not by the Holy Writ but by the humanity of the bedpan. "Why do we love our vermin?" he asks at the end of his autobiography. "Do our souls need dirt, lice, rats, and puddles and woe?" And he replies:

> We caress and stroke our rotten, starved years because the dream requires it. You who have pondered Joseph's interpretation of Pharaoh's dream consider this: the seven lean kine that stand in the hot river Nile will always devour the seven fat ones—aye, seven again; it is the sign of pestilence and famine—but there is more food here for the despairing, the niggard heart than in the tenderest grass and herbs.

Lizzie Dahlberg, the squalid quack and chin-scraper, is the redemptive figure in the autobiography, not so much as a symbol of the self-sacrificing mother so dear to our national folklore but as an equivalent of Ivan Ilytch's sanctifying servant who "cannot make those subtle distinctions between a man in his social and decorous clothes and in his honestly defecating necessities." Dahlberg's retrospective acceptance of his mother is thus tantamount to an acceptance of his loathed self—his Jewishness, his fatherlessness, his wormy childhood—and, finally, of his hypocritical flesh.

Richard Wright and the
Communist Party

In 1920, H. L. Mencken reviewed for *Smart Set* Mary White Ovington's *The Shadow*, a "bad novel" which the pundit used as an object lesson for black writers. After summarizing its improbable plot and commenting on the superiority of black music to black literature (largely polemics and lyrical verse), he advised Miss Ovington "to forget her race prejudices and her infantile fables long enough to get a true and unemotional and typical picture of her people on paper." Only then would she "achieve a respectable work of art" and serve the cause she believed in.

The fact that Mary White Ovington was not black undermined Mencken's injunction, but it did not invalidate a remarkable statement in which he defined the as yet unwritten great black novel and its Negro author.

> The black man, I suppose, has a fairly good working understanding of the white man; he has many opportunities to observe and note down, and my experience of him convinces me that he is a shrewd observer— that few white men ever fool him. But the white man, even in the South, knows next to nothing of the inner life of the Negro. The more magnificently he generalizes, the more his ignorance is displayed. What the

Originally published in *New Letters*, 38, no. 2 (Winter 1971), 170–181. Reprinted with the permission of *New Letters* and the Curators of the University of Missouri–Kansas City.

average Southerner believes about the Negroes who surround him is chiefly nonsense. His view of them is moral and indignant or, worse still, sentimental and idiotic. The great movements and aspirations that stir them are quite beyond his comprehension; in many cases he does not even hear of them. The thing we need is a realistic picture of this inner life of the Negro by one who sees the race from within—a self portrait as vivid and accurate as Dostoievsky's portrait of the Russian or Thackeray's of the Englishman. The action should be kept within the normal range of Negro experience. It should extend over a long enough range of years to show some development in character and circumstance. It should be presented against a background made vivid by innumerable small details. The Negro author who makes such a book will dignify American literature and accomplish more for his race than a thousand propagandists and theorists. He will force the understanding that now seems so hopeless. He will blow up nine-tenths of the current poppycock.

This literary redeemer, Mencken warned, would have to take care to avoid the wrong literary models: "The place to learn how to write novels is in the harsh but distinguished seminary kept by Prof. Dr. Dreiser."

Some half-dozen years later, Richard Wright, a young black man who would ultimately fill these specifications, discovered the *Prefaces* of Mencken in the Memphis Public Library. Mencken, who had probably insulted the South more flagrantly and vehemently and colorfully than any other American writer, was subject to editorial attacks in all of the Southern newspapers at that time. Here was a rambunctious man striking out at everything sacred to Americans— political, social, religious—and "fighting with words . . . using words as weapons . . . using them as one would a club." The self-taught boy who had just managed to finish eighth grade learned from Mencken the names of writers he would soon read: Poe, Conrad, France, Dostoevsky, Mark Twain, Anderson, Lewis—and above all, Dreiser. "All my life," Wright wrote later, "had shaped me for the realism, the naturalism of the modern novel, and I could not read enough of them." It excited him to think that men all over the world were fighting against oppression—that he wasn't alone in his rebellion. The discovery of Mencken encouraged him to become a writer, and the reading of the realists mentioned by Mencken pointed Wright in the direction of Communism.

Wright's account of his arrival in Chicago in 1927 resembles the experiences of other men and women in real life or in literature who come to the Big City from the provinces. One thinks, for example, of the heroine of Dreiser's *Sister Carrie* (a novel Wright read with deep interest) or the hero of *An American Tragedy*. Chicago wasn't a vision out of the *Arabian Nights* as it was to Clyde Griffith, but it was exciting and frightening enough. Wright was astonished at first by the indifference of the white Chicagoan to the black newcomers, but in time he saw that his people had only exchanged masters—the Bosses of the Buildings for the Lords of the Land.

Wright described the impact of Chicago very eloquently in "How Bigger Was Born," and later he speculated on the gains and losses attending the black migration from the rural South to the Northern cities. Observing the misery of the urban black, the white man might wonder why the Negro had abandoned his Southern shack for an urban slum. Wright likened the black migration to the white man's breaking out of the "slumberous feudal world" to take the risks of what William James called "unguaranteed existence." In leaving the South, the Negro acted on "the same impulses" that motivated the white western activists who left the known for the unknown. He shared the hopes as well as the corruptions and psychological maladies of white men, but in the "cold industrial North" there existed a "saving remnant of a passion for freedom," and that was worth a good deal to Richard Wright with his secret ambitions.

So we find Wright in the Chicago of the late 1920s leading two lives simultaneously—one literary and intellectual, the other social. In a flat running with cockroaches, he read Stephen Crane and Dostoevsky and Gertrude Stein's *Three Lives* (a book that struck him as forcibly as it had Sherwood Anderson). His chief problem, with the advent of the Depression, was not in finding enough books to read but in finding jobs—or rather holding on to them. Thousands of other boys and young men went through similar experiences during the Thirties. They worked as porters, bill collectors, dishwashers, hospital orderlies, post office workers, counselors (these were some of the jobs Wright had); but few listened so attentively to the jive talk of the urban blacks, observed the behavior at rent parties, or watched the expressions on the faces of unemployed men and women as they resisted evictions or stood up to the police.

Wright described his attitude at this time (between 1927 and

1931) as one of "watchful wonder," and his desire increased "to measure accurately the reality of the objective world so that I might more than meet its demands." He was old enough and mature enough to record the Depression and to respond to events that practically determined he would become a writer. The fat years for the Chicago blacks—which began in 1924—came to an end in 1929; they felt the onset of the long slide downward at least a year before white Chicagoans discerned the full impact of the economic collapse. Negro-owned banks were the first to fail, black workers the first to be fired. By 1932, the Black Belt was in the depths of deprivation. In and out of jobs during this period, Wright watched the relief kitchens being set up, watched middle-class relief officials interviewing their unemployed clients, saw how quickly the inchoate and confused mass of people developed feelings of solidarity as they anxiously waited in the employment offices or helped one another in the streets. "I was slowly beginning," Wright recalled, "to comprehend the meaning of my environment; a sense of direction was beginning to emerge from the conditions of my life. I began to feel something more powerful than I could express. My speech and manner changed. My cynicism slid from me. I grew open and questioning. I wanted to know."

And then one of those events occurred that have a kind of Horatio Algerish significance. A case worker assigned to the Wright household discovered Richard Wright. This chance meeting with the wife of a Chicago sociologist, Louis Wirth, brought Wright to the university where he met Wirth—and, more important, Wirth's assistant, Horace Cayton—a black intellectual who had arrived in the Black Metropolis via the Northwest and who was to become one of Wright's closest friends.

Cayton, in his autobiography, *Long Old Road* (1963), tells about his friendship with Wright and how the massive sociological data gathered by the Chicago sociologists helped to provide the ballast for *Native Son*. It was somehow appropriate that Wright should write the introduction to St. Clair Drake and Cayton's impressive study of Chicago Negroes, *Black Metropolis*, for he was doing something equivalent in his fiction. This is not to say that he would not have written his books without the assistance of the Chicago school. There were other goads, as we shall see, to his imagination.

•

The story of Wright's connection with the actual or would-be Communist world in the early Thirties is familiar to anyone who has read his autobiographical writings. In 1932 he became involved with the Chicago John Reed Club, an organization sponsored by the Communist Party in 1929 to coordinate the activities of radical artists and writers. Wright had heard Communists haranguing crowds in Washington Park, but it was not until a white social worker invited him to a meeting that he came to know any of them. Suspicious at first, he soon warmed up to people who, he felt, regarded him as a person only incidentally black. The Marxist literature they gave him to read demonstrated to him that the black downtrodden formed only a portion of the oppressed toilers. Some of the artists he met at the club were to become as famous as himself—men like Nelson Algren, Jackson Pollock, Ben Shahn. Most of the members were simply young people looking for cultural stimulation. In this sympathetic environment Wright began gradually to find his own voice amidst the rhetoric and clichés of revolution. Not surprisingly, he joined the Party.

Wright's autobiographical remarks on the John Reed Club of Chicago and his subsequent dealings with the League of American Writers are all tinted a little, but essentially his account is reliable and only suffers from revealing omissions. The first national conference of the John Reed Clubs met in Chicago, May 29, 1932. The unpublished minutes of that conference both complement and qualify Wright's recollections of the internal schisms and factional fights within the Chicago John Reed Club.

The temporary chairman of the conference was the same Jan Wittenber who served as the model for Jan Erlone in *Native Son*. (It was through him that Wright had joined the John Reed Club in January 1932). Wittenber, a member of the artists' faction of the CP, sided with those John Reed members who preferred to entrust all questions of politics to the "militant leadership of the Communist Party." His description of the club's activities shows the kinds of work other members of the John Reed Club (and presumably Richard Wright) were engaged in that year.

However, his almost poignant summary of purposeful activity makes no mention of reaching out to the Negro masses, nothing about bringing in young proletarian writers like Richard Wright. The 1932 conference boiled down to such questions as the proper approach to fellow-traveling intellectuals like John Dos Passos or Edmund Wilson, or debates on the danger of Left sectarianism as against a too-latitudinarian approach to writers and politics. Most interesting and portentous, the minutes indicate implicitly if not explicitly that individualists in the local clubs already distrusted the Central Party and the New York writers in particular, high-powered intellectuals from the East, who dominated the conference. Clearly, even in 1932, the CP ran the show; and clearly the New York contingent wanted to exclude the inexperienced and uninfluential "boys" (as Mike Gold called them) and to make the John Reed Clubs attractive to big names. As Wright knew well, the reconstitution of the clubs did not take into consideration the needs and interests of black artists.

Until the late Twenties, the "Negro Question" for the Party was primarily a political and economic one—that is, until Stalin initiated the principle of a separate black nation in the United States. Of course, the Party line vacillated. The policy of black self-determination, maintained between 1928 and 1934, was played down during the Popular Front period (1934–1939) only to be revived briefly following the Nazi-Soviet Pact. After Hitler invaded the USSR, the Party line switched again. At no time during these years, however, did the Party exercise much influence on the majority of American blacks. When Wright joined the CP, it numbered about 16,000, of whom barely more than a thousand were Negroes.

Some black Communists considered the notion of a separate black state within the United States highly unrealistic, as well as smacking of a kind of Red Jim Crowism. All Party people agreed, however, that the Party had failed to reach the black proletariat and that Negro artists were partly to blame. As one black leader put it in 1928:

> There is little in recent Negro poetry that would lead one to believe that the poets are conscious of the existence of the Negro masses. There is no challenge in their poetry, no revolt. They do not echo the lamentations of the downtrodden masses. Millions of blacks are suffering from poverty and cruelty, and the black poets shut their eyes! There is not a race more desperate in this country than the black race, and Negro poets play with pale emotions!

He added that most Negro writers were simply petit-bourgeois opportunists or black decadents or cowards.

This animus lay behind the Party's attempt to recruit black writers who would inject Marxist militancy into black writing and give the lie to those who played the role of the "Meek Moses" and "Black Hamlet"—who shunned protest and refused to confront the revolutionary traditions of the Negro people. So it was that in 1932–1933, when Wright was working with the John Reed Club in Chicago, the Party singled him out as the type of proletarian revolutionary artist—free of the bourgeois taint—it had been seeking. Here was someone who could "eradicate the distorted stereotypes of the Negro people prevalent in American literature and drama" and write about the struggle of the masses. To the Party at this time, middle-class intellectuals like Walter White and W. E. B. Du Bois were traitors. It looked to writers like Wright to lead black America's fight against the "foes of culture and progress."

Wright was very receptive to this appeal in 1932—and with good reasons. He saw Communists not only fighting for Negro rights but also seeking to uproot racism within their own ranks. They pushed blacks into Party work (Wright was elected president of the John Reed Club without his knowing why); they nominated Negroes for political office, dramatized the black man's problem, risked social ostracism and even physical violence in behalf of black people. No political party since the Abolitionists had challenged American racial hypocrisy so zealously.

Wright's explanation of why he left the Party makes it abundantly clear at the same time why it had such a hold on him when he joined it and why he remained a radical after he left the Party in the early Forties. He says (and this is probably true, although how conscious he was of this reason is hard to say) that as early as 1932 he felt the Party oversimplified black experience. But the Party *had* a program, an ideal, and he, Richard Wright (this was his function as he saw it then), would tell the Communists how the common people felt. He would also tell the black masses of the sacrifices the Communists were making for them. What notions Wright held about the Black Republic at this time is hard to say, but the white Jewish lawyer's description of American blacks in *Native Son* may suggest a clue: "They are not simply twelve million people; in reality, they constitute a separate nation, stunted, stripped, and held captive within this nation."

Wright wrote at length about his resentment toward the Party, but these are retrospective comments. He remained in the Party, it should be noted, long after most of his literary friends had left it, even while he chafed under Party directives. That was the burden of his article "I Tried to Be a Communist." In this piece and in his contribution to *The God That Failed*, he drew a picture of a manipulating, opportunistic, sectarian-ridden Communist leadership whose ultimate purpose in bringing in intellectuals and writers was simply to turn them into instruments of propaganda—to convert them into "weapons."

He joined the Party, he tells us, when it still distrusted intellectuals and was sensitive to all manner of heresies and deviations, and almost from the beginning Wright began to challenge the Party line. He opposed the liquidation of the John Reed Clubs in 1935 and the Party decision to substitute in their place a more controllable literary organization, the League of American Writers. (The clubs had become almost quasi-autonomous, and the Party leadership feared the club magazines might open their columns too freely to left-wing deviationists.) In 1937 Wright was certainly the Party's most illustrious proletarian author. All the same, it interfered with his literary work by imposing on him various extraliterary tasks. Still, if Wright (as he said in 1944) had become disenchanted with the Communists, if not their cause, as early as 1937, he continued to serve the Party faithfully even after 1939—a fact he omitted in his 1944 piece.

For example, in 1937 he wrote an essay entitled "Blue-Print for Negro Writing" in which he called upon black writers to stop distrusting each other and pled for "unity with all the progressive ideas of our day, the primary prerequisite for collective work." To achieve a progressive unity, to arrive at "a thorough integration with the American scene," the novelist needed a theory that would account for the "meaning, structure, and direction of modern society." Without this theory, the writer floundered. Once the Negro writer responded to the Marxian vision, he was granted "a sense of dignity" which "no other vision could give." It restored to him "his lost heritage, that is, his role as a creator of himself."

These were very fine words, so far as the Party theorists were concerned, and they praised the author of *Uncle Tom's Children* and *Native Son*—although Party critics were by no means unanimous in their opinions of the latter novel. When Wright declared that Marxism aided the writer to create the world in which he lived, that it restored his role "as a creator of himself," he was already treading on dangerous ground. Perhaps he thought the Party would be pleased with his formulation, but it is conceivable that even then he already suspected it might not accept his rather subjective notions about *his* world and the deliverance of his private self. Constance Webb's book on Wright lists excerpts from a talk entitled "Personalism" he delivered at a midwest conference in 1936 or 1937. These also contain heretical ideas. There is no question that the Party would have preferred Wright to supplement his themes of Negro exploitation with prophecies of white/black proletarian solidarity along the lines followed by Paul Peters and George Sklar in *Stevedore*. In this play, an embattled group of black New Orleans longshoremen are eventually joined by their white brothers in common resistance against the capitalist foe. Black proletarian and white proletarian, two massive figures featured in the *New Masses* cartoons, standing arm in arm—that's what the Party wanted.

The possibility of the black man's legitimate hatred for capitalist exploitation existing side by side with hatred for whites of all political creeds never occurred to the Party leadership. Neither did it occur to them that they might be regarded as carriers of the racist virus. It is not unlikely that in the late Thirties Wright himself was living a kind of double intellectual life. One side of him—the black Marxist, very likely a true believer in the Party's fight against its enemies at home and abroad—contributed useful articles and poems and stories to the Party press. The other and private side tried to explain and define the meaning of being black in white America, tried to discover his own identity and, in effect, to create himself.

After he left the movement, the Party accused him of refashioning "the truths of his own life in a distorted and destructive image." They said the Richard Wright of 1934 was not the Richard Wright of 1944; in short, Wright lied when he wrote, "I Tried to Be a Communist." Wright was not lying, and he really did try. His hidden and perhaps repressed opposition to the Party came out in *Native Son*, if not before.

The instant success of that novel, its worldwide coverage, the author's bona fide Communist affiliation meant that Party critics almost of necessity had to praise it. So far as the Party was concerned, *Native Son*, with the exception of *The Grapes of Wrath*, was the most important fictional work of the decade. Yet even the Communists could not pretend *Native Son* was ideologically flawless, as the gingerly criticism of the novel in the files of the *New Masses* attests.

Officially the Party "rejoiced" with the Negro people in hailing the "magnificent artistry" of *Native Son*. It had its shortcomings, to be sure. One critic regretted "the absence of characters who would balance the picture by showing Negroes whose rebellion against oppression is expressed in constructive mass action rather than in individual violence." Another thought the trial scene too long, and really unnecessary, for it only stated what had already been dramatically shown. To this legitimate objection he added, rather cautiously, that *Native Son* was not "an all-inclusive picture of Negro life" in America.

Other critics, however, took a more serious view of Wright's ideological lapses. The unfriendly critique came down to the following set of objections. The artist can't assume his task is completed after he has drawn his material from the physical world; subject matter of this sort is not axiomatically a true picture of reality. The author must build upon his aesthetic perceptions if he is to achieve a broader fidelity. Aesthetics must be informed by politics. Is Bigger Thomas a representative of his people? Wright says he is—but the conception of Bigger is aesthetically false and politically confused:

> In *Native Son* Bigger is a frustrated, anti-social individual who commits anarchic acts of violence in his blind rebellion against capitalist society. It is politically slanderous to contend that Bigger Thomas is the symbol of the Negro people. Consequently it is an esthetic falsity to select a character who is atypical and to make him the protagonist of a novel that deals with the bitter persecution and exploitation of a minority people in bourgeois society.

Furthermore, Wright made Communists out to be insensitive fools like Jan and Mary. Even Boris Max never really understands Bigger, and is frightened by Bigger's vision of himself. Not a single white character, in fact, has any appreciation of what is going on in Bigger's mind.

Bigger dies defeated by society—not a fitting conclusion from the point of view of socialist realism, which usually posits a sunrise or a dawn at the end. Even sympathizers of the exploited blacks would hesitate to accept Wright's justification of Bigger's behavior—"a repellant mystical confession of 'creation.' " And if readers in the movement were not persuaded, how would the bourgeois subscribers to the Book-of-the-Month Club respond?

To such ideologues, it did no good to point out that Wright did not address himself to that larger Communist reality or write to soothe the feelings of the Book-of-the-Month Club readers. He had urged black writers to write about what they knew and nothing else. His subject in *Native Son* was the Bigger Thomases of America. He was writing about a boy who had to hate in order to remain human, but of course such psychological or existential considerations cut no ice with the Party. Quite rightly, given its assumption, it saw something subversive and dangerous in *Native Son*.

By 1940 Wright had ended his literary apprenticeship. Literature had been his vehicle for discovering the world outside him and, more important, himself. Communism afforded only one of the roads to that territory from which the young Richard Wright had been excluded. But he had not succeeded in reconciling, either in his work or in his mind, the streams of influence that accounted for *Native Son*: Marxist universalism and black nationalism. He paid lip service to the former, or, rather, he believed in it, acted on it, but he *felt* black nationalism. It touched something deeper in his nature. Wright spoke from the heart when he said the Negro writer is "called upon to do no less than create values by which his race is to struggle, live and die. . . ."

Reds, Whites, and Blues:

The Life of Langston Hughes

The first volume of Arnold Rampersad's biography of Langston Hughes ends in 1941, with Hughes painfully recovering in a California hospital from an "unspeakable illness" (it was gonorrhea). He was on one of the bottom sides of his up-and-down career, evicted from his Harlem apartment (his subtenants had neglected to pay the rent) and dogged by the right-wing press, and by publicity-seeking politicians, for his alleged Communist Party ties. As proof, his persecutors kept citing a notorious poem, "Goodbye Christ," that he had dashed off in Moscow nine years earlier, in which the Christ co-opted by "Kings, generals, robbers, and killers" is asked to make way for "A real guy named / Marx Communist Lenin Peasant Stalin Worker ME." In vain Hughes insisted that he never was a Communist, that his target had been corrupt religion, not Christ himself. The press repeated its calumnies; and his radical pals chewed him up for knuckling under to the reactionaries. It would take another fifteen years of compromise and accommodation before he was allowed, in Rampersad's words, "to survive on acceptable terms as a writer and continue his lifelong service as an artist to his race."

The second volume of Arnold Rampersad's biography of Langston Hughes exhibits the virtues of his first; that is to say, it is rich in detail, consistently intelligent, stylishly written, and full of acute

Originally published as a review of Arnold Rampersad, *The Life of Langston Hughes*, volumes 1 and 2, in the *New Republic* (October 10, 1988), 34–38.

observations about the mind, the times, and the work of Langston Hughes. If it seems less intrinsically interesting than its predecessor, that is because only a few events in the second half of Hughes's life match in intensity and excitement the extraordinary episodes of his formative years: young Langston's traumatic interactions with his Negro-hating father and his self-absorbed, histrionic mother; the day in a Kansas church when he waited for the infusion of Christ's abiding grace and faked a conversion; the "grand tour" of Africa as a mess boy on a freighter followed by his down-and-out days in Paris; his rapturous immersion in the Harlem scene and his part in its "renaissance"; his term of gilded bondage to a spooky white patron or "Godmother," as she wanted to be called, shrewd, benevolent, tyrannical, and wrapped in her mystique of black primitivism; his collaboration and irreparable rift with Zora Neale Hurston; his euphoric sojourn in the Soviet Union in 1931; his journalistic stint in Republican Spain six years later.

These are the bare bones of the biographical narrative about the adventures and misadventures of a writer, spiritual cousin of Peter Pan and Augie March, whose immediate forebears on his mother's side had been distinguished black leaders. The bloodstained shawl of his grandmother's first husband, killed at Harper's Ferry, was a family relic, and the child's elders never let him forget his sacred obligation to "The Race." As Rampersad tells it, there was something almost providential in the fateful interventions of white and black associates at certain critical junctures of Hughes's career, in the overcoming of his doubts and hesitations before giving himself totally to Afro-America.

The thirteen-year-old boy, receptive to the sermons and gospel music he heard in a black church, waited for the flashing illumination of Christ, but had to fake the conversion that never came. The talented Harlem poet gratefully accepted the help of Carl Van Vechten and the even more disinterested support of a rich Californian. For a time he submitted to the gilded bondage of his "Godmother." When he broke with her, an act of redemptive rebellion, he went into shock. But he could not resist the pull of his vocation: to be a poet bonded to his people, speaking for them and to them, drawing sustenance from them.

The making of the race poet is the central theme in *I, Too, Sing America* (vol. 1). A lonely, reserved boy escapes through books into fantasy. He acquires a facility with words, takes what he needs from his literary models (Sandburg, Whitman, Du Bois, McKay, among others) without being overwhelmed by them. Gradually he comes to sound like nobody but himself. An original note can be heard in a high school poem about one Susanna Jones, whose face, when she is dressed in red, is "like an ancient cameo / Turned brown by the ages. / Come with a blast of trumpets, / Jesus!" Thoughts on black antiquity also inform one of his most quoted poems, "The Negro Speaks of Rivers" (a response, Rampersad believes, to his father's contempt for "niggers" and poets), which equates his own soul with the primordial rivers of the world. The best of the poems that follow register deeply felt emotions unspoiled by artifice or bombast; the least satisfactory are likely to be throbbing hymns to blackness or truculent political declarations no better or worse than much of the protest poetry published in the Twenties or Thirties.

Hughes reached his apogee, Rampersad persuasively argues, with *Fine Clothes to the Jew* (1927), "his most brilliant book of poems, and one of the more astonishing books ever published in the United States—comparable in the black world to *Leaves of Grass* in the white." It also got a comparable reception. The title, lifted from one of the lesser poems in the volume ("When hard luck overtakes you / Nothin' you can do / Gather up yo' fine clothes / An' sell 'em to de Jew"), was misunderstood (Hughes was an unequivocal philo-Semite); and reviewers in the black press pronounced *Fine Clothes* disgusting and degenerate, "reeking of the gutter and sewer."

To be misunderstood is not invariably a sign of greatness, but in this instance the blinkered critics were too deeply offended by unseemly vignettes of the black underclass to recognize a literary event. A radical language experiment, a kind of sustained blues akin in mood and tone to the grieving songs of Bessie Smith and Billie Holiday, *Fine Clothes* marked the author's deepest penetration of black culture. One has only to compare its chants of misery with his fine poem "The Weary Blues," written in 1920, to notice a shift in perspective. In the latter, Hughes had artfully linked "the lowly blues to formal poetry" and yet seemed somehow remote from the singer in the poem. The poet seems almost a voyeur; he says he "heard that Negro sing, that old piano moan." By 1927, however, he had become his performers, was privy to their secrets, their sense of loss and pain and desolation. Seldom thereafter, even in *Montage of a Dream Deferred* (1957) and *Ask Your Momma* (1961), was Hughes able to project these intangible feelings so unaffectedly and at such a pitch of concentration.

I Dream a World (vol. 2) opens with Hughes once again breasting the current of history, but not making much headway. War is about to break. The Cold War lies beyond, and thereafter the civil rights movement. He crisscrosses the country, lecturing to black students, visiting friends. He publishes volumes of poetry and fiction, edits anthologies, writes plays, operas, songs, always hoping for the big success that never comes. He surfaces, sinks, resurfaces. Only eventually would he arrive in calmer waters, still not rich, but respected and honored by an international audience.

In 1941, however, such recognition was a distant prospect. Hughes had no such expectations. A battered and self-described "literary sharecropper," made wary by adversity, in 1941 Hughes began his slow waltz (to use Rampersad's figure) "from the embrace of the left." The fellow traveler had no quarrel with the Soviet Union, and he could never expunge the memory of his joy on entering a country where racism was officially proscribed. But when his political ties threatened his livelihood, he decided the time had come to withdraw unobtrusively from suspect organizations labeled "un-American" by the right wing. As he remarked later, "Trying to run a major career on a minor income is something." This capitulation, which entailed self-censorship and reneging on old friendships, did not prevent his being hauled up before the McCarthy committee in the next decade. Appearing as a "cooperating witness," he denied that he had ever been a Communist or an atheist, affirmed his patriotism, and disarmingly retracted the sentiments of his radical juvenilia. Hughes got through the patronizing interrogation without having to grovel or name names, but as Rampersad says, he had nonetheless "surrendered," however "honorably," and the humiliation rankled.

Hughes joined the war effort, and contributed his share of patriotic doggerel to whip up black enthusiasm for the antifascist cause, but this did not silence his denunciations of the ubiquitous Jim Crow. His concession to political orthodoxy was tactical, not ideological. It was undertaken to keep the loyalty of a black constituency that had never warmed to his Marxist and antichurch rhetoric. A radicalism is detectable in his writing then and later, as the savage and mournful verse in the posthumously published *Panther and the Lash* attests. For Hughes, racial issues had always superseded politics, or at least subsumed it. The stories, poems, and plays that he wrote during and after the war are shot through with sardonic and despairing comments on the disparity between the national cant about freedom and the squalid reality that belied it. On the day that Berlin fell, he found himself riding across Oklahoma aboard a Jim Crow car, segregated from the celebrations of his fellow Americans.

Hughes hadn't entirely abandoned what he called "the dream deferred," a Whitmanesque version of "spiraling upward and outward toward a freer, fuller life for all," but persisting racism and black anger chilled his hopes. He caught, Rampersad writes, "the unmistakable sounds of cultural change" in the black music floating out of Harlem's bars in the late Forties. Swing, with its "sweetened, whitened strains," was being displaced by " 'be-bop' jazz," traditional lyrics by nonsense language. To Hughes's sensitive ear, these changes denoted "the growing fissures in Afro-American culture, the myth of integration and American social harmony jarred by a message of deep discord."

At about this time, in 1948, Hughes bought a house in Harlem, his first and only permanent residence. He had finally come home, after his literal and metaphorical peregrinations. From his early youth he had been haunted by his ancestral links with the white community (personified by white great-grandfathers on both sides of his family) that had denied kinship to him and his distinguished black forebears, the theme of two of his best-known poems, "The Cross" and "Mulatto," and of his powerful story "Fathers and Sons." The prophet of negritude (and so recognized by his African literary confreres) was fascinated by the blurring of racial boundaries, by the ambiguities and ironies of "passing." But drawn as he was to white friends and patrons, and notwithstanding the happy interludes he spent in white company, it was Harlem, the bastion of blackness, where he came to feel most at ease. His decision to plant himself there could be read as a declaration of fealty to the black part of his divided heritage.

"Harlem" already signified for Hughes what "Manahatta" had meant to Whitman. It was both a place and a poetic invention, a promiscuous urban scene where one could be alone in and part of the crowd, a compost heap that fertilized his imagination. Hughes, the good brown literatus, relished its noisy streets, the jukes and the bars, the music, "not at all abashed" (as Whitman might say) by pimps, prostitutes, and drunks, and comfortable as well as respectable hard-working Harlemites. This mélange of emotions about Harlem and its inhabitants he incarnated in his incomparable Jesse B. Semple—Simple to his friends—whom many of Hughes's admirers consider not only his most striking creation, but also a folk hero of immense social and literary importance.

Rampersad's pages about the Simple books are among the best in his work. He shows how the character that Hughes casually introduced into his Chicago *Defender* column in 1943 as "My Simple Minded Friend" gradually exfoliated into a distinctive person and eponym, into an authentic black voice. Boyd, the narrator of the Simple sketches, is educated, a bit on the prim side, and starchy in his locutions like the straight man in a minstrel show, but he is also Simple's friend and confidant. He pays for his beer and sympathizes with his grievances, even though, unlike his larky bar companion, he has internalized a strain of the white middle-class ethic. Together, as Rampersad observes, they equal Langston Hughes, or as Hughes himself puts it, "myself talking to me. Or else talking to myself."

But it is Simple who wins out in the contest between Hughes's black rebellious side and his passive, liberal, white alter ego, Simple who blurts out opinions far more subversive than the revolutionary clichés that Hughes published in the radical press—dark thoughts about perdurable prejudice, racial mixing, even daydreams about the destruction of the white race. And although Boyd chides him for making blanket indictments (after all, Simple knows there are many fine white people, and he loves Mrs. Roosevelt), Simple usually gets the last word. "You are the most *un-Negro* Negro I know," Simple tells Boyd. "You ought to be a race leader. White folks would love you." Boyd replies, "I'm only trying to look on both sides of the question." "To do which," counters Simple, "you have to straddle *both* sides of the fence. Me, I stand on one side and look on the other—and all I see over there is white. On my side, is me. Sitting on the fence is you." "I didn't build the fence," Boyd answers. "Then tear it down," says Simple.

•

In identifying himself with Simple, Hughes was continuing his long seriocomic feud with the black bourgeoisie, among whom were the men and the women who had brought him to notice, and who continued to regard him as a beloved, if erring, son. Accused in the 1920s of writing "gutter" poetry that confirmed in white minds the stereotype of the primitive, lawless "nigger," Hughes had replied for himself and the "Niggerati" (Zora Neale Hurston's designation for his rebellious coterie) in a rhapsodic manifesto: "We younger Negro artists who write now intend to express our individual dark-skinned selves without fear or shame. If white people are pleased we are glad. If they are not, it doesn't matter. . . . If colored people are pleased we are glad. If they are not, their displeasure doesn't matter either."

Thirty years later, however, it did matter. The portrayal of blacks as murderous crazies by writers of the next generation deeply distressed Hughes. He was particularly critical of Richard Wright, whom he blamed for setting the ugly pattern, and of Wright's literary heirs, who simply substituted "modern stereotypes" for old ones. Out of allegiance to his fellow writers, Hughes at first refrained from attacking them in print. He had come of age at a time when the black intellectual elite frowned upon rudeness and vulgarity, and he rather fancied a touch of lawlessness and iconoclasm. What stuck in his craw were the "foulmouthed militants," the distorters of "the Negro image." And he singled out for special scorn the black writer who adopted "the confessional approach to literature," indulged in self-pity, resorted to profanity and "near pornography," and exploited white guilt on his "lonely crusade towards the best seller lists."

These reproofs of his juniors, Rampersad notes, were not entirely disinterested. Hughes was envious of their financial and popular success. He was troubled and puzzled by the acclaim given to *Invisible Man* and *Go Tell It on the Mountain*, which seemed to him pretentious and overwritten, and he showed little awareness of the motives and the compulsions that fathered them. Once Lawrence had shaken him up, and he couldn't entirely escape the influence of Eliot and Joyce, but he thought of himself primarily as an entertainer of and a spokesman for his race, not as an intellectual. He made no effort to read and study the literary gods of the moderns. Not surprisingly, Baldwin and other like-minded writers treated him as a black chauvinist and gifted has-been who had "stopped thinking."

Rampersad monitors the running debate rather than plumping for either side. Without committing the biographer's unpardonable sin of selling out his client, he concedes that Hughes did fritter away his energies on minor tasks, and took on too many assignments in his search of the fame and the cash so long denied him. He quotes without comment Ralph Ellison's assertion that Hughes was "incapable of sustained labor on a single, epic enterprise." But he rejects Baldwin's ultimate put-down: that Hughes never managed to reconcile his "social and artistic responsibilities." To write for and about the unsophisticated, to explore the folk mind, requires real artistic skills, and is not inconsistent with writing professionally. Hughes urged black writers to be writers first, "colored" second, "even while dealing with racial material." But he added the significant caveat that this objective was unattainable without "a deep confidence in blacks and love of them." For Rampersad, Hughes was "one of the few black writers of any consequence to champion racial consciousness as a source of inspiration for black artists."

The concept of negritude or "soul" (as Hughes preferred to call it) was very much in the minds of black intellectuals in the Sixties and Seventies. Still, the militants were not about to canonize a writer who, regardless of his previous services to non-white peoples in America and abroad, invidiously contrasted the credo of the ultranationalists with genuine pride and love of race. All his life Hughes had condemned the extremes of black and white chauvinism, pondered the pros and cons of integration, and distrusted the optimism of the integrationists, black and white. Yet he had always felt comfortable with his white friends, and never quite relinquished the Whitman-inspired vision of harmonious heterogeneity. The split between the followers of Malcolm X and the protagonists of nonviolence disheartened Hughes, because he could identify himself with both parties. Lacking either the will or the energy to throw himself actively into the struggles of the Freedom Fighters now agitating the South, he compromised by dedicating his gospel musical, *Jericho-Jim Crow*, to the young who marched and picketed and petitioned "to help make a better America for all, and especially for citizens of color."

In 1966 Hughes presaged his own withdrawal when he dispatched Jesse B. Semple and his wife, Joyce, to the suburbs (a kind of living death for the Harlem denizen who said he preferred wild men to wild animals and neon signs over bars to nature's sunsets) and brought his series to a close. Savoring his honors, Hughes continued to lecture and to publish practically to the moment of his death in the following year. The country was at war, and there was no joy in Harlem. At his funeral, his friends arranged a jazz concert that ended with the playing of Duke Ellington's "Do Nothing Till You Hear from Me."

With the completion of this admirable biography, it is possible to get a handle on this elusive figure, who repelled intimacy and remained a puzzle even to his closest friends. Rampersad's Hughes is a worldly-wise innocent, a cunning naif, eager for praise and affection but guarding his privacy, secretive about his sexual habits, drawn to mother and father surrogates. He thinks a good deal about food and is "a veteran at accepting hospitality." (One can get along in the world, he advises young Ralph Ellison, by being nice to people and letting them pay for your meals.) Neither hero nor saint, he can be impulsive (decreasingly so with age), courageous, affable, mischievous, disingenuous, occasionally unfeeling and malicious, and, thanks to many blows and rejections, something of a cynic and fatalist. "Maybe you might be soft outside," he writes in his journal, "but you got to be hard inside." He is tempered, rather than twisted, by the humiliations he swallowed at considerable emotional cost.

Rampersad's study contains a few slips (Mary McCarthy will be surprised to find herself and Dwight MacDonald listed with Lillian Hellman and other "illustrious leftists" whose presence at the noisy 1949 Waldorf Astoria "peace" gathering offset the "few well-known anti-communists" who heckled the sessions). And specialists will disagree with, or wish to qualify, some of Rampersad's judgments on Hughes and his contemporaries—his portrait of Alain Locke as a feline and self-serving conniver, for example; or his treatment of the Hughes-Hurston imbroglio (slightly slanted in the former's favor) over the disputed authorship of a play; or the way he handles the issue of Hughes's ambiguous sexuality.

Does it really matter whether Hughes was asexual, heterosexual, homosexual? To the biographer, it must matter. Rampersad scrupulously reports the surmises of Hughes's friends and acquaintances, and decides, given the want of concrete evidence, that the question must remain forever moot. Perhaps so, but Rampersad's accounts of Hughes scrambling to discourage marriage-minded women, and the examples he provides of his bland evasiveness and reticence about his personal affairs, offer hints of unexplored answers.

Indeed, Rampersad is a little evasive himself when it comes to "explaining" Langston Hughes, the man and the writer. What he thinks about him remains implicit in what Hughes says and does. Rampersad leaves it pretty much up to the reader to draw his own conclusions. He adroitly blends Hughes's varied writings into the biographical narrative, but he attempts only sparingly to probe them for clues to the secret man. He fully records how the writings were received decade by decade, but holds back in his assessment of Hughes as a man of letters. Often illuminating in his readings of single poems, and in his analyses of the small body of Hughes's most original and finished work, Rampersad is sometimes not miserly enough in his use of superlatives, and he is too noncommittal on the stream of slack verse that Hughes turned out so effortlessly.

Such reservations count for little, however, when measured against Rampersad's achievement. He may not have penetrated Hughes's core of secrecy, but he comes closer than anybody else to making sense of a very complicated personality and an unusual literary talent. And he shows, unintentionally, how oblivious most white readers still are to the history, to the social and cultural geography, of black society in the United States. Written without stridency or partisanship, this life of Langston Hughes (and this is not the least of its many distinctions) illustrates once again how American Afro-American literature really is, and why it is both illogical and misleading to treat it as if it existed in some alien and exotic dimension far away from our own.

The "Inky Curse":

Miscegenation in the White American Literary Imagination

To dramatize my lurid title, I begin by quoting from and paraphrasing a letter written in 1889 to Richard Watson Gilder, editor of the influential *Century Illustrated Monthly Magazine*. The writer was Maurice Thompson, a Georgia-born novelist and poet who, after serving in the Confederate Army, had settled in Indiana, where he had studied law and become a minor man of letters.[1] Thompson publicly applauded the abolition of slavery, but in the 1880s he became obsessed by what he called "the first steps of negro influence in art" and "the final rush of the African to absolute domination."[2]

The circumstance which prompted the letter was Gilder's rejection of Thompson's astonishing long poem, "A Voodoo Prophecy," which the self-styled "squire of poesy" found unsuitable for his readers.[3]

Gilder had good reasons for his misgivings. The speaker of Thompson's poem, "the prophet of the dusky race," recalls how his people had been torn from their African homeland and doomed to the lash and manacle. Now mastered by a "black and terrible memory," a "tropic heat" still bubbling in his veins, still quintessentially savage, the prophet spurns the white oppressors' "whine / Of fine

This paper was presented at the Colloquium on "National Identity, Miscegenation and Cultural Expression: A Comparison between the United States and Brazil," held at the Maison des Sciences de l'Homme, Paris, March 25 and 26, 1982. It was published in *Social Science Information*, 22, no. 2 (1983), 169–190.

repentence" and warns of the day when their whiteness will darken under him.

> You seed of Abel, proud of your descent,
>   And arrogant, because your cheeks are fair,
> Within my loins an inky curse is pent
>   To flood
>   Your blood
> And stain your skin and crisp your golden hair.

Filled "with nameless dreams of lust," the prophet vows to taint "snowy limbs" and "blood's patrician blue":

> Yea, I will dash my blackness down your veins,
>   And through your nerves my sensuousness I'll fling;
> Your lips, your eyes, shall bear the musty stains
>   Of Congo kisses
>   While shrieks and hisses
> Shall blend into the savage song I sing.

Roasted in his "passion's hottest fire," its cities razed, its fields turned into deserts, America will be Africanized and the "Prince of Darkness, rule the world at last."[4]

So much for the argument. Thompson had to speak out "in my rugged way," he explained to Gilder, to check the "rapidly swelling menace of miscegenation." He blamed neither the Negro (toward whom he professed the kindest feelings) nor the "respectable whites" for this collective crime. No, the responsibility lay with chattel slavery and the "awful sin of our ancestors." Because of their "unspeakable whoredom," the national blood was being polluted and the United States was in danger of becoming a "sad mulatto country."[5]

According to popular folklore, it is said, Indians and blacks were pre-Adamites, Satan or the Snake and the black gardener in Eden, Cain the first "amalgamationist," and miscegenation the sin which let loose the Deluge.[6] Appropriately in Thompson's poem, the prophet's "fetich"—a serpent—"lolls its withered lip / And bares its shining fangs" at the prospect of blackening white skin and crisping golden hair. In the prophet's words, "I scarce can hold the monster in my grip / So strong is he, / So eagerly / He leaps to meet my precious prophecies."[7] Here is the "black rapist" with a vengeance, the polluter of the American Garden.

The fear of miscegenation expressed in Thompson's masturbatory poem had a long history, but the word itself was only twenty-five years old in 1889 when he wrote to Gilder. It entered the English language with the publication of *Miscegenation: The Theory of the Blending of Races Applied to the American White and Negro* (1864). The anonymous author of this tract combined two Latin words, *miscere* (to mix) and *genus* (race) to denote the abstract idea of the mixture of two or more races. Since he was arguing for the mixing of blacks and whites in particular, he suggested another concocted word, *melaleukation*, from the Greek words *melas* (black) and *leukos* (white), as a more exact rendering of his meaning, but conceded it was too hard to pronounce. "Miscegenation" would have to do as a substitute for "amalgamation"—then the common term in antebellum America for black/white sexual unions, but, according to the author, a misnomer. "Amalgamation" properly signified "the union of metals with quicksilver."[8]

The author of *Miscegenation* resorted to anonymity, he explained, in order to escape "contumely" and "abuse"—an understatement if there ever was one. Hardly any white American in 1864 agreed with his novel thesis: that the redemption of an imperfect white race depended upon the infusion of Negro blood. People had been lynched for saying less. Moreover, the pamphlet appeared at a crucial phase of the Civil War when the subject of race was an especially emotional issue.

Here in brief is its argument:

1) The human race is essentially one, and the strongest, handsomest, and most creative branches are the most hybrid.

2) Whatever power and vitality the American "race" possesses derives not from the Anglo-Saxon strain but from other and different nationalities.

3) Weak, flaccid, dyspeptic white America requires a strong admixture from the passionate and emotional darker races and the imaginative and spiritual Asians.

4) The vigor of the Confederacy is largely owing to the intimate association of Southern aristocrats with blacks, the degeneracy of the "poor whites" to their exclusion from physical contact with black slaves.

5) Irish women and Southern girls in particular have an affinity with black men—and vice versa.

6) The salvation of the United States rests on the Negro. Eventually a brown America will emerge—and a good thing, too.

Not surprisingly, the pamphlet created quite a stir among the pro- and antislavery partisans until it was discovered to be a hoax. Its authorship is now ascribed to David Croly, an Irish-born journalist and father-to-be of Herbert Croly, founder of the *New Republic*. He and his backers had hoped to embarrass the Lincoln administration by identifying it with "nigger-lovers" and racial pollution. The plan to undermine the president's bid for reelection failed, but Croly's word "miscegenation" stuck and retained its disreputable connotations.[9]

Given the black stereotype held by generations of white North Americans and deeply rooted in the folk imagination, the popular association of miscegenation with the shameful and criminal— above all with the "unnatural"—seems almost inevitable. White was beautiful; black, ugly, devilish, sinful. The African had appeared to the first English observers as a species of ape, limited in intelligence and lustful. Cruder expressions of this sentiment gradually softened into euphemism, but respectable savants for several centuries buttressed vulgar prejudices with a weird mélange of scientific misinformation. No wonder that the Puritan clerisy, the Founding Fathers, the celebrators of America's Manifest Destiny, the champions of the melting pot never included blacks in their dreams of a triumphant and regenerate society. As the historian Winthrop Jordan observed:

> A darkened nation would present incontrovertible evidence that sheer animal sex was governing American destiny and that the great experiment in the wilderness had failed to maintain the social and personal restraints which were the hallmarks and the very stuff of civilization. A blackened posterity would mean the basest of energies had guided the direction of the American experiment and that civilized man had turned beast in the forest. Retention of whiteness would be evidence of purity and diligent nurture of the original body of the folk. Could a blackened people look back to Europe and say they had faithfully performed their errand?[10]

The "blackening," not the "reddening" of the nation was to be feared. Before the importation of Negro slaves, Indian aborigines for a brief time had posed a threat to white racial purity. The dire possibility of New England settlers becoming "Indianized," to use Cotton Mather's term, alarmed the Puritan theocracy. Yet even in the seventeenth century the "tawney" Indian stood higher in the Great Chain of Being than the Negro. In contrast to the "lascivious African," Indians were popularly regarded as sexually passive. Nor was Indian "blood" deemed such a polluting ingredient. If the "half-breed" in literature often figured as the embodiment of treachery, cowardice, and revengefulness, he appeared less "unnatural" than mulattoes, seemed to have simpler and less ominous components and to be more easily assimilated into the master race.[11]

The word "mulatto" stems etymologically from "mule." Like the mule, the mulatto was considered the product of an unnatural union. I dwell upon the animal imagery, because it is a key element in the outer and inner history of miscegenation in North America. It was widely believed that the African in his original state displayed a beastlike ferocity and indolence. Once domesticated, the Negro could be trained to play the spaniel and to be affectionately indulged.[12] "Impure" blacks, on the other hand—their blood curdled by white admixture—could sometimes turn into a different sort of beast, perhaps cleverer than the pure black by virtue of the white input but nonetheless a "mongrel." The traits of a purebred animal could be predetermined. The mongrel was always an uncertainty because of his unlicensed begetting. By analogy, a purebred black was safer and more reliable than the sinister mulatto.

Yet despite the white man's allegedly instinctive revulsion against "unnatural and inordinate copulation" between the races, increasing numbers of "mixt," "spurious," and "mongril" offspring[13] in the English colonies spurred the passage of strong antimiscegenation laws by the middle of the seventeenth century. How stringently they were enforced then and later differed from period to period and place to place. A recent history of white and black "amalgamation" in the United States shows that until the 1850s, free mulattoes in the lower South—especially in Charleston, S.C., and in New Orleans—were in varying degrees a privileged and protected group, a buffer between the slave population and the outnumbered whites. They acquired property and in some instances passed with white connivance into the white community. In the upper South, however, and in the northern and western states, the slightest percentage of blackness made the mulatto irrevocably "Negro."[14]

Northern attacks against slavery in the 1830s tightened restrictions against all free persons of color in the South as Southerners grew defensive about their "peculiar institution." But notwithstanding the "scientific" evidence of Negro inferiority proffered by proslavery advocates, the mixing of races continued unabated and the number of mulattoes kept increasing until the Civil War.[15] Thereafter, the breaking up of the plantation system and the death of thousands of Southern white males in the war lessened the close proximity of blacks and whites. What tolerance had previously existed for racial mixing virtually ended after growing numbers of Southerners began to interpret the Confederate defeat as a sign of God's anger with a people who had indulged in the criminal mingling of races. Ancient prejudices of the most virulent sort awakened in the decades of the 1880s and 1890s. Once again the Negro became in the minds of white extremists the concupiscent ape, the wild beast, the putative rapist dominated by uncontrollable sexual passion. New "scientific" discourses reinforced the fears of black contamination that pervade "A Voodoo Prophecy"[16] and what Leslie Fiedler has called "the semi-obscene literature of Southern racists."[17]

Respected Northern scientists, be it noted, sanctioned the racial opinions expressed in this literature. The great and much beloved naturalist Louis Agassiz, the internationally esteemed craniologist Samuel George Morton, the nation's leading paleontologist, E. D. Cope, were Negrophobes. They subscribed to the widely held view that blacks were physically revolting, irredeemably inferior, and (as Agassiz put it) "incapable of living on a footing of social equality with the whites, in one and the same community, without being an element of social disorder."[18] Miscegenation in their minds threatened society no less than incest. "We cannot," Cope warned, "cloud or extinguish the fine nervous susceptibility and the mental force, which cultivation develops in the constitution of the Indo-European, by the fleshly instincts, and dark mind of the African." How then to account for the increase in the mulatto population? Agassiz offered one answer to a correspondent in 1863: unfortunately the natural repugnance of whites for blacks proved insufficient to withstand the blandishments of light-skinned mulatto girls whose unabashed sexuality weakened the inhibitions of young Southern whites. Once slavery was abolished, this kind of unnatural breeding would cease and the sickly mulattoes die off. But he drew a fearful picture, not unlike Maurice Thompson's, of a once "manly population descended from cognate nations" giving way to "the effeminate progeny of mixed races, half Indian, half negro, sprinkled with white blood. . . . How shall we eradicate the stigma of a lower race when its blood has once been allowed to flow freely into that of our children?"

The visibility of dark-skinned Negroes made them easy to spot and therefore to exclude. Not so persons one-sixteenth or one-thirty-second black who slipped under the color bar and passed undetected into the white community. The arch-Negrophobe Thomas Dixon gained a nationwide readership at the turn of the century by playing on a national fear that in time distinctions based on color might be fatally blurred. "The future American," Dixon warned through a thinly disguised surrogate, "must be an Anglo-Saxon or a mulatto. . . . This Republic can have no future if racial lines are broken and its proud citizenship sinks to the level of a mongrel breed." A single drop of Negro blood, another character says, "kinks the hair, flattens the nose, thickens the lip, puts out the light of intellect, and lights the fires of brutal passions."[19]

To Dixon and other radical racists, the condoners of racial mixing and advocates of political and social equality for Negroes implanted "impossible desires for time and eternity." As a Southern clergyman remarks in Dixon's novel *The Leopard's Spots* (1903): "You cannot seek the Negro vote without asking him to your home sooner or later. If you ask him to your house, he will break bread with you at last. And if you seat him at your table, he has the right to ask your daughter's hand in marriage."[20] Dixon may have shortened the leap from ballot box to bedroom, but he was not far off the mark in charging that even liberal spokesmen on the race issue stopped short of genuine social equality in black-white relations.

An episode in the novel melodramatically illustrates Dixon's point. The son of George Harris, the proud and courageous mulatto who figures prominently in *Uncle Tom's Cabin* (Dixon cleverly and maliciously makes his novel a sequel to Stowe's), has become after the war the protégé of the scholar-statesman Senator Lowell of Massachusetts. Harvard-trained, handsome, gifted, young Harris is encouraged by his benefactor to right the wrongs of his race. He is a welcome guest at Lowell's Boston home until Harris has the temerity to ask the senator for his daughter's hand. Lowell is astonished and disgusted. "To be perfectly plain with you," he tells Harris, "I haven't the slightest desire that my family, with its proud record of a thousand years of history and achievement, shall end in this stately old house in a brood of mulatto brats!"

Harris winces and springs to his feet "trembling with passion."

> "I see" [he sneers] "the soul of Simon Legree has at last become the soul of the nation. The South expresses the same luminous truth with a little more clumsy brutality. But their way is after all more merciful. The human body becomes unconscious at the touch of an oil-fed flame in sixty seconds. Your methods are more refined and more hellish in cruelty. You have trained my ears to hear, eyes to see, hands to touch and heart to feel, that you might torture me with the denial of every cry of body and soul and roast me in the flames of impossible desires for time and eternity."[21]

White liberals had no ready answer to this cry of despair. However offended they were by Dixon's violence and vulgarity, they were no less reluctant than he was to sink, as he put it, "into the black waters of Negroid life!"

George Washington Cable, William Dean Howells, and Mark Twain were less affected than Dixon by local and sectional prejudices and socially determined revulsions. Even these moralists, however, as they preached equality and tried to deal honestly and fairly with the black presence, could not suppress their distaste for racial mixing.

Cable, born in New Orleans, a Confederate veteran, broke with the Southern consensus on the race question by defending the Negro's civic rights and campaigning against the crippling handicap that kept the Negro from sloughing off the debasements of slavery. He ridiculed the so-called racial instinct. Indeed, his audacity in raising the miscegenation issue with "unsouthern" intent angered radical racists everywhere in the South—especially in New Orleans, where the Creoles resented what they took to be his imputation that they were of mixed blood. Eventually Cable's views aroused such a hullaballoo that he was virtually driven out of the South.

Cable's enemies considered him a crypto-Yankee miscegenation-ist. He was nothing of the kind.[22] He differentiated public rights and social intimacy and neither wanted nor expected blacks to enter into the private lives of whites. On the question of miscegenation (that "bedraggled word," he called it), Cable sometimes sounded like a more refined Maurice Thompson. He spoke in one place of the Negro's "repugnant" physical traits. Slave songs "varied the inner emotions and passions of a nearly naked serpent-worshipper."[23] The feelings of a black woman character in his best novel, *The Grandissimmes* (1880), are distilled through ages of African savagery, through fires that did not refine but blunted and blackened, through a past that included dirt, fetishism, and debauchery. Cable differed principally from radical racists like Dixon in arguing that the denial of civic rights to blacks promoted the very miscegenation they feared.[24] Jim Crow laws encouraged illicit racial unions by making them exciting and mysterious. Give blacks the privileges enjoyed by white Americans, Cable argued, and they would keep to themselves.[25] Racists demanded black docility, but by degrading the blacks, they degraded themselves.

In *The Grandissimmes*, Cable drew an ugly picture of miscegenation while trying not to offend the sensibilities of his audience. The "shadow of the Ethiopian" darkened his novel, but sentimental and sugary episodes vitiated its power. His tale of miscegenation's sad legacy—of mutilation and murder—ends with happy marriages. After depicting the ostracism of proud and cultivated people of color by their white kinsmen in New Orleans, and after relating how a mulatto stabs a white man to death, Cable can still praise God for "love's young dream." It is almost as if he trusted good manners and a decent civility to exorcise the sins of the fathers.

Howells, Cable's Northern admirer, took somewhat the same line in his one work of fiction dealing with the touchy theme of racial mixing: *An Imperative Duty* (1893). Like Cable, he believed in the primacy of culture over color. Nevertheless, he treats miscegenation gingerly at best. When his heroine in that novel is apprised of her Negro "taint," the consequence of some "ancestral infamy," she is shocked to her very marrow. Yet because she is imbued with the agonized conscience or "dutiolatry" of New England, she feels obliged to merge with the Negro community even though its members appear "hideous to her." As Howells elaborates: "their flat wide-nostrilled noses, their out-rolled thick lips . . . seemed burlesques of humanity, worse than apes, because they were more like." Fortunately, the hero—who acts upon Howells's insight that we hate those we have wronged or thought ill of—reassures her. He has never hated these poor creatures, he tells her, and hence he cannot hate "their infinitesimal part in her." In *An Imperative Duty* Howells the realist too easily evades the problem by dispatching his miscegenationists to Italy where, apparently, the "touch of the tarbrush" is of no consequence.[26]

For all his sympathy, Howells like most Americans was a "racialist" if not a "racist." He relished in this novel and elsewhere the "playful primitivism" in the "dog-like" blacks. All of them "shine with good nature and good will." They show a "barbaric taste in color." Even the heroine of his novel, who is one-sixteenth black, has an "irresponsible" side. The attraction the hero feels for her does not come from his "moral sense," which he has blotted out for a time. In fact, he feels a little revolted upon learning of her ancestry. What draws him to her, Howells hints, is her attenuated primitivism, the "remote taint of her servile and savage origin,"[27] and he is a little disappointed when the "tragic mask" of her New Englandism supervenes after their marriage.[28]

It is easy to smile at Howells and his contemporaries for their skittish treatment of miscegenation, but considering the genteel climate of the day and the currency of racial stereotypes, it could hardly have been otherwise.[29] Abolitionists had pictured the South as one vast brothel. When Howells wrote his novel, stories of planters violating their black women, selling their own children for profit—enormities which excited the indignation as well as sexual fantasizing of many antebellum Americans—no longer inflamed the Northern literary imagination. For Richard Watson Gilder and his kind, miscegenation was a nasty business and certainly an unsuitable literary subject.

And so it was for their Southern counterparts. But whereas most Northern writers had no firsthand knowledge of interracial unions, Southern writers did. Miscegenation for them was a fact of life enmeshed in family histories. They were under pressure, if they mentioned it at all, to minimize or extenuate it. This was understandable, too, for miscegenation conjured up patriarchal sins, incest, sectional guilt, ancestral racial fears. It was safer to attribute the hundreds of thousands of mulattoes in the South after the Civil War to the licentiousness of Yankee soldiers or the "white trash." Only a few of the white Southern-born writers of any distinction addressed themselves (and then only guardedly) to the forbidden theme. One of them was Mark Twain, and he did so with characteristic indirection.

His novel *The Tragedy of Pudd'nhead Wilson* might be described as a melodramatic and sardonic fairy story in a pseudorealistic setting. It opens with the birth of two boy babies, both white but one of them technically Negro. His mother, the slave woman Roxy, was (I quote Mark Twain) "to all intents and purposes as white as anybody, but the one sixteenth of her which was black outvoted the other fifteen parts and made her a negro." In charge of two almost identical infants—one the acknowledged son of a prosperous slaveholder, the other fathered by a man equally rich and well-born, Roxy switches their identities in the cradle. She thereby starts a train of action that ends only after the black-white usurper has murdered his foster father, been unmasked by the clever white hero, and sold down the river.

In this genially bitter tale, Mark Twain subjected the institution of slavery and the slaveholder's mentality to his most withering irony, but like Cable he was also questioning, perhaps inadvertently, racial stereotypes themselves. If Roxy's son could pass undetected and the legitimate white child turn into a "white nigger" unable to "endure the terrors of the white man's parlour" and excluded from black companionship because of his restored status—then what was a white man, what was a white woman? How could one be sure who were "the 'real' white Americans, North or South"?[30] Did not the impossibility of determining precisely when a person could be declared white or black undermine the American social structure?

Mark Twain camouflaged the subversive burden of his fable of miscegenation and mistaken identity by shifting some of the white community guilt on to the imposter, Roxy's son (it is an open question whether his comeuppance derives from his white or black attributes) and by resorting to melodramatics and farce. All the same, *Pudd'nhead Wilson* might serve as an illustration of what the critic William Bedford Clark has called "a paradigm of the basic myth of miscegenation as it recurs throughout the course of post-bellum fiction."[31] That paradigm goes something like this. First, a preoccupation with collective guilt and God's retribution against a sinful people. Second, the identification of the sin with slavery and the caste system. Third, the role of the mulatto as both victim and avenger. Fourth, the ambiguities surrounding mulatto identity, the placelessness of people neither white nor black. Noticeably absent from Clark's model (aspects of which I have already touched upon or alluded to) is the obsession with pollution and the darkening of the white race.

Pudd'nhead Wilson reveals no signs of this obsession, although Mark Twain's curious notebook entry "Whites under feet" by 1895 hints of an apprehension not found in his published works. Given his Southern background and his practice of never publicly deviating too far from the national consensus, his reluctance to speak candidly about miscegenation is understandable. Comstockery flourished in these years, and the treatment of any sexual theme, not simply miscegenation, inhibited would-be realists. Mark Twain confined his comments on sexual matters to the smoking room. Not so the three twentieth-century writers—all of them Southern—I want to take up very briefly now, although they, too, show a certain constraint in dealing with miscegenation.

First, William Faulkner. His feelings about racial mixing were more intense than Mark Twain's, and his shifting and unresolved attitudes toward his mulatto characters more openly and agonizingly dramatized. From the beginning to the end of his literary life, Faulkner adhered to a conservative view of Negro-white relations. Never a radical racist of the Dixon stripe and acknowledging the essential place of the Negro in the Southern literary landscape, the Negro in his early work had not yet assumed a central role in the Yoknapatawpha plot of Southern damnation and redemption. In time Faulkner gave more thought to "the estrangement of the races." His Negro characters became more individualized, and the mulatto in particular he singled out as the avenger-victim—the most wronged and the most to be feared. One part of him seemed to respond to engrained phobias, "the inherited fear of blood-mixture," that eventually all Americans would be the descendants of Africans.[32]

I say *seemed*, since all references to miscegenation are conveyed or intimated by his characters; the reader can only infer from them what Faulkner's own views were. His fiction articulates two equally balanced and conflicting positions: that black blood stains and corrupts, and that the mulatto (avatar of his race's capacity for suffer-ing, passivity, and endurance, at once ennobled and damned by his white ingredients) is a forerunner of the time when the two races will no longer be estranged. The latter position, I suspect, was not one Faulkner welcomed, nor did he ever radically depart from the racial attitudes of the conservative white community. However, no writer before or after him explored so boldly the miscegenation "myth."

The theme of racial pollution is more explicitly spelled out in a few unpublished fragments by Thomas Wolfe, a writer Faulkner professedly admired, some time between 1920 and 1922. Wolfe was then studying to become a playwright, and the "tender subject" of race (too important, he declared, to be killed by "public squeamish-ness") was very much on his mind:

All about us are members of a savage and inferior race. When they were brought here, their skins were black. Now the skins of some—a great many—are yellow; there are a few [who] are almost white. Can you deny it? What folly! It walks by you in the streets like a great plague. It is, and is everywhere. Simply look around you and begin to count. You know this thing. You know many others like it; why then do you con-fine your conversation to decorous trifling: why do you skim along the surface when the great, dark, passionate currents of life are sweeping on down there beneath your feet?[33]

The play he was writing "dealt with the decay of a powerful South-ern family in the days following the Civil War." The last heir is a "quadroon negro," the child of the eldest son and a mulatto. Wolfe writes:

The decay of the family is thus terribly climaxed. This of course is the sore spot in our life here in the South—the forbidden tree of conversa-tion and exposure. Nevertheless it is damnably true. One is sickened and disgusted at the inanity and cowardice of editor and parson who spend their time denouncing flapperism, short skirts, dancing, and so on, as the summum malum of our society. Here's something very much like a yellow plague walking on our streets; there are as many yellow skins as black ones and for this the white man is solely to blame.[34]

Significantly, the race cancer is not in the blacks but in "the dis-contented mulattoes who feel, with justice, that they are neither fish nor flesh.[35] More terrible still is the contemplation of the inevitable result if this amalgamation continues. But with admirable and resolute idiocy we refuse to look on that side."[36]

The Dixon-like alarums of young Thomas Wolfe about the "plague" faded out of his later writing, and no "tragic mulattoes" figure in his novels. Descendants of mixed marriages are in the background, however, and in a passage he deleted from *Look Homeward Angel*, he describes the feelings of a town worthy as he watches the copper-skinned cook, who is also the "mother of his two sons," preparing breakfast. Black sensuality and the mysterious attractiveness associated with the "dark lady" in American romantic fiction are evoked in the "tall powerfully molded negress of thirty-eight years." By this time, Wolfe had reduced the "Negro problem" to "a sexual one." The Southern white man's antipathy toward blacks derived from his envy of Negro potency. This simplistic explanation offered in a passage he excised from *Of Time and the River* closes with the hope that "lynching bees" and the castration of blacks following "the occasional roasting parties in the public square" would cease. Yet Wolfe's condemnation of brutal racism, his scorn of white hypocrisy and rage at the exploitation of blacks by white employers coexist with his belief in black inferiority and the deleterious results of racial mixing.[37]

As Wolfe was pondering these matters, Allen Tate outlined *his* thoughts on the Negro question in response to a letter from Lincoln Kirstein, then publisher of the *Hound & Horn*, a literary quarterly. Why, Kirstein asked, did the Southern Agrarians omit the Negro from their discussions? Tate gladly explained. They had been "vague" because there was no "solution" to it. Given the realities of Southern life, the "inferior race" had to yield to the "superior race" if order were to prevail. Outside observers (Tate was outlining the "conservative" Southern position on race) tried to upset that order in the name of "social justice." In so doing they drove the South to deny the Negro the "legal justice" he certainly would obtain if liberal and Communist agitators (who used the blacks as cat's-paws for their ulterior designs) would only stop exacerbating economic and political frictions between the races. In a stable South where "the dogma of racist integrity" was maintained, the Negro might expect "legal justice" in all cases save one: the "rape of a white woman."

Tate's exception hinged on his distinction between a Negro man's "miscegenation" with a white woman and its reverse:

> If a white woman has a negro child, then negro blood has passed into the white race. Our purpose is to keep the negro blood from passing into the white race. . . . The general dogma is simply that white blood passing into the negro race ceases to be white. You may ask why this is not so when the white woman bears a mulatto child. It *is* so in fact, but the threat to white racial integrity is greater. For it is upon the sexual consent of women that the race depends for the future.[38]

It was also a question, Tate continued,

> of moral symbolism . . . based upon the psychology of sex and of maternity. The moral symbolism requires that the source of life shall not be polluted. The psychology of sex says that a man is not altered in his being by sexual intercourse, but that the body of a woman is powerfully affected by pregnancy. A white woman pregnant with a negro child becomes a counter symbol, one of evil and pollution.

After reflecting on the works and opinions of these writers and of others I have not mentioned—Robert Penn Warren and William Styron come to mind—it can be seen that anxieties over "racial integrity" (to use Tate's euphemism) go deeper than parochial prejudice.[39] Mulattoes in the fiction of Mark Twain, Cable, Faulkner, Wolfe, and Tate are not the apelike rapists of Thomas Dixon and Thomas Nelson Page. The infusion of white blood makes them literally "family," whereas undiluted blacks are "family" only by affectionate designation. Fictional mulattoes, furthermore, occupy an uncertain place in the Southern social order. As Wolfe says, they are neither fish nor flesh, and this very indefinableness accounts for the mysterious aura which frequently surrounds them and for their own confused sense of identity.

The critic W. B. Clark finds in "the alienation and uncertainties of mixed blood" and "the fictional mulatto's search for self-definition" a parallel to a larger theme: "the plight of 'modern' man in general."[40] And so it may be. But conceived of in this way, the victim of miscegenation becomes a "convenient emblem" of an identity crisis. Miscegenation as *fact* is submerged in more ghostly issues like original sin.

Implicit in the writing I have been discussing are the following propositions. 1) Racial problems involving blacks and whites are insoluble. 2) Miscegenation at bottom is the consequence of "individual sinfulness" aggravated "by the opportunities for sin which slavery and the subsequent oppression of the black man afforded members of the Southern community."[41] Ergo, 3) economic, political, and sexual exploitation are simply the residue of flawed human nature. Hence the black community can be symbolized as the jungle of error through which the white pilgrim must wander and from which he seldom emerges unscathed. However sympathetically portrayed, the mulatto—a figure akin to the Wandering Jew—becomes a supernumary in a white theological pageant. Individual responsibility dissolves into universal complicity. The victim may be a mulatto, but the villain is human nature.

Such an all-encompassing indictment amounts to an evasion of sorts, a convenient way to explain, if not to justify, a good deal of mean and nasty behavior. The record of white-black interaction in this country from colonial times to the present (much of it still buried in court proceedings, travelers' accounts, letters, diaries, and the like) furnishes poignant examples of cruelty, prejudice, sadism (read "Original Sin"). It also points to unexamined anxieties, racial fantasies, self-deceptions. What lies behind that repeated and tiresome question, "Would you like your daughter to marry one?" is the assumption, sometimes avowed, sometimes unspoken, of white superiority.

Faulkner comes pretty close to the reality of the subrational concern for "white purity" implicit in this question in *Absalom! Absalom!* Charles Bon says to his half-brother, Henry Sutten: "so it's miscegenation, not incest, which you can't bear." Henry doesn't answer. "You are my brother," Henry says. Charles replies, "No I'm not. I'm the nigger that's going to sleep with your sister." Then Henry shoots him.[42] A fear of the "inky curse," I believe, echoed through the corridors of Faulkner's mind, and no "sacramental system" could exorcise it.

The apocalyptic terrors evoked by the imminence of racial "pollution" are no longer publicly entertained as they were in the time of Thomas Dixon and Maurice Thompson, and it is hard to believe that scarcely more than a century ago, a Democratic Party parade in Indiana "featured a group of young ladies carrying the banner,

"Fathers, save us from nigger husbands."[43] Interracial unions today are numerous enough to be commonplace. But the old apprehensions still obtain. The majority of neither race is persuaded to let the process of natural selection take its course without aids or barriers. Antibusing legislation, organized support for segregated schools, law and order crusades may not be solely aimed at the spirit of integration, but they surely indicate the persistence of color prejudice and the power of the appeal for white homogeneity.

As a literary subject, miscegenation—at least for Southern writers—is said to be exhausted, but then it seems never to have been addressed very thoughtfully or without constraints and indirections by any white writer. The immense literature of race contains comparatively very little about miscegenation in all of its many ramifications, and writers have tended to handle it with tongs. And this continues to be true despite the noticeable relaxation of racial taboos and the new and complex relationships—especially among the professional classes—resulting from interracial marriage.

Admittedly, I have been discussing only one side of the miscegenation story in the United States—the white side in which the black component is essential but subordinate. Told from a black perspective, the story would widen and deepen. It would touch on the complex and contradictory attitudes of dark-skinned blacks toward the lighter skinned, the mulattoes' own conception of themselves in terms of the color spectrum, the differences between the black woman's and the black man's views on interracial mixing, the ethics of "passing," and the like. Fuller and more profound explorations of these and other themes will doubtless be forthcoming. My candidate for the Great Miscegenation Novel would be some black Cervantes steeped in his heritage while distanced enough to see the subject in its absurd as well as tragic dimensions and inclined to cut through the casuistry, solemnity, and emotional inflation that so often seep into white fiction whenever interracial sex is an issue.

Over the centuries, antimiscegenationists have inspired and welcomed a vast amount of bogus science.[44] They have presumed that the attraction a member of one race might feel for another could be short-circuited by legislation and have resorted to the silliest subterfuges and jugglings of evidence in their efforts to escape the inescapable fact that racial "purity" and racial "pollution" are figments of frightened minds.

The black author I envisage will be no "Voodoo prophet" holding a torch to Western civilization, but a satirist and poet alert to the preposterous disparity between illusion and fact in the literature of racism and prepared to give the age-old lore surrounding the "Inky curse" a thorough and wholesome ventilation.

Notes

1. O. B. Wheeler, *The Literary Career of Maurice Thompson* (Baton Rouge: Louisiana State University Press, 1965).
2. Letter from M. Thompson to R. W. Gilder, May 7, 1889. Century Collection, New York Public Library.
3. Wheeler, *Maurice Thompson*, 98.
4. Quoted in ibid., 99–103.
5. Thompson to Gilder, April 30 and September 7, 1889.
6. G. Frederickson, *The Black Image in the White Mind: The Debate on Afro-American Character and Destiny, 1817–1914* (New York: Harper and Row, 1971), 88–89.
7. Wheeler, *Maurice Thompson*, 103.
8. *Miscegenation*, Introduction.
9. For a detailed history of this episode, see S. Kaplan, "The Miscegenation Issue in the Election of 1864," *Journal of Negro History*, 34 (April 1949), 274–343.
10. W. Jordan, *White over Black: American Attitudes toward the Negro, 1550–1812* (Baltimore: Penguin, 1969), 543.
11. I use the word "ominous" advisedly. Herman Melville in 1849 likened the blood of the nation "to the flood of the Amazon, made up of a thousand noble currents all pouring into one." Thirty years later (Melville would have appreciated the irony), Mark Twain could refer to the "mulatto" waters of the Mississippi. By that time, the mulatto had become in the American literary imagination a symbol of black victim and black avenger now dissolved into the national bloodstream, the visible reminder of the nation's guilt and a term resonant with dark meanings.
12. Melville satirized this conception in his story "Benito Cereno," in which the amiably obtuse sea captain associates black slaves with friendly dogs and describes their women as "unsophisticated as leopardesses; loving as doves." See L. Karcher, *Shadow over the Land: Slaves, Race, and Violence in Melville's America* (Baton Rouge: Louisiana State University Press, 1980), 134.
13. Jordan, *White over Black*, 164.
14. J. Williamson, *New People, Miscegenation and Mulattoes in the United States* (New York: Free Press), 1980.
15. "We have now nearly four millions of these serfs among us. They are increasing in a ratio unknown to the white race. Not only this, but . . .

they are imbibing the energies and taking the color of the superior race. They now range all the way up the scale from the jet black to the offspring of quadroons. Does anybody flatter himself that the usually sullen . . . mulatto has no more ambition, nor more energy of mind, than the African proper. Do not the faces show that they have? The fact that the cross of two antagonistic bloods makes them short lived, as a class, has demonstrated to physiologists that they are the worst class of inhabitants a country can have." From the *Wheeling Intelligencer*, quoted in M. Myers, "Thoreau and Black Emigration," *American Literature*, 53 (November 1981), 384.

16. Aversion to racial amalgamation was strengthened in the second half of the nineteenth century by influential apostles of Neo-Darwinism like Herbert Spencer, Joseph Le Conte, and Nathaniel Southgate Shaler. While not using "black inferiority" as an excuse to justify discrimination against blacks or call for their expulsion, they reinforced sentiment to keep the races apart. Neo-Darwinists agreed that unsupervised blacks regressed to their primitive origins, that it would take eons before the saving remnant among them might be safely absorbed. See R. Banniser, *Social Darwinism: Science and Myth in Anglo-American Social Thought* (Philadelphia: Temple University Press, 1979), 189ff.

17. Leslie Fiedler, *Love and Death in the American Novel* (New York: Criterion, 1960), 395.

18. The quotations of Agassiz and Cope are taken from S. J. Gould, *The Mismeasure of Man* (New York: W. W. Norton, 1982), 36–42.

19. T. Dixon, *The Leopard's Spots: A Romance of the White Man's Burden—1865–1900* (New York: Doubleday Page, 1903), 244. Knowledgeable people thought they could detect the Negro taint in the damasked cheek, but stories were rife of black babies born to unsuspecting parents. Kate Chopin's much anthologized story, "Desirée's Baby," is based on this folk fear.

20. Dixon, *The Leopard's Spots*, 398.

21. Ibid., 397.

22. L. Freedman, *The White Savage: Racist Fantasies in the Postbellum South* (Englewood Cliffs, N.J.: Prentice-Hall, 1970), 99–117.

23. G. W. Cable, "Creole Slave Songs," *Century Magazine*, 30 (April 1886), 810.

24. "A hundred years we have been fearing to do entirely right lest something wrong should come of it; fearing to give the blackman an equal chance with us in the race of life lest we might have to grapple with the vast, vague, afrite of Amalgamation; and in all this hundred years, with the enemies of slavery getting from us such names as negrophiles, negro-worshippers, and miscegenationists; and while we were claiming to hold ourselves rigidly separate from the lower race in obedience to a natal instinct which excommunicated them both socially and civilly; just in proportion to the rigor, the fierceness, and the injustice with which the excommunication from the common rights of man has fallen upon the darker

race, has amalgamation taken place." G. W. Cable, *The Silent South*, ed. A. Turner (Montclair, N.J.: Patterson Smith, 1969), 102.

25. G. W. Cable, *The Negro Question* (New York: Scribner's, 1890), 44.

26. William Dean Howells, *An Imperative Duty* (New York: Harper & Brothers, 1893), 85, 144–145. A comment on Mediterranean tolerance for interracial mixture is in order. The old English canard "the niggers begin with Calais" is symptomatic of the Anglo-American vulgar notion that whiteness becomes muddied in the Mediterranean populations, that the Portuguese are mongrels, the Levantine people not really white, and that even the Italians and French are not overly fastidious about commingling with "wogs." Swarthy skins were long suspect in the United States. A foreign accent or a turban could facilitate the "passing" of the bogus "European" or "Asiatic," abet "pollution," and turn white America into "another Mexico." Mulattoes, a Northern soldier observed during the Civil War, were sometimes "very beautiful" and looked "more like voluptuous Italians than Negroes." L. Litwack, *Been in the Storm So Long: The Aftermath of Slavery* (New York: Knopf, 1979), 265, 129.

27. Howells, *An Imperative Duty*, 149.

28. A. W. Amacher, "The Genteel Primitivist and the Semi-Tragic Octoroon," *New England Quarterly*, 29 (June 1956), 216–217.

29. For hostile reviews of Howells's novel, see T. W. Ford, "Howells and the American Negro," *Texas Studies in Literature and Language*, 4 (Winter 1964), 530–537.

30. Freedman, *The White Savage*, 107.

31. W. B. Clark, "The Serpent of Lust in the Southern Garden," *Southern Review*, 10 (Autumn 1974), 810.

32. See Irving Howe, *William Faulkner: A Critical Study* (New York: Random House, 1952), 121. In *Absalom! Absalom!* the progenitor of the mixed breed which will spread over the western hemisphere is Colonel Sutpen, and his last living descendant is a "hulking young negro man in clean faded overalls and shirt, his arms dangling, no nothing in the saddle-colored and slack-mouthed idiot face." Faulkner, *Absalom! Absalom!* (New York, Modern Library, 1951), 370.

33. Thomas Wolfe MSS (Folder 1208), Houghton Library, Harvard University.

34. T. Wolfe to G. P. Baker (c. June 22), Wolfe MSS, University of North Carolina.

35. "Some of these [mulattoes] were about half white, some almost white, leaving it difficult to distinguish where the one ends and the other begins. To one unaccustomed to see human nature in this guise, it excites feelings of horror and disgust. It has something in it so contrary to nature, something which seems never to have entered into her scheme, to see a man neither black nor white, with blue eyes, and a woolly head, has something in it at which the mind recoils. It appears that these people instead of abolishing slavery, are gradually not only becoming slaves of themselves,

but changing color." Mrs. Anne Royall, *Sketches of History, Life and Manners in the United States* (New Haven, Conn., 1826), 101. This passage is cited by Simone Vauthier in her very perceptive essay, "Of African Queens and Afro-American Princes and Princesses: Miscegenation in *Old Hepsy*" (Publication du Conseil Scientifique de la Sorbonne Nouvelle, Paris III [1968], 105). The mulatto thus conceived becomes "uncanny" in the Freudian sense, neither real nor unreal, at once mysterious and threatening. Such a view did not always maintain. In Walter von Eschenbach's thirteenth-century Grail romance, Parzifal's father, while soldiering in the heathen orient, falls in love with a black queen. He leaves her pregnant, and she gives birth to a son of two colors.

36. Wolfe to Baker (see note 34).

37. See P. Reeves, *Thomas Wolfe's Albatross: Race and Nationality in America* (Athens: University of Georgia Press, 1968), 18 ff.

38. Quoted in L. Greenbaum, *"The Hound & Horn": The History of a Literary Quarterly* (The Hague: Mouton, 1966), 145–149.

39. See L. Casper, "Miscegenation as Symbol: Band of Angels," in *A Collection of Critical Essays*, ed. Robert Penn Warren (New York: New York University Press, 1965), 140–148.

40. Clark, *Serpent of Lust*, 821.

41. W. Sullivan, "The Fathers and the Failures of Tradition," *Southern Review*, 12 (Autumn 1976), 763.

42. Faulkner, *Absalom! Absalom!*, 357–358.

43. Eric Foner, *Free Soil, Free Labor, Free Men: The Ideology of the Republican Party before the Civil War* (New York: Oxford University Press, 1970), 263.

44. The extent and influence of this literature—much of it by redoubtable scholars and scientists and never adequately collected and assessed—represents an astounding record of credulity, prejudice, and self-deception. Anthropologists, neurologists, physiologists, ethnologists, geneticists, eugenicists contributed to the hodgepodge of misinformation, as did the random commentary of travelers, clergymen, novelists, politicians, psychologists, phrenologists, and what have you. In addition to the works cited here, see W. Stanton, *The Leopard's Spots: Scientific Attitudes Toward Race in America, 1815–1859* (Chicago: University of Chicago Press, 1960), and Daniel Kevles, *In the Name of Eugenics* (New York: Knopf, 1985).

· III ·

Bostonians

The magisterial reserve associated with Boston and Cambridge was still discernible when I landed there in 1933. The scions of Old Boston I encountered at Harvard and elsewhere seemed to me a distinct breed. I liked their understated humor and alternating suavity and bluntness, the way they dressed and talked, their domestic rituals, eccentricities, and gusts of civic courage. I also thought some of them hidebound, starchy, insular, and smug—an opinion I must have derived in part from satirical novels on Boston Brahmins, Menckenian attacks on Boston prudery, and the recriminations of liberal writers against the Bostonians they held responsible for the executions of Sacco and Vanzetti. But for a midwesterner like me, soaking in American history and literature, Boston was holy ground; so not surprisingly many writers I eventually wrote about had Boston connections.

Three who figure in this section are by my criteria immutably Boston and display in varying degrees the attitudes, attributes, and actions that to me betray a Puritan inheritance: anxiety over the choice of vocation, a penchant for self-deprecation, fear of failure, an agonized conscience, and flurries of rebelliousness. George Santayana, who made much of his Catholic and Mediterranean foreignness, would appear to be an exception in this company of Yankees, but he tried even more strenuously than Henry Adams did to purge himself of the Puritan contagion he had contracted during his long exposure to Boston. For both, Boston was more than a place: it was also a state of mind.

Two Boston Fugitives:
Dana and Parkman

The words "pilgrimage," "voyage," "journey," "quest" almost routinely appear in discussions of American literature. Our writers constantly seem to be wandering over prairies and forests, crossing real and imaginary oceans, launching desperate expeditions. They go in search of their own identities, track down private incarnations of reality, project themselves into historical and even primordial pasts and into unknown futures.

This essay concentrates on two travel narratives not ordinarily associated with the metaphorical voyages of Poe, Melville, Hawthorne, Whitman, Emerson, and Thoreau. Both are "Boston" books rather than "Concord" books, which is another way of saying that their authors were conservative gentlemen inattentive to messages from the Over Soul. Nevertheless, Richard Henry Dana's *Two Years Before the Mast*, anonymously published in 1840, and Francis Parkman's *The Oregon Trail*, serialized seven years later, are animated by the same "extra-vagrant" westward-turning impulse Thoreau spoke of in his essay "Walking": "Eastward I go only by force; but westward I go free. I must walk to Oregon, and not toward Europe."

Of the two books, Dana's is the greater achievement, but it is less profitable to approach them as rival adventure narratives than as extraordinarily interesting examples of a kind of writing, often unrecognized by American readers, that is best categorized in William

Originally published in *American Literature, Culture, and Ideology: Essays in Memory of Henry Nash Smith*, ed. Beverly R. Voloshin (New York: Peter Lang, 1990), 115–132.

Spengemann's phrase, "the poetics of adventure."[1] The "poetic adventure" might be defined as a vague and shifting genre lying somewhere between the plain factual narrative (for example, the five-volume report of a United States exploring expedition by Dana's and Parkman's contemporary, Captain Charles Wilkes) and narrative purportedly factual but wafting off into fiction and fantasy like Poe's tale of Arthur Gordon Pym. Both *Two Years Before the Mast* and *The Oregon Trail* can be read as autobiographical yarns. Both grow out of the journals kept by their respective authors, and yet they have much in common with the land and sea novels of Fenimore Cooper—a writer, incidentally, in whom both Dana and Parkman delighted—and even metaphysical travel in the vein of Poe and Melville.

It comes as no surprise, then, that Emerson was charmed by Dana's book or that Melville virtually absorbed it. Just as romance writers borrowed the forms and conventions of travel literature, so by the 1840s travel-adventure had incorporated fictive or novelistic devices into ostensibly truthful accounts; seascapes and landscapes that reflect the narrator's state of mind while accelerating the action; portraits of people whose characters and personalities affect the logic of events; and artfully related episodes of suspense. These devices are not hard to detect in *Two Years* and *The Oregon Trail*, but I shall consider the two books primarily from an extraliterary perspective—as expressions or consequences of what might be called ancestral influences and vocational pressures.

ii

Both Dana and Parkman, scions of old Boston families well known to each other, were "Brahmins," a term popularized by Dr. Oliver Wendell Holmes and later defined by Parkman as "a progeny of gentlemen and scholars from the days of the Puritans." Both were sons of well-known fathers and the beneficiaries of a complex social order. The Parkmans were much richer than the Danas, but young Richard and young Francis got the best educations Boston could provide and had equal recourse to the distinguished people of their time and place. Both grew up in a Federalist/Whig milieu not unlike that of Cooper's, and the conservatism they absorbed in their youth deepened with the years. All the same, on the eve of their coming of age, they seemed to have experienced some of the fears and mis-givings felt by many of their New England contemporaries[2]—and not merely the dissenters—when faced with the problem of voca-tion. They knew what was expected of them: to put aside their ado-lescent daydreams and prepare themselves for a respectable busi-ness or profession.

But although they had little in common with the visionaries in the Brook Farm community, neither was ready or eager to slip into the Boston harness, and like other young gentlemen who doted on Byron and Scott and Cooper, their fancies turned to simpler and less restrictive worlds. Theodore Parker speaks somewhere of "the impetuous ardor that sometimes sleeps beneath the habitual cold-ness of New England," and William Dean Howells of "the anti-Puri-tan quality which was always vexing the heart of Puritanism." Their observations should be kept in mind when we think of nineteen-year-old Dana and twenty-three-year-old Parkman embarking on their adventures. Yet the impulse to break away from ancestral Bos-ton in both of these writers was balanced by an equally powerful urge to come back to it. The conflict between home and outland in *Two Years* and *The Oregon Trail* creates in each a tension that deter-mines its narrative pattern.

A comparable tension was already present in the early Indian captivity narratives. The Puritans knew very well the lure of the unlicensed wilderness, the possibility that errant sons and daugh-ters might become "Indianized" in unsupervised forest spaces.[3] That was one of the reasons they preferred to move collectively into un-settled territories. Only the regenerate white hunter who had learned the ways of the forest without succumbing to its abomina-tions and then had returned to the settlements with his forest-knowledge and his white Christian values intact was held up as the proper model. The narrators of *Two Years* and *The Oregon Trail*, as we shall see, did not return unscathed from their travels in trans-Boston America and their passages into the self, but neither did they become white Indians or renegades. They had never severed their ties with home throughout their voyaging or dropped their suspi-cion of the uninhibited life that repels as it attracts. Habits, preju-dices, and moral assumptions implanted in them may have been temporarily stretched, but the two Bostonians clung, like Natty Bumppo, to their social identities and the tenets of their fathers.

The principal reason Dana, then a Harvard undergraduate, gave for going to sea as a common sailor was eyestrain. Presumably it was to restore his eyes that he turned down an easier job of supercargo on a voyage to India and elected instead to sail before the mast. Was it fear that the chores of the supercargo might task his eyesight? Or did the prospect of staying under the eyesight of his elders make him decide against it? Parkman was also bedeviled by eyestrain, not to mention indigestion and insomnia. To be sure, his venture to the Great Plains marked the first step of a plan, dating back to his sophomore year at Harvard, to write the history of the Anglo-French conflict in North America, yet in his case, too, some legitimate excuse like ill-health or bad eyes may have been required to justify a temporary reprieve from duty, that stern mother of Boston.

Dana and Parkman were not the first or last Yankees to take time off for strenuous recuperation.[4] Timothy Dwight, one of the Connecticut Wits and later president of Yale, had to work himself nearly to death before he permitted himself to hike and ride through New England and New York and write a four-volume account of his travels far livelier than his patriotic but dreadful epic poem, *The Conquest of Canaan*. Young Emerson also had his bout with sore eyes, his eyes "refusing to read" as he agonized over his vocation. But perhaps Dana and Parkman were the most gifted of the untranscendental types whose "eye problems" had transcendental implications. Romantic poets and philosophers of their day often lamented the loss of the child's heavenly vision. Men's eyes were so glued by the gum of a materialistic civilization that they could not "see" and were to that degree diminished. "What we are," Emerson wrote, "that only can we see." In order to recover their lost vision, to correct, so to speak, the spiritual squint, it was necessary to undergo an experience equivalent to Thoreau's in Walden Pond: to take "voyages," whether in Concord or elsewhere.

Now, Dana and Parkman temperamentally and philosophically belonged to the rational camp. Neither could be labeled an idealist, much less a transcendentalist, but perhaps they were trying to recover, if not the wholeness of childhood, at least a return to the time when mind and body, flesh and spirit, were not divided. The sailors and trappers and Indians and South Sea islanders they encountered, most of them childlike men, natural and unsophisticated, could be said to have approximated for them the antique peoples who flourished before modern civilization separated thought from feeling. Dana and Parkman were drawn to outdoor men, so different from the effete sprigs of Boston. It never occurred to them, however, to join their company.

iii

Dana's book tells of his 150-day voyage from Boston to California via Cape Horn, August 1834 to January 1835; his life on the California coast from January to May 1835, collecting and curing hides; and his return voyage, May to September in the same year. It was based on a diary Dana kept, he says, to show what a sailor's life was all about. After he finished the manuscript, in which he spared no details in describing the hard lot of the common seaman, he thought it prudent to remove passages dealing with the sexual relations between sailors and Indian women and said nothing, as a friend reminded him, of the "beautiful Indian lasses" with whom he had consorted in his "humble abode in the hide house." An older and more decorous Dana later explained the reason for the omissions: "The dangers to a young man's moral purity, and to his nicer sentiments, as well as to his manners, are more to be dreaded in such a life, than gales, mast-heads and yard-arms."[5]

Such pomposities are rare in *Two Years.* The writing throughout is concrete and lucid and devoid of affectation no matter whether the subject is a storm or an iceberg, the mysteries of seamanship or the technique of curing and loading hides. Dana had the power mentioned by Poe, the "power of verisimilitude," that our best writers seem to have, the ability to describe a process accurately, to dramatize it, and while doing so to disclose themselves. In a review of Dana's book, Emerson observed, "Though a narrative of literal prosaic truth, it possesses something of the romantic charm of Robinson Crusoe," and shortly after he wrote to a friend, "He was my scholar once, but he never learned this of me, more's the pity." But perhaps Dana did—at least more than Emerson realized—because for Dana, as well as for Dana's classmate Henry Thoreau, plain facts, as Emerson had taught, contained a special poetry and needed no rhetorical adornment. They simply had to be "seen."

How does Dana keep the routine of process from becoming monotonous? For one, he punctuates his narrative with illustrative adventures, anecdotes, character studies—and by these artful assertions builds up suspense. The *Pilgrim*, an appropriate name for both ship and author, weighs anchor for her voyage around the Horn to California. Promptly the lubberly narrator gets seasick and vomits up his shore food, a symbolic as well as literal purgation, before he acquires his sea legs and is restored by a diet of salt pork and biscuit. "Now my lad," the cook tells him, "you are well cleaned out; you haven't a drop of your 'long shore swash aboard you."

The narrator is on a new tack, and before he reaches the California coast, he has been educated by his exposure to fundamental events: by death at sea, with its attendant sensations and consequences, by the vagaries and indifference of nature as well as its terror and beauty. He becomes hardened to weather, to the work discipline of the ship, its dirt and brutality, and its comradeship, too. Above all, he experiences the pride of the professional and the veteran, the pleasant feeling of superiority

> in being able to walk the deck, and eat, and go aloft, and compare oneself with the two poor miserable pale creatures staggering and shuffling about decks, or holding on and looking up with giddy heads, to see us climbing to the mast-heads, or sitting quietly at work on the ends of lofty yards. A well man at sea has little sympathy with one who is sea sick; he is apt to be conscious of a comparison which seems favorable to his own manhood.

Once in California, the hard, tedious labor of collecting and loading hides begins. Dana the Yankee remains serenely and robustly ethnocentric (to him, Mexicans are a worthless if charming lot, the Muscovite sailors from the North greasy tallow-swilling oafs), but the shipmates and un-Boston types he encounters on the coast challenge his Boston parochialism. The storm-tossed youth who has watched a seaman being flogged (he will later agitate against cruelty to seamen in a powerful pamphlet), who has observed the ocean in its gay, somnolent, and ferocious moods, successfully completes his rite of passage. The landlubber is converted into a salt.

All through *Two Years* Dana plays on the dialectic between sea and land—a theme Melville will treat with greater imagination and force—and the impulse to escape from and return to Boston. Away from home, thoughts of Boston arouse nostalgia and guilt. He worries lest his long absence endanger his career, and while he likes and sympathizes with his shipmates, he never loses his sense of social distance. The attraction of the sea and adventure, in short, is not strong enough to detach him from familial commitments. Still, a note of reluctance creeps into the account of his homecoming. Boston gentlemen seem to him pallid and emaciated, the women mere shades. And long after he has resumed his domestic and professional burdens, he seeks outlets for his questing spirit in more curtailed and oblique ways than sailing before the mast: in travel or in steering for low dives in Halifax and New York City where, dressed in his sailor's togs, he accosts prostitutes and urges them to give up their erring ways.

Dana's father sent a copy of *Two Years* to Fenimore Cooper along with a note in which he observed that if the voyage did not cure his son's eyes, it would at least fit him for an active life. But as Henry Adams wrote of Dana in his *Education*, "the freshness of the great lesson faded away," and Dana submitted to Boston: "he affected," Adams recalled, "to be still before the mast, a direct, rather bluff, vigorous seaman, and only as one got to know him better one found the man of rather excessive refinement trying with success to work like a day-laborer, deliberately hardening his skin to the burden, as though he were still carrying hides at Monterey."

Adams did not quite do justice to the stubborn, nay-saying side of Dana, his willingness, for example, to challenge his fellow conservatives on the slavery issue, but American literature did lose a promising writer when Dana opted for the Law, Family, and Episcopalianism after the striking success of his book. The gentlemen amateur adventurers who followed him, men like Theodore Roosevelt and Owen Wister, also allegedly preferred the company of rough men—sailors, trappers, guides, cowboys—over that of a middle-class would-be gentry, but they never tested themselves so rigorously as Dana did or as Dana's slightly younger contemporary, Francis Parkman.

iv

Parkman resembled Dana in certain respects, but he was essentially a different sort of person, and *The Oregon Trail*, for all its virtues, lacks the existential drama of *Two Years*. In Dana's book, the narrator seems fully conscious of his risk. He really is in danger of cutting himself off; his very identity is at stake. The prospect at once thrills and alarms him. Will he, indeed, ever succeed in returning home? Can one ever "go home again"? The clash between Boston and non-Boston is real. It figures in the very structure and content of the work.

The Oregon Trail, on the other hand, is an episode in a carefully planned career of a young man who, on the surface at least, knows what he is about. The narrator, as Howard Doughty puts it in his fine study of Francis Parkman, is a "sportsman-ethnologist on holiday." One feels that Parkman's land trip never threatens his sense of himself or more than dents the armor of his preconceptions. When you travel by land, Washington Irving remarked,

> there is a continuity of scene, and a connected succession of persons and incidents, that carry on a story of life, and lessen the effect of absence and separation. We drag, it is true, "a lengthening chain" at each remove of our pilgrimage, but the chain is unbroken; we can trace it back link by link; and we feel that the last of them still grapples us to home.

But, Irving continues,

> a wide sea voyage severs us at once. It makes us conscious of being cut loose from the secure anchorage of a settled life, not merely imaginary, but real, between us and our homes—a gulf subject to tempest, and fear, and uncertainty, that makes distance palpable and return precarious.[6]

Parkman never broke the lengthening chain to Boston, but he lugged it pretty far. *The Oregon Trail* is a young man's first major literary experiment in transmuting the "raw material of direct observation" without dulling its authority; it is also the author's calculated response to a self-imposed challenge. He may be less openly at war with society than the narrator of *Typee*, but he also betrays Byronic yearnings[7] and he is clearly off on more than a hunting holiday. His objective is the camp of the Oglala Sioux, Parkman's counterpart, it might be said, of Melville's Marquesan valleys; and the way to that goal, and the retreat from it after several weeks of intimate living with the Indians, is strewn with physical and mental obstacles that test the narrator's manhood. He and his companions face fierce storms and dangerous encounters. Attacks of dysentery leave him so weak he can hardly stay on his saddle. Throughout his ordeal, he keeps his stiff Boston demeanor and is decidedly offish toward most of his fellow Americans surging westward in the fateful year of 1846. He regards them as boors with whom he has nothing in common. Yet his actions often belie his snobbish reserve, and he finds merit in specimens of a class he theoretically disdains.

Parkman's guide, Henry Chatillon, is a good example of what Melville was to call "the kingly commons." A natural gentleman with an instinctive courtesy, he is extraordinarily proficient in the arts of the plains, a great hunter and natural leader. Like Natty Bumppo, one of Parkman's favorite characters, he has not sunk into the savagism Parkman observes in the majority of mountain men and is the ideal guide for what Doughty calls Parkman's "backward journey in time."

Unlike Dana, Parkman had prepared himself for his journey. During his college years, he had ventured into the wilds of New Hampshire and Maine in search of old forts and battlefields. He had trained himself to withstand the rigors of the western wilderness, become an expert marksman, and learned horsemanship under the instruction of an ex-circus rider. Again and again he had forced himself to the point of exhaustion on hiking and canoeing trips.

Nor was this preparation for his backward journey confined to the New World. The European tour he undertook in 1843–44 also figured in the design of the North American epic incubating in his mind. It introduced him to Roman Catholicism and enabled him to appreciate the spirit that animated the Church in Canada, if not its policies. More important, it clarified his conception of his embryonic chronicle, its opportunities and responsibilities. Europe's dense history offered rich bounties to the historian, but its origins were doubled in myth and inaccessible to him. North America was comparatively unstoried, but its past was still visible. Hence, the knowledgeable and imaginative investigator could write with some validity about an early stage in civilization in which nature still dominated man.

To accomplish this task, however, the historian had to have a firsthand acquaintance with the geography and topography of North America, its forests, rivers, mountains, all its physiographic features. More than that, he had to *see* and *feel* what the early explorers saw and felt. And above all, he had to know the aborigines whose true character, Parkman believed, had been distorted by literary interpreters. As he put it in a passage deleted from the final version of *The Oregon Trail*: "Having from childhood felt a curiosity on this subject, and having failed completely to gratify it by reading, I resolved to have recourse to observation. I wished to satisfy myself with regard to the position of the Indians among the races of men; the vices and virtues that have sprung from their innate character and from their modes of life, their superstitions, and their domestic situation."

Parkman's first "impulse toward ethnological inquiries" (if he is writing autobiographically, as I believe he is, in *Vassal Morton*) came from his delighted reading, while still in college, of Augustine Thierry's romantic and immensely popular history of the Norman conquest of England, the opening chapters of which show how various races came to occupy Europe. Morton "soon began to find an absorbing interest in tracing the distinctions, moral, intellectual, and physical, of different races, as shown in their history, their mythologies, their languages, their legends, their primitive art, literature and way of life." Ethnological studies would "enable him to indulge his passion for travel" and "make him intimate with the most savage and disgusting barbarians; in short, give him full swing to his favorite propensities and call into life all his energies, body and mind."

Thierry's racial premises must have left their mark on Parkman, although his conclusion that Indian character "is more rigid and inflexible than that of other savages" was also supported by current theory. Much as he admired Cooper as an interpreter of nature and the creator of heroic characters, he considered Cooper's Indians with few exceptions "either superficial or falsely drawn." In *The Oregon Trail*, most of the Indians are fatally corrupted by contact with whites. They tend to be squalid, dirty, and insolent. Even the comparatively untainted Sioux are ferocious and gluttonous and treacherous, their life mean and paltry, their warfare satanic, their habits disgusting. This devastating indictment of an entire race was hardly mitigated by Parkman's concession that Indian depravity was no match for "the utter abasement and prostitution of every nobler part of humanity, as I have seen it in great cities, the centres of the world's wisdom and refinement."

That Indians are uncivilized and doomed to extinction was a commonplace in Parkman's day, but the harsh portrayal of Indian character did not sit so well with those who may have accepted their disappearance as inevitable but who contemplated the spectacle with sadness and shame. Herman Melville, fresh from Polynesia, praised *The Oregon Trail* in an anonymous review but firmly dissented from Parkman's opinion that any white man familiar with Indian ways would be as indifferent to "the slaughter of an Indian" as the slaughter of a buffalo. "It was too often the case," Melville wrote, "that civilized beings sojourning among savages soon come to regard them with disdain and contempt." Such an attitude seemed to him indefensible and "wholly wrong."

Not surprisingly, critics in our post-Freudian age have detected an ambivalence in Parkman's view of the Indian, and many passages in his journals of the western trek seem to bear them out. Consider, for example, the portrait of the Sioux warrior, not yet poisoned by contacts with whites, whose *nom de guerre* was "the Panther."

He was a noble looking fellow. As he suffered his ornamented buffalo robe to fall in folds about his loins, his stately and graceful figure was fully displayed; and while he sat on his horse in an easy attitude the long feathers of the prairie cock fluttering from the crown of his head, he seemed the very model of a wild prairie rider. He had not the same features with those of other Indians. Unless his face greatly belied him, he was free from the jealousy, suspicion, and malignant cunning of his people. For the most part, a civilized white man can discover very few points of sympathy between his own nature and that of an Indian. With every disposition to do justice to their good qualities, he must be conscious that an impassible gulf lies between him and his red brethren. Nay, so alien to himself do they appear that, after breathing the air of the prairie for a few months or weeks, he begins to look upon them as a troublesome and dangerous species of wild beast. Yet in the countenance of the Panther, I gladly read that there were at least some points of sympathy between him and me.

Parkman's love-hate relation with the Indian remained a constant in his writing, and his "snake-eyed" and "lynx-eyed" forest prowlers are at once odious and admirable, "vicious and dangerous" yet mysteriously attractive animals. The English critic Harold Beaver observes in a perceptive essay[8] that Parkman was not the first or last to contemplate with obvious pleasure "these 'graceful' yet vigorously muscled athlete-warriors," objects, he suggests, of "sexual contemplation" aesthetically disguised: Cooper and Melville could compare the "matchless symmetry" of their Mohawk and Marquesan Apollos to Greek statues. But Parkman, Beaver thinks, underscored his distrust of Indians and Indian-ness while repressing the erotic attraction he felt for handsome copper-colored men and his self-described fits of "burning desire" to mingle with "niggers, Indians and other outcasts of humanity."

The sadism and ferocity cum voyeurism Beaver finds in Parkman's journals and to a lesser extent in the 1847 serialized version of the narrative were largely eliminated or toned down when it appeared in book form two years later as *The California and Oregon Trail*. For example, Parkman excised a passage in which he sighted a medicine man "perched aloft like a turkey buzzard, among the dead branches of an old tree." The narrator muses:

> He would have made a capital shot. A rifle bullet skillfully planted, would have brought him tumbling to the ground. Surely, I thought, there would be no harm in shooting such a hideous old villain, to see how ugly he would look when he was dead, than in shooting the detestable vulture which he resembled.

Parkman also eliminated most of the references to the "abominable indecencies" of the Indians that studded his journal account and provoked his strong revulsion against such flagrant violations of New England values: sexual propriety, hard work, cleanliness, and thrift. Beaver thinks that Parkman paid a fearful price for his adherence to his ancestral code, and he connects Parkman's much discussed physical breakdown—his partial blindness, heart pangs, arthritis, insomnia (now posthumously diagnosed by Parkman scholars as psychosomatic)—with his resistance to the blandishments of forest and Indian.

This is not the place to pursue these ill- or well-founded conjectures, but surely *The Oregon Trail*, an apprentice work, invites speculation about Parkman's allegedly "schizoid personality." As he heads home from the iniquitous Eden of the Sioux, he is both relieved and pained. He regards the white settlements and patches of forest he passes through with "unmingled pleasure," rejoices in their "sights and sounds," and yet he also notices "tokens of maturity and decay where all had before been fresh with opening life" and looks "back regretfully to the wilderness behind us."

But however genuine this expression of sadness at leaving it, and despite his contempt of Boston foppery, a comment by an editor of *The Oregon Trail*—that Parkman "steadily weakened" as he moved westward in space and backward in time, and only began to recover en route to civilization—is pertinent. "How near to good is what is *wild*," Thoreau exclaims, after describing how "our Northern Indians eat raw the marrow of the Arctic reindeer." Young Parkman, who watched his Indians feasting on raw buffalo and found it "no attractive spectacle," did not agree: "Some were cracking huge thigh-bones and devouring the marrow within; others were cutting away pieces of liver, and other approved morsels, and swallowing them on the spot with the appetite of wolves. The faces of most of them, besmeared with blood from ear to ear, looked grim and horrible enough."

Parkman returned to civilization and, like Dana, to his work, but unlike Dana, he did not undertake his labors out of a sense of duty. He had caught a glimpse of the primordial world of raw nature and rawer men that enthralled and depressed him, yet like Daniel Boone, some of whose descendants he encountered in Missouri, and like Leatherstocking, he had recovered some kind of primitive manna from this ethnographic excursion. Perhaps it was this benison that helped to keep him going during the pain-racked years as he slaved over his monumental History. The mementos of the Sioux camp—a shield, lance, bow and arrows, medicine pouch—hung thereafter on the walls of his study.

The Oregon Trail was both an apprentice work and a rehearsal for his masterpiece that unfolded volume by volume in the next four decades. The beginner was given to rhetorical posturing, hyperbole, studiedly "literary" set pieces, and the pathetic fallacy. His mountains "frowned" or lit up "with a benignant smile." Theodore Parker had good reason to fault his friend's book for its "lack of severity of style," and, as William Taylor notes, examples of "ornate or mannered prose" are not hard to find even in Parkman's mature work.[9] But when we come across pointed and vigorously written passages in the notebooks Parkman kept during his western journey and to wonderfully expressive pages in the book itself, the classic Parkman is foreshadowed: the master of the panoramic scene, the superb narrator, the colorist and portraitist, the dry and sardonic humorist, the matter-of-fact observer.

The way to the Sioux village, writes Howard Doughty, "unlocked the more fundamental resources of Parkman's imagination." As he turned from personal to narrative history, from *The Oregon Trail* to *The Conspiracy of Pontiac* and then on to the successive volumes which chronicle the rise and fall of New France, his imagination expanded. The historical mode gave him the necessary latitude to incorporate theretofore separately treated themes and experiences—travel, Sir Walter Scott, ethnology, Boston, the forest, race—into one sustained narrative. The biases and penchants displayed in his first book still showed up in the History, notably his conception of Indian character, but in the History the Indian motif is heard within a complicated orchestration of other themes: imperial rivalries, missionary faith, and individual exploit; and the historian is readier to balance Indian treachery and bloodthirstiness with Indian pride and passion and dash he found wanting in nineteenth-century white America. The "irreclaimable son of the wilderness" (so he referred to the Indian in *The Conspiracy of Pontiac*), "the child who will not be weaned from the breast of his rugged mother," now glides and floats in a forest setting reminiscent of Cooper's. He waits in ambush and butchers his foes and arranges elaborate ceremonials of torture, but Parkman also discerns "the germs of heroic virtues mingled among the vices," and he can commend the Indian soul, "true to its own idea of honor, and burning with an unquenchable thirst for greatness and renown." What is more, Indians are now enmeshed in the gigantic issue on which hinges the fate of warring empires. They are doomed, of course, by their rigidity, by their incapacity for reflection and abstraction, but for a brief interval the Indian in his "native wilds" (not, Parkman hastens to add, "the beggarly frequenter of frontier garrisons and dramshops") wins his admiration.

V

Parkman the Bostonian may have seen a design in the extinction of the Indian and the defeat of the French. But if he understood with his head, his heart entertained disquieting reservations. It was a good thing for human liberty, his History testified, that Wolfe on the Plains of Abraham turned back the Bourbon monarchy and balked the ambitions of the Roman Catholic Church. In so doing he cleared the ground for free enterprise and democracy. But the long-term consequences of Wolfe's victory were not altogether pre-possessing for a man who demanded more from civilization than locomotives and cotton gins. American enterprise destroyed the American wilderness, Parkman's alter ego, Vassal Morton declares, without creating in its place the "polished landscape" associated "with poetry, art, legend, and history." Perhaps, he concedes, the nineteenth century is better than the middle ages as shopkeepers are an improvement over cutthroats, but he prefers the chivalric code ("fantastic and absurd on the outside," like Don Quixote, "but noble at the core") to the business code of State Street. And it is worth pondering why this quintessential Bostonian should identify himself more closely with the French explorer La Salle, that intrepid monomaniac and spiritual cousin of Captain Ahab, than with any other of the larger-than-life figures of the History.

For all of his celebration of physical fortitude and his disdain for Boston's unheroic fops and crafty entrepreneurs, however, Parkman, like Dana, spoke for Boston, and never more so than when denouncing his fellow citizens for not living up to their Puritan heritage. Both Parkman and Dana kicked over the traces and roamed for a time in unfenced space, but like good Puritan sons they came back to the sacred ground, readier to adapt to Massachusetts ways without being entirely reconciled to life in the Hub of America.

This was especially so in Dana's case. Out of sight of his mentors, he had lived more unconstrainedly than Parkman did on his tour, and he suffered more guilt as a consequence. Back in Boston he contrived a double life for many years, one very proper, the other most improper—"cruising" (to use his word) the city's brothels and dives in his seaman's garb. Robert Lucid, editor of Dana's journals, sees these dangerous excursions as Dana's unconscious wish "to undermine his association with the respectable world," while out-wardly conforming to it and contemplating his concupiscence, Lucid says, with "transports of self-loathing."

Parkman's apostasy, if it deserves that name, was less bizarre and more covert, and it took an exclusively literary shape. Dana, having given up the option of becoming a writer, had no other literary outlet save his private journal. Parkman, who was and remained a man of letters, found a kind of surcease in the act of writing, despite the agonies he had to undergo; for in depicting the struggles and ordeals of would-be empire builders who kept driving themselves on in the face of indescribable hardships and the ever-present possibility of death by torture, he could convey both his own baffled aspirations and his heroic achievements and, in effect, write his apologia to the world.

Neither Parkman nor Dana, so far as I know, knew or cared very much about Nathaniel Hawthorne, whose fictional kingdom seemed to hang suspended between dream and reality, but their lives are illuminated in Hawthorne's ghostly parables. One of Hawthorne's archetypal plots has to do with the attraction and fearful risk of unlicensed experience. His questors, once outside the precincts of the settled and habitual, become "unsettled." Having caught a frightening glimpse of their undisguised selves, they are apt to think or behave sacrilegiously. Now, Dana and Parkman kept their eyes fixed on home base even as they orbited it and hence did not suffer the penalties Hawthorne meted out to his unpardonable sinners. But they had seen enough of the profane to vex their Puritan hearts, and if they were never "weaned from the breast" of rugged Mother Boston, neither were they able thenceforth to nestle comfortably upon it.

Notes

1. See his *The Adventurous Muse: The Poetics of American Fiction, 1789–1900* (New Haven: Yale University Press, 1977). I am much indebted to this innovative book.

2. See Henry Nash Smith, "Emerson's Problem of Vocation—A Note on 'The American Scholar,' " *New England Quarterly*, 20 (1939), 52–67.

3. This theme is most fully developed in Richard Slotkin's *Regeneration Through Violence: The Mythology of the American Frontier* (Middletown, Conn.: Wesleyan University Press, 1973).

4. Including, among others, Charles Eliot and William James. "In New England," observes H. M. Feinstein, "illness had considerable utility. It provided social definition, sanctioned pleasure, prescribed leisure for health, protected from premature responsibility, forced others to care, and ex-

pressed inadmissible feelings while protecting vital personal ties." *Becoming William James* (Ithaca: Cornell University Press, 1984), 205.

5. This note and other references to Dana's life are taken from Robert F. Lucid's introduction to *The Journal of Richard Henry Dana, Jr.*, vol. I (Cambridge, Mass.: Harvard University Press, 1968), xv–xli.

6. Quoted in Spengemann, *The Adventurous Muse*, 58.

7. See Parkman's amateurish but revealing autobiographical novel, *Vassal Morton* (1856).

8. "Parkman's Crack-Up: A Bostonian on the Oregon Trail," *New England Quarterly*, 48 (1975), 84–103.

9. "A Journey into the Human Mind: Motivation in Francis Parkman's *La Salle*," *William and Mary Quarterly*, 3d ser., 19 (1962), 220.

Portrait of a Failure:

The Letters of Henry Adams

Henry Adams is a rare bird in American letters: rich, autonomous, and socially unassailable; descendant of presidents, secure within the genteel Establishment, yet holding himself aloof from it; historian of his country, toward which he felt a proprietary concern; and, by his own reckoning, "a failure in politics and literature, in society and in solitude, in hatred and in love." For many intellectuals, *The Education of Henry Adams* defined their predicament. They relished its irony, learning, and worldly tone, and saw in Adams's gloomy appraisal of his age and its prospects a corroboration of their discontents. Today his catastrophic imagination is tuned to current fears, and he continues to draw strong responses from both admirers and detractors.

The best introduction to Adams is still Ernest Samuels's biography, published in three volumes between 1948 and 1964 and now issued in a one-volume abridgment. "My aim," Samuels writes in the preface, "has been to bring Adams's personality and career into sharper focus than the detailed treatment of the earlier volumes permitted." Nothing has been lost in the retelling, and much has been gained. The life unfolds lucidly and without authorial finger-wagging; the discussions of Adams's writings blend happily with the narrative of his literal and intellectual wanderings. Henry

Originally published as a review of Ernest Samuels, *Henry Adams*, and J. C. Levenson et al., *The Letters of Henry Adams*, vols. I–VI, in the *London Review of Books* (January 25, 1990), 13–14.

Adams, who called biographers assassins and equated biography with strychnine, could not have found a more sympathetic interpreter. The modicum of poison in this wise and artful book has been gently administered.

Samuels is one of a team of scholars headed by J. C. Levenson (himself the author of an innovative study of Adams) who after an arduous stretch have brought out Adams's letters—more than four thousand pages of them—in six impeccably edited and annotated volumes. Besides enriching the stock of informal American literature—for embedded in them are novelistic episodes and passages of power and beauty—the letters constitute a kind of epistolary autobiography that complements Adams's more reticent memoir.

The *Education*, although written in the confessional vein of Augustine and Rousseau, blotted out—Adams was more voyeur than stripper—as much as it revealed about its subject. He described it as a meditation on "the direction, tendency or history of the human mind, not as a religion, but as fact." But it has also been read as a ruse to forestall murderous biographers, a didactic nonfiction novel (the mannequin hero a character bearing the name of its author), an apologia, a covert message to the Happy Few. The letters qualify the self-revelations of the *Education* and fill in its gaps. They don't "tell all"—that wasn't Adams's style—but they do trace the changes in his fortune and disposition, how he came to be "Henry Adams." Some merely record encounters with friends, household business, travel plans, social gossip, and the like. They are sprightly enough but not of much import. A number of others, no less vivacious and salted with malice, are vents for his antipathies: namely, parvenus, political enemies of the Adams family, congressmen, reformers, mongrel breeds, Irish-Americans, and above all Jews, whom he loathed, feared, and half-admired to the point of mania.

To say, as the editors do, that Adams conflated the word "Jew" with "banker" and "gold" scarcely does justice to the intensity of his revulsion. Figuratively speaking, banker Pierpont Morgan was also a "Jew," but one socially within the pale. The international Jewish bankerhood were not; nor were the clever "spiteful" Jews Adams occasionally consulted or patronized. Only grudgingly did he concede to the persevering Bernard Berenson a measured intimacy.

His phobia or "humour" can be diagnosed as an aggravated case of a prejudice shared in varying degrees by other "improvised Europeans" like Henry James, Edith Wharton, George Santayana, T. S. Eliot, and Ezra Pound. His interpreters haven't ignored or condoned his obsession, but neither have they explored its possible bearing on other aspects of his thought and personality. He seems to have looked upon Jews as an unsavory mix of the "oriental" and the "modern," quintessentially commercial, ugly harbingers of an ugly future. He detected their handiwork in every war and panic, and studied them as barometers of social disintegration. Observing the Jews and the Moors in Spain gave him, he quipped, a more liberal view of the Inquisition. The presence of 450,000 Jews in New York City alone, "doing Kosher," proved to him that "God himself owned failure."

Such extravagances were consistent with his adopted pose. The very act of letter writing, he pointed out, tended to exaggerate "all one's mistakes, blunders and carelessness. No one can talk or write letters all the time without the effect of egotism and error." Yet obviously he saw no harm in flourishing his biases before indulgent friends. And indeed, from ebullient youth to sententious old age, his letters were performances of the sort intended to entertain, condole, advise, inform, rebuke, or merely blow off steam, the contents often less noteworthy than their stylish packaging. He appeared to be watching himself as he enacted a series of roles: Conservative Christian Anarchist, éminence grise, Cosmopolite, Licensed Scoffer.

One of them pretty much superseded the others by the mid-stage of his life: that of the bored and languid philosopher-worldling, quick to discern the signs of universal rot. He has learned to laugh at abominations and to measure men and events by their entertainment value. (It says a lot about him that the most frequently recurring words in the letters are variants of "amuse.") Educated by experience and well acquainted with failure and grief, he has lived long enough to be caught up by his own destiny and finds "a summer-like repose" in accepting his fate, "a self-contained, irresponsible, devil-may-care indifference to the future as it looks to younger eyes; a feeling that one's bed is made, and no one can rest on it till it becomes necessary to go to bed forever. . . ." This stoic pose is comically at odds with the histrionic player who overreacted to real and fancied crises and likened himself at the crest of his powers to a "corpse," a "ghost," a stranded "wreck." An apter representation was Saint-Gaudens's caricature of him on a bronze medallion, the domed head in profile attached to the body of a bristling porcupine.

"My dispute, or rather my defense against self-criticism," Adams wrote to Barrett Wendell in 1909, "is that our failures are really not due to ourselves alone. Society has a great share in it." The letters orchestrate this theme of self-exculpation. He comes of age only to discover that politically speaking "the House of Adams" is "buried" and "beyond recovery." History in the guise of Andrew Jackson and U. S. Grant had seen to that. Ancestral traits presaged the family's decline. The Adamses had good reason to think well of themselves (they had "held in succession every position of dignity and power their nation could give"), but they were a stiff lot, resistant to change and ill-equipped to compete with the upstarts who took over the country after the Civil War. His disdain for these black-guards made him no less critical of his forebears, who, given their virtues, weren't "built on the large self-sufficing scale" of the great Virginians. "The New Englander," he decided, "is, and always was, narrow, nervous, and self-distrustful often, always introspective, un-easy, and till lately, intolerant."

Accordingly, he and his friends had been fatally conditioned by their inheritance and culture—by Unitarianism, by Harvard Col-lege, and by the Boston that "cankered our hearts." At twenty, he already felt his youth had been taken away "by force of arms." How sad that he couldn't be "gay and fascinating, and that everyone should think me old and mannered"—but then there wasn't much point in trying to be what one wasn't. Fifteen years on, he was doing his best not to become the most odious of all things, the Bostonian "intellectual prig." After another thirty years, he pinpointed his "vice" as "self-depreciation," his "moral weakness" as "self-con-tempt." And in an often-quoted letter to Henry James, he classified himself *Type-bourgeois-bostonien*, ineradicably respectable by the very nature of things. Lineage and upbringing determined his fail-ure and, so he wanted to believe, extenuated it.

Yet the letters also show that the hapless pawn willed his alien-ation from America, elected to abandon the scholar's lot for Wash-ington glitter and to place worldly success and proximity to power above literary achievement. His "failure," if it can be called such, lay in undervaluing his gifts. John Jay Chapman blamed Adams and his fellow "dilettanti" for admiring America too much and despising her too much: "They could not help bowing the knee to success, though they did so with a sneer upon their lips." The letters bear him out. Adams made much of his so-called anarchism ("As a man of the world, I like confusion, anarchy and war"), but the "man of sense" shied from "the policies of disaffection" and suffered the powerful "imbeciles" who lacked, he said, brains, education, and courage. From start to finish he remained a political and economic conservative. Still, it hardly makes sense to imply that the author of a multi-volume history of Jefferson's and Madison's administrations (a work Chapman pronounced superior to the histories of Macaulay and Trevelyan), and of other memorable books, hadn't fulfilled his promise.

Denied the public role he felt entitled to play (Justice Oliver Wendell Holmes said Adams wanted a diplomatic appointment handed to him on a silver platter), he fashioned a career out of himself and became perforce a literary artist, a philosophical travel writer. "My notion of Travels," he wrote to John Hay, "is a sort of ragbag of everything: scenery, psychology, history, literature, poetry, art; anything, in short, that is worth throwing in; and I want to grill a few literary and political gentlemen with champagne."

That's not such a bad summation of his books and many of his letters. Lighthearted, lyrical, clever, and comparatively unbuttoned, the best display a wonderfully sensitive eye for landscape and topography and a seismographic intelligence. Like Alexander Kinglake and Evelyn Waugh, he resorted to comic hyperbole; like Mark Twain, he dramatized his disenchantments and was a great one for sweeping half-facetious generalization: Greece was a fraud, Poland dreary, Australia a bore, Japan primitive, Java a "disappointment," India "a huge nightmare, with cobras and cows." Everywhere he journeyed *impayable* tourists amused and disgusted him. The American "Cook tourist" he runs into on the Syrian plains

is sometimes a presbyterian, and interested in the facts of Christ's biography, and the evidences of tradition; she—almost always it's a she, three to one—talks about it at table d'hôte. She comes in caravans of twenty, fifty, a hundred, three hundred, at a time, personally conducted, in clouds of dust, in storm and tempest,—crusaders without an object or a faith or an idea—and goes away with a stock of associations, every one of which is grotesque in its want of relation with the things supposed to have been seen.

After his wife's suicide in 1885, unmentioned in the *Education* and only touched upon in his letters, Adams notified his condolers that he was finished, smashed, a washed-up man sated with sorrow and beyond pain: yet his letters from foreign parts don't sound very disconsolate. A large number were addressed to Elizabeth Cameron, the young and beautiful wife of a Pennsylvania senator. He had begun to write to her effusively, almost flirtatiously, in 1886 while traveling in Japan. Several years later he was patently lovesick. The long and detailed letters he sent her—a travel diary, really—amounted to an oblique courtship, the rueful lover striving to divert his mistress, dazzle her by his brilliance. And what he couldn't quite bring himself to declare directly he conveyed transparently in letters to her daughter, Martha. Martha should know that Dobbit, as she called him, felt "very dull and stupid without her." He loved her very much, thought of her all the time, and yearned to play Prince Beast to her Princess Beauty. Some "naughty man" had "stolen my gold sword and silk-stockings and silver knee-buckles," so he couldn't come after her, but if she would come to him, she might help him "to write beautiful history in my big library."

To none of his other correspondents did he expose himself so unabashedly, and never again did he break out of his Prufrockian reserve. Thereafter "Mrs. Cameron" was his trustworthy confidante and he her respectful and solicitous courtier. His bootless infatuation may well have deepened his belief in the spiritual superiority of her sex. The bare-bosomed women he encountered in Japan and Samoa had proved to his great relief that sexuality need not be licentious, as it so often was in disreputable France. In time, he would pay homage to the Virgin, Elizabeth Cameron translated into the vital and all-forgiving gothic mother-goddess.

News of engagements, marriages, and accouchements filled his letters. He even dreamed he was going to have a baby, an amusing revelation, he wrote to Mrs. Cameron, "of my own mind and character," and came to depend on his "coop" of "nieces," genuine and honorary, who coddled him and to whom he dispensed cynical aphorisms on matrimony, husbands, and children:

> We all know that every woman repents marriage, and that they mostly
> wish their husbands and children were dead, or suffering life-sentences
> in the state's-prison for their cruelty to Women with a capital W. Still,

with all this notorious, there is probably some temporary and fitful pleasure, as in alcohol and cream-soda, in the vice of marriage. . . .

Take some fellow of your own age, keen as a rat, selfish as a shark,
restless as a wasp, and put all your sympathy into him, for he needs it,
and in the long run will make it worth your while, even if he doesn't
return it. . . .

Children are an illusion of the senses. They last in their perfection
only a few months, and then, like roses, run to shoots and briars.

Their "Uncle Henry" also took it upon himself to educate them,
but the polishing, it would appear, went no further than taking
them to Europe and supervising excursions to museums and
churches. One would hardly gather from his letters to them—or to
close English friends like Charles Milnes Gaskell, Sir Robert Cun-
cliffe, and Cecil Spring Rice—that the gamut of writers he casually
and aptly quoted or alluded to seriously engaged him. Not one letter
contains an extended passage on a literary work. His test for a storyteller, a "trivial sort of animal," was that he or she be amusing and
superficial. Presumably he demanded more from great poets. In
general, his one-shot judgments sound as if they were tossed-off
bits of persiflage. Thus Dickens's "cockneyism" fretted his "temper
beyond endurance." Kipling was "vulgar." The books of Huysmans
and Mallarmé, and "Verlaine's expiring gnashings of rotten teeth,"
were the "refuse of a literary art which has now nothing left to study
but the subjective reflection of its own decay." Henry James knew
nothing about "Woman," because "he never had a wife." William
Dean Howells always slipped up when he dealt with "gentlemen
and ladies," whereas Adams's friend John Hay demonstrated in his
novel *The Bread-Winners* that he understood not only women but
also "ladies; the rarest of gifts."

On the subject of history, Adams spoke with the force and conviction of a professional who knows his business. Clearly he didn't
consider history writing as one of the lesser exercises of the imagination, but rather as a masculine activity exempt from the charge
of frivolity. History, he reminded his student, Henry Cabot Lodge,
was "the most respectable and respected product of our town." A
career in history might well lead to "social dignity, European reputation, and a foreign mission to close." It paid no such dividends to
Adams, for whom it remained a gentlemanly avocation, but he held

onto his dream of bringing history closer to a "fixed science," and he anticipated the moment when "psychology, physiology and history would join in proving man to have a fixed and necessary development as that of a tree and almost as unconscious."

Adams studied the Germans for method and professed to rank logic and thoroughness higher than knowledge and style, but the injunctions on good writing scattered through the letters belie him. He believed at bottom that history was an art and the historian "little better off than a novelist, with imagination enfeebled by strapping itself to a fact here and there at long intervals." The letters in which he expounded on the craft of writing history, biography, and political articles would make a useful little treatise. Especially revealing are those he wrote to his brother Charles in 1867 when he still thought it possible to influence public discourse. Give the barbarians plain stuff without big or useless words, he urged him: "They will listen to us when we know how to speak." "I abhor from my deepest soul," he wrote, "every attempt to make a thing what it is not; to write for men as if they were children; to varnish a plain story with a shining and slippery polish; to make use of traps in which the readers' attention may be caught, and the idiot may be waxed into ideas. Let those do such work who like it. No man who knows what a true style is, will condescend to use such upholsterer's art." A proper style "should fit the matter so closely that one should never be able to say that the style is above the matter—nor below it." He commanded his protégés to omit, cut, strike out the superfluous, "though the flesh is weak and shrinks from the scissors."

Adams preached his gospel of creative omission long after he had given up on the democracy that had rejected him, his family and his class. The letters once so supple and fresh grow stiffer and more formulaic. As friends drop like "hit birds," his condolences serve as excuses to rehearse his own woes. ("We have always been the victims, never the causes. Disease, Insanity, Vice, Stupidity, have ruined our lives.") Every crisis, convulsion, catastrophe has for him both cosmic and personal implications, whether it be the Dreyfus affair (needless to say which side he was on), the death of Queen Victoria (which aroused bitter recollections of the London years when the Adamses never "received from her or any of her family so much as a sign of recognition"), or the Boer and Russo-Japanese

Wars that to him proved the accuracy of his and brother Brooks's geopolitical calculations. Consulting their Doomsday Book, they prophesied a time not far distant when accelerating technology would outstrip the "thought-power" to control it.

The late letters refer to honors proffered and pleasantly declined ("As I grow older and idiotic, people become civil and complimentary"), but they don't suggest that recognition surprised him. He counseled "silence" volubly and was very social in his "solitude." Twelfth-century music brought him surcease, careering around the French countryside in an automobile lifted his spirits, and his interest in science remained undiminished. By 1910 he had lost any desire to tamper with the fraudulent system that kept him solvent. Best "keep our tempers," he wrote to Brooks, "and try to make the machine run without total collapse in catastrophe, so that it may rot out quietly by its natural degradation." Having survived a stroke which occurred ten days after the *Titanic* went down, and having buried most of his friends, he faced the coming horrors with equanimity. He monitored his business affairs, made "frightful grimaces" in an effort not to think about the war, and increasingly summoned up the past. After the United States joined "the great Community of Atlantic Powers," thus accomplishing "the great object of my life," he was prepared to reconcile himself to a ruined world.

The next-to-last letter he wrote was to Elizabeth Cameron. Cool, affectionate, elegiac, it touched on "this wretched war" that "has swept our literary class out of existence and threatens to carry our whole leisure class after it." But he was already turning his back to the future. Before he died, he read through his diaries and burned them. Had he suspected that his most intimate letters were destined for public exposure, no doubt he would have pressured their recipients to do the same. Fortunately he did not.

Pilgrim's Progress:
George Santayana

George Santayana may at last be emerging from a long period of unsalutary neglect, if these two books turn out to be straws in the critical wind. Santayana has never been without his acolytes, but the beautiful writer who charmed and needled his contemporaries, challenged a whole set of philosophical, religious, and political orthodoxies, and inspired one of Wallace Stevens's noblest poems, "To an Old Philosopher in Rome," is only a name to the general reader. It is to be hoped that the forthcoming MIT edition of his complete works will help to change all that.

Persons and Places, Santayana's three-part autobiography, and the first of MIT's planned nineteen volumes, was originally published in sections—the first in 1944, the last in 1953, one year after his death. Now impeccably edited and embellished by rare photographs, its omitted passages and marginal headings restored, and superbly introduced by Richard Lyon, it appears in the one-volume form in which Santayana intended it be read. And what he left out by design or simply forgot is supplied by John McCormick in the fullest and most informed biography of Santayana to date.

Even with these volumes, though, it's still not easy to grasp the protean author concealed in the luxuriant foliage of his works.

Originally published as a review of George Santayana, *Persons and Places: Fragments of an Autobiography*, and John McCormick, *George Santayana: A Biography*, in the New Republic (May 18, 1987), 28–32.

Those works range across a wide area of genres and categories—poetry, aesthetic treatises, literary criticism, cultural and social commentary, fiction, Platonic dialogues, political disquisitions, autobiography—all marked by a learning, acuteness, vivacity, and stylistic felicity rarely encountered in our jargon-ridden days, and all feeding into the mainstream of a humanist philosophy. Santayana wasn't a system builder. Nor do his pages, in Wallace Stevens's words, "offer themselves for sensational summary."

Still, from his sonnet sequences (1883–1904) through *The Sense of Beauty* (1896), *Interpretations of Poetry and Religion* (1900), *The Life of Reason* (1905–06), and *Skepticism and Animal Faith* (1923), to the culminating four-volume *Realms of Being* (1927–40), Santayana addressed himself to a central issue: the relation between man and the universe. To dissolve old antinomies, he would, as McCormick puts it, "keep together mind and body, and simultaneously marry a theory of the ideal to an unyielding belief in the primacy of matter"—an aim, needless to say, uncongenial to both the transcendentalist and the positivist.

One can only speculate on the connections between Santayana's personal history and his materialistic idealism. Outwardly his life, if initially traumatic, was placid enough. His Spanish mother had married a Bostonian, George Sturgis, while residing in the Philippines. Left with three children after her husband's death in 1857, she removed to the Boston of his family until 1862, when, during a visit to Spain, she married Augustín Ruiz de Santayana. George, born in Avila in 1863, was the only issue of that union. Five years later, his mother returned to Boston with her Sturgis children, leaving George in the care of his gentle and free-thinking father. He lived in Avila for eight years. Then his father took him to Boston, and after a short interval went back to Spain. Santayana's adjustment to his new surroundings; his responses to his half brother and half sisters and to his Sturgis relatives; his years at the Boston Latin School and at Harvard College, from which he graduated in 1886; his trips to Europe, where he reestablished ties with his father and pursued his postgraduate studies in philosophy; his brilliant career in a distinguished Harvard department from 1894 until he left the United States in 1912; and the ensuing forty years in England and on the Continent—all are engagingly recounted in his memoirs, but with significant omissions.

It almost seems as if his candor, the charm of his style, the very volubility of his disclosures, were calculated to mislead investigators of his private history. He wanted his memoirs ("rambling recollections," Lyon aptly calls them) to be read as a mix of "satire and gossip," not as "confessions"; posterity would have to judge him by his other books, by the legitimacy of his sentiments and ideas. And that is precisely the way he is judged in McCormick's fine new biography. The biographer supplements his running elucidations ("ruthless" summaries, he calls them) of Santayana's invitingly quotable books with extracts from unpublished letters, essays, and marginalia that tell of episodes and convey opinions unmentioned or only hinted at in the memoirs. Thus a new and more vulnerable Santayana peers out from behind the suave, ironic autobiographer who achieved his serenity at some emotional cost. No other study of Santayana blends so perceptively the facts of his life with his intellectual divagations.

Santayana described *Persons and Places* as a "retrospective voyage." The metaphor is more than a cliché. He once claimed Hermes as his patron god; it might just as well have been Poseidon, for he was an oceanic traveler in both his literal and his mental migrations. Between 1872, when he was uprooted from his Spanish homeland, and 1912, when he quit the American shore for good, he crossed the Atlantic thirty-eight times. Age, not to mention two world wars, slowed down his comings and goings but did not deter his intellectual forays. Travel fortified his skepticism, kept his mind flexible and open to new ideas, taught him, he said, to "forgive the world everything except the ignorance of thinking its conditions alone possible or alone right." It also corroborated his view of existence as an "endless flux" beyond human control, and prompted an aloofness to events "mechanically produced" and irremediable. "It is better to put up with things," he advised, "than to be responsible for them."

The voyager's strategy was to stay unattached in his "cockleshell," but to make himself comfortable wherever he found anchorage, to respect the mutability of friendship, and to "maintain the dignity of a guest." The wandering "visitor" cherished solitude too deeply to immerse himself in the "inhuman" world, and he died, appropriately enough, at the convent-clinic of the Blue Sisters in

Rome. Nature, he wrote, "framed me for a recluse." Yet the earth, if "a barren, treacherous and intractable waste for mankind," was also "tempting and beautiful and swarming with primitive animals not possible to tame but sometimes good to eat" and "possible to exploit."

Such sentiments come curiously from one who confessed that he had "never been adventurous" and needed quiet in order to feel free, but there was something of the adventurer in his nature. The quiet man relished tales of rascals whose "impudence" and "knowledge of things" appealed to his mocking spirit, and whose indifference to pain and tragedy matched his own.

This isn't to say that he was a covert picaro, a Sinbad the Sailor or a Felix Krull—only that he made the most of his brains and connections, and usually landed on his feet. He was never really poor, despite his frequent references to family "poverty" (at worst it was a genteel deprivation) during his precollege years, but he appreciated the efficacy of money—"the petrol of life," he once called it—without ever wishing to emulate the men who devoted their lives to making it. Young Santayana felt no qualms about sponging off his rich friends. "I don't find poverty at all a burden," he wrote to a college classmate, "but rather a stimulant. Besides I sponge systematically and on principle, not feeling my dignity compromised thereby any more than if I were a monk or a soldier." There is nothing cynical in that declaration; he repaid material debts in a different tender. After he had acquired a comfortable competence, he gave away large sums, often secretly.

All the same, Santayana doesn't seem to have reflected on the sheer amount of intangible privilege and material prosperity that it took to live unencumbered by possessions in clean, well-lighted places high above the muck of the world. He rode on the destructive element like a cork. Even his admirers were sometimes chilled by his avoidance of "human contagion," and by his apparent imperviousness to suffering—a charge he took seriously, and rejected. He wasn't heartless in his personal relations, but neither was he given to brooding over catastrophe. From "a broad cosmic view," he wrote, "destruction is only the shady side of progress. Like natural death it is inevitable; and though we regret it when premature or needlessly painful, there would be as much sentimental folly in disallowing it as in mourning the coming on of night or of autumn."

Such conclusions followed logically from a Lucretian belief in nature's inexorable and impersonal processes. They might also have sprung, McCormick surmises, from a selfish wish to remain uninvolved in sticky social issues. Santayana couldn't ignore political and social upheavals or devastating wars. They saddened as much as they inconvenienced him. But the "genuine skeptic" refused to take sides in the cat-and-dog rivalry of contesting ideas—Communism, fascism, liberalism. Each was "capable of prevailing in the world." He had more positive things to say about his blessed triad—tradition, authority, order—and about the kinds of society most conducive to "organized, harmonious, and consecrated living" and to the unconfined freedom of the mind. Wars, "furious factions," above all anarchy in any form constituted the great threat to "well-ordered polity." Like Ortega y Gasset, he appreciated the fragility of civilization and condemned the presumptions of rabid egalitarians oblivious to the immense and painful efforts it took to create it. Unlike Ortega, however, his passion for order on occasion led him, McCormick notes, "to see 'Order' where other observers saw criminal usurpation and abuse."

For reasons not entirely clear, I suspect even to Santayana himself, he identified the "Jewish spirit" as one of the disorganizing tendencies in modern life. McCormick finds this strain of thinking aberrant, "unworthy," indeed "scarcely comprehensible" in the author of *The Life of Reason* and *Realms of Being*, but he doesn't fudge its implications. It derived in part, he suggests, from Santayana's exposure to the Roman Catholic catechism and to the anti-Semitic attitudes prevalent in the English and American upper classes.

Until the 1930s his guarded aspersions tended to be more flip than rancorous. He had evidently thought a good deal about the Jews and their place in history. He revered Spinoza and approved of austere Talmudic intellectuals absorbed in the affairs of the mind and unsullied by commerce. For their worldly anti-types, the German and American magnates who "tried to masquerade as gentiles," he had only contempt:

> They had no roots in the earth, in the race, in the traditions, or in the religion of their countries. They were surface phenomena, as are actors, professors, critics, journalists. While they remained humble artisans or

solitary thinkers, like Spinoza, they could live content and blameless in the crevices of the Christian edifice; but when they grew mighty, they could only hasten its ruin, and the ruin of their own power over it.

By the 1940s Santayana had come to dote on the scurrilities of Céline, and to express in private letters his annoyance with Jewish upstarts—he charged them with taking over and manipulating the literature, arts, and sciences of their host countries—and with quarrelsome messianic Jewish radicals. McCormick offers evidence (an unpublished "surreal" and self-defensive sketch for a film or a play cryptically entitled "A Preface Which May, or May Not, Be Projected") to suggest that as late as 1950 Santayana was trying to exorcise his bias, but he feels obliged to conclude stiffly that "Santayana's anti-Semitism reveals an astonishing failure of the imagination and either willful disregard of fact or willful ignorance."

At Harvard, where Jews were few and conventional anti-Semitism was the rule, Santayana had shown no overt signs of this antipathy. He, too, had felt incurably foreign and stood out, McCormick happily puts it, as "a ripe mango among Jonathan apples." His Boston ties, however, enabled him to pass into an inner society from which his Jewish and Irish-Catholic classmates and students were barred, and to mask his feelings of marginality by taking part in socially prestigious activities, such as acting in Hasty Pudding shows and contributing to the *Lampoon*. At the same time, he was getting much more out of his courses than he indicated. In trivializing this period as years of "spiritual penury and moral confusion" and deprecating his education in the manner of Henry Adams, he was being unfair to himself and to his college.

The autobiographer of *Persons and Places* depicts the Harvard student and teacher as an exile, or as a kind of Spanish spy. Eventually he challenges the "influential persons" by writing pessimistic verses, by "being indiscernibly a Catholic or an atheist," by attacking Robert Browning, by ducking his administrative duties, by choosing the company of rich, happy-go-lucky undergraduates over that of the "intelligentsia." Played down or omitted are the stages of his intellectual maturation and the unsingularity of his poses and tastes. Others besides himself rebuked the Philistines and swore by Ruskin, Arnold, and Schopenhauer. In short, he was never more "American" than when he capitalized on his exotic origins, sported a cape, and with kindred spirits rejected vulgar materialism, the machine, and the mob.

Thus his decision to give up teaching and strike out for Europe—a move possibly hastened by the retirement of William James, the death of his mother, and the assurance of a modest legacy—wasn't a sudden impulse. It was the long-planned scheme of a would-be expatriate. And it may have been fathered as well by a motive unrecorded in his memoirs. Daniel Cory, Santayana's protégé and secretary, reports his remark that in his Harvard days he must have been an unconscious homosexual, and that others "must have suspected something unusual in his make-up." His awareness of this silent disapproval, he told Cory, was one of the reasons he decided to leave. (McCormick has other explanations for but no doubts about Santayana's more than "unconscious" homosexuality—certainly latent, possibly overt.)

Whatever prompted him to go, America looked at from Europe grew increasingly shadowy for Santayana as fact and loomed larger as idea. He had never known, he later confessed, "the deeper layers and broad currents of American life." His knowledge of the United States during his residence there had been confined mainly to "Harvard College, a part of Boston, an occasional glimpse of New York." Not surprisingly, his account of American society and the American mind was partial and opinionated. Once out of Yankeeland and free to indulge pent-up irritations, he had many pungent things to say about the New England in which, by his own account, he had been so long incarcerated.

The animadversions in *Persons and Places* are satirical, funny, and good-humoredly malicious. Santayana's Catholic sensibility suffocates in the Protestant milieu, as he disdainfully observes a half-formed society "groping after its essence." His Boston is a "moral and intellectual nursery, always busy applying first principles to trifles." He associates it with abandoned spinsters, a feeble and complacent religiosity, and hollow moralizing. Fortunately, a "cultivated inner circle" provides an oasis in the Unitarian Sahara. Its members—a select society "not haunted as yet by the specter of decline, of war, of poverty, of a universal bureaucracy, and of a vulgar intelligentsia"—share his interest in "poetry and art, religion also . . . sport, fashionable society and travel, good wine and good books."

This conservative Europeanized set has managed to retain some of the vitality and simplicity of antebellum Boston and stands in marked contrast to the washed-out scions of the old merchant gentry, who aren't hard or crude enough to survive in the era of big business, who rot before they can ripen, and who strike him as "confused, amateurish, out-of-focus, and violently useless."

The Last Puritan, a fictional meditation on the Boston-Cambridge ambience of Santayana's youth and its "agonized conscience," is his most widely read statement about this group of *fin-de-siècle* Harvardians, civilized and gifted but of no use to the world. McCormick's chapter on Santayana's novel traces its slow exfoliation from the seedbed of memory and experience. Oliver Alden (the name is a composite of Cromwell and the irresolute hero of Longfellow's poem) "peters out," like other members of Santayana's doomed generation, because he can neither capitulate to the prevailing values nor muster enough strength or courage or intelligence to break out of his "spiritual vacuum." His tragedy, as explained by Santayana, lies in the fact that "he was superior to the world, but not up to his own standard"—and that he knew it. A throwback to his Puritan forebears and carrying a heavy load of duty, he lacks, like Melville's Ahab, "the low enjoying power." "Touched with divine consecration," he dies a martyr to his unlivable ideals. Santayana used the occasion of the novel to expound his anti-Puritan brand of regimented hedonism, but he recognized elements of Oliver in himself and confessed admiration, "even envy," for his hero. The Last Puritan is an affectionate brickbat tossed at the country he had been delighted to leave.

Nowhere is his ambivalence more evident than in his various disquisitions on the American "genteel tradition," a term he coined in 1913 (in *Winds of Doctrine*) that was to gain wide currency after the publication of *Character and Opinion in the United States* (1920) and *The Genteel Tradition at Bay* (1931). It referred particularly to an inherited intellectual tradition, literary and religious, totally out of keeping with the realities of American life, and to its priestly preservers. The discrepancy between American ideals and practices is pinpointed in a much-quoted sentence: "The American Will inhabits the skyscraper; the American Intellect inhabits the colonial mansion." Santayana was saying, in effect, that the highbrows were flogging a dead horse. "Old genteel America," handicapped by its "meagerness of soul, thinness of temper and its paucity of talent, and constitutionally unhappy," had nothing in common with the hearty, playful, animal America of jazz bands, football games, and "cheerful funerals." This was the real America he enjoyed and ridiculed, the "trunk" of the nation sundered from its "head," a society fatiguing but less obnoxious to him than its bloodless appendage.

Santayana's condescending comments on the derivative and sapless culture of the gentility, and his contemptuous references to the "intelligentsia" and "professors," anticipated fiercer assaults by others in the years ahead, but they also blurred his not so distant cousinship with the objects of his satire. Admittedly, the now generally forgotten guardians of culture were in most respects his opposites, although not all of them were quite so straitlaced, parochial, conventionally religious, and sexually innocent as he and others made them out to be. It would be hard to imagine any one of them writing the extraordinary letter to a classmate that McCormick quotes, in which the twenty-four-year-old Santayana lists his sexual options (wet dreams, masturbation, pederasty, whores, seductions and mistresses, marriage); or acknowledging the divinity of the "Dionysiac inspiration"; or espousing Santayana's particular strain of philosophical materialism.

But something of their Boston tone can be heard in his dismissal of those ill-educated "specialists" of the Academy who "by sheer effrontery make themselves tyrants in their respective fields," and in his remarks on the young rebels of the Twenties ("too much freedom, too much empty space, too much practice in being spontaneous when there was nothing in them to bubble"), and in his dig at the Lawrences and the Gides, who had "openly and conscientiously written down robbery, murder, adultery, and sodomy among the unalienable rights of man." He stuck to his Tocquevillian conviction: "Culture if profound and noble must remain rare; if common it must become mean."

At first glance, Santayana's critique of America and its culture might be taken as merely another clever and trenchant put-down, similar in spirit to the overviews of European visitors who came to sneer and found America wanting in all the essentials that make life endurable. But the cosmopolite was less unsympathetic and less detached than he appeared to be. His superciliousness was not only self-protective; it also served to conceal the intensity of his off-and-on quarrel with the "place" he held responsible for disinheriting him morally from his Spanish birthright. No indifferent outsider would have sustained the quarrel over such a long period. McCormick thinks that Santayana belongs outside "a predominantly American tradition," and that to place him in it "would violate his thought and work."

I think that America represented for Santayana a part of the truth. He relied on its realities to counteract what he called his "umbilical contemplations," to keep him from floating off to an "imaginary Atlantis." From the very American philosopher William James he acquired, he says, "a sense for the immediate, unexplained, instant fact of experience." In Emerson (the one American writer, with the possible exception of Whitman, he seems to have known really well, and with whom he carried on an extended debate) he found support for his belief that nature could not be apprehended directly, but only through symbols and visible signs.

Had he read with any attention the American writers he belittled or glancingly referred to or failed to mention at all—Hawthorne, Thoreau, Poe, Melville, Henry James, Edith Wharton, to name a few—he might have discovered unsuspected affinities between himself and these literary pilgrims who had gone off on real or imaginary voyages. Since the early nineteenth century, Europe had been a way station for them, a necessary stopping point in their spiritual itineraries—but seldom "home." For Santayana, the case was reversed. "Home," if anywhere, meant Europe; the United States was his catalyst and adversary, but was indispensable to his development. Although "outside" the American tradition, he remained a part of it, no matter how persistently he denied the relationship.

The ideal society for this self-styled "high Tory" had disappeared forever with the early Greeks. He would have been happiest, he said many times, living under a system "essentially idle, aristocratic, and contemplative—in a word, utterly un-American," but he was too sensible of the dynamics of change to hunger for the irrecoverable. Obviously, he could never feel at home in a country whose culture he arbitrarily split into antithetical components, one borrowed and desiccated, the other crude and adolescent. Yet he watched with keen interest the fortunes of a republic still, by his cultural measurements, in its swaddling clothes—not yet fully conscious of its capacities for good and ill but already an economic and political force.

Santayana had rather fixed notions about national character. Americans, as distinguished from their pale intellectual spokesmen, tended to be energetic, good-humored, innocent, generous, and technically competent—traits that boded well for the future of the nation. At the same time, they lacked historical memory, and were glad rather than "ashamed of having always to begin afresh." They wanted to foist their own democratic tradition on older ones and to refashion "all human souls" after their own image. Trusting fondly in a benign destiny, they went about "daily building faith over a sleeping volcano"; committed the preservation of intellectual independence and "moral initiative" to a second-rate body of teachers, clergymen, poets, and artists; and concentrated on the "multiplication of mechanisms."

Luckily, America was "full of mitigations of Americanism." Santayana saw auspicious signs in its institutions, "jumbled and limping" and untransplantable though they were, and took special note of the American spirit of "free individuality" and "free cooperation," by-products of historical circumstance, perhaps, and imperfect and self-serving in their operation, but still safer props for a world order than organized fanaticisms. In the end, he would settle for American dullness rather than suffer through religious and political despotisms. By the close of the Second World War, he was half-persuaded that the United States had the power and techniques to stabilize the international economy. So long as it refrained from interfering with the "peace and liberty" of its neighbors, it might become "the secular arm of Reason in checking unreason" and provide the world with what it most needed: "not a religion with a militant mission," but a government "to serve and keep order, not to dominate where it has no moral roots."

Characteristically, Santayana didn't allow his hopes to overshoot possibility. He had great respect for limits and boundaries, great distrust for utopian thinking in any form. He remained a skeptical spectator rather than an activist, on the grounds that the philosopher's business was not to change the world but to aspire to self-discipline and inner harmony. Edmund Wilson wasn't the first to sense something unpleasant in this detachment, achieved in part, he thought, by Santayana's avoiding "indiscriminate human relationships." Santayana seems too snugly ensconced in the churning universe, his affections too narrowly circumscribed. And yet his lifelong pursuit of the truth and his adherence to unpopular doctrines qualify this imputation. A social and moral purport is latent in everything he wrote. He instructed as he entertained.

Santayana's critics have felt uncomfortable with his ideas, his personality, his literary style. For a philosopher he wrote indecently well, incurring suspicion by the very felicity of his language. Sometimes the manner and tone of his beguiling sentences do seem to vitiate their substance; nor does it extenuate his mean and feline prejudices to say that they could be amusingly couched. Such reservations, however, don't apply to his conservatism, deep and abiding and often offensive to liberal minds, but seriously argued and free of cant. Unlike many of the misnamed "conservatives" of today, ignorant of their ignorance, he was alert to valid arguments in ideas and programs at odds with his own.

He deserves to be read in the same open-minded spirit in which William James read him. There was much in Santayana's attitudes and thought that was uncongenial to James, yet he "literally squealed with delight" at the "imperturbable perfection" with which his younger colleague—and "with so impudently superior an air"— challenged the Harvard consensus. "Truth," Santayana once remarked, "is only believed when someone has invented it well." How his ideas and intuitions will come to be rated by professional philosophers remains to be seen, but the "inventions" of this exact and elegant writer and master of epigram, whether believed or not, assure him a high place in American thought and letters.

· IV ·

Critics
and Writers

I pay tribute in this section to three writers who were important to me for professional and personal reasons.

I read Randolph Bourne for the first time in 1942 while preparing a lecture on the so-called Little Renaissance (1907–1917) when artists and poets and reformers rejoiced in the prospect of their country's cultural coming of age. The generous hopes of these young visionaries evaporated after the USA entered World War I, and Bourne, the most responsible and farseeing of them all, despaired and died. He figured briefly in *Men of Good Hope* and more prominently as a hero-prophet in *Writers on the Left*, and I cherished what Edmund Wilson called Bourne's "moral passion" and "mastery of expression."

Wilson's *Axel's Castle* introduced me to literary modernism. Thereafter I read everything he wrote and usually subscribed to his literary judgments. His life and work almost became my avocation. Unlike most of his writer friends, he had been a reader of American literature since childhood, and we made a game out of mentioning the titles of obscure books we hoped the other hadn't heard of. When he was gathering material for his *Apology to the Iroquois*, I drove him around upstate New York and between stops tried to dredge up his memories of the Thirties. He recalled those times with reluctance, thought the whole subject of writers and Communism a dreary one, and didn't think much of my account of it. Although he thought better of my essay on his Civil War book, he never stopped lecturing me or correcting my mistakes.

When I began to teach at Smith College, Eudora Welty's fiction was sparsely represented in American literature anthologies. Her first collection of stories, *A Curtain of Green*, which I read in the early 1940s and recommended to my students, ushered me into an exotic yet earthy fictional territory previously unmapped in my literary geography. The smoke of the Southern past hung over it. Her small universe, hard and definite and magical, too, reminded me of Hawthorne's antique New England. Its inhabitants were more unmanageable than his and appeared to go about their business without authorial supervision, but she was always invisibly watching them.

The Man of Letters in American Culture

Edmund Wilson was one of the last and most impressive examples of an American literary type which—though it could hardly be said to have flourished in the United States during the last century—had at least managed to plant itself precariously in the national landscape. Wilson's death in 1972 and the death of Lionel Trilling in 1975 marked the end of a literary species, *criticus generalis*, the Arnoldian critic who views culture, in Trilling's words, as "the locus of the meeting of literature with social actions and attitudes and manners."[1] The disappearance of Wilson and Trilling from the cultural scene coincides with the so-called crisis in the Humanities, with what has been described as the increasing remoteness of "humanistic enterprises" from common human concerns, or "the larger events of the world."[2]

Educators have been pointing out the unwillingness of students to undergo the strenuous preparation that the humanities require. They have noted the abrupt swing to the "hard" and "soft" sciences (the problem-solving disciplines), the obsessions with the present (which discourage attention to the legacies of the past), and the polarization of "high" and "popular" culture as the gap widens between specialized academic scholars and the public. It no longer seems possible or desirable to master the technicalities of a subject

Originally published in *The American Future and the Humane Tradition: The Role of the Humanities in Higher Education,* ed. Robert E. Hiedemann (Associated Faculty Press, 1982), 60–76.

and at the same time try to influence the social and aesthetic values of an age.

This unassigned task was once undertaken (how consciously and with what success it is hard to determine) by men like Wilson and by some of his immediate predecessors and contemporaries. They encouraged their readers not to compartmentalize social and political and aesthetic matters, and although they differed markedly in style, manner, and point of view, they were generalists able to acquire assorted learning, predigest it, and present it attractively to a receptive and widening audience hungry for random enlightenment.

ii

The conception of the man of letters as a kind of secular priest, "a spiritualized literary authority responsible for the intellectual and spiritual well-being of a nation,"[3] can be traced back at least as far as the early 1800s. He was expected to act as well as to be, to stand, Lewis Simpson tells us, in his indispensable book, for "the disciplined use of words in writing and speaking," and "to provide moral guidance of society." He was a citizen of a literary republic, a "commonwealth of learning" coeval with the realms of Church and State, where everyone was "sovereign" yet "under the jurisdiction of every other."[4] During the antebellum years, a small number of New England authors and scholars constituted something approximating Coleridge's notion of a "clerisy." This constellation of poets, novelists, historians, essayists, and theologians often disagreed on fundamental issues. A consensus on politics and culture could hardly be expected among a group so diverse as Andrews Norton, George Ticknor, Margaret Fuller, R. H. Dana, Elizabeth Peabody, Theodore Parker, Orestes Brownson, Francis Parkman, Bronson Alcott, Henry Thoreau, J. R. Lowell, Horatio Greenough, Sylvester Judd, Frances Bowen, R. W. Emerson, Nathaniel Hawthorne, *et al.*; but each was a cultural activist, a promulgator of ideas consecrated to the vocation of letters. For a "golden day" they offered themselves as civilizers and moral guides to an educated constituency. They instructed and edified and entertained, screened and domesticated foreign intellectual imports, and did their best to raise the level of popular taste.

All the efforts, however, failed to check an irresistible tendency toward cultural leveling which Tocqueville thought was inevitable in democratic societies. Pre–Civil War America lacked the tradition and the social basis of a unified culture, and the much touted spread of literacy and public education simply reinforced the values of a materialistic and utilitarian-minded society. The reading public in Jacksonian America subsisted largely on a diet of religious and political periodicals and upon books "easily procured" and "quickly read." Clerical watchdogs stood ready to pounce upon works of the unsanctified imagination. Emerson might celebrate the Scholar but his "Man of Letters" was "gravelled in every discourse with common people," and "treated as a trifler" when he went to the attorney's office or the carpenter's shop.[5] His status had not risen appreciably with the grocers and carpenters by the end of the Civil War.

At this point, the men of letters who had come of age on the eve of that war (including such figures as Henry James, Henry Adams, W. D. Howells, E. P. Whipple, T. W. Higginson, J. G. Holland, R. H. Stoddard, E. C. Stedman, H. M. Alden, R. W. Gilder, T. B. Aldrich), found themselves trying to straddle two worlds: the defunct agrarian republic, already showing the effects of technological change several decades before 1860—but still decentralized—and the modern continental nation moving with a harsh grinding of gears toward an organized and integrated state. Some New England writers had long complained about the provincial and anarchic character of the national culture which had no intellectual center and depended upon a handful of isolated men of letters and a scattered reading class. How to harness wasted human energy, how to make the imprecise precise, how to establish aesthetic as well as moral standards were questions that troubled them before 1860. The Civil War, they hoped, would give them a nation at last and secure for their class a cultural hegemony comparable to the political and economic hegemony of the new men of power. Yet they were also the inheritors and transmitters of the traditional values of individualism and freedom that pervaded the localism they decried. Although they welcomed "secular nationalism" as the will of God to advance virtue, intelligence, and power, they cherished many of the values of the old civic culture.[6]

It soon became clear how little their talents and virtue and ideals would be put to use in the redemption of the nation. The materialism they had deplored in the era of Jackson and his successors deepened into something uglier during the Gilded Age. However much they had found to complain about in the prewar society, at least they had been at home in it. Neither they nor the younger generation of scholars and literati felt so secure in postwar America and turned away from its squalor and violence. The vulgarity of the new rich disgusted them as much as the corruption of the spoilsmen; the condition of the industrial working class quickened their fears more than their sympathies; and the streams of immigrants pouring into clotted cities aroused ancestral dread of unassimilable strangers taking over the country. Hence, for the remainder of the century they tended to become retrospective, to glance back nostalgically to an unspoiled and homogeneous America, and to reassert in the very teeth of the realities that appalled them their faith in unchanging moral values, inevitable progress, traditional culture. As editors of magazines for the middle-class readership (the largest and most influential segment of which were women) or as essayists and critics, they could not hope to reach the populace, but they could and did uphold the beacons of Beauty and Idealism and proclaim the standards of "good taste." Even those men of letters who chafed at editorial censorship—James and Howells, for example—were compelled by the facts of American life (and very likely by their own inner reticences) to comply with the going codes.

Writers and scholars differ in their evaluations of the accomplishments of the genteel men of letters and in their conceptions of what they stood for,[7] but the consensus on genteel ideas and practices might be broken down into the following generalizations.

First, although a number of them became figures of note in literary circles and sought and enjoyed the friendship of rich or prominent people, they were without real authority and influence in public life when compared to the leading English men of letters who moved easily between the realms of academic scholarship, government service, and literature.

Second, rather than instructing and correcting their readers in the manner, say, of Dr. Oliver Wendell Holmes's breakfast table Professor, or irradiating them as Emerson could, they catered to public taste and for all their high-minded declarations assented to their customers' cultural preferences. The literary wares they wrote and sold contained nothing indecorous or threatening to middle-class verities.

Third, with a few notable exceptions, they seemed incapable of addressing, much less comprehending, the critical issues of their times (technological innovations, the race question, urban problems, science, the new role of women, trade unionism, etc.) or of mediating the silent conflict, as Ludwig Lewisohn put it, "between the sense of life and civilization of the native Anglo-Saxon people and a divergent sense of life and scale of values brought by the yet inarticulate masses of later immigrants."[8] Rarely did they touch upon or articulate effectively the thought of major segments of the population.

Fourth, the Atlantic Ocean became for them a *cordon sanitaire* or filter preserving American ideals from noxious intellectual and aesthetic contagion. If some of them shared Matthew Arnold's preference for French critical methods and eventually (1898) established their own tepid equivalent of the French Academy,* their real loyalties were to the ancestral culture of England (in all its literary, political, and ethical ramifications) and to the gods of the New England pantheon. They closed ranks against naturalism, against literary experimentalism and social heterodoxy, against any movement or work that might endanger (in Henry Van Dyke's indicative phrase) "the spiritual rootage of art."[9]

Fifth, they formed a clubbable and complacent enclave, fulsomely praised each other's books, exchanged encouraging letters, and filled the middle-class magazines with sketches, appreciations, literary dicta, and autobiographical and biographical chitchat.

The point of view expressed in these assertions has been vigorously challenged by Professor Howard M. Jones. The work of the genteel men of letters, he declares, has "been often more traduced than analyzed" by those "who see the history of the arts from 1865 to 1915 principally as a battle between the emergent and admirable modernity and a senescent and deplorable romanticism." They were not, he concedes, "geniuses" and fell into the sentimentalism they tried to avoid; but by insisting on the importance of technique, style, structure, form, clarity—on the *craft* of writing—and by understanding and "illuminating the technique to increase the reader's

*The Institute of Arts and Letters.

pleasure," they performed a needed service. The most mature and serious of the theorists, like W. C. Brownell, did not regard mere expertise as an end in itself but rather as an essential ingredient for a disciplined idealism.[10]

Not many of them, it is true, matched Charles Eliot Norton in scholarship, broad culture, or diversity of interests. Still, the majority were well-read and capable of turning out readable essays in lucid prose. Modern readers may find the tone of their literary pieces, their conscious and unconscious mannerisms, their genteel slickness less ingratiating than the readers of their own day presumably did, but they were not charlatans. They seem to have had a genuine love of literature, and their essays and reviews are free of the jargon and muddy language not unprevalent today.

Both the criticism and defense of the genteel man of letters and most discussions on the American "Establishment" they allegedly represented (viz., the cultured community, universities, and magazines of the Eastern seaboard) have been vitiated by the habit of lumping them in a single category. Most generalizations blur important distinctions, and the attempt to place figures as diverse as E. P. Whipple, J. R. Lowell, T. W. Higginson, W. D. Howells, J. G. Holland, R. H. Stoddard, E. C. Stedman, H. M. Alden, R. W. Gilder, H. W. Mabie, W. C. Brownell, Brander Matthews, H. T. Peck, and Henry Van Dyke under a single rubric ignores essential distinctions. They differed markedly in age, background, range, literary insight, writing skill, and receptivity. It is not enough, said the *Times Literary Supplement* reviewer of Henry May's *The End of American Innocence* (the most frequently cited book in any discussion of the "custodians of culture"), to list names and stud one's book with "potted" quotations, not enough to generalize when so little specific information is furnished about the actors: "it is usually more interesting to know why men said what they did, than merely the fact of saying it."[11]

The genteel bookmen and critics are unlikely to be restored to popular favor even after we have come to know more about them individually and collectively. We might, however, be able to talk more confidently about their relation to each other and to their younger contemporaries and perhaps be able to answer certain unresolved questions. For example, how did the man of letters after the Civil War come to terms with the fact of his own unimportance—if, indeed, that is how he saw himself? Did he adhere to the dictates of his high mission—to direct, guide, educate even when his writing was offensive or, more likely, irrelevant to the general public? Did he act out his role of tastemaker for his audience—the educated and culture-aspiring portion of the middle class—taking care not to offend but rather to articulate and defend its values? Did he take on this responsibility a bit cynically at times? Did he ever feel guilty about his acquiescence to their preferences and taboos? Did he sometimes express his dissatisfaction by assailing, ridiculing, or shocking his readership?

The clubbableness of the genteel men of letters has been noted and ridiculed. Perhaps a greater understanding of their isolated position might explain why they craved approbation and support from their cozy fraternity. Some of them, like Gilder, Alden, and Brownell, attained power and influence in the literary world and attached themselves to an important and well-to-do segment of the middle class. But they had lost the independence of Emerson's bolder generation; they were less daring and idiosyncratic, more fearful of eccentricity. And even when they did not share the prejudices of their public, they felt obliged to eliminate language and ideas and situations that might offend it. By the 1880s and 1890s, the ideal of the literary vocation seemed more remote than ever from the realities of a commercial civilization.

Yet if these dispensers of cultural nutriment for middle-class consumers closed their ears to "the coarse dialect of the people," they were more attuned to the rhythms of the age than perhaps they themselves realized and to the industrial expertise and machine discipline which seldom if ever engaged their thoughts and whose products they deprecated.[12] The functional uncluttered style of standard post–Civil War prose became the hallmark of the professional writer. It was the prevailing style of the man of letters. His books may not have engaged the sweaty multitudes, but it was not because he wrote in a convoluted way or resorted to an "aristocratic jargon." It was because he directed literary allusions and references to persons and places at cultivated insiders. Perhaps it was the literary man's dependence on this audience that prompted Charles Dudley Warner's misgivings about the role of the cultured man in American society.

Warner, Mark Twain's friend and one-time collaborator, and editor of the *American Men of Letters* series, could understand why the cultured man had distanced himself "from the sympathies of common life." Accustomed to "a refined society" and the beneficiary of books and travel, it was inevitable that "affinities of taste" should separate him from the culturally impoverished. But "by what mediation," Warner asked, "shall the culture that is now in the possession of the few be made to leaven the world and to elevate and sweeten ordinary life?" Unless culture was diffused, "working downward and reconciling antagonisms by commonness of thought and feeling and aim in life," social discord (he was writing in 1873) might end "with mutual misunderstandings and hatred and war."[13] Matthew Arnold had touched on this theme a few years earlier in "Culture and Anarchy." There he referred to the "great men of culture," the "true apostles of equality," with their passion to spread throughout society "the best ideas of their time," and he defined their function as well as anyone ever had: "to divest knowledge of all that was . . . diffuse, abstract, professional, exclusive; to harmonise it, to make it efficient outside the clique of the cultivated and learned, yet still remaining the best knowledge and thought of the time, and a true source, therefore, of sweetness and light."[14] But as W. C. Brownell, one of Arnold's disciples, pointed out years later, the American lettered class was too small, too unmagnetic, too removed from contact with the many to fulfill this lofty mission.[15]

Arnold remained a commanding presence in American intellectual life despite his condescending statements about the irreverence, want of distinction, and careless expression of the English language in the United States. Howells and Mark Twain considered such remarks unbecoming from one so out of touch with American society. Others resented what they felt to be his sarcastic tone or they questioned his religious orthodoxy. But Arnold proved useful both to the genteel men of letters and to those who now began to challenge their cultural authority. The former found many of their own opinions embodied in his persuasive prose—the importance of a natural aristocracy, the untrustworthiness of the masses, the necessity for standards, order, and discipline, the relation between beauty and morality, the obligation to preserve cultural continuity. The latter, even as they disowned some of Arnold's principles and practices, clung to Arnoldian assumptions on the role of the man of letters as critic. That is to say, the critic not only established aesthetic categories and made literary judgments; he also concerned himself with the social and moral dimensions of literature, evaluated the author as well as the work, and observed how cultural contexts might influence, even determine, what and how a writer writes.

iii

Edmund Wilson grew up in an intellectual climate strongly influenced by Arnoldian ideas. Some he accepted; others he qualified or rejected, but Wilson and his generation had more in common with the genteel Victorians than has commonly been supposed and his quarrel with his literary fathers produced a creative tension rather than a violent rupture. He acknowledged this link with his predecessors at a time when many of his literary associates in the radical camp were making fun of William Dean Howells's insipidity and attacking the neo-humanism of Paul Elmer More and Irving Babbitt. Wilson also cheered on the innovators and iconoclasts. But owing, perhaps, to his family background, his Princeton education, and his devotion to literature, he could never yield himself to the romantic release of the Twenties with the abandon of some of his friends. He tinctured his ridicule of the Old Guard's timidity and fear of modernism with an acknowledgment of their slighted virtues.

In 1915, Randolph Bourne, writing in the *New Republic,* had warned against the revival of gentility in a new and deceptive form. The younger writers, having destroyed the gods of their elders, were in danger of succumbing to "the terrible glamor of social patronage," to the uncritical receptiveness of "the liberal audience" that tames as it appreciates. What they needed above all was a "new criticism . . . created to meet not only the work of the new artists but also the uncritical hospitality of current taste"; it would insist on "clearer and sharper outlines of appreciation" by the public and "the attainment of a richer artistry" by the writer. Such criticism had to be "intelligent, pertinent, absolutely contemporaneous" and at once "severe and encouraging." The ideal practitioner Bourne had in mind was the artist "turned critic" whose notions of "literary art" combined "a classical and puritan tradition with the most modern ideas."[16]

A decade later, Edmund Wilson—who like Bourne found the older critics inhospitable to new ideas "and a little spitefully disconsolate" but who also like Bourne admired the "intellectual acuteness and sound moral sense" of the best of them—was preaching Bourne's doctrine. "When we look back on the literary era which preceded the recent renascence," he wrote in 1926, "we are surprised, after all that has been written about its paleness, its tameness and its sterility, to take account of the high standard of excellence to which its best writers attained." He included examples of the "best" (Henry James and Stephen Crane) and "even novelists of the second rank" (Howells and Cable), along with such critics as W. C. Brownell, Irving Babbitt, and Paul Elmer More. Although less "emancipated," they exhibited "certain superiorities over our race of writers today" and "possessed a sounder culture than we; [although] less lively, they were better craftsmen. They were professional men of letters, and they had thoroughly learned their trade."[17]

Wilson's professional career began with the witty yet serious pieces he published in *Vanity Fair* between 1920 and 1923. Three years earlier he had submitted "a burlesque biography of an imaginary man of letters" which delighted the editor, Frank Crowninshield. When Wilson returned from the war, Crowninshield made the young author of this "brilliant satire on the literary memoirs of the 'Nineties' " a managing editor, and for the next few years Wilson was introducing such names as Brieux, Freud, Gertrude Stein, Proust, Eliot, Bergson, and Cocteau to *Vanity Fair* readers. Even at this stage he seems to have awed his admirers by virtue of his literary facility and learning, although they considered him a bit too intellectual and cold.

In retrospect it can be seen that Wilson during his *Vanity Fair* days—and thereafter as a literary editor of the *New Republic* and contributor to the *Dial,* the *Freeman*, and other magazines—was trying in his own way to bridge the gulf between what his older contemporary, Van Wyck Brooks, had called "Highbrow" and "Lowbrow" and he called the "refined" and the "vulgar." His principal concern then was an art "become increasingly private and privileged at the expense of its responsibility."[18] This Arnoldian concern persisted. It derived in part, I think, from something akin to a Puritan sense of stewardship, for although Wilson, no less than the Young Intellectuals, rejected Puritanism in the Menckenian sense of that misunderstood term, his self-appointed role of culture-bearer had a ministerial aura. Wilson bristled when his friends professed to discern a religious strain in his makeup. He always proclaimed himself a staunch anti-Christian and saw no connection between his personal kindness—the willingness with which he encouraged, counseled, and assisted his friends—and religion. Certainly he never condoned their literary faults or puffed a book out of friendship. But he was not so different from the Emerson who embraced letters and scholarship as a vocation. In his own way he was consecrated to his calling of "critic." He refused to flatter or cajole or soothe his readers. Rather, he lectured to them, diverted them, corrected and set them straight, tried to make them intellectually regenerate.

The question of what constitutes an audience for the man of letters and how he regards this audience is always ambiguous. His attitude toward the consumers of his literary wares is conveyed in the tone of his prose, by his vocabulary, by what he takes for granted and by what he feels it necessary to explain. These indicate the degree to which he sympathizes or identifies himself with his readers' values and assumptions. Apparently Howells felt ambivalent toward the class with which he was professionally and socially linked. Lewis Simpson has perceptively spelled out the dilemma of this troubled man, at once a *theoretical socialist* and a *practical aristocrat* whose dream of a republic of letters in a truly equalitarian society was dashed by his awareness that he and his fellow writers had no ties with "all the toilers of the shop and field."[19] Most of Howells's literary associates derived their income and loyalties from the propertied middle class. Their distance from the populace inspired no guilt, only, at times, a sense of foreboding that a widening class rift might end in social violence. Their public—and Howells's—was primarily the informed, aspiring, decent, religious old-stock America not irretrievably mired in materialism.

This was precisely the public from which many of Wilson's literary generation sprang and which they enjoyed shaking up. Like Emerson, they resented the agglutinated Crowd and made no effort to redeem it. (Bourne had recommended that "this younger generation" approach demos "with a certain tentative superciliousness.")[20] But they felt refreshed by its presence, if only because the Crowd seemed closer to life than did respectable society. The genteel men of letters had cringed at both the meretricious and the vital manifestations of the "vulgar," hence the etiolated quality of their writing.

Wilson's literary generation (Paul Rosenfeld, Waldo Frank, Stark

Young, Gilbert Seldes, Allen Tate, Kenneth Burke, R. P. Blackmur, Malcolm Cowley, Burton Rascoe, to name only a few) challenged the ideas and biases of the genteel tradition. Although some of them at times wrote and behaved extravagantly and treated cultural subjects with what would have seemed to their precursors a shocking irreverence, they were committed to literature and the arts and open to technical and intellectual innovation. They neither apologized for their country nor turned to Europe for its imprimatur. E. E. Cummings, Gilbert Seldes, and other appreciators of comic strips, jazz, vaudeville, burlesque, and Charlie Chaplin films welcomed the popular culture rejected or ignored by their stodgy predecessors and wrote their apologies for crudity. Some of them hoped to produce a new breed out of the Highbrow and Lowbrow, more beautiful and vigorous than either. Others explored hitherto neglected strata of their society and posed the energy, wit, and color of popular culture against the killjoy gentility of the Fathers.

Wilson tried to maintain a balance between these two positions. And because he was able to enter into the minds and persuasively articulate the points of view of even those writers and critics he disagreed with, he early established a reputation for being disinterested and resistant to partisanship. He encouraged his friends' excursions into the world of vaudeville, musical comedy, comic strips, and film (his own contributions bear out Gilbert Seldes's opinion that Wilson, had he chosen to do so, might have surpassed all the interpreters of the Seven Arts); but his hope for a national "renascence" in the Twenties rested not only on his confidence in the talents of his own generation but also on the legacy of the rejected one. He could not in good conscience unreservedly condone the assault against the fogies or sentimentalize noisy vulgar America or discover poetry in advertising or wash his hands of American civilization and flee to Paris.

Not that he was a chauvinist (he despised the vogue of literary nationalism current in the late Thirties and in the next two decades). All the same, he took seriously the obligation to do something for American culture, to improve it and bring credit to it. Hence his tributes to those critic-allies and men of letters who first challenged the tastes and edicts of the literary Establishment, cleared away cultural rubbish, and discovered new talent.

For example, there was John Jay Chapman—moralist, literary

critic, poet, political reformer—the patriot who offended professional patriots, the free-souled literary adventurer who discovered and accepted and put to use Old World culture without denigrating his own country's potentialities. To him, "the great writers of the past were neither a pantheon nor a vested interest. He approached them open-mindedly and boldly, very much as he did living persons who he thought might entertain or instruct him." Chapman "hammered out" his style "into an instrument of perfect felicity, limpidity, precision and point" and could take one's breath away "by laying hold of the root of some subject, by thrusting through, with a brusque gesture, all the familiar conventions and pretensions with which it has been enclosed."[21]

Mencken was another. Wilson contrasted the energetic and intelligent polemicist with the "unexceptional editors" of "those feminine magazines" who seemed "invariably to have worn like white shirt fronts impressive-sounding triple names (with a second family name in the middle) that were almost guarantees of mediocrity." Mencken performed a necessary service when he smashed the "false reputations" of the 1890s and early 1900s and introduced in their place the writers of "solid and serious" work. He showed "the positive value of our vulgar or colloquial heritage" and supported "the cause of an American national literature in independence of English literature, and the cause of the contemporary American ideas as against the ideas of the last generation." But Mencken—the man of letters as bruiser—impressed Wilson less than the stylist, the concocter of a kind of journalistic poetry.[22]

With Van Wyck Brooks his relation was deeper and more complicated, for in many respects Brooks seemed to him the exemplary man of letters. Wilson and Brooks had similar backgrounds; both dedicated themselves to literature and disdained the commercial spirit. What Wilson especially esteemed in the older man was his solicitude for his country—never more in evidence than when he was itemizing its cultural liabilities. "You were almost alone," Wilson has F. Scott Fitzgerald say to Brooks in an imaginary dialogue, "when you first began to write, in taking American literature seriously—in appraising it as rigorously as possible, in comparison with other literatures, and in exhorting us to better our achievements." In the same dialogue, Brooks is surely speaking for Wilson when he says of the genteel writers he has been accused of undermining that they "usually followed their art with a very high sense of dignity, so that even their journalism sounds like the work of serious men of letters." Throughout his uneven career, Brooks addressed himself to what Wilson considered a central American problem: how "to adapt European culture to the alien condition of American life and to cultivate from our own peculiar and un-European resources an original culture of our own." Neither in his early phase, when he was defining America's "spiritual poverty," diagnosing the "malady of the ideal," and castigating its victims, nor in his later elegiac phase did Brooks solve that problem or overcome his deficiencies. He was not sufficiently interested in literature as art; he adhered to the tastes of his youth, distrusted modernism, ignored politics, theology, philosophy. But Wilson honored him for upholding "the old enthusiasm for culture along with republican ideals," for being "the first modern literary historian to read through the whole of American belles-lettres" instead of limiting himself "to some special figure or corner."[23]

These reflections—and to them could be added Wilson's judicious appraisals of Poe, Paul Elmer More, James Gibbons Huneker, and others—suggest the conception of the man of letters he aspired to. As objectified by Wilson himself, he need not be a philosophical critic, a refined analyst of unerring judgment, or a polymath, but he ought to have immersed himself in the life of the present as well as past culture and to have tried his hand at poetry, fiction, and drama in addition to criticism. The man of letters read the works he discussed in their original languages and never resorted to translations. He wrote in a jargon-free English, did not reject the designation "journalist," and would have agreed with Eliot's observation that a healthy society requires a sufficient number of minds capable of permeating society with the " 'fresh thought' of which Arnold speaks."

Wilson never equalled Eliot in fineness of perception. His opinions of poems and poets were frequently more idiosyncratic than just, and the religious dimension of human experience escaped him. Yet, Wilson's critics were off the mark when they dismissed Wilson as a mere popularizer. He was, of course, much more than that, although the art of popularization is not a negligible one. Wilson's exposition of books and ideas reflected a rigorous and disciplined intelligence as well as consummate literary skill, and he was readier than Eliot (whose audience in his later years was pretty much confined to a bookish minority) to address minds less refined than his own. He wanted to make literature as liberating for others as it had been for him, "to contribute a little [as he put it] to the general cross-fertilization, to make it possible for our literate public to appreciate and to understand both our Anglo-American culture and those of the European countries in relation to one another."[24]

It was the canonical Eliot rather than the eclectic Wilson who captured the Academy, and today the humanist man of letters has a hard time making himself heard in a world in which science and sociology and the entertainment media preoccupy the kinds of intelligences that once found what they wanted in literature.[25] In his first important critical book, *Axel's Castle,* Wilson refused to accept Paul Valéry's pessimistic prediction about the future of literature. The passage is worth quoting:

> Literature, acording to Valéry, has become "an art which is based on language as a creator of illusions, and not on language as a means of transmitting realities. Everything which makes a language more precise, everything which emphasizes its practical character, all the changes which it undergoes in the interests of a more rapid transmission and an easier diffusion, are contrary to its functions as a poetic instrument." As language becomes more international and more technical, it will become also less capable of supplying the symbols of literature; and then, just as the development of mechanical devices has compelled us to resort to sports in order to exercise our muscles, so literature will survive as a game—as a series of specialized experiments in the domain of "symbolic expression and imaginative values attained through the free combination of the elements of language."[26]

When Wilson was writing *Axel's Castle,* he could not conceive of a literature reduced to "a sort of game with no relation to other intellectual activities."[27] Thirty years later, his vocation of man of letters coming to an end and increasingly disinclined to read (or at least to write about) contemporary fiction and poetry, he turned away from a literary scene that more and more had begun to follow Valéry's scenario and from an America in which he no longer felt at home.

iv

In 1952, Allen Tate outlined the responsibilities of the man of letters at a time when language was debased "by the techniques of mass control." Not only did he have the moral obligation to preserve the vitality and reality of language ("to which the rest of culture is subordinate"); he also had to "discriminate and defend the difference between mass communication, for the control of men, and the knowledge of men which literature offers us for human participation." Tate said: "Communication that is not also communion is incomplete. We *use* communication; we *participate* in communion." His man of letters reflected the general intelligence and remained uncommitted "to the illiberal specializations that over the nineteenth century proliferated into the modern world." More than most he was affected by shattering social and cultural transformations and found it hard to stick to his job—to recreate and apply literary standards, preserve the integrity of language, and restrain the impulse to escape from society. In order "to be more effectively literary," the man of letters had to "be more than literary," to be ready to condemn the "usurpations of democracy that are perpetuated in the name of democracy."[28]

Wilson might not have approved of the sacerdotal tone of his friend Tate, but he could have been the sitter for Tate's man-of-letters portrait. He had a hard time meeting the moral obligations Tate set down, especially during the social and political convulsions he lived through. Usually Wilson assumed an above-the-battle stance during the literary wars and recorded the aesthetic and ideological contentions of the moment disinterestedly and with good humor. His contemporaries admired and respected his intelligence, his learning, his literary skills, and yet saw him at the same time as a somewhat forbidding figure who coldly surveyed their antics even as he participated in them. In many ways (other than political) he remained socially and culturally conservative and held on to certain values and attitudes of his father's generation. He tried and largely succeeded in seriously addressing himself to an audience still puzzled by the literature of modernism if not downright hostile to it. He believed in cultural standards and hierarchies and never expected to see great works of literature (in Tate's words) "consumed by entire populations."[29] He spurned commercialism in every form and guarded his independence. All in all, he was not so far from Emerson, who regarded the vocation of Scholar or Man-Thinking or Man of Letters in a quasireligious sense. The vocation demanded devotion and sacrifice of some sort, not a retreat from society but active participation within it, an imperviousness to worldly blandishments. It placed disinterested curiosity, the Arnoldian ideal, above religious or political absolutes. It enlisted the man of letters in the fight against what Wilson called "the gulf of illiteracy and mean ambitions."

By the end of the Thirties, Wilson had already begun to lose hope in the prospects of a flourishing republic of letters. As writers became politicized, the literary brotherhood and sisterhood he had spoken for and nourished split along ideological lines. Writers were judged by the criteria of political affiliation and party allegiances, not by the intrinsic merits of their books. Relevance of subject in the eyes of the politically committed superseded aesthetic considerations. Writers were asked to choose sides, even to denounce friends, or risk excommunication. Disgusted by this sort of partisanship, Wilson gave up politics. Thereafter and until his death, America gradually became more foreign and alien to him. His old constituency fell away or was fragmented into a series of specialized interpreters. The arts were becoming private, technical, hermetic, and so were the vocabularies contrived to explain them.

The qualities of mind, the discrimination and learning, and the social aims that distinguished the ablest of our professional men of letters are no longer in much demand. The new "academic experts" and "culturati" and the "mass media pundits" are a different breed. The latter (perhaps not all that different from their counterparts of a half-century ago) are a class of transmitters hooked up to the knowledge and communication industries. The first do not address themselves to a general audience but to a restricted and donnish readership of peers, and they employ a technical vocabulary beyond the reach of the uninitiated. They seem to be less concerned with demonstrating the continuities between past and present than in pointing out the discontinuities; they have made themselves the subject of their discourses. Whatever can be said for or against the star performers of much recent criticism, they bear little resemblance to Edmund Wilson—the "introductory critic," as René Wellek calls him: "middleman, the expositor and chronicler of literary events" who educated "several generations of readers."[30]

The passing of Wilson signalizes the gradual disappearance of the journalist-humanist, the type of "second-order," not "second-rate," critical intelligence that, according to Eliot, is responsible "for the rapid circulation of ideas."[31] It coincides with the disintegration of the Republic of Letters in which Wilson served as a kind of minister of culture, if not a pontiff. He flourished at that point in America's coming of age when literary modernism required an explicator and defender, someone who was at the same time steeped in the culture of the audience he was seeking to enlighten. No such audience exists today, no comparable resistance to the new.[32] And one would be hard put now to name a living critic who duplicates Wilson's rigorous and disciplined intelligence, his curiosity, his irascibility and good humor, his critical method (not so much analytical or philosophical as explanatory and judgmental), and his openness to minds less refined than his own.

Like his counterparts before and after him, he might have elected sincerely or cynically to legitimate the tastes of his readership. He might have thumped the "boobs" in the style of Mencken, or sneered at "middle-brows" and addressed himself only to the enlightened few. Instead, he chose to inform and to speak out, to write about what interested him or what he thought to be important, even though it might bore or antagonize readers accustomed to blander fare. No more than Thomas Mann, a writer he did not especially relish, would he have the man of letters living in "pompous isolation." His forays into social action lessened in number, if not in intensity, during the last two decades of his life, but he never forgot, while speaking to the educated reader, "that yawning gulf of illiteracy and mean ambitions"[33] into which his America might sink.

Although Wilson was writing at a time when "values" and "meaning" had not been declared "invalid" or "exploded" and when the biographical or historical slant in literary criticism still commanded a qualified support, the man of letters had even then become a marginal figure in American culture. Neither he nor the other citizens of "that holy society," as Auden called the Republic of Letters, could have affected appreciably the shape of things to come. Yet their presence added immeasurably to the intellectual vitality of the country, and their faith "in the assimilating function of words and letters"[34] at least afforded an alternative to the current institutionalizing and specialization of the arts. The absence of these obsolete generalists impoverishes us all.

Notes

1. Lionel Trilling, "The Moral Tradition," *New Yorker,* 25 (September 1949), 18. Cited in J. H. Raleigh, *Matthew Arnold and American Culture* (Berkeley and Los Angeles: University of California Press, 1961), 243.

2. Sherman Paul, *Edmund Wilson: A Study of Literary Vocation in Our Time* (Urbana: University of Illinois Press, 1965), 34.

3. Lewis P. Simpson, *The Man of Letters in New England and the South* (Baton Rouge: Louisiana State University Press, 1973), 29.

4. Ibid., 25.

5. *The Journals and Miscellaneous Notebooks of Ralph Waldo Emerson,* XII (1976), 51, and XI (1975), 375.

6. See Morton Keller, *Affairs of State: Public Life in Late Nineteenth Century America* (Cambridge: Harvard University Press, 1977), 35, 43.

7. For example: Van Wyck Brooks, *America's Coming-of-Age* (New York: B. W. Huebsch, 1915); *Letters and Leadership* (New York: Huebsch, 1918); *New England: Indian Summer, 1865–1915* (New York: Dutton, 1940); *The Confident Years: 1885–1915* (New York: Dutton, 1952); Thomas Beer, *The Mauve Decade* (New York: Knopf, 1926); Ludwig Lewisohn, *Expression in America* (New York and London: Harper & Bros., 1932); Henry May, *The End of American Innocence* (New York: Knopf, 1959); Warner Berthoff, *The Ferment of Realism: American Literature, 1884–1919* (New York: Free Press, 1965); Gordon Milne, *George William Curtis and the Genteel Tradition* (Bloomington: Indiana University Press, 1956); Kermit Vanderbilt, *Charles Eliot Norton, Apostle of Culture* (Cambridge: Harvard University Press, 1959); Howard M. Jones, *The Age of Energy: Varieties of American Experience, 1865–1915* (New York: Viking, 1971); Larzer Ziff, *The American 1890's* (New York: Viking, 1966); John Tomsich, *A Genteel Endeavor: American Culture and Politics in the Gilded Age* (Stanford: Stanford University Press, 1971); Henry Nash Smith, *Democracy and the Novel: Popular Resistance to Classic American Writers* (New York: Oxford, 1978).

8. *The Story of American Literature* (New York: Modern Library, 1939), 84.

9. E. W. Morse, *The Life and Letters of Hamilton W. Mabie* (New York: Dodd, Mead, 1920), 116.

10. Jones, *The Age of Energy,* 216, 241–242, 233, 221.

11. *Times Literary Supplement* (December 23, 1960), 828.

12. Jones, *The Age of Energy,* 222–223.

13. *The Relation of Literature to Life* (New York: Harper & Bros., 1897), 117–119.

14. Arnold, "Culture and Anarchy," in *The Portable Matthew Arnold,* ed. Lionel Trilling (New York: Viking, 1949), 499.

15. *Democratic Distinction in America* (New York and London: Scribner's, 1927), 23. Quoted in Raleigh, 117.

16. Randolph Bourne, "Traps for the Unwary," in *The Radical Will: Ran-*

dolph Bourne, Selected Writing, 1911–1918, ed. Olaf Hansen (New York: Urizen Books, 1977), 480–484.

17. Edmund Wilson, *The Shores of Light: A Literary Chronicle of the Twenties and Thirties* (New York: Vintage Books, 1961), 245.

18. Paul, *Edmund Wilson,* 34.

19. Simpson, *The Man of Letters,* 103–104.

20. Bourne, *Selected Writing,* 483.

21. Edmund Wilson, *The Triple Thinkers: Twelve Essays on Literary Subjects* (New York: Oxford, 1963), 156.

22. Edmund Wilson, *The Bit Between My Teeth: A Literary Chronicle of 1950–1965* (New York: Farrar, Straus and Giroux, 1965), 30–33.

23. *The Shores of Light,* 144, 152, 412; *The Bit Between My Teeth,* 554.

24. *The Bit Between My Teeth,* 5.

25. John Gross, *The Rise and Fall of the Man of Letters* (New York: Macmillan, 1969), 285–287.

26. Edmund Wilson, *Axel's Castle: A Study in the Imaginative Literature of 1870–1930* (New York: Scribner's, 1969), 284–285.

27. Ibid., 285.

28. Allen Tate, "The Man of Letters in the Modern World," in *Collected Essays* (Denver: Alan Swallow, 1959), 379–393.

29. Ibid., 387.

30. René Wellek, "Edmund Wilson (1885–1972)," *Comparative Literature Studies,* 15 (March 1978), 110.

31. *The Sacred Wood,* quoted in Gross, *The Rise and Fall of the Man of Letters,* 236.

32. See Daniel Bell, *The Cultural Contradictions of Capitalism* (New York: Basic Books, 1976), 3–30.

33. Wilson, "A Preface to Persius," in *The Shores of Light,* 273.

34. Simpson, *The Man of Letters,* 254.

American Prophet:
Randolph Bourne

If the name Randolph Silliman
Bourne is now even faintly recognizable to the general reader, it is
likely to be associated with "the tiny twisted unscared ghost" ele-
gized by Dos Passos in *U.S.A.* Dos Passos had a penchant for martyrs, and his tribute to the radical pacifist who opposed American
entrance into President Wilson's war memorialized both a man and
a legend.

Bourne was born in Bloomfield, New Jersey, in 1886, the same
year as his friend Van Wyck Brooks, and died at thirty-one in the
influenza epidemic of 1918. A severe birth injury which curved his
spine and disfigured his face doubtless determined to a large degree
the formation of his character and disposition. "The deformed
man," he was later to write in "The Handicapped" (1911), "has all
the battles of a stronger man to fight" and none of the advantages
granted to the well-favored. His self-respect is stunted, for he is
never sure whether his difficulties are owing "to his physical disabil-
ity" or "to his weak will and character." Yet there are compensations
for bearing "a crooked back and an unsightly face." Friendships
become more precious. Denied certain "physical satisfactions," he
can "occupy the far richer kingdom of mental effort and artistic

Originally published as a review of Olaf Hanson, ed., *The Radical Will: Randolph Bourne,
Selected Writings, 1911–1918*, in the *New York Review of Books* (November 23, 1978),
36–40. Reprinted with permission from the *New York Review of Books*; copyright 1978 by
Nyrev, Inc.

appreciation." And having undergone the neglect and anguish of the handicapped, he can identify with the "despised and ignored" and "begin to understand the feelings of the horde of the unpresentable and the unemployable, the incompetent and the ugly, the queer and crotchety people who make up so large a proportion of human folk."

After his graduation from high school in 1903, he was forced to go to work instead of attending Princeton, where he had been accepted, and earned his living by playing the piano and taking on joyless jobs for six years until his savings and a scholarship enabled him to enter Columbia College. There his intellectual maturity and literary ability quickly brought him the recognition he craved and the indispensable "friends" (the "persons, causes, and books") that "are chosen for us by some hidden law of sympathy." He had come to Columbia to prepare himself for a career as a "cultivated 'man of letters,' " but finding the English department embalmed in a genteel past, he was converted by such teachers as John Dewey and Charles Beard (as he put it in an autobiographical sketch) "to a fiery zeal for artistic and literary propaganda in the service of radical ideas." While he was still an undergraduate a series of his articles published in the *Atlantic Monthly* (1911–1912) marked him, in Van Wyck Brooks's words, as "the flying wedge of the younger generation."

These high-flying pieces caught the spirit of the "confident years" (roughly the decade preceding America's entrance into the First World War) when, Bourne wrote, "the muddle of a world and a wide outlook" combined "to inspire us to the bravest of radicalism." By "us" he meant his iconoclastic contemporaries then beginning their irreverent examinations of the culture and politics of the period dominated by the pompous conservatism of William Howard Taft and the hollow Bull Moose rhetoric of Teddy Roosevelt. Walter Lippmann spoke for all of them when he announced in 1912: "We have a world bursting with new ideas, new plans, and new hopes. The world was never so young as it is today, so impatient of old and crusty things."

The struggle against the forces of inertia was being carried on in a number of cultural and social fronts by artist-rebels, reformers, and college professors, but it was Bourne's distinction to spell out the special prerogatives and obligations of the so-called younger generation, to present it as "the incarnation of reason pitted against the rigidity of tradition." Youth welcomed experiment; the elderly, devoid of the "scientific attitude," feared it. Old men fell back on the shibboleth of "experience" while youth saw it merely as "a slow accretion of inhibitions." For most people, Bourne thought, "experience" stopped at twenty-five:

> As their youthful ideals come into contact with the harshness of life, the brightest succumb and go to the wall. And the hardy ones that survive contain all that is vital in the future experience of the man—so that the ideas of older men seem often the curious parodies or even burlesques of what must have been the clearer and more potent ideas of their youth. Older people seem often to be resting on their oars, drifting on the spiritual current that youth has set going in life, or "coasting" on the momentum that the strong push of youth has given them.

Hence it behooved "Youth" whose "vision is always the truest" to be not less radical, but more radical—to keep a generation ahead of the times so that its ideas would not be obsolescent when it assumed control of the world. Bourne envisaged a leadership which constantly checked its thinking with the facts of life and retained the "fine precipitate" of youthful spirit—sane, strong, aggressive, flexible, receptive. "To keep one's reactions warm and true is to have found the secret of perpetual youth, and perpetual youth is salvation."

Uncertain of his own role in the clash of generations, Bourne studied sociology for a year after his graduation before his academic life came to an end. He had hoped for a teaching job at Columbia but had to settle in 1913 for a traveling fellowship which gave him an impression-packed tour of a Europe ready to burst apart and a sense of what American civilization had not yet but could become.

Upon his return, Bourne joined the ambitious pragmatists on Herbert Croly's *New Republic* as the specialist on city planning and education. Croly and Bourne were followers of Dewey, and Bourne's pieces on the Gary, Indiana, "work-study-play" schools and his other educational articles bore the Deweyan stamp. He also sketched portraits of American types (sometimes tenderly, more often sardonically) and commented on such topics as sociological fiction, reformers, organized labor, industrial relations, and middle-class radicalism. But soon after the first German successes the magazine began to side with the Allied powers. Bourne, hating any sort of jingoism, appalled by the futility of the killing, found himself increasingly jarred by Croly's editorial line. The inevitable rupture was signaled by Dewey's articles attacking the "moral innocency" and "inexpertness" of his former disciples, who had once, Bourne said, "taken Dewey's philosophy almost as our American religion."

Dewey's support of American intervention on the side of the Allies was a deep disappointment. His dismissal of the antiwar position as "a somewhat murky belief in the existence of disembodied moral forces," painful in itself, also exposed to Bourne the hollowness of that "instrumentalist" philosophy which he had championed as late as 1915—the same "practical instrument" with which the Youth-vanguard was to have solved the problems of the age. Dewey chastised the antiwar party for placing emotion over intelligence and ideas over specific purposes, for nurturing "political motives" rather than creating "social agencies and environments." Bourne countered by charging that Dewey's "instrumental use of intelligence for the realization of conscious social purpose" might work well enough in peacetime but that war invalidated choice or what Dewey called "creative intelligence." Hence, he wrote in "The War and the Intellectuals" (first published in the *Seven Arts*), the *New Republic* intellectuals could neither realize "conscious social purpose" nor control events. If the proper course was to accept the inevitable and try to direct it, as Dewey maintained, then Bourne had the right to choose what seemed inevitable to him, that is, conscientious objection.

As the war hysteria intensified Bourne found fewer outlets for his unpopular notions. The *Seven Arts,* a magazine addressed to "the many unknown who are hidden and pinned down in sordid corners of America," published Bourne's antiwar articles, until it ceased publication altogether in 1917, and he continued to appear in the *Dial* and elsewhere until his death. But when the United States entered the war, Bourne went into seclusion, although there is no evidence that federal agents hounded him and stole his papers or that during his last days he was poor and embittered, as the legend had it.

•

Since his death in 1918 Bourne has been "rediscovered" a number of times and cited on occasion to corroborate political and cultural programs of action he very likely would have repudiated or qualified. A number of books and articles and several collections of his writings appeared in the Sixties[1] which corrected misconceptions and offered a balanced appraisal of his thought. Now Olaf Hansen, a young German scholar and lecturer on American social and literary culture at Frankfurt University, has compiled a new anthology. With a preface by Christopher Lasch and a forty-five-page introduction by Hansen, it is the fullest and most representative collection of Bourne's work in print. The selections are arranged under four categories that pretty well subsume Bourne's life and work: "Youth and Life: In Search of a Radical Metaphor"; "Education and Politics"; "Politics, State and Society"; "Portraits, Criticisms and the Art of Reviewing." Each section is introduced by an extended headnote. Hansen omits some pieces appearing in previous collections but includes twelve hitherto unpublished ones.

Hansen's interest in the literary consciousness of Bourne's generation and American radical thought makes his approach to Bourne somewhat different from that of most of Bourne's other commentators.[2] Marxism, he notes, had only a "negative attraction" for the American radical intelligentsia. Something of Marx's "moral indignation" seeped into their "humanistic social philosophy," but finding his ideas inapplicable to American conditions, they advanced alternatives of their own that were comparable if not equal to his in scope and coherence. Bourne's work, Hansen believes, can be read as one kind of radical alternative to Marx. His cross-section of Bourne's published and unpublished writing holds up for examination not only a mind but an intellectual tradition as well.

The new anthology also suggests why Bourne, like Emerson, was able to attract adherents from opposing intellectual camps and how a generation's culture hero can turn out to be one of its most searching critics. He spoke for the international working-class movement and the abolition of class war through socialism, yet was hypersensitive to all authoritarianism, whether Marxist or bourgeois. "Intellectual radicalism," he wrote in 1916,

> should not mean repeating stale dogmas of Marxism. It should not mean "the study of socialism." It had better mean a restless controversial

criticism of current ideas, and a hammering out of some clear-sighted philosophy that shall be this pillar of fire. The young radical today is not asked to be a martyr, but he is asked to be a thinker, an intellectual leader. So far as the official radicals deprecate such an enterprise they make their movement sterile. Yet how often when attempts are made to group radicals on an intellectual basis does not some orthodox elder of the socialist church arise and solemnly denounce such intellectual snobbishness. Let these young men and women, he will say, go down into the labor unions and socialist locals and learn of the workingmen. Let them touch the great heart of the people. Let them put aside their university knowledge and hear that which is revealed unto babes. Only by humbly working up through the actual labor movement will the young radical learn his job. His intellectualism he must disguise. The epithet "intellectual" must make him turn pale and run.

Suspicious of utopian notions and impressed by Walter Lippmann's *Drift and Mastery,* with its vision of a scientific government run by a managerial elite, Bourne still yearned for an organic social order, a loving community, and the free development of the self. The pragmatist with his ironical cast of thought allied himself with the more fervid insurgents on the *Seven Arts* and wrote confidently about a cultural takeover by the radical Youth Party. Even during his darker moments, as he watched the young intelligentsia "making themselves efficient instruments of the war-technique," he clung to the hope that the "skeptical, malicious, desperate, ironical mood" of a few malcontents "may actually be the sign of more vivid and more stirring life fermenting in America today." Yet he never underestimated the power of constraining social forces or the vulnerability of the young to the silent coercions of institutions.

Bourne constructed no systematic social theory, and despite his wide reading in sociology his interests tended to be literary and aesthetic. Hence, Hansen observes, his "freedom from the restrictions of theoretical order" allowed him to follow his ideas to the point of their negation, to hold in balance dramatic oppositions, and to maintain "the unresolvable paradox of existence." There were no solutions in Bourne's philosophy. "Is" and "ought," the event and the antecedent idea never fused. In his most optative mood, he felt "the dark undercurrent" of forces that worked against individual self-sufficiency and troubled his dream of community.

He set forth the politics of this unrealized society in pronouncements about the condition of the civic arts (architecture and town planning) and literature in the United States. "From the chaos and ugliness of American cities," Bourne wrote, "flows too palpably our economic and human waste." Art signified to him an "aesthetic correlative" for "social hunger." Creative expression occurred only within creative communities, themselves not simply the consequences of social engineering but of a reinterpretation of culture itself. How "legal and economic barriers" might be surmounted and the communal ideal implanted and sustained he did not attempt to explain. Nor could he reconcile his fascination for group art (pageants and masques, choral singing and dancing, the *unanimisme* of Jules Romains, and the like) with his ineradicable distaste for the vulgarities of mass culture.

Many of the essays included in *The Radical Will* contain attacks on the older generation, especially the genteel critics, editors, and academics who dominated the cultural scene with their tepid ethics, moral unction, want of passion, and fear of the new and disturbing. Bourne ascribed their failure to propagate "the best ideas of their time" to their practice of a kind of "applied virtue" which had nothing to say about "caste and race and economic equality." Against their shifty evasions, Bourne pitted, even after his disenchantment, the idealistic and experimental "malcontent" minority.

He is usually treated as the spokesman and prophet for this radical contingent, and so he was; but he was also its wary strategist and supervisor. He took on the responsibility of alerting the young to their self-deceptions and sentimentalities, and he anxiously scanned the shades of the prison house about to close around them. They had less to fear from collisions, he warned, than from invitations to compromise, and a good deal of his writing pinpointed the traps society planted to ensnare them in.

To Bourne, the family epitomized the coercive world. Although not entirely deleterious, for it provided a salutary routine, it inculcated moral opinions of dubious value and suppressed "natural and beautiful tendencies." Education simply continued the inhibitory process initiated by the family, chilling the ardent and preparing robots for a robot society. Thereafter economic pressures could be counted upon to stifle any lingering eccentricity. Conditioned now to the herd's instinctive suspicion of the unusual, the novice slowly withdrew "into an ideal world of phrases and concepts and artificial attitudes." He internalized the dogmas of family and conspired in his own defeat. Bourne completed the sad scenario by elaborating on the sinister inducements to comply and collaborate: opportunities for reputable pleasure-seeking, the "terrible glamor of social patronage," the uncritical receptiveness of "the liberal audience" that tamed as it rewarded.

Undoubtedly these thoughts derived in part from Bourne's relation to his own straitlaced family and the frustrations growing out of his "physical misfortunes." He was a misfit in more ways than one, shut off (he intimates in his letters) from many kinds of human intercourse because of society's dread of aberration. Coming to terms with these "physical misfortunes" enabled him to see his humiliations "in the light of those of other people" and to formulate in his essay "The Life of Irony" the precepts to which he attributed his own survival.

The Ironist (a composite of Montaigne, Arnold and Veblen) opened his mind to all experience and tested ideas in the light of disinterested observation. The most unself-righteous of democrats, he acknowledged kinship with the damned human race, and although he disposed of outworn ideas with forgivable malice and encouraged idiots to hang themselves on their own words, he was no cynic and was never brutal or overbearing. Since the Ironist always saw the other side and shunned the polarities of good and evil, he could be neither optimist nor pessimist. "In his world," Bourne wrote, "there is no privileged caste, no aristocracy of sentiments to be reverenced, or segregated systems of interests to be tabooed."

He opposed to the Ironist, during the war hysteria, the intellectuals who were unable to endure "contradictory situations" or live with incompatible ideas, who retreated to "safer positions" and adjusted to the "old tyrannies." Feeling inferior to men of action and deceived into imagining that they possessed a greater influence than they had—indeed that they controlled events—the intellectuals renounced thought for action and boasted it was they who willed America into war. Bourne likened them to drunken or incapacitated officers on a reeling ship with the crew pouring on the coal. While they tinkered and dreamed, the real rulers—their hands on the ma-

chinery of power—hypnotized "loosely floating 'public opinion.'"
"Our fallacy," he wrote in an unpublished manuscript in 1917,

> in trusting to either labor or capital to save civilized Europe from a
> world-war lay in ignoring the isolated persistence of this third power—
> the military caste, to whom both were merely means to an end, the one
> as food for powder, the other as sinews of war. The *Défaillance* of one
> was no worse than the other. In our disillusionment and chagrin, we
> must recognize that the attitudes of the Socialists and of the Great illu-
> sionists were equally sentimental. While they were educating the peo-
> ple, the Emperors were drilling their soldiers. Proletarians, bankers, sci-
> entists, poets, business men—all the numberless classes that did not
> want war—these had the sentiments. The Emperors had the guns.

But for Bourne, the "cowardly middle-classes" had to bear the
cost of their "faint-hearted negligence" and to learn bitter truths:
"there was no such thing as automatic progress"; the "keynote of
social 'progress' is not evolution but the overlapping of the generations, with their stains and traces of the past . . . the struggle of the
old to conserve, or the new to adapt." Bourne had not expected the
intellectuals to be "martyrs and heroines," but he blamed them for
failing to be "fiercely and concentratedly" intellectual enough, for
not hammering out a "constructive socialist analysis and criticism
of industrial relations."

It is hard to conceive of Bourne or the saving remnant of "malcontents" being able to systematize his visionary brand of pragmatism.
How was the socialized order with its promise of maximum individual freedom to be realized, and by whom? No enlightenment would
come from the "masses," for all their energy and vitality. Once he
had looked to the gifted minority to eliminate society's "terrible
stupidities" and achieve a synthesis of freedom and order. But when
these gentlemen socialists and college teachers and writers suc-
cumbed "to an almost incurable neurosis of herd-fear," Bourne had
to qualify, if not entirely abandon, his expectations for Young
America.

ii

Had Bourne lived, Van Wyck Brooks surmised, he would have
turned increasingly to "the problems of evoking and shaping Ameri-

can literature," but if Brooks meant by this an abandonment of economic and political concerns, he did not reckon sufficiently with the fundamental radicalism of his tougher-minded friend.

Aesthetic considerations, it is true, invariably entered into Bourne's assessments of writers as diverse as Henry James, Dreiser, Mencken, and Upton Sinclair; and he demanded of "fictional sociology" not only that "its sociology be sound and true" but also that its "message" be implicit and unobtrusive. All the same, his reviews, critical pieces, random sketches, satires, and literary maxims betray the social thinker and reformer not primarily concerned with the formalistic problems of the arts. A good critic challenged "the uncritical hospitality of current taste." According to Bourne, Mencken possessed "moral freedom, a passion for ideas . . . vigor and pungency of phrase," but spent so much time attacking that he became a moralist and a bore; criticism ought to "discriminate between what is fresh, sincere, and creative and what is merely stagy and blatantly rebellious." Bourne wanted a "literary art which will combine a classical and puritan tradition with the most modern ideas . . . minds with a touch of the apostolic about them and a certain edge—a little surly but not embittered." He called timidity the reigning fault and regarded the "terrorism of 'good taste' " as more deadly "to the creation of literary art than is sheer barbarism."

Dreiser, the subject of two sympathetic and probing analyses, was a case in point. "For Dreiser," Bourne wrote, "is a true hyphenate, a product of that conglomerate Americanism that springs from other roots than the English tradition." Innocent of the genteel canons, groping and wistful, he was the "very human critic of very common human life" and the recorder of what was pathetic and vacuous yet energetic and appealing about lower-middle-class America. For the sake of his realistic and unprurient treatment of sex, his powerful handling of American themes, his refusal to tack on happy endings and punish the wicked, Bourne tolerated Dreiser's slovenly style, "his lack of nuances, his apathy to the finer shades of beauty, his weakness for the mystical and the vague."

In many ways the most winning and attractive side of Bourne was his openness to cultural differences, his solicitude for the immigrant cut off from his own culture and in danger of being converted by the melting pot process into a faceless philistine. His idea of cultural cosmopolitanism was embodied in the expatriate whose "expansion involves no shameful conflict within him, no surrender of his native attitude." He envisioned a "Trans-National America" which supplied the new immigrant with a national culture while inspiring him to retain the old and current culture (but not the political loyalties) of his ancestral country.

These are only some of the ideas which might have preoccupied him had he survived the 1918 epidemic. It is almost impossible to imagine him a Communist. It is less difficult to think of him as a cultural critic and social commentator planning new strategies for a fallible intelligentsia and constantly reminding them that "vision must outshoot technique."

He died before he could establish himself as a major literary force and left hardly more than a pile of fragments. Yet in them we can find analyses of what we now call the "identity crisis" and of what it means "to grow up absurd" that are more acute than much social commentary we now read. Bourne's prophetic and hortatory tone can become tiresome. He was too ready to educate, announce, denounce. He was far too hopeful about the potential influence of the intellectual in politics. He experienced too much too fast and tried to get it all down without sufficient reflection.

Yet as Hansen brings out in his illuminating introduction, and as the selections in *The Radical Will* demonstrate, this elitist democrat, this socialist who distrusted society, this pessimistic optimist, sensitively registered the cultural and ideological vibrations of his times. He remains perennially interesting and "discoverable": the maverick *clerc* out of tune with his own class and the anonymous public (although never disowning them) and in search of what he called "that imagined audience of perfect comprehenders."

Notes

1. *War and the Intellectuals: Essays by Randolph S. Bourne, 1915–1919,* ed. Carl Resek (New York: Harper Torchbook, 1964); *The World of Randolph Bourne,* Lillian Schlissel (New York: Dutton, 1965); John Adam Moreau, *Randolph Bourne, Legend and Reality* (Public Affairs Press, 1966); Christopher Lasch, *The New Radicalism in America, 1889–1963* (New York: Knopf, 1965), 69–103; Sherman Paul, *Randolph Bourne* (Minneapolis: University of Minnesota Press, 1966).

2. See his *Be·vufstseinformen literarische Intelligenz: Randolph Bourne, Herbert Croly, Max Eastman, V. F. Calverton und Michael Gold* (Stuttgart: J. B. Metzlersche Verlagsbuchlandlung, 1977).

Clytie's Legs:
Eudora Welty

Eudora Welty's fictional territory stretches as far as the Northern states of her native America, and to Europe too, but its heartland is Jackson, Mississippi, and its environs, a country more accessible and neighborly than Faulkner's Yoknapatawpha. The dust and heat are the same, the people comparably rooted and earthy. Yet Faulkner's South, for all of its authentic particularity, is a space larger than life in which a magnified cast of performers carry out fated acts. His stores, workplaces, forests, houses, monuments, jails, and churches are the setting for a sprawling historical spectacle that violently unfolds to the accompaniment of rhetorical music.

Jefferson, Mississippi, is the center, Faulkner once said, of a "cosmos" inhabited by people whom he could move around "like God." Eudora Welty's people live mostly in, or near, small free-floating towns like Morgana, with its water tank and courthouse and its "Confederate soldier on a shaft" that resembles "a chewed-on candle, as if old gnashing teeth had made him." They go their own ways and are not haunted by history. You can find them in a scruffy beauty parlor (scene of "The Petrified Man") where Leota says to her "ten o'clock shampoo-and-set customer: 'Reach in my purse and git me a cigarette without no powder in it if you kin, Mrs. Fletcher,

Originally published as a review of Eudora Welty, *The Optimist's Daughter, One Writer's Beginnings*, and *The Collected Stories of Eudora Welty*, and Peggy Whitman Prenshaw, ed., *Conversations with Eudora Welty*, in the *London Review of Books* (May 2, 1985), 15–16.

honey . . . I don't like no perfumed cigarettes.' " They frequent drug-stores, depots, old ladies' homes, woods, and river bottoms, and congregate at funerals. Some are quiet and withdrawn; some chatter incessantly. They eat Milky Ways and hamburgers, drink Coca-Cola and Memphis whiskey, and bear the names Stella-Rondo, Missouri, Woodrow Spights, Powerhouse, Edna Earle, Wanda Fay, and Mrs. Marblehall—the last a club woman, member of the Daughters of the Confederacy, who will sing on request "O Trees of the Evening"—"in a voice that dizzies other ladies like an organ note, and amuses men like a halloo down the well."

Because Eudora Welty shies away from lofty and portentous themes, her characters are less likely than Faulkner's to be snatched into a metaphysical empyrean. She doesn't, as Henry James would say, "cultivate the high pitch and beat the big drum." What interests her is not so much their existential dilemmas as their physical and moral landscape, the enclosing objects, in which she allows herself virtually to disappear: their domestic lives, conversations, clothes and kitchens, the food they eat, the flowers they grow, the cars they drive. The process by which she invests herself in otherness is something akin to the effect produced by the "mysterious contraption," the stereopticon, in her story "Kin."

In that story, the narrator recalls the Sundays she spent as a child in the house of Uncle Felix, and how she and her uncle, after the heavy midday dinners, would pore over the "picture cities" in the stereopticon slides. As they studied the strollers on checkered pavements, islands in the sea, volcanoes, the Sphinx, these scenes, she says, were "brought forward each time so close that it seemed to me the tracings from the beautiful faces of a strange coin were being laid against my brain." And as she watches Uncle Felix "with his giant size and absorption . . . looking his fill," it appears to her "as though, while he held the stereopticon to his eyes, *we* did not see *him*." Nor do we see her, the individual Eudora Welty, the author with a Jackson habitation and a legal identity. What we see are a series of fictional slides of people and places and occasions, all transmuted from personal experience, and standing—as she says in one of her interviews—"for what your life has meant to you."

The more self-centered and confiding writers become, the less likely we are to know them. Although insistingly, sometimes touchingly, and more often tiresomely *there,* they hide themselves in their own ink. Writers more sparing in their self-revelations, while unable to obliterate the thumbprint of their uniqueness, their special tone and voice, can be tacitly revelatory. Their selfness is buried in the bodies of the worlds they create.

"I do not comprehend all that I am," St. Augustine wrote, and he followed this declaration with the question "Is the mind, therefore, too limited to possess itself?" Eudora Welty conveys self-possession by self-dispersal, not by consciously, or even unconsciously, concocting an instantly recognizable "personality." Rather, she defines and displays herself in the act of seeping into other minds and bodies. This is not a vampirish invasion but a kind of Keatsian entering-into, passive and affectionate, inspired by curiosity, wonder, and love—rarely by hate. She may be likened, at least in this respect, to the Whitman who chronicles the incubating self nurtured by the sensuous world:

> There was a child went forth every day,
> And the first object he looked upon and received
> with wonder or pity or love or dread, that object
> he became.

The "old drunkard staggering home" from a tavern outhouse in Whitman's poem, the schoolmistress and quarrelsome boys, the "barefoot negro boy and girl," the changes he notes in city and country, have their counterparts in the Mississippi depicted in Eudora Welty's recent account of her literary "coming forth."

Made up of three lectures delivered at Harvard in 1983, *One Writer's Beginnings* is a meditation on the making of a secular and earth-bound writer. It includes some facts about herself undivulged in her reported "conversations" over the past four decades, but adheres tenaciously to the dictum "a writer's life belongs to the writer." Biographical information unrelated to her work, and some that is, is none of the public's business. Hence, *One Writer's Beginnings* confines itself to her literary genesis, to the influence of family, school, and travel on a sponge-like consciousness—how she listened and learned to see and finally found "a voice." In these glowing recollections the town and society of Jackson spring back to life like castle dwellers in the fairy tale who, frozen to stone for aeons, resume their activities after the enchanter's spell is broken. The accounts of little girls dressed in taffeta and clutching five-cent coins in "hot white gloves," the trips to the Carnegie Library, the summer expeditions—long voyages, really—in the family car to visit her mother's and father's people in West Virginia and Ohio, furnish "hints, pointers, suggestions" to the future storyteller.

Respectful of solid things, integrated and bolstered by parental supports, she knows her "home," her "Place." She has studied and internalized local space, acquired standards, models, canons of order and discipline from her family and from literature, music, and photography. Thus accoutred, she can reach those points of "confluence" (a powerful word for her) where real and visionary rivers pour into each other. In Emily Dickinson's lexicon, "Circumference" was the line dividing knowable earth from the Eternity of Blank; the transmundane could only be guessed at from cryptic messages of birds, or slants of light and other disturbing visitations. With Eudora Welty, reality and illusion merge without divine condescension or malediction. Dream is palpable, reality ductile to the cherished minorities of her stories, the ones responsive to "the old stab of wonder," quick to catch the signals unheralded by thunderstorms and lightning: a rain-soaked letter, the appearance of a solitary heron, a key falling on a wooden floor, a touch of the wrist.

If the magical moments in Eudora Welty's fiction derive from "the living world," which forms, she says, "the vital component" of her "inner life," they are nonetheless separate and secret. "You must never betray pure joy," the American girl in "The Bride of the Innisfallen" thinks to herself—"the kind you were born and began with—neither by hiding it or by parading it. And still you must tell it." Eudora Welty tells it by communicating the feelings of ecstasy or insight that her adventurous characters experience but can't convey.

The ability to absorb and retain what has been seen and heard, to become many persons without losing hold of the underlying self, is a gift and an art, but perhaps even more a matter of discipline. From her earliest years, Eudora Welty frames and chronologizes, corrects her perspective through books, one of her conduits to the trans-Jackson world. Many of her childhood memories point to the nascent writer. In one, the seven-year-old reader lies on the floor deep in the conglomerate richness of the ten-volume set *Our Wonder World*. In another, she lists the contents of her father's library drawer: a kaleidoscope, a gyroscope, "an assortment of puzzles composed of metal rings and intersecting links and keys chained together." The barometer hanging on the dining room wall of the Welty house also deserves mention, because, thanks to her self-described "strong meteorological sensitivity," storms, floods, high winds, and heat precipitate or complement the action in many of her stories. So does the camera. It taught her to coalesce *One Time, One Place* (the title of the "Snapshot Album" of Mississippi photographs she took during the Depression) without violating the dignity of her subjects, and to reread objectively the history of the faces revealed by the dumb camera's unblinking eye.

But these instruments are primarily aids to register rather than to encompass the ephemeral. Photography, she acknowledges, can train the writer "to click the shutter at the crucial moment." It teaches "that every feeling waits upon its gesture," but the camera is finally only a tool. To reach the hidden dimensions beyond its scope, the writer must fall back on the artifice of words, however unstable their meanings, words ostensibly clear or neutral but twistable into the ambiguous and sinister. In the story "Circe" the enchantress remembers her greeting to Odysseus and his crew: " 'Welcome!' I said—the most dangerous word in the world." Colors seem to have special connotations for her: black, blue, green, red (fairytale colors), and particularly "gold" and "golden," and their equivalents, "corn-colored," "yellow," "honey." These colors resonate with magic and expectation: they are hues of the self, for what the self puts into words is what it has sucked up from the "thick," as she would say, of its background.

The ultimate mystery of a personality or object, however, lies beyond mannerisms of speech or physical identifications like the shape of a nose or the color of eyes or hair. It can never be divined by the word alone, only approximated. The cascade of similes pouring through her pages might be taken as a tacit concession of the impossibility of "making reality real," of impaling it on a phrase, because reality is not contained in a single vision. But, through simile and metaphor, she nonetheless keeps shaving closer to the Thing-in-Itself, a perpetual grasping at the indefinable. "Nothing is." Everything suggests something else. And yet she trusts the veracity of images, luxuriates in the plenitude of analogy.

Her style is the style of a storyteller who wishes "to set a distance" between herself and what she is observing. This feeling may signify

Weltyan reserve as well as a belief in artistic detachment, but it does not lead her to blur her fictive outlines or to prettify unpretty things. She is not at all squeamish about mud, stains, blood, river slime, dirty necks, dandruff, sweat. Her speakers have their own idiosyncratic vernacular, and her prevailing narrative voice, devoid of affectation or strain, is equal to recording varieties of behavior from the refined to the gross. She can evoke the truly vulgar, be unexpectedly shocking. Her exercises in the grotesque may seem less bleak or threatening (and more credible, too) than Nathanael West's or Flannery O'Connor's, but they are blackish enough, downward in their humor, and occasionally brutal. Who can forget Clytie, drowned in a rain barrel, "with her poor ladylike black stockinged legs upended and hung apart like a pair of tongs."

Hawthorne, T. S. Eliot said, had "the firmness, the true coldness, the hard coldness of the genuine artist." Eliot's observation applies equally well to Hawthorne's admirer, Eudora Welty, although others who have noted this similarity scant her differences from Hawthorne in style and temperament. She is not an allegorist, and her settings, even the myth-pervaded Morgana of *The Golden Apples* and the Natchez Trace of *The Robber Bridegroom*, are recognizably Mississippian and have little in common with his self-styled "fairy precincts." His voice and accents sound in the words of his characters; their thoughts are filtered through his own. Her stories buzz with the conversations of individualized persons whose talk seems to have been taken down by some hovering amanuensis.

Both these writers accommodate depravity in their moral systems, distrust the antinomian impulse, are not mystical about mystery. Their fantasies exhale from things. Neither is indulgent toward the "good," or ready to abrogate the laws of consequence. Both are secret observers, Hawthorne often furtive and voyeuristic, Eudora Welty the tactful and sympathizing spy. Both care for what Henry James called the "deeper psychology" in their probes into human relations, their contemplations of blinkered and partial lives. Each spells out the penalties awaiting those who get lost in their private visions.

Relishing the babble of life, Eudora Welty neither loses her "abiding respect for the unknown" nor relaxes her attentiveness to the obsessions and hallucinations of her eccentric or dim-witted or half-mad characters. They are often more alive, possess more "self," than their safe-and-sane detractors and patronizers, although she knows that dreamers risk a loss of self once their orbitings bypass the human community. Uncle Daniel in *The Ponder Heart,* insulated from the actual by his fantasies, drifts off to cuckoo-land. Circe, the unchanging daughter of the gods, is fated to repeat her gyrations, because she is unable to grieve or to feel sympathy.

Pain in Eudora Welty's stories is often, if not necessarily, a catalyst for insight. Her most fully realized characters are likely to be "wanderers," adventurers, who expose themselves, in Hawthorne's phrase, to "fearful risks," and, whether doomed or not, wring a "strange felicity" from their unlicensed excursions. Usually these brief encounters with the elemental are comprehended only dimly if at all by the participants, and they do not emerge from them unscathed or uninstructed. "No Place for You, My Love" is about a man and a woman, strangers to each other, who find themselves stranded in New Orleans on a hot summer evening, ride into the country in a rented car toward some possible intimacy, and joylessly return to their starting points: yet both have felt something momentous and irrecoverable. After spending the afternoon improperly with a Tennessee coffee salesman, Ruby Fisher in "A Piece of News" reads a paragraph in the newspaper he has left behind of another Ruby Fisher who "has had the misfortune to be shot in the leg by her husband this week." Given a sudden glimpse into her secret self, she fantasizes her own death at the hands of her husband in a state of shame and bliss. In "Death of a Travelling Salesman," the feverish salesman in the presence of a "mysterious quiet, cool danger" lacks the "simple words" that would have allowed him "to communicate some strange thing—something which seemed always to have just escaped him." But for Ellen Fairchild in *Delta Wedding,* "one moment told you the great things, one moment was enough for you to know the greatest thing." These radiant events are less "epiphanies" (for Eudora Welty a pretentious term which is without Joycean reverberations) than eruptions of self-awareness.

The climactic moment in *The Optimist's Daughter*—in form, a long story, she says, "even though it undertakes the scope of a novel"—occurs when Laurel McKelva Hand finds her dead mother's breadboard in a kitchen cupboard. A middle-aged war widow, she returns to her Mississippi birthplace in time to watch her recently remarried father die, and to confront Wanda Fay, his obnoxious wife. Toward this young woman (a "ball of fluff," as Helen McNeil calls her in a fine introduction to the novel, but hard as nails) Eudora Welty shows an unexpected hatred. The "scored and grimy" breadboard Laurel rescues as she prepares to leave the "desecrated" family house for good is to Wanda Fay "the last thing anybody needs." To Laurel it is a correlative of her supplanted mother, of her husband, killed in the Pacific war, who lovingly made it, and of the "whole solid past" she has not yet managed to resolve or put behind her. Wanda Fay, that piece of perdurable grit, is the key element in the confluence of events that emancipate Laurel from her daughterly obsessions. "For there is hate as well as love," Laurel reflects, "in the coming together and continuing of our lives."

On numerous occasions Eudora Welty has defined the difference between the autobiographical and the personal. Perhaps *The Optimist's Daughter* is the fullest demonstration of that distinction, for it virtually replicates many of the memories she sets down in *One Writer's Beginnings*. Her father, she tells us, energetically practiced optimism. Her mother, born like Laurel's in the West Virginia mountains, never felt quite at home in the Mississippi flatlands. Doubtless Eudora Welty's biographers will have much to say about these and other similarities, but, as she has declared many times, Becky and Judge McKelva are not Mrs. and Mr. Welty, nor is Laurel—angry and wounded by her father's absurd second marriage, guilty about her mother, and still grieving for her lost husband—modeled on Eudora Welty calm and sure of herself in Jackson. What is autobiographically factual in the novel, then, is of less consequence (a point made by Helen McNeil and by Eudora Welty herself) than "the kernel of privately felt experience out of which the narrative developed." Her characters have expropriated her emotions, and she is dramatizing a literary problem and resolving it. Wanda Fay, all appetite, a scary portent of the future, has no memories and is penned in with her appalling self. Laurel, buoyed by memory, can flow into others; she redeems and is redeemed by it.

"A sheltered life," Eudora Welty remarked, "can be a daring one as well." The word "sheltered" connotes something quite different from "insulated," "isolated," "beleaguered," "secluded." Some writers have found all they required in a circumscribed society without feeling tyrannized by the familiar, but a refusal, as she has said, "to move mentally or spiritually or physically out of the familiar" can signify "spiritual timidity or poverty or decay." An "open mind and receptive heart" make her fictional terrain a Chekhovian rather than a Bloomsbury enclave. She was sheltered, if you will, by family influence inimical to class snobbery or venomous racialism. Her circle of friends and teachers may have been wanting in sophistication, but it was understanding enough to encourage a questing intelligence. The community in which she grew up was sufficiently open-ended and diverse to satisfy a writer not content with the mere paraphernalia of local color. Her real subject is natural violence and fallible people, the fools and cranks and misfits, the shy and the bold, the dreamers and the literal-minded, with whom she sympathetically and humorously identifies.

Apparently nothing was lost on the child exposed to the gossiping of her elders and delighted by the strains of comedy in Jane Austen, Dickens, Edward Lear, Twain, and Ring Lardner. These very different writers must have alerted her to the comic possibilities of her own Mississippi microcosm and colored her benign aspect of the human menagerie. But her affection for the common lot is touched—to paraphrase her out of context—with a grave if seldom belittling irony, and her sympathy for the rebellious, the injured, and the passionate is unsentimental and controlled. Emotion which in softer sensibilities is likely to spill over she restrains in the trammels of form.

Her justly admired story "A Worn Path" could easily have turned maudlin and gone soft; directness, irony, and humor preserve it and keep it taut. Phoenix Jackson is a frail black woman with a faltering memory and eyes "blue with age." She makes a tasking expedition from her place "away back," as she puts it, "off the old Natchez Trace" to the city where she goes to get some "soothing" throat medicine for her grandson who has swallowed lye. She tells the hospital attendant, after momentarily forgetting why she has undertaken the quest:

> My little grandson, he sit up there in the house all wrapped up, waiting by himself. We is the only two left in the world. He suffer and it don't seem to put him back at all. He got a sweet look. He is going to last. He wear a little patch and peep out holding his mouth open like a little bird.

The story is dredged of tearfulness, because Phoenix herself is too indomitable to be pathetic. Undeterred by her filmy sight, she deals cheerfully and resolutely with her trials—thorny bushes, a barbed wire fence, a log, a scarecrow, a dog, a tumble in a ditch, not to mention mirages of her own making. Her gestures are "fierce" and soldierly. Likened by the author to "a festival figure in some parade," she moves "in a little strutting way" and is as much at home in the pinewoods as the "foxes, owls, beetles, jack rabbits, coons and wild animals" she importunes to stay out of her path. There is something of the trickster in her, too, for although she is civil rather than obsequious in coping with white people, she exploits their solicitude and complacency. She is even ready to slide into her apron pocket a shining nickel dropped by a young white hunter, or to extract another five cents from the hospital nurse in order to buy a paper windmill for her waiting grandson. But she accepts this donation "stiffly," and it is her "fixed and ceremonial stiffness" of body and spirit that prevents this story from melting into pathos.

Stephen Dedalus, in one of his aesthetic harangues, describes a process by which the artist's personality "finally refines itself out of existence" through the dissolvent of his imagination. Once this mystery, a purification of life, is accomplished, the artist, Stephen says, is left "like the God of creation . . . within or beyond his handiwork . . . indifferent, paring his fingernails." In contrast to this rather grandiloquent affirmation is Eudora Welty's more modest and human aim: to be "invisible" but not "effaced." She is to be looked for, not in blatant self-advertising confidences, hints, and nudges, but in the metaphorical clues she drops, which are the exposures of a disciplined sensibility. From them we can deduce a history of a life. One might say her writing, spun out like the web of a "noiseless patient spider," is not about but of herself. At bottom, the beauty and astonishment of her fiction, as Emerson might say, is "all design." For it is by design, by her calculated disclosures, that this storyteller makes herself and her writing powerful and free.

History
and Fiction

The articles in this section are more variations on a theme that runs through much of my written work: the companionship of history and literature. My treatment of historical episodes and the players involved has often, and without premeditation, had a literary or extrahistorical dimension, just as a good many of my literary essays and reviews are history-flavored.

This isn't to say that I have conflated history and literature or, for that matter, disagreed with Stendhal's contention that the historian's first qualification is to have no ability to invent. I prefer history pruned of myth and authorial reflection. Although I don't bristle, as some historians do, when authors of historical novels smudge the boundary between fact and fiction and even claim that their fictions are "truer" than the professional historian's facts, I have found most historical novels unsatisfactory both as history and as fiction.

All the same, there are the dazzling exceptions. I believe professional historians impoverish themselves by making fidelity to fact their touchstone in evaluating historical fiction no matter how well or badly it is written. More than a few American writers have been blessed with what Henry James called "historical sympathies and affinities" and Allen Tate "a peculiarly historical consciousness." I take this to mean, among other things, the power to reconstruct and inhabit a place in historical time, to identify with it almost viscerally and extract its essence.

Fictionalizing the Past

"Saucy lictors

Will catch at us like strumpets, and scald rhymers

Ballad's out a' tune. The quick comedians

Extemporally will stage us, and present

Our Alexandrian revels. Antony

Shall be brought drunken forth, and I shall see

Some squeaking Cleopatra boy my greatness

O' th' posture of a whore."

A kind of novel is being written today that may be best described as extrafictional or pseudohistorical. More fiction than fact, it boldly mixes historical events and real personages with invented ones—usually with satirical intention. The historian John Lukacs calls it "novelized history," for want of a better name, but it might just as well be labeled "factitious" or "sham" history, for it is contrived and synthetic. It is not written to instruct or to illuminate or to recreate the American past. It makes little use of myth or legend. History in such novels furnishes props for the fictive decor. The authors employ as principal characters people who were or are history-makers themselves and imagine them as they might have been but were not. History itself may feed the plots, but it is history idiosyncratically conceived as burlesque, parody, hallucination. "Novelized history," whether it denigrates or celebrates, usually trivializes. It is present minded and future oriented rather than backward looking, its account of the past derisive rather than affectionate or forbearing or contemplative. Its purpose is ulterior.

Novelized history is likely to be written during periods of fear and social dislocation when the fictive imagination is susceptible to catastrophe and nightmare. At such times the writer is encouraged to read his own terrors into the cosmos and almost obsessively sniffs

Originally published in *Partisan Review*, 47 (1980), 231–241.

the rot and evil of his times. Not invariably, but often, the writer will present his wasteland in the form of black farce, as Nathanael West did in his lunatic novel of the 1930s Depression, *A Cool Million*—a burlesque on American would-be Hitlers and on the hypocrisy of the American gospel of success. Among West's targets were John D. Rockefeller, who claimed to have run his business according to the Golden Rule, and Calvin Coolidge, author of the imperishable piece of wisdom, "When men are out of work, unemployment results." The special quality of West's brutal and disdainful parody is suggested in a passage from Herman Melville's novel *Pierre,* quoted by West's biographer: "in the hour of unusual affliction, minds of a certain temperament find a strange, hysterical relief in a wild, perverse humorousness, the more alluring from its entire unsuitableness to the occasion." West, however—unlike the writers I am about to discuss—used the historical scene only as a backdrop for his fable. He invented grotesque parodies of unnamed but real people (he had President Coolidge in mind and a well-known fascist demagogue), but although history becomes nightmare in his fiction, he does not write what I have defined as novelized history.

Writers of novelized history are likely to find more popular and lucrative subjects in the "visitable past," to borrow Henry James's term, than in remote times about which most modern readers seem to know or care little. Their books do not have much in common with such historical novels as *The Confessions of Nat Turner* or *Burr,* whose authors take liberties with facts but who manage all the same to evoke the historical shudder. William Styron's story of a slave insurrection seemed all too topical to some readers. It was denounced as a covert defense of racism and triggered an insurrection of its own. Yet Styron's formulation of a shadowy historical personage, however distorted it might seem to his critics, is what he calls it: a "meditation" on history, an exercise of the historical imagination by a novelist contemplating the inner lives of characters rooted in antebellum America. Gore Vidal's *Burr* appears to be a tour de force, more adroit than deep; in fact, it is a considered judgment of a personality and an age by a writer for whom American history is virtually a family affair. It might be said of Styron and Vidal, as H. B. Henderson III wrote of their distinguished predecessors, that for both "History becomes myth, a collection of traditional tales which are timebound yet possess contemporary relevance and emotional force."

The same with considerable reservations applies to Beryl Bainbridge's *Young Adolph,* a ferociously comic account of Hitler's brief sojourn in Liverpool, England, shortly before World War I (an invented episode that brilliantly foreshadows the subsequent career of the clownish and warped hero as well as some of the horrific events associated with his name and times) and to Jerome Charyn's *The Franklin Scare*—"A Novel About the True Life and War-Time of Franklin Delano Roosevelt, Eleanor Roosevelt, J. Edgar Hoover, and a Sailor Named Oliver Beebe."

Charyn's book has the earmarks of novelized history. It is a scandalous story of backstage official Washington in 1944, a kind of scabrous equivalent of William D. Hassett's *Off the Record with F.D.R., 1942–1945,* which Charyn, I suspect, used as one of his sources. It is full of the gossip about the Roosevelts' domestic life and the rivalry of government agencies. It contains allusions to popular songs, baseball players, newspaper columnists, and the like. Yet what might well have become simply another exercise in black comedy and the studiedly perverse turns into an evocative fantasy. The action is hyperbolic, the characters dreamlike, the true and apocryphal blended, but if Charyn distorts and caricatures the traits of his notables, he neither cheapens nor sentimentalizes them.

We see them through the eyes of Seaman Oliver Beebe, a cross between Billy Budd and the Good Soldier Svejk. He is F.D.R.'s barber and surrogate child; Fala's caretaker and companion to Eleanor Roosevelt (a comic yet noble figure as impressive in her way as "The Boss"); he is diner-out with his "Uncle Edgar" Hoover, whom Charyn transforms into a wonderful wizard-like presence, half Caligula, half Robin Hood; he is an object of fascination to Stalin and the Russians and a "Rasputin in seaman's dress" to Churchill and the British. Involved willy-nilly with crazies and whores, Trotskyists and fascists, and a veteran of sexual encounters with his sister, Oliver throughout retains his natural goodness and tact and fidelity and his fondness for Tootsie Rolls without ever discovering how his sexual indiscretions could have brought down the Administration. Charyn relates Oliver's odyssey in an inventive style, simple and declarative, that is appropriate to his hero's bluntness and simplicity. He is witty and funny but never smirks at the reader or hits him over the head.

Candidean books of this sort are often disquieting not merely because they handle sacred cows sacrilegiously but because they give the outrageous a tragicomic dimension and make moral judgments profanely. Hence they are received with more gingerliness and less delight than slick spoofs like E. L. Doctorow's *Ragtime,* which is not at all disturbing. A few grouches here and abroad panned *Ragtime* when it came out, but reviewers all across the critical spectrum scarcely found words enough to express their delight in Doctorow's "viscerally satisfying" achievement, which "read like a streak," "altered one's view of things," and "managed to seize the strands of reality and transform them into a fabulous tale."

Ragtime has already been scrutinized sufficiently to see what ingredients went into its concoction. John Lukacs sums up Doctorow as a highly talented trickster who fails to make history come alive because he has no "subtle feel" for it and lacks the gift of authentic novelists like Edith Wharton or F. Scott Fitzgerald to convey a deep and intense vision of an age through imaginary characters. He writes, says Lukacs, "sheer movie stuff." And perhaps that is the best way to look at *Ragtime* as the episodes unroll under the author's hovering camera eye. Its sets are expensive and accurate. Parts of the film-cum-novel have been shot on location, and the actors really look like the people, famous and anonymous, they are intended to represent. Written in an archly simple prose and salted with sex and violence and zany humor, *Ragtime* is a pastiche of highbrow and popular: a novel of Kleist; biography and autobiography: a game of names (some of them easily spotted, others a little harder) for readers to play; and a star-studded cast of honest-to-God historical figures—financier, industrialist, courtesan, anarchist, explorer, savant, magician, monarch—all mingling higgledy-piggledy and staring out of the pages as if from the brown-tinted rotogravure section of an old newspaper.

Since a good many of Doctorow's appreciative readers have been conditioned to look upon the current American scene as a continuing Johnny Carson show where entertainers, athletes, and professional celebrities sit side by side prominent writers and politicians and scientists, the journalistic license with which he exhibited his luminaries must not have seemed very unusual to them. Today a vast audience is privy to the sex life, medical history, and "agonizing decisions" of presidents and basketball players. Persons of consequence have become the intimates of everybody, yoked in the popular mind by their mutual recency. There is nothing new, of course, in the public's relish for behind-the-scenes behavior of famous and notorious people, but for a long time the source of rumors about them was the gossip column and the gutter press. Then at some point, it may have been shortly after World War II, men and women in the news were subjected (or they accommodated themselves) to a new kind of exposure. Suddenly Ike and Mamie, Jack and Jackie, Lyndon and Lady Bird, Dick and Pat, along with the lesser fry, became characters in a national "All in the Family" TV series. Even before the horrendous Sixties and Seventies, Americans of all ages had learned from the media to regard the eminent as their familiars.

Their curiosity and their appetite for the "low-down" extended beyond the private lives of the famous to the important events the famous ostensibly participated in and affected. The secrecy surrounding American military and diplomatic adventures and certain undiscussed phases of domestic politics—especially those growing out of the Vietnam war and Watergate—encouraged lurid speculation about what was really going on behind closed doors. Unsavory revelations (some of them pretty wild) dug up by investigative teams inspired even wilder fictions. Here was incontestable proof of national rottenness, fresh evidence to buttress the texts of a hundred profane moralists. What could supply more relevant themes for "apocalyptic parody" with its helter-skelter sequences, its jumbling of historical facts, its cartoon characters, and its kaleidoscopic narrative line?

Robert Coover's *The Public Burning* comes directly out of this frenetic ambience. An oversized parody lit up by coruscating verbal fireworks and at moments savagely comic, it has none of the funny-funny humor of genial *Ragtime* or the offbeat comedy of *The Franklin Scare*. Coover is out to get America and scorns Doctorow's calculated palliatives. His countrymen are as "perverse, rapacious, atavistic" as Cooper's half-savage frontier renegades, "civilized in externals but savage at heart" like Melville's John Paul Jones. Whitman's dark diatribe against American corruption in 1871 might serve as a motto for *The Public Burning*: "the dominance of greed, the hell of passion, the decay of faith, the ceaseless need of proph-

ets." Coover's America is all this and more, but although he flour-
ishes the shreds and tatters of his research, his findings corroborate
a predetermined conclusion. He is less historian than social pathol-
ogist.

The novel's action is compressed into three days of June 1953.
Ethel and Julius Rosenberg's ordeal will culminate in a Grand National Lynching Bee, for they have collaborated with the Phantom,
the epitome of everything alien and evil, and relinquished to him
and his minions America's Holy Grail—the Bomb. It is a time of
fearful tensions at home and elsewhere. The nation's troops are
stalled in Freedom's War, and Joseph McCarthy cries treason to receptive ears. In this atmosphere of mass hysteria with the population terrified by threats of nuclear attack, the Rosenbergs are framed
by the Power Structure and condemned to be electrocuted in Times
Square while the world looks on. The traitors who disarmed the
USA and conspired to kill our soldiers in Korea must suffer the
vengeance of a wronged people. After delays and crises, the "burning" takes place.

Vice-President Richard Nixon is Coover's informing intelligence.
The story crazily unfolds in his monologues, and most of the other
leading actors—Eisenhower, the Rosenbergs, Judge Kaufman, Supreme Court justices, politicians, and a supporting cast of thousands—are revealed through his feverish consciousness. Authorial
reflections provide additional commentary on the developing nightmare, as do Coover's dramatic "Intermezzos." The president delivers
a fireside chat on "The War Between the Children of Light and the
Sons of Darkness" and later turns down Ethel Rosenberg's plea for
clemency: the Rosenbergs, in "A Last-Act Sing Sing Opera," refuse
to cooperate with the government and protest against their illegal
and vindictive penalty as the "Chorus" of public opinion assails the
two culprits. At various points the National Poet Laureate, *Time*
magazine personified, delivers his messianic messages based "on
inner vision and imaginary 'sources' " and articulates in racy *Time*-
ese the vision of the Republic.

Presiding over the entire extravaganza is Coover's mighty incarnation of America, Uncle Sam, a composite of Sam Slick and Sut
Lovingood. Uncle Sam is Coover's *deus ex machina*. He harangues
his children with floods of vicious, exuberant, and scatological tall
talk when their spirits sag. Randy, hard, rapacious, bigoted, violent,

revengeful, he is the essence of frontier humorist with a dash of Lyndon Johnson and the Texas of Mailer's *Why We Are in Vietnam.* When he passes into the souls of his chosen political heirs, they absorb his manifest unpleasantness. Only the Phantom, felt but never seen, dares stand up to him, and the struggle between these two titanic powers locked in comic-book contention is not decided until the public burning of the Rosenbergs. Will Nixon become Uncle Sam's anointed son and assume the presidency? Or is Uncle Sam too disgusted with his vacillating and pusillanimous servant who tries to be all things to all men? Only after Nixon is violently and redemptively sodomized by his angry but forgiving paterfamilias is doubt dispelled.

The Public Burning, among other things, is a study in the excremental grotesque and a jaundiced version of the Rosenberg case. It is history as "happening" with real performers drafted to act in a Coover Spectacular. Here is Ike looking like his Norman Rockwell portrait, blue eyes, sandy hair, the face America loves. He has reading problems and troubles with Mamie. He is the uncomplicated yet canny fellow who is only comfortable drinking and playing poker with his cronies and watching cowboy movies. And there is Nixon, lover of cottage cheese and ketchup, a caricature right out of a Herblock cartoon or *Mad* magazine. His eyebrows meet. He is afflicted with afternoon shadow. He is forever sweating and stinking. Yet Coover's Nixon, unlike any of the other characters in the novel, is examined in depth and not always unsympathetically. A sensitive and self-mortifying little man peeps out occasionally from under the hard mask. In his fantasies, he can identify with the Rosenbergs, for he too is an outsider trying to ingratiate himself with his tormentors. But he is also vindictive and cowardly, and his moments of insight about his superiors and inferiors and the shabby trial are followed by explosions of fatuity: dreams of converting America into a continental suburbia, visions of himself as an international hero. Coover, in complete command of Nixoniana and committed to smashing Nixon to smithereens, will finally not concede his humanity even though it is sometimes hard to distinguish Nixon's voice from his own. As for the Jewish couple whose trial bedevils Nixon's inner life as it advances his political fortunes, Coover is hardly the ardent advocate. He sees them as dreary innocents, decent enough and poignant but middlebrow in their tastes and not very smart. Their guilt or innocence is of less consequence to him than the mania of their traducers.

To convey the flavor of the Cold War era, Coover floods his novel with topical allusions both familiar and esoteric and like Doctorow counts on the pleasure his readers may derive from identifying such *Zeitgeist* indicators as Bobo Olsen, Christine Jorgenson, Luke Appling, Clark Kent, Bojangles Robinson, Johnny Mack Brown, Martha Raye, Irving Saypol, James Hagerty, Young Widow Brown, Punjab, David Greenglass, Dick Button, Lionel Stander, Dale Carnegie, and James Montgomery Flagg. He revives hoary political jokes and ramsacks newspapers, literary texts, songs—more than a decade of popular culture—for tags to authenticate his assault against a squalid and haunted society. The Great American Joke, reiterated in Coover's clever parodies of radio entertainment, hangs on variations of the failure of potency. Uncle Sam's humor is crude and brutal, because crudity reminds Americans of the good old days when Columbia was full of piss and vinegar and answered her critics with a sock on the jaw.

A hodgepodge of names and songs and allusions to forgotten incidents may provoke nostalgic recollection, but the denseness and fluidity of the past are not recaptured through necrologies. Coover is a dazzling performer, witty, inventive, intelligent, and his novel is full of powerful moments: the scene, for example, in which a crowd tumbles out of a three-dimensional horror film into an equally phantasmagorical Times Square. I take it that the burning of the Rosenbergs is intended to represent only one fantastic chapter in the fantasy of history, that like the movie crowd we awaken from our private nightmares into the nightmare of history. The idea, if not new, is brilliantly objectified.

Yet for all his dogged research and literary gifts, his fantasy of national convulsion is a waste of talent. Even serious parody cannot be sustained for over five hundred pages. The Rosenberg case plainly told is horrific enough without the garnishing of an obscene pseudohistorical Pageant of America. In *The Public Burning*, the impious entertainer crowds out the moralist. And whereas Coover the moralist sees all the sins of America reflected in the mirror of the media, Coover the entertainer is unable to resist punning and quipping like mad and indulging in the kinds of verbal gymnastics typical of the Luce publications he is ostensibly scourging. He turns into a bore.

The example of Coover prompts the melancholy thought that even angry oppositionists, like the musical purist who finds to his disgust that he's been humming some noxious commercial jingle, are infested by the culture they execrate. What is more, they seek reassurance from it and inadvertently become collaborators. Gore Vidal once wrote that American writers today are power obsessed and that in a society without a "moral, political, and religious center," there is a tremendous temptation "to fill in the void" with one's presence and to achieve a "crude celebrity." To write a merely "excellent" novel, intellectually and aesthetically satisfying, is of no consequence to demos, "indifferent to literature" and reachable only "by phenomena, by superior pornographies, or meretriciously detailed accounts of the way we live now." As an example, Vidal cited Norman Mailer, an honorable artist, who finding his best work ignored by a thick-witted public and "unduly eager for fame," clowned for attention. This judgment, made before *The Armies of the Night* appeared, is even more applicable to a number of Mailer's less remarkable contemporaries who in their quest of a larger readership turn mystagogues and allow their ideas, in T. S. Eliot's disparaging words, "to run wild and pasture in the emotions."

For such writers, history as conceived of in the recent "docudramas" offers a splendid way to attract popular notice. We live at a time when real events are hardly distinguishable from imaginary or "pseudo" ones. Movies and TV films seem not only to provide the scenarios for actual deeds of violence and crime (terrorists hijack a plane carrying among other passengers a troop of beauty queens) but also dictate the behavior of criminal and victim. Plots of everyday dramas reported in the press grow increasingly improbable and melodramatic. A rich Texan is believed to have arranged the execution of his son-in-law, the latter himself suspected of murdering his wife, the Texan's socialite daughter. The case inspires a book arguing the culpability of the father, and he in turn sues the publisher and author. Meanwhile the book has been sold to the films, and when a famous director arrives to observe the trial, accusers and accused respond histrionically to his presence and play their assigned roles like professional actors. It is almost as if the movie scene has become the reality, as if the Texas story or the one about the mother convicted of killing her two children (the subject of two books) or the exploits of the "Son of Sam" are not really graspable until translated into media language.

Philip Roth, the novelist, expressed this idea some years ago in a much quoted passage. The modern writer, Roth said, "has his hands full in trying to understand and then describe, and then make *credible* much of the American reality. It stupefies, it sickens, it infuriates, and finally it is a kind of embarrassment to one's imagination. The actuality is continually outdoing our talents and the culture tosses up figures almost daily that are the envy of any novelist." Perhaps this sense of monstrous quotidian "actuality" accounts for his own sometimes amusing but heavy-handed parody, *Our Gang* (1971), in which President Trick E. Dixon and his White House entourage blather over the abominations they have promoted. Starting with the premises of the Nixon administration, Roth manufactures an extended black joke almost as grotesque as Coover's. His imaginary situations—a massacre of the Boy Scouts, an invasion of Denmark (pornographic center of the world), exposure of plotters—are hardly less fantastic than the stories pouring out of the media to an audience conditioned to regard history, past and present, as lurid entertainment made up largely of plots and conspiracies.

The conspiracy theme has a long history in America. Charges of subversion have been used with good effect against Masons, abolitionists, Catholics, Negroes, Jews, Communists, fascists, and capitalists. It is particularly compelling for temperaments impatient with complexity and receptive to cut-and-dried polarities. In this time of foreign and domestic machinations, the conspiracy obsession gathers strength and quickens imagination. J.F.K. and Martin Luther King were obviously the victims of plotters, and literary sleuths have demonstrated how insiders did in Abe Lincoln. But why stop there? The Garfield business looks pretty fishy ("disappointed office seeker" indeed!), and don't tell us that Leon Czolgosz pulled off the McKinley caper by himself. To American Manichaeans, irrespective of class, the Kingdoms of Light and Dark that President Eisenhower held forth on in Coover's novel have been contending since the Pilgrims landed. The Devil foments mischief in literal or metaphysical hideouts, and Mr. Big, his protean American agent who figures so prominently in crime fiction, orchestrates the shenanigans of the "Interests" and the Mafia and the CIA.

"The situation of our time," W. H. Auden wrote, "surrounds us like a baffling crime," and the resourceful practitioners of novelized history find "private faces in public places" less inviting "than public faces in private places." By converting recent enormities into fiction and capitalizing on the conspiracy motif, these writers stand not only to increase the sale of their wares but also to revenge themselves against a society hungry for personalities and indifferent to all but "relevant" subjects. The demolition of Richard Nixon is one of those subjects, the story of the fall of a tinhorn Cataline from high place that ends not in tragedy, not even in pathos, but in bathos. It evokes no somber reflections. The groundlings pelt the ousted trickster with garbage. "Quick comedians" mock his speech and gestures and convey his heinousness through parody. How seriously the parodists take themselves it is hard to say, since they can either claim or disclaim a moral burden in their spoofs. Do they see themselves as the unacknowledged interpreters of events if not the legislators of mankind? Do they believe that their X-ray vision really does disclose the cancer in the body politic?

It has often been asserted that the serious writer with "tyrannous eye" and sense of felt life is better equipped than historians to explore the "hidden corridors" of history. Unbaffled by the plethora of facts which inhibit the historian who must eliminate to see, he is ostensibly endowed with the power to detect designs and read meanings in the contemporary flux. But what happens to the "antennae of the race" when current reality embarrasses the literary imagination and the balked writer can no longer distinguish the real from the meretricious and the fake, when the fictional historians of our "low dishonest" decades have to compete with unfrocked politicians, ex-White House aides, newspaper reporters, and former undercover personnel—not the most clairvoyant elucidators of the postwar years?

The inventive fantasies of Doctorow, Coover, and company are denser but not intrinsically more interesting than the self-justifying ones of Spiro Agnew, E. Howard Hunt, William Safire, John Dean, and John Erhlichman. Both groups compound the contemporary confusion or grossly simplify it. The Washington-based novels may be nothing more than *romans à clef,* packages of vendible gossip that enable their authors to cash in on their exposures to power in high places. They may have little literary substance. Yet they possess the kind of verisimilitude to be found in some of the popular "docu-dramas" and the film variations on the theme of Watergate into which they are so readily convertible. Novelized histories are less adaptable to the media, but perhaps they have a value other than their literary merits. Treated as artifacts, they might conceivably offer some clues to the historian or novelist of the future seeking to fathom a type of sensibility (circa 1975) for whom American history was camp or junk and pertinent only in so far as it lent itself to farce or traced the course of national degradation.

The Unusable Man:

An Essay on the Mind of Brooks Adams

Brooks Adams has been dead for more than twenty years now, but there are still many people in Boston and Cambridge who remember this eccentric and arrogant man, the last of the children of Charles Francis Adams to survive. His nephews and nieces recall his gruff manner and his penchant for saying shocking things at dinner parties, his love of argument, his endless jaunts to watering spas, his fondness for the Scottish lays he compelled his niece Abigail Adams to memorize. To some people, it seems, he was known as a crank, "that damned fool, Brooks," and Boston never quite accepted the man whom, during the fiery days of '96, it had ostracized as a dangerous incendiary. Even his brother Henry, certainly closer to Brooks than to any other member of his family, saw a mulish streak in the youngest Adams, and continually cautioned him not to kick so violently against the obnoxious aspects of American life they both loathed but to which Henry had become resigned.

Brooks never became resigned to anything, no matter how vehemently he boasted to Henry that he had. He remained the rebel, the unreconstructed individualist, knowing all the time that he was an anachronism, an "unusable man," as his niece put it, preaching to uncomprehending ears. The few times in his life when he did manage to interest a small audience always astonished him, and he

Originally published in *New England Quarterly*, 21 (1948), 3–33.

would sometimes announce with a curious air of triumph to Cabot Lodge or to Henry that he was not a maniac. "I feel I am not mad," he wrote to Lodge in 1894 as if to reassure himself. "I am after all like other men. I am not the victim of an illusion. I am not a man with a maggot in my brain—and all the years when I have been wandering from New York to Jerusalem speculating on the causes which seemed to be crushing the world, I have not been morbid, crazy or ill." This is the cry of the "unusable man," the prophet in the wilderness, and it is only after we have discovered more about this misplaced American that we can understand his despair. It is agonizing to believe that one has a revelation that one's contemporaries are incapable of responding to, and Brooks Adams's eccentricity and neuroticism were aggravated if not actually produced by what he chose to regard as the blockheadedness of his fellow citizens.

Adams took some consolation in the thought that posterity might find some merit in his views and even wrote to Henry in a moment of pride, "I shouldn't wonder if I had quite a reputation after I'm dead," but his recognition has come slowly. It is ironic that Vernon Louis Parrington, whose political philosophy he would have found completely repugnant, should be one of the first to write favorably about him. Parrington's essay was genial but thoroughly misleading, and most of his successors have erred in taking literally Henry's joking reference to his brother as a "Jeffersonian, Jacksonian Bryanian democrat," a judgment which clashes with almost everything Brooks Adams ever wrote. While an immense literature has grown up about Henry, Brooks (if we except the valuable introduction by Charles Beard to *The Law of Civilization and Decay* and R. P. Blackmur's perceptive essay which appeared some years ago in the *Southern Review*) has received only the most cursory treatment and that of a very inferior sort.

That Adams might be a more considerable person than the historians had supposed was made clear in Mr. Blackmur's essay and also in the few pages which Mr. Matthew Josephson devoted to Adams in his book *The President Makers* (1940), where he appears for the first time as a flamboyant and somewhat sinister figure. The quotations Mr. Josephson cites from Adams's letters to Theodore Roosevelt reveal the imperialist and the Darwinian, the snob and the frustrated aristocrat. According to Mr. Josephson, Brooks Adams had become, after a brief flirtation with political reform, the historical theoretician and international strategist for the younger group of statesmen who came into power during McKinley's administration. Adams's speculations on trade routes, international exchanges, and the historical responsibilities of peoples were extremely congenial to men like Roosevelt, Lodge, and Beveridge, and although Mr. Josephson makes far too much of Adams's influence, he is correct in pointing out the similarity between the ideas of Adams and the neo-Hamiltonian expansionists who were cheered by America's reviving nationalism and who sought to substitute the martial values for the spirit-destroying materialism of plutocrat and socialist. Roosevelt and Lodge shared Adams's distaste for what T.R. called "the lawless capitalist" and "the Debsite type of anticapitalist." They too believed in the "Stewardship" principle, in the desirability of a public-spirited but aristocratic elite of skilled administrators representing the nation as a whole and jealous of its honor.

It is rather surprising that Adams's geopolitical speculations have not attracted more attention during the last decade (Harper's recent reissue of *America's Economic Supremacy* seems a little belated), for Adams was one of the first American strategists of *Realpolitik* to be taken seriously by the Germans, and his remarks on America's place in the world and her future course with Russia make less eccentric reading to us than they did to his provincial contemporaries. It seems likely, however, that as his papers become available, he will become less important as an authority on the dynamics of international change and more interesting as a kind of American phenomenon, a complement to his brother Henry whose ideas he helped to shape and who furnished him, in turn, with his only sympathetic audience.

ii

From his birth in 1847 until his death eighty years later, Adams lived a life that was not, on the surface at least, very different from the lives of his older brothers; that is, he was graduated from Harvard College, married well, traveled extensively, and wrote from time to time on public issues. But he seems to have been a chronically dissatisfied man, conducting a one-man mutiny against the world as he found it. He never attained the popular success of his brothers Charles and John Quincy, to whom apparently he never felt particularly drawn, nor could he acquire the disciplined resignation of Henry, who taught himself to stare into the horrid abyss of the future without quivering.

As a young man Brooks hoped for political preferment or at least for some post of power and authority, and persisted in his ambitions for a much longer time than Henry. With the retirement of his father from politics, he lost for a time his last intimate connection with the men guiding American affairs, and it was not until Lodge and Roosevelt came into the ascendant during the Nineties and Henry began to move in the Washington orbit that he once again found access to the inner circle. Out of office himself, he still had the pleasure of knowing and advising men who were in. He enjoyed playing the role of the amateur statesman and offered his ideas and services to properly oriented people in Washington who had the wit to appreciate his expert counsel. It is not too much to say that Adams's pessimism about the future of the country fluctuated with his friends' political successes and failures.

During his early years after his father had returned from his post as minister to England, Adams practiced law, served as private secretary to his father when the latter represented the United States on the Alabama Claims Commission, and married Evelyn Davis, the sister of Mrs. Henry Cabot Lodge. For a short time he flirted with the Mugwump reformers, but he quickly repudiated their ideals as sentimental and unrealistic, and from the Nineties on, he developed his particular brand of romantic conservatism which distinguished his writings from this time until his death.

We cannot be sure what influences or forces changed Adams from a genteel reformer to a hard-headed geopolitician, but this much seems clear. After his marriage he retired from the active practice of law and began to write history. Fortunately for him, he was not obliged to earn his living, for, as he remarked to Henry, he was too original a person to survive in a world that protected a man only if he joined a guild and listened to him only if his ideas were stolen. The reception of his first book, *The Emancipation of Massachusetts* (1887), convinced him that the public was far stupider than he had dreamed possible, and from this time on he played the misunderstood prophet with gusto. Ostensibly the book was a ferocious attack on the Puritan founders of Massachusetts Bay, whom Adams excoriated as monsters, sadists, and hypocrites. So, at least, Boston interpreted the book. But Adams, in letters to Cabot Lodge, Henry Adams, and William James, protested that such was not his intention at all. "What I feel the lack of," he wrote to Lodge, "is appreciation of the unity of cause and effect in the notices I see of my book. It is really not a history of Mass. but a meta-physical and philosophical inquiry as to the actions of the human mind in the progress of civilization; illustrated by the history of a small community isolated and allowed to work itself free." He insisted that he could have done the same for any other similar community: "This is not an attempt to break down the Puritans or to abuse the clergy, but to follow out the action of the human mind as we do of the human body. I believe they and we are subject to the same laws."

Whether or not Adams was justified in censuring his audience or in confiding to Henry that no one seemed bright enough to review him, his explanations to his friends clearly show that already he was thinking along the lines he was to develop most completely in *The Law of Civilization and Decay* (1895). He was attempting to show, as he told William James, "that mind and matter obey the same laws and are therefore probably the same thing." In this same letter he outlined one of his cardinal theories and defended his historical approach:

> My dear sir, the deepest passion of the human mind is fear. Fear of the unseen, the spiritual world, represented by the priest; fear of the tangible world, represented by the soldier. It is the conflict between these forces which has made civilization. And it is the way in which the problem has worked itself out which interests me. . . . If you mean I have given a side, it is very true; I can't conceive what is meant by impartial history, any more than impartial science. There are a set of facts; your business is to state them accurately and then criticise the evidence, and draw a conclusion; and at the same time, if you can, throw in enough interest to sugar-coat the pill. I have tried to show what I believe to be the crucial point of a certain phase of development, and then to show that what is true of this is universally true. . . . I have perhaps erred in making the story too personal, but the temptation to try to interest your audience, I admit, is too strong for me; and I can't resist the desire to make all the men and women as real to other people as they are to me.

The explanation to James is most revealing, for it helps to show what prompted Brooks Adams to apply his theory on a larger scale; it also offers a hint of what he took to be the function of the historian.

The initial result of his first political fiasco was to send him to Europe and to a set of experiences which he later cherished as the most rewarding of his life. Europe, the Near East, and afterward India not only confirmed and expanded the ideas he first propounded in America but opened up the endless vistas of a past which even his mercenary and vulgar contemporaries, he told Henry, could not desecrate. In 1888 he began his introduction to the middle ages, his discovery of the meaning of the Gothic, and what he described to Henry as "the heart of the great imaginative past." At a cathedral in Le Mans, the meaning of the mass and the medieval spirit struck him with a strange intensity, and it was here that he received the impetus to go on to Jerusalem, to Syria, and to see "what it was that made the crusades" and "the remains of the age of faith." In Jerusalem, at Beaufort, at the Krals, and "most of all it may be," he reminisced to his brother, "in that tenderest of human buildings, the cathedral of the Templars at Tortosa, I suppose I had an intenser emotion than I could ever have again."

Out of these experiences came *The Law of Civilization and Decay*, perhaps his greatest book and as much a glorification of the preindustrial age of fear and of the imagination as it was a demonstration of the inexorable movements of the trade routes and money centers. Simultaneously with this sudden and ravishing illumination came the numbing realization of what it all portended. In the past he read the degeneration of the present and glimpsed the chaos toward which he saw his own world rapidly heading. The revelation heightened his nostalgia for an age forever closed, and increased his disgust for the age in which he found himself entrapped. His subsequent writing can be understood only in the light of this dilemma.

Long before his European adventure, Adams indicated that his sympathies lay with the obsolescent standards of a defunct past rather than with the capitalistic ethic of his own America. As early as 1874, he confessed a strong distaste for Benjamin Franklin's doctrines of self-interest. "No man who has elevated ideas of morality," he wrote to Lodge, "is willing to put the duty he is under to keep his word of honour to the account of profit and loss." Franklin's morality was perfectly suited to

> counter jumpers but well I know that George Washington would never have indulged in any such calculation nor yet would have been proud to become the preacher of such small ware if he had. I never said Franklin wasn't useful—so is the constable and so are your account books—but you don't set the constable by the side of your God nor make a bible of your ledger—though many folks have no other.

These assumptions he developed more fully some years later in a remarkable essay on Scott and Dickens in which Adams made out his case for the preindustrial man.

According to Adams, Scott expressed the ideals of the noneconomic man while Dickens spoke for the economic man. Scott's heroes, and we may assume they are Adams's too, are extremely brave, hold honor more precious than life, display the utmost naiveté about money matters, and cling fervently to an ethic which, on the eve of the industrial period, is becoming obsolescent. The soldier-hero, the religious enthusiast, the loyal retainer (creatures of the age of fear) are ennobled by Scott, and the attributes which characterize them, he believes, derive from a decentralized, rural, police-less society. Only the courageous and the physically strong can flourish in this kind of world. But when these conditions disappear, Adams continues, with the rise of the industrial community in the eighteenth century, a new and timid social stratum comes to power (creatures of the age of greed), differing from the preceding one as the organism of the ox from the wolf. Charles Dickens is its chronicler. Where the antique world of Scott had singled out courage as the "essential quality of the ruling class," in Dickens's novels the prevailing trait is a kind of scaredness, the fear of a timid class that has applied craft and guile to the struggle for survival rather than valor. "Accordingly," Adams concludes, "when Dickens wished to personify force he never did so through the soldier, or the swordsman but through the attorney, the detective, or the usurer."

Beginning with *The Law of Civilization and Decay* and continuing in books, articles, and letters, Adams ranged the idealized types from the age of faith against the mercenary and unheroic figures of his own day. He deplored this world of Dickens, a world devoid of statesmanship, of art, of manners, of adventure, even while he traced its inevitability. Hence his attacks against plutocrats, bankers, Jews—collectively subsumed in the word "gold-bug," the quintessence of everything vile and rotten in his generation.

The "gold-bug" for both Brooks and Henry was an epithet and conveyed no exact designation. The gold-bug or Jew or banker (he used the words interchangeably) embodied the spirit of the modern, the genie of money. Essentially they were poetic conceptions personifying the forces of commerce. In his more rational moments, he recognized that "to hate the gold-bug is not the attitude of the historian. The gold-bug sucks because he is a gold-bug, and nature causes him to suck." He also knew perfectly well, as Henry did, that the family income depended on the sovereignty and well-being of the money changers. But history had also persuaded him that the money power had poisoned his world. "I never should have hated Wall Street as I do," he wrote to Henry in 1896, "if I had not just dug the facts out of history, and convinced myself that it is the final result of the corruptest society which ever trod the earth. I tell you Rome was a blessed garden of paradise beside the rotten, unsexed, swindling, lying Jews, represented by J. P. Morgan and the gang who have been manipulating our country for the last four years." This is a romantic statement and typical of the naive oversimplifications to which so-called realists are often susceptible. That a money power existed, that it exerted an influence dangerous to a democratic people, was certainly true, and many thousands of Adams's contemporaries agreed with this view, but Brooks, and Henry too, attributed to international finance an almost occult energy and pervasiveness which hardly differed from the fantasies of the primitive populists they ridiculed.

Brooks Adams's mightiest effort to overcome the legions of gold came in 1896, when he lent some tangible and much moral support to the Democrats. He had spent the last year in India studying reverently, almost ecstatically, the vestiges of a warlike, poetic, and imaginative culture. Modern India, with its crumbling shrines, its commercialized temples, its vulgar, arrogant officialdom, epitomized for him the deteriorating effects of the money economy on human institutions, and he returned to Quincy full of resolves to strike at gold if the opportunity arose.

The campaign of 1896 seemed to offer that opportunity. In a long and interesting series of letters, Brooks recounted to Henry what he later referred to as the last great servile insurrection. It was characteristic of Adams that he should quixotically associate himself with the Nebraska farmers (a group as obsolete, he believed, as the Templars and the English monks) while at the same time having no respect for the populists or their candidate Bryan, "one of the very most empty, foolish, and vain youths, ever put in a great crisis by an unkind nature." He informed his brother that the election of Bryan would mean revolution, for the bankers would never let him assume office even granting the remote possibility that he could win the election. Bryan was only a clever agitator, he reported to Henry, with no understanding of economics, and he early came to the conclusion "that the Republicans had better win" over the "honest incompetents" of the silver movement. Adams had everything to lose by a Bryan victory. The Adamses' estate had gone on the rocks in '93, and a Democratic administration, as he told Henry, "would disarrange many things which have taken me three long, harassing years to get in order." Adams had backed the conservative movement within the Democratic camp, but he was not prepared to support actively "a raving Populist stump speaker" and his bobtail following.

Believing as he did that the country and the family fortunes would remain safer with McKinley as president, Adams could still enjoy the spectacle of the struggle ("it is like a cold bath, it is like looking into a heavy surf where you know you must plunge") and take the most exquisite pleasure in the consternation of the goldbugs. The Republicans, moving "in their course like a squad of police against a mob," had everything on their side. Mark Hanna, Adams mentioned to his brother, took two millions out of one Boston office building alone during the first week of August 1896. And yet the Democrats, lacking "ability, or judgment, or capacity of any kind" and led by an "empty vessel," still managed to keep the election in doubt and terrify business. The violence of the agrarian storm astonished him:

> I have never seen so impressive a sight as the election. A rising of miserable bankrupt farmers, and day labourers led by a newspaper reporter, have made the greatest fight against the organised capital of the world that has ever been made this century—or perhaps ever. . . . No

money, no press, no leaders, no organization. Amidst abuse, ridicule, intimidation, bribery—against forces so powerful and so subtle that they reach the bravest and most honest men in the country.

Brooks, as a gesture, sent money to Chicago and induced Henry to do the same, but he reluctantly reached the conclusion that the gold-bug must retain control until the inevitable rot should set in. "Henceforth," he wrote to Henry, "the old travesty of popular government must be abandoned and the plutocracy must govern under its true colors." Nature had so constituted the gold-bug mentality that it alone could survive; the rest were mere anachronisms, the rejected, animals "who might have done well in the glacial or the torrid or some other age, but who can't live now." And the worst of the defeat, Adams lamented, was the absolute impossibility of a renaissance:

> Out of it all observe, that for the first time in human history there is not one ennobling instinct. There is not a barbarian anywhere sighing a chant of war and faith, there is not a soldier to sacrifice himself for an ideal. How can we hope to see a new world, a new civilization, or a new life. To my mind we are at the end; and the one thing I thank God for is that we have no children.

iii

During the exciting days of '96, Adams had been reflecting on other subjects besides silver and gold, and in the closing years of the century he continued his European travels, watched carefully what he believed to be the signs of decay in the British empire, studied the campaigns of Napoleon, for whom he developed an intense admiration, and scrutinized the great Russian state sprawling to the eastward. It was at this time that he thought through the ideas embodied in his next books, *America's Economic Supremacy* (1900) and *The New Empire* (1902). These ideas can be reduced to the following axioms: 1) that "man is an automatic animal moving along the paths of least resistance" without will and dominated by forces over which he has no control, and that what is true of men is true of nations; 2) that "by nature, man is lazy, working only under compulsion," and that "when he is strong he will always live, as far as he can, upon the labour or the property of the weak"; 3) that the history of nations is simply the success or failure of adaptation (the flexible live; the rigid die) and that "intellectual variations are the effect of an attempt at adaptation to changing external conditions of life"; (4) that since the life of nations centers on the fiercest competition (with war as the extreme form) and since nations "must float with the tide," it is foolish for men to talk of "keeping free from intanglements. Nature is omnipotent." Nations either respond to challenges or decline. There is no standing still.

The corollary economic laws worked out by Adams made national survival depend upon energy and mass, or, to put it in another way, upon concentration and the cheap and efficient administration of large units. "From the retail store to the empire," he wrote, "success in modern life lies in concentration. The active and economical organisms survive: the slow and costly perish." Throughout the history of man, Adams decided, civilizations have expanded or receded according to their control of trade routes and their access to mineral deposits; but military and commercial successes frequently destroyed national traits responsible for engendering these successes, and newer and more virile nations rose upon the ruins of the old. As society comes to be organized into "denser masses," he reasoned, the "more vigorous and economical" unit "destroys the less active and more wasteful." Hence the modern state, if it is to survive, must move in the direction of collectivism, whether private or state. Political principles for the realist become less important than success in underselling one's rival. Victory in the war of trade depends, in turn, upon ready access to raw materials and a cheap, efficient administration.

> Political principles are but a conventional dial on whose face the hands revolve which mark the movement of the mechanism within. Most governments and many codes have been adored as emanating from the deity. All were ephemeral, and all which survived their purpose became a jest or a curse to the children of the worshippers; things to be cast aside like worn-out garments.

Adams's attitude toward governments rested finally upon the degree to which they could exploit material and human resources and survive in the continuous struggle between nations. To see him solely as an antiplutocrat and a radical, as some have done, is to oversimplify as well as to misconstrue his true position. The clue to his character and the explanation for his various stands are suggested by his dual role of romantic and conservative. In the first, he glorified the preindustrial man, lashed out against the money power, and identified himself with the obsolete organisms who retained the vestigial attributes of the age of faith. In the second, he played the ambitious opportunist, the lover of power, the geopolitical schemer mapping the course of his country's destiny and bolstering the status quo. These two seemingly antithetic guises were actually complementary.

As a historian and a realist, Adams knew that to protest against the change in the character of society was foolish, and that the sensible man adjusted himself even in a world for which he felt himself unsuited. He saw no reason why he should make himself a martyr to gold. "Only those who have a faith to die for want to suffer," he wrote to Henry, who needed no convincing. "I see no future to this thing but a long, sordid, slow grind lasting, may be, indefinitely, with no hope of anything better, and no prospect of what you call anarchy, even supposing anarchy an agreeable condition." The wise strategy for the philosopher in a dying world was to survive as comfortably as he could. "If I believed in a god, or a future, in a cause, in human virtue right or wrong, it would be another thing; but I have not enough lust for martyrdom to want to devote myself to misery simply for the sake of suffering." One did not have to make one's peace with the gold-bug to endure in his society.

Given the stupidity of the average man, certainly one of Adams's primary postulates, and the iron laws of history, the sheer task of staying alive was difficult enough to preoccupy any man. He knew for certain that the world was disintegrating, and he had no faith, as we have seen, in man's ability even to comprehend the complexities of modern living. Man moved instinctively toward self-gratification by the shortest possible route, the "human mind so constituted that whatever benefits an individual seems to that individual to benefit the race." What his grandfather had discovered about the people who spurned his services, Adams professed to have discovered about his own generation: that the American people rejected the great dream of his idol, George Washington, of a "constructive civilization," that science and education only aggravated the problem since man was not, as John Quincy Adams at first hopefully surmised, an intelligent, rational animal. Science only permitted man to "control without understanding." It hastened the process of disintegration since "an education of conservation was contrary to the instinct of greed which dominated the democratic mind, and compelled it to insist on the pillage of the public by the private man." With such human stuff to work with, no government could evolve "capable of conducting a complex organism on scientific principles." Democracy was by its very nature disintegrative, "an infinite mass of conflicting minds and of conflicting interests, which, by the persistent action of such a solvent as the modern or competitive industrial system, becomes resolved into what is, in substance, a vapor which loses its collective intellectual energy in proportion to the perfection of its expansion."

These conclusions (which illustrate again the Adams brothers' fondness for applying the second law of thermodynamics to human institutions) spelled ultimate disaster for the race; but Brooks nevertheless felt that a strategy might be worked out whereby America's prosperity and potential supremacy could be at least temporarily sustained and which could once more revive the old heroic virtues. As a property holder and a gentleman he opposed the thrusts of populism, socialism, and trade unionism. As a statesman and an economist, on the other hand, he saw the policies of the plutocracy, with their unintelligent domination of the banks and the courts, as suicidally stupid and leading straight to revolution. His criticism of the rich, therefore, must in no sense be interpreted as adventures in muckraking, but as warnings to a class in danger of being overthrown by forces within and without. Most of his writings after 1896 should be seen as lectures to the members of his own class on the tactics of survival. Governments, he says, are not accidents but growths "which may be consciously fostered and stimulated, or smothered, according as more or less intelligence is generated in the collective brain." In modern society their duration depends upon the successful application of Adams's talismans: consolidation, conservation, administration.

Adams's domestic ideas were radical enough to anger most of the conservatives, but as he turned more and more to the international scene around the turn of the century, an apparent inconsistency began to appear in his writings which disturbed even Henry, always in close rapport with his brother. Adams had started as a young man in the Mugwump camp and had worked with the New England reformers of the "Goo Goo" variety. He had refused to support James G. Blaine, "the continental liar from the state of Maine," and for some time had plumped for Cleveland, a conservative Democrat who wanted, as Adams saw it, to scale down a revolution-provoking tariff and maintain sound money. He came out flatly at this time against the McKinley tariff as a device by capitalists to destroy capitalism; for it was the oppressive protective duties, he felt, that indirectly lured the ignorant into supporting confiscatory and socialistic financial schemes like the unlimited coinage of silver. Harrison in 1892 he labeled a gold-bug. Cleveland steered a path between socialism and plutocracy, and Adams supported him for that reason. And then, rather dramatically, Brooks Adams, the anti-gold-bug, the secret sympathizer of the populists, the man who wanted to see McKinley hanged in front of the White House, became one of the Republican administration's strong supporters.

Actually the shift was not so bewildering as an innocent populist who had read *The Law of Civilization and Decay* as an anti-gold-bug tract might have supposed, and Henry, out of sympathy with Brooks's new jingoistic phase, need not have been surprised. This book, as Adams pointed out to Lodge in 1894, did trace "the origin, rise, and despotism of the gold-bug," but he advocated no heretical monetary theories and had seen silver as a feasible solution only in so far as it might be controlled by conservative businessmen in the Democratic party. Adams feared revolution in 1896 and thought that an intelligently controlled silver policy might reduce its threat by relieving the impoverished farmers. His pamphlet on the gold standard published in that year (described by Samuel Bowles of the influential *Springfield Republican* as "perhaps the most insidious and powerful argument ever made in demonstration of the ruinous consequences of silver demonitization") provided useful ammunition for the anti-gold-bugs. But he found no difficulty in coming to terms with the other side a few years later, because his own friends, the imperialists, were moving into positions of power. The war with Spain had alleviated the pressure at home by opening up new markets. Surplus production could now be handled without tampering with the monetary system. Adams announced his change of views at a press interview in 1898:

The party which takes advantage of the opportunity afforded now for the nation to advance and takes its place as a power in the world, is bound to be victorious, no matter what its name, and the men and parties who are content to stand still, and who cannot see that the country has outgrown the system of government which did very well a century ago, will be swept aside. I believe in the war . . . and in the policy of expansion which it forced the nation. I am an expansionist, an "imperialist," if you please, and I presume I may be willing to go farther in this line than anybody else in Massachusetts, with, perhaps, a few exceptions.

Certain world patterns were beginning to take shape that called for a different strategy. From 1898 to 1912 Adams was eager to provide it.

iv

From his studies and travels, Adams became convinced by the early Nineties that the old European balance of power was beginning to shift. Watching the money centers moving further westward from Lombard Street to Wall Street, always a sign of impending convulsion and revolution in Adams's prognosis, he calculated that the United States stood at last upon the threshold of a new era. By 1897 (a crucial date in the Adamses' chronology when Pittsburgh steel began to undersell European steel) America was on its way to becoming the greatest creditor nation in the world. The rapid liquidation of British assets abroad—the dissolution of the British empire was a favorite theme of both Brooks and Henry—had placed tremendous demands upon the supply of American specie. But owing to the superb and remarkably efficient reorganization of American industry through the great trusts, we met our obligations and then proceeded to undersell Europe. In addition to our clearly superior manufacturing facilities and our rich endowments of natural resources, especially the all-important minerals, our prohibitive tariff, formerly assailed by Adams, permitted us to pay for the losses suffered temporarily in the trade invasion abroad. We were carrying on the war of commerce with commendable energy, impoverishing European farmers, reducing the profits of Europe's industry, excluding large, potentially productive areas from European penetration, and, in general, making our position economically unassailable.

For the moment Adams could support the party of the plutocrats and the trusts. "The trust must be accepted," he said in 1901, "as the corner stone of modern civilization, and the movement toward the trust must gather momentum until the limit of possible economies has been reached." Not only did he feel that the trust produced more cheaply and efficiently than small concerns, reducing waste and providing low prices for the consumer, but he saw the trust also as a form of western collectivism which would meet the challenge of the collectivist peoples of the east. He summarized his ideas when he wrote to Lodge:

> I must honestly and seriously believe that we are now on the great struggle for our national supremacy, which means our existence. I believe, from years I have given to the study of these matters in many countries, that we must be masters or we must break down. We must become so organized that we can handle great concerns and vast forces cheaper and better than others. It is fate. It is destiny. I believe that, unsatisfactory in many ways as our present system is, the overthrow of McKinley, or even the failure to strengthen his administration, would be a blow to our national life.

After his conversion to McKinleyism in 1900, he saw no reason McKinley's administration should not go down "as the turning point in our history. As the moment when we won the great prize. I do believe," he assured his friend Lodge, "that we may dominate the world, as no nation has dominated it in recent time." In this happy and aggressive frame of mind, the country's prospects looked particularly good. To Henry he wrote:

> I look forward to the next ten years as probably the culminating period of America. The period which will hereafter be looked back upon as the grand time. We shall likely enough, be greater later, but it is the dawn which is always golden. The first taste of power is always the sweetest.

His temporary good spirits did not delude him into the belief that America's ultimate future was any brighter, "but the bloom," he concluded, "will last our time. We have vitality enough for one generation at least—perhaps more. And we shant last that long." A trip to Spokane in the spring of 1901 provided more evidence of America's incredible energy:

> The journey was tiresome [he wrote to Henry] but very interesting. I came home straight, and sat most of the time in an observation car. It is no use for the world to kick, the stream is too strong, nothing can resist it. Beginning on the crest of the rockies the tide flows down into the Mississippi valley, and then across to the eastern mountains in an ever increasing flood, with an ever heightening velocity. At last you come to the lakes and Buffalo. There, I take it, modern civilization reaches its focus. No movement can keep pace with the demand; no power can be found vast enough. . . . No one who has watched that torrent from its source on the Divide to its discharge in New York Bay can, I think, help feeling the hour of the old world has struck.

Confident in America's destiny, close to his friends Lodge and Roosevelt, and eager to receive information or offer what he considered to be sound advice, his utterances took on a magniloquence, a bellicosity, and a fervor which he showed neither before nor after.

Both Roosevelt and Lodge understood geographical necessities; they shared Adams's distaste for plutocrats and socialists and appreciated the soldierly virtues. But it was Roosevelt who seemed particularly attuned to Adams's aggressive message and who most clearly reflected the influence of his scholarly friend. From the time of Roosevelt's sympathetic review of *The Law of Civilization and Decay* until the days of the Bull Moose party, Adams closely followed T.R.'s career. He had sympathized with Roosevelt's ambitions in 1896, for Roosevelt too felt the pain and frustration in a gold-bug age, and he had advised his friend to sell himself. "It is of course a poetical conception to fight and die for what is right, what is pure and true and noble, but after all is it not the dream of a poet, or at least a poetic age? Is not to live the first, the most pressing demand of nature; and to live must we not bend to nature? Can anything be wrong for us to do which is imperiously demanded by the instinct of self-preservation?" After Roosevelt had temporized with Wall Street and found himself by accident in the White House, Adams congratulated his protégé as the new Caesar:

> "Thou hast it now: King, Cawdor, Glamis, all—" The world can give no more. You hold a place greater than Trajan's, for you are the embodi-

ment of a power not only vaster than the power of the empire, but vaster than men have ever known.

You have too the last and rarest prize, for you have an opportunity. You will always stand as the President who began the contest for supremacy of America against the eastern continent.

Roosevelt, in short, was to carry out the policies of McKinley, whose death Adams deeply regretted, and whom he now described as the best president since Lincoln. McKinley had kept pace with the times, changing his cabinet after the war, reorganizing the army, checking Russia and Germany in the east without causing a panic, and revising America's trade policy. Roosevelt must continue and implement these achievements or we were doomed. This was to be the theme on which he continually harped to the new president and which lay behind all of his subsequent counsel, on both foreign and domestic relations.

Dreams of peace, Adams had long argued, were the will o' the wisps luring nations to destruction. Human destiny called for war. Nations destroyed or were in turn destroyed. Our trade methods actually despoiled the world, whether or not they were intentionally devised to do so, and if we meant to retain our commercial hegemony, we had to face the facts. If we played the braggart, "rich, aggressive, and unarmed," we would most certainly be stripped by our adversaries; nor could we cautiously withdraw. "If we retreat from our positions," he wrote Henry in 1901, "we might keep the peace, but I fancy our retreat would mark our culmination. It would mark the point you are always speculating about when America would be overweighted by the combination of all Asia from the Atlantic to the Pacific. It would be all Asia then, Europe would be absorbed." For the certain success of the new American push, Adams added one more proviso. Our political administration would have to be as flexible, up-to-date, and energetic as our economic; our political machinery would have to be recast into a cheaper, more elastic, and simpler form. Finally, we would have to develop a new kind of administrator, well-trained, audacious, and disinterested.

Now, by their very natures, the rulers of American society were specialists whose skill in aggrandizing themselves and whose heroic devotion to their own interests incapacitated them for public service. The ideal administrator represented no special interest but all the interests, and his mind was not bounded by the narrow concerns which made the capitalist unfit to rule a vast, complex, and centralized economy. Unfortunately, America, said Adams, had no administrators, and in 1903 his letters to Henry are filled with apprehensive references to this dearth of trained personnel:

> We need a new deal of men and we need it very bad, and everyone agrees with it. Only we can't raise the men. . . . As I see it, everything is ripening for a plunge. We must have a new deal, we must have new methods, we must suppress the states, and have a centralized administration, or we shall wobble over. The most conservative as well as the most radical seem to agree to this.

Adams used the analogy of the "new high steel building" to suggest the powerful, compact, administrative system he had in mind. "Our whole civilization," he warned, "must consolidate to match the high building."

> In daily life we have outgrown the specialist, and for that reason the specialist fails and is a positive danger. We are now attempting to produce the generalizing mind. We are attacking administration scientifically. If we succeed in training the next generation right, and their nervous systems do not give way under the strain, we shall, likely enough, pull through and land a big fish . . . the change is represented by the steel cage of thirty or forty stories. Everything has to pass onto the basis of steel from a basis of brick and stone. It means a social revolution going down to the family and up to the government.

An intelligent administration subordinated the indispensable monopolies to the service of the state, obviating the necessity of a biased judiciary (which hastened the movement toward revolution), and taught the people how to obey and take responsibility. Adams's dream envisioned a kind of modified state socialism, run along the lines of a big modern corporation, with a trained and conservative elite solidly in control, a powerful but amenable industrial aristocracy, and an orderly responsible electorate. "The older I grow," he wrote to Henry, "the more I am convinced that the administrative mind is the highest vehicle of energy, and that is what makes the power of the soldier, for the soldier must also be an administrator." The time was rapidly approaching, he hazarded with more prophetic insight than he usually showed, "when we shall be reorganized by soldiers." From 1900 his cry was for discipline—a disciplined Business, a disciplined Nation, a disciplined Home. "Life is tolerable," he concluded, "under any form of orderly government."

Adams placed his hope in Roosevelt as the man who might bring about the necessary administrative reforms. He welcomed his incumbency and remained in close touch with him until T.R.'s death. Roosevelt, he thought, at least approximated the ideal type of administrator, despite his occasional aberrations, his volatility, and his penchant for addressing hard-bitten party men as if they were Groton boys. He too shared Adams's disgust for "moral platitudinizing" about war ("hogwash without admixture," Adams called it) and feared the loss of national virility if the feminists had their way. Adams backed Roosevelt, admitting all of the latter's limitations, not only because of his sincerity and honesty, but because Roosevelt represented the kind of intelligent conservatism which, through limited concessions to reform, would preserve their class and protect the country. Writing to the president in 1903 about the railroad problem, he remarked:

> I think all conservative men owe you and the Attorney-General a great debt—for it is your policy or State ownership. There is no middle course. In a word, to live, this country must keep open the big highways leading west, at equitable rates, and must command the terminus in Asia—if we fail in this we shall break down.

Throughout Roosevelt's administration, Adams constantly advised him on the railroad issue. His own affairs happened to be involved here, but he saw the arrogant and irresponsible practices of the roads, supported by what he regarded as a stupid and reactionary judiciary, as an invitation to social convulsion as well as an injurious blow to our foreign interests. "I apprehend that we are entering on a social revolution," he wrote Roosevelt in 1906, "which must either wreck or reorganize our society. The community, or the monopoly must control prices, and therefor all wealth." Under Taft, Adams was now certain, the gold-bugs had regained lost ground; it was for this reason that, in 1912, he urged his friend to seek a third term and save the country. "This two term business," he agreed with his grandfather, was "vicious and preposterous Jeffersonian rot," and as Roosevelt seemed to respond to Adams's ideas, he grew more excited about his campaign for reelection. He warned Roosevelt that he was attempting to defeat the strongest and best defended entrenchment in the world and that the gold-bugs would treat him no better than an anarchist. But then, he concluded, "it has always been so":

> I think I know this thing to the bottom. What I want, and have always wanted, is order and authority, and we can have neither unless the law is equally enforced. Capitalism, as always, seeks unequal enforcement of the law—or privilege. Just now, to get privilege, they use the courts, as they are using the Commerce Court to upset the Interstate Commerce Commission. To attain this immediate end they expose the courts to popular attack, as the vested slave interest did the Dred Scott Case. Capital always will. But in so doing it undermines the foundation of order. It works chaos. And chaos is straight before us.

These ideas he presented in greater detail in his *Theory of Social Revolutions* (1913), which reflected the 1912 campaign as *The Law of Civilization and Decay* embodied the issues of 1896. As Adams saw it, Roosevelt's job, if he was elected, was to rebuild a broken-down administrative system, unable to cope with modern complexities, in a scientific way. He could not succeed by making emotional speeches against the bosses. Bryan and his followers had failed in a similar contest because they relied too much on emotion, and Roosevelt's task was immeasurably more difficult than Bryan's.

> The question [he told Roosevelt] is whether we can construct a central administration strong enough to coerce those special interests, or whether they can prevent such a consolidation. Call it what you will: empire, dictatorship, republic, or anything else, we have the same problem which Caesar had in Rome when he suppressed the plundering gang of senators led by Brutus, who murdered him for it. We must have a power strong enough to make all the interests equal before the law, or we must dissolve into chaos. All of these special interests are now banded against you in Chicago and they are capable of anything, including murder.

After Roosevelt failed to win the Republican nomination at Chicago, Adams advised him not to run independently and to bide his time, but to Henry he confided his disappointment. Roosevelt had tried hard, but his mind was not elastic and he never fully understood the issues; with a tenth of Caesar's ability he faced problems ten times as difficult. Adams found the emotion of the Bull Moose crusade extremely distasteful, and the antics of Roosevelt and his followers reminded him of "these volatilized women who run about in motors and can't keep still." Henry was sure by this time that Roosevelt's mind had "disintegrated like the mind of the country," but Brooks still believed that some use remained in his erratic friend even though Teddy made "plenty of mistakes" and was "as headstrong as a mule."

Adams had never really approved Roosevelt's brief alliance with the Progressives ("They do not know what they want and, if they were told what must be done, they would run like rabbits"), but as Roosevelt moved back again to reality and began his crusade against Wilson and unpreparedness, Adams warmed up considerably. The war he had predicted in 1903 had already embroiled Europe and threatened to drag in the United States. American participation at this time would be disastrous, he told Roosevelt in 1914, because only by remaining neutral could we reconstruct our obsolete political system and defend ourselves. A German victory he thought preferable to an English, "for Germany will not dare attack us with the English fleet on her flank, whereas England, I suspect, if she has the better, must control our competition on the sea if she is to carry her debt and feed her people." The Germans, at least, might teach our plutocrats and our mercenary proletariat that "we men owe a paramount duty to our country." Our salvation lay in substituting for the money standard of Wall Street the military standards of West Point.

By 1916 Roosevelt's chances for the presidency were slim, but Adams thought he might carry enough influence to have himself appointed Secretary of War or see to it that a man like Leonard Wood got the job. He wanted to see a series of military schools on the order of West Point set up all over the country in which "obedience, duty, and self-sacrifice" would be taught "on a great scale." If Roosevelt succeeded in this all-important assignment, which was nothing less than changing the moral values of people raised for two generations on the gospel that money is the chief end in life, he would have made his greatest contribution to the nation. "Our troubles," according to Adams, "now arise from the false standards of our people. Is it not logical for men to reason that if money is the only end in life, then peace at any price is a sound policy?"

Roosevelt, however, could not prevent the reelection of Wilson, the president who had become for Adams a "flagrant ass" and the symbol of our national disunity. He detected the hand of his old enemies, the Bankers, behind the League of Nations and suspected that Mr. Schiff was "somewhere near the focus of the hell-broth." Adams should have realized by this time that his recommendations had little chance of being taken seriously, but he could not resist the temptation to preach in spite of Henry's pointed remarks that he avoid didacticism; he still felt obliged to warn his uncomprehending and bemused contemporaries. In the debates of the Massachusetts Constitutional Convention in 1917 and 1918, he unfolded all of his favorite arguments and admonitions: the necessity of national supremacy and the subordination of all special interests to the collective will; the dangers which would follow from our failure to collectivize in the face of European tendencies; the tyranny of the courts as brakes on progress; the importance of a flexible bureaucracy which could administer without obstruction ("All modern government means administration, and that is all it does mean"); the certainty that "everything is to be cured by the concentration of power in some one who really will protect the whole community, the interest of all of us"; the natural inequality of men and the inevitable concomitant, competition; the necessity of recasting our society and girding ourselves for the future struggle which is most certain to occur.

These ideas, amusingly and sometimes brilliantly elaborated in the Massachusetts debates, drew polite applause but no one pretended to know what he was talking about. Only one person really understood Adams's remarks, the person who had provided his first and most sympathetic audience—his brother Henry.

V

Henry had been following Brooks's strenuous theorizings from the beginning and had found little to disagree with. Always more reserved and skeptical, if no less pessimistic, than Brooks, he still found his brother's economic analyses stimulating and instructive;

indeed, his own thinking was frequently so similar that it is sometimes hard to discover which brother anticipated the other. Although Henry refused to take credit for the ideas in *The Law of Civilization and Decay,* he exhibits many of Brooks's pet preconceptions, not only his loathing for the gold-bugs, Jews, and socialists, but his views on the inevitability of some kind of state socialism. Both brothers predicted the bankruptcy of England, Henry with more regret, for he did not share Brooks's inveterate hatred of England or accept his vision of an American empire. America, he felt, could not manage its own concerns, much less the world's (a view which Brooks returned to), and Henry preferred to see Germany and Russia direct the machine after Britain went under. But Henry's geopolitical speculations resemble Brooks's in large part (he too believed "that superiority depends . . . on geography, geology and race energy"), and he accepted unchanged Brooks's hypothesis of civilization:

> All Civilization is Centralization.
> All Centralization is Economy
> Therefore all Civilization is the survival
> of the most economical (cheapest)

Henry's heavy correspondence with Brooks, earnest for the most part and without the veneer of flippancy that characterized most of his other correspondence, is merely one indication of their close intellectual relationship. "We are too much alike, and agree too well in our ideas," Henry remarked to a friend. "We have nothing to give each other." Both used different methods to approach identical ends and acted upon each other as counter irritants or whetstones. Each submitted favorite hypotheses to the other and criticized the other's ideas with brotherly candor.

Brooks had a younger brother's respect for Henry's genius and the highest admiration for his literary talents. *Mont St. Michel and Chartres* he called "the best literary production of America, if not Europe, at least upwards for two generations," and he took a family pride in this "gem of thought, of taste, of execution" which redeemed his generation. "I perhaps alone of living men can appreciate fully all that you have there," he wrote to Henry, "for I have lived with the crusaders and the schoolmen." Of the *Education* he was less certain, although he allowed that it was perhaps "the broadest and, in many ways, the best thing you have ever done." His criticisms or recommendations seem a little cryptic to the outsider, but apparently he felt that Henry had not written the last half on the scale of the first and had "tried to relieve the shadow." Brooks may have meant by this last remark that the "failure" of Henry's life was not seen clearly enough as an individual reflection of a general predicament: man's tragic inability to adapt himself in a changing universe. Such a meaning is certainly suggested in Brooks's reply to Henry after receiving his essay "Phase." Here he recommended that the *Education* be rewritten on the basis of this radical theorem:

> You have at last overcome your obstacle. Here is unity whereby to measure your diversity. The theorem which should precede the experiment. Your education has been the search for the "new mind." The contrast you wish to draw is the absolute gap between the thing nature demands and the human effort. If you can strip from your book all semblance of personal irritation against individuals, eliminate the apparent effort to write fragments of biography, and raise the story of your life to the level in dignity of the vast conception against which you are to measure the result, you will have created one of the master-pieces of literature, psychology and history. But I can only say again to you what I have said before . . . that this is a huge and awful tragedy.

Henry had begun to complain to Brooks in 1908 about failing powers of mind, and his brother's praise and encouragement must have been especially welcome. Brooks assured him that his work had steadily improved and that his best work, like his grandfather's, had been done after sixty. "The only trouble with you," he wrote, "is the trouble he felt and we all feel, that is an increase of mental power as the bodily power declines. I suffer from that myself."

As for himself, Adams noted that he was losing his "faculty of expression" and that he could not rid himself "of that rigid, didactic and school-mam manner, which drives me to frenzy but which holds me like a vise." Certainly Henry wrote far better than Brooks. He was more successful in presenting systematically and meticulously his well-considered ideas, sustained, as Mr. R. P. Blackmur says, by an all-pervasive imagination. But it should be added that Brooks knew perfectly well the strength and limitation of his method. Always deferring to Henry and regarding him as one of the greatest minds of his age, he nevertheless stoutly defended his own kind of writing against his brother's criticisms. He never thought of his books as being history or literature in the strict sense. They were written for an "occasion," for crises, and the times were too crucial to allow him the luxury of being a mere chronicler. History for him had no particular interest unless a practical lesson could be extracted from it:

> I try to present a method, not an historical study. I use history as little as possible, and only as illustration. Anyone can gather facts if they only have a plan upon which to arrange them. Hence I have a perfectly plain task, very narrowly limited. I have to state a theory or a method. I have to illustrate it enough to be understood. . . . I have to take a definite starting point, and I have to deduce a practical conclusion bearing on our daily life. I have last of all to be ready at the precise moment when the catastrophe is impending evidently—or I shant be read.

Henry and Brooks clearly differed in method—Brooks choosing to be didactic and active, Henry noncommittal and passive—but they saw eye to eye on laws of social change and the probable future of the world.

After Henry's stroke and gradual debilitation, Brooks foresaw his brother's death and recoiled from the prospect of being left alone, the last of his generation. Writing to Henry in the spring of 1915, he reminisced:

> And as I look back through the long series of years to the days when I was a schoolboy and you used to take me to walk in England, more than fifty years ago, I wonder more day by day what it has all been about and why I am here at all. You have been closer to me than any other man, I suppose, and I cannot with equanimity contemplate parting with you. At this moment my whole life rises before me. I am a coward. I do not want to stay till the last. You must wait and keep me company.

A few months later he wrote almost shyly:

> You have helped both of us over many a wet place in our path. . . . It is my birthday—so I may be forgiven an emotion. You always were the best of us four brothers—you are so still now that we are reduced to

two. I wish I could have done more to justify my life—but I think I have done nearly my best—good or bad, the best part has been yours ever since I was a boy. And now, as an old man, I look at your worth and thank God that you have redeemed our generation.

Brooks's last tribute to Henry was his long introduction to the latter's *Degradation of the Democratic Dogma* in which he reiterated his and Henry's theory of exhaustion of resources by waste and its human equivalent. The introduction was mainly an account of John Quincy Adams and, by indirection, of Brooks himself, for he had come gradually to identify his own career with that of his grandfather. In 1909, while he was preparing a biography of John Quincy Adams that he never published, he wrote to Henry that Washington and their grandfather were

> the only two men who ever conceived of America as a unity and tried practically to realise their idea. They failed and with them our civilization has failed. Adams stood alone because no one else saw the sequence of relations. He felt this and the sense of failure made him bitter and morbid.

Brooks and Henry, facing the same problem, had failed too. No one ever understood their grandfather, Brooks concluded, and "no one will ever understand us—but he was right: and we are right."

Brooks Adams died in 1927, the same arrogant, blunt, audacious man that he always was, with a few years to spare before the crackup he anticipated and had hoped to escape. With him died his prejudices that were later to crop up in uglier forms and his yet unfulfilled predictions. He had wanted to serve his countrymen, for he never seemed quite able to resign himself to the pessimistic implications of his own message, but they responded neither to his promise of national glory nor to his threats of disaster. He had much to suggest which was pertinent and valuable, but he always stood aloof from the democracy he wanted to save and believed that men were "doomed eternally and hopelessly to contend" against a blind and purposeless universe. And yet he did not gloat over the world's destruction as Henry Adams liked to do. He made a great show of being fatalistic and of enjoying the *Götterdämmerung*, but behind the façade of scientific detachment can be discerned a prevailing sympathy for man in his uneven contest with nature.

Theodore Roosevelt as Cultural Artifact

Four gigantic presidential heads, the work of the American-born sculptor Gutzon Borglum, look out from the granite wall of South Dakota's Mt. Rushmore. Washington, Jefferson, and Lincoln cluster clubbably on their mountain eminence, but does the head of Theodore Roosevelt, replete with a cleverly simulated pince-nez, belong in this godlike company? Borglum thought so, and not merely because he believed in and practiced the Rooseveltian gospel of the "strenuous life" (Americans, he complained, didn't live vigorously enough) or because Roosevelt had been a personal friend. He simply considered him a great man, an "all-American President" under whose aegis two oceans had been linked and the United States transformed into a world power. Borglum saw nothing incongruous in wedging him between Thomas Jefferson, whom Roosevelt held in reserved contempt, and Abraham Lincoln, whose fondness for unclean stories Roosevelt deplored but whom he nonetheless revered.

The finished stone portrait of Roosevelt was dedicated in 1939. By that time his name had been pretty well preempted by the then occupant of the White House, his fifth cousin and husband of a favorite niece. In fact, Roosevelt's deflation had started even before his death in 1919, partly because his misalliance with the Progressives had disappointed Republican stalwarts and pleased only a ve-

Originally published in *Raritan*, 9 (Winter 1990), 109–126.

hement minority of the voters he had captivated during his glory years, the people, as he put it, "who make up the immense bulk of our Nation—the small merchants, clerks, farmers and mechanics." Rejected by party conservatives in his bid for the presidency in 1912, he went on a kind of political binge that distanced him from the middle-of-the-road consensus and left the radicals unconvinced of his sincerity. Just as George F. Babbitt, the eponymous hero of Sinclair Lewis's novel, rejoined the Good Citizens' League after his brief revolt against the credo of Zenith, so Roosevelt after his own insurgency happily returned to the Republican fold to spur the crusade against Woodrow Wilson, the IWW, and the "Bolsheviki." Had he lived he would certainly have blocked the presidential nomination of his antithesis, pliable Warren Gamaliel Harding, the "bloviating" senator from Ohio, whom he had seriously contemplated as a possible running mate in the 1920 elections.

Whether the man President Harding eulogized as the "mighty hunter" and "the most courageous American of all times" could have worked his old magic on an electorate fed up with moralistic harangues now seems unlikely. The epithets lavished upon him by his celebrators—"genial giant," "Colossus," "Cid of the West," "Great Heart," "Mr. Valiant," "the Lion"—had a comical ring in America's Babylonian Twenties. He had always recoiled from what he took to be the cynicism of Henry Adams and Henry James; he hated irony and had harsh words for Mark Twain's dark novel, *A Connecticut Yankee in King Arthur's Court*. "There is nothing cheaper," he wrote in 1907, "than to sneer at and belittle great men and great deeds and great thoughts of a bygone time." Sentiments of this sort, not to mention his calls to civic duty, didn't thrive in the debunking atmosphere of the jazz age.

In that decade, Roosevelt's "gloriously simple world" disappeared. H. L. Mencken's portrait of him as a calculating, anti-democratic politician, the "national Barbarossa" philosophically akin to the kaiser, set the tone for the negative reappraisals to come. Historians and social critics over the next twenty years did more than question his liberal credentials. They also detected in the words and attitudes of this "perfect *representative* of the middle class of prewar America" (so John Chamberlain dubbed him) the signs of an incipient native fascism. By the end of World War II, however, the hostile stereotypes of Roosevelt—the unmagnanimous adversary, militant imperialist, coiner of platitudes, slaughterer of innocent beasts—had begun to be qualified or rejected in biographies and monographs, especially after the publication of his letters in eight fat volumes.

A revised portrait of Roosevelt as the far-sighted pragmatist and constructive conservative suited the national temper of the 1950s. Even Edmund Wilson, who thirty years earlier had ranked him low in the scale of presidents, conceded in a review of Theodore Roosevelt's correspondence that he had been "unfairly eclipsed" by Woodrow Wilson and "Franklin D." Now he found that he could sympathize "to some extent with Roosevelt in his doctrine of 'practical politics,' his insistence that the uncompromising kind of reformer, who refused to yield anything to expediency, can never put through his reforms." Since Wilson wrote these words, revisionists, in redressing several decades of T.R. baiting, have moved far beyond his measured approval.

There is still no firm consensus, but I doubt that many historians today would quarrel with Oscar Handlin's summation of Roosevelt as "the first modern chief executive of the United States" or deny the efficiency of his administration. He has been called "the greatest activist in the history of the American presidency." Truly or not, he saw himself as the steward of the whole nation, preserver of its natural resources and its spiritual and bodily well-being. The series of regulatory acts passed by the Congress with his strong backing left displeased both radical reformers and Big Business, but not the public, receptive to Roosevelt's doctrine of "applied idealism" and content to stay in the middle of the road. His advocates especially commend his tactful and moderate diplomacy. They see him as the first president to deal confidently and comfortably with the heads of foreign powers, the first to ensure America's future role in global politics.

Roosevelt's stock continues to fluctuate on the political exchange in an era of White House adventurism and Noriega's Panama, and his recent co-option by President Bush—who describes himself as "an Oyster Bay kind of guy" and surmises that he may "turn out to be a Teddy Roosevelt"—could send Republicans and Democrats alike back to their history books. Roosevelt was no Lincoln (I think his most ardent partisans would concede as much), but he was one of our more spectacular and entertaining presidents, the most obstreperously boyish (his enemies would say "insane" or "manic"), and for all of his thousands of personal letters and twenty volumes of packaged views about everything under the sun, not easy to plumb. Perhaps the sheer mass of memorabilia and conflicting commentary that has accumulated about him, much of it self-spawned, impedes discernment. From this detritus, would-be interpreters construct their own Roosevelts.

Mine is a pastiche drawn from many sources but chiefly from the letters. I see him as the scion of old money (though the terms *aristocrat* and *patrician* often applied to him seem to me malapropos), an American "gentleman" with a strongly developed civic sense, ambitious for glory but—perhaps because he had no need of it—disinclined to claw his way up the political ladder. He learned early to compromise, to accept small defeats on the way to larger victories, even if that sometimes demanded the repudiation of former allies and a certain amount of truckling, though never to the extent of frequenting barrooms or kissing proletarian babies. Probably no other American president loved his job so much, felt more pleased with himself (his expressions of humility have a hollow ring), or pursued his goals with greater insouciance. Uninhibited, politically canny, temperamentally optimistic, he was blessed with an untroubled faith in his own rectitude. He liked to fight and to win; no one ever questioned his physical courage. If Justice Holmes's comment on Owen Wister's gushing memoir of Roosevelt ("the talent he depicts is that of a first class megaphone and not of a statesman") sounds unfair, his judgment of the man who appointed him to the Supreme Court does not: "R. was more or less a great man no doubt but I think he was far from having a great intellect."

But I don't want to debate the pros and cons of T.R.'s presidency, to concede or dispute his greatness, or to contrast him invidiously with other American presidents. My interest here is his reputation and how he acquired it. Why was he once widely judged to be the greatest and best-known American of his day—indeed, the incarnation of America? What was it about him and his times that contributed to his acclaim?

I believe he had a lot to do with his translation into the American "superstructure." Before the onset of the professional image-makers (that is to say, roughly from his election to the New York State Assembly in 1881 until at least 1917, when he tried but failed to raise a division of troops to fight in France), Roosevelt served very effectively as his own press agent. He was the first ex-president to publish his autobiography. His political, historical, and literary writings, not to mention his voluminous correspondence, constitute among other things a campaign of self-promotion, a sustained "Song of Myself."

"I celebrate myself and sing myself," chanted Walt of Manahatta, "And what I assume you shall assume / For every atom belonging to me as good belongs to you." Roosevelt delivered a comparable message to the electorate, although I suspect he would have shared his atoms more reluctantly than the Good Walt did. Both were histrionic and self-loving, but in other ways the two singers were quite antithetical. Whitman envisioned an American democracy composed of all races and occupations, a union of loving comrades. Roosevelt's Americanism, though resistant to nativist bigotry, had little to do with equality and brotherhood. Rather, in Edmund Wilson's words, "it was a concept he had to invent as an antidote to those tendencies in American life he found himself sworn to resist," tendencies that might be subsumed in the words Anarchy and Slouch. Whitman the loafer was passive and mystical; he dissolved into the experiences of his countrymen. Roosevelt despised anything loose, disorderly, slack, lawless, soft. Both celebrated strenuous deeds, but Roosevelt, unlike Whitman, acted out his fantasies in the public glare, and the public took the uncommon man into its collective heart as it never did Whitman.

Mark Twain often noted the paradox of an America ostensibly attached to leveling principles yet enamored with rank. "Scoffing democrats as we are, we do dearly love to be noticed by a duke, and when we are noticed by a monarch, we have softening of the brain for the rest of our lives." At home, "precious collisions" with the rich and the well-born were no less treasured, especially if the one on high were affable and gracious. Roosevelt capitalized on his upper-class affiliations, his dress and accent, his cartoonable mannerisms. It didn't take him very long to learn that the very presence of a dude in the rough-and-tumble political arena attracted attention. And when that dude happened to be quick-witted, belligerent, and demonically energetic (someone said Teddy "used adjectives like hammers"), he was bound to stand out in the crowd of big-city machine politicos and populist "Jackasses" from the west.

A Roosevelt biographer mentions his subject's "genius for publicity." Mark Twain, himself no slouch at self-promotion, made the same point less silkily at the end of Theodore Roosevelt's administration. "Mr. Roosevelt," he wrote then, but prudently didn't publish, "is the Tom Sawyer of the political world of the twentieth century; always showing off; always hunting for a chance to show off; in his frenzied imagination the Great Republic is a vast Barnum circus with him for a clown and the whole world for an audience; he would go to Halifax for half a chance to show off, and he would go to hell for a whole one."

Twain's remark was flip and simplistic but not wildly beyond the mark. Other ironists felt the same way, appalled and exhausted by the supercharged Roosevelt, whose ideas seemed to spring from his nervous system. Henry Adams and his inner circle (Gore Vidal brings this out in his novel *Empire*) found him refreshing if often irritating, and as impressive in his way as a spouting geyser. Reporters chronicled his tireless round of horseback rides, walks, and rock climbs, his swimming, boxing, and shooting. The public delighted in his furious spasms of activity. Never before had there been a president who was such a provocative phrasemaker, such a fist-thumping, arm-waving, toothy jack-in-the-box, yet withal dignified, powerful, and purposeful—and a little dangerous, too.

Roosevelt did more than tolerate the larger-than-life image of himself; he cultivated it. Less visible was the T.R. whose intimates addressed him as "Theodore" (he disliked being called "Teddy"), who played tennis (but forbade photographers to take pictures of him in his sissy tennis clothes), dressed for dinner, and displayed an almost feminine sweetness toward his family and close friends. What the public saw Roosevelt wanted it to see: the broncobuster, soldier, hunter, crime fighter—the moral exemplar and protector of the national domain who reigned in an era of good feeling. E. L. Doctorow captures the Rooseveltian euphoria in his novel *Ragtime*:

> Patriotism was a reliable sentiment in the early 1900s. Teddy Roosevelt was President. The population customarily gathered in great numbers either out of doors for parades, public concerts, fish fries, political picnics, social outings, or indoors in meeting halls, vaudeville theatres, operas, ball-rooms. There seemed to be no entertainment that did not involve great swarms of people. Trains and steamers and trolleys moved them from one place to another. That was the style, that was the way

people lived. . . . Women were stouter then. They visited the fleet carrying white parasols. Everyone wore white in summer. Tennis racquets were hefty and the racquet faces elliptical. There was a lot of sexual fainting. There were no Negroes. There were no immigrants.

Omitted from this postcard vignette (besides Negroes and immigrants, as Doctorow notes) are riots, strikes, scandals, and exposés. Yet none of these disquieting signs seem to have tarnished T.R.'s luster. The nation was advancing, and he was leading the charge. Everything was "Bully!" The president was "De-lighted."

When he left office, Roosevelt had already become a national artifact, a popular possession. Henry Cabot Lodge, one of the crowd of well-wishers who saw him off on his African safari in 1909, assured the ex-president that the American people were following the "minute accounts of [his] progress" in the daily press "as if it were a serial story" and "with all the absorbed interest of a boy who reads 'Robinson Crusoe' for the first time."

Roosevelt kept this public well informed of his comings and goings. He rarely missed the chance to advertise his invariably newsworthy opinions. "What funnily varied lives we do lead, Cabot!" he had written to Lodge back in 1889. "We touch two or three little worlds, each profoundly ignorant of the others. Our literary friends have but a vague knowledge of our actual political work; and a goodly number of our sporting and social acquaintances know us only as men of good family, one of whom rides hard to hounds, while the other hunts big game in the Rockies." A decade later, the whole country was inescapably privy to selected portions of his political, social, and literary worlds. Each of his subpublics focused on a different Roosevelt: the politicians on the unpredictable and slippery officeholder and -seeker; the literary and scholarly community (historians, explorers, naturalists, museum people) on the reputedly omniscient polymath with a photographic memory.

Of the assorted "Teddys," a few in particular caught the fancy of his national audience and inflated the Roosevelt myth. I shall concentrate on two of them, the Hunter and the Soldier. I believe he cultivated these two images more assiduously than he did his other personae—the Christian Gentleman, the Practical and Sane Reformer, the Peacemaker, the Man of Letters, the Conservationist—all subsidiary roles comprehended by his conception of the Hunter and Soldier.

A 1919 cartoon of him shows the retired president seated in his den. Heads of wild beasts deck the walls. He looks uncomfortable in repose and appears about to stir. Is his unease a presentiment of what's to come? (Roosevelt confessed in his autobiography that he was devoted to *Macbeth* but indifferent to *Hamlet*.)

Half derisively, half affectionately, the newspapers reported his African expedition. Cartoons showed jungle animals running in terror at the mere rumor of Teddy's presence. In one spoof, a "man-chewing" tiger explains to a jealous cobra how he intends to face the barrage of snapping Kodaks and yield up his "sinful soul with a mean snarl." Teddy in caricature is a comic figure, his huge teeth bared, no less animal than the buffalo, rhinoceroses, elephants, zebras, and giraffes he relentlessly pursues.

Of all the big game he tracked and killed, the bear was probably most closely associated with his prowess and personality, thanks, in part, to the reporters and camera crews who accompanied him on his publicized bear hunts. Mark Twain wickedly parodied one of them. It culminated, according to the newspaper account he quoted, with the president dashing into a canebrake, dispatching the bear at twenty paces, and then gleefully hugging the guides. (In Twain's version, Roosevelt has slain an exhausted cow, despite her touching plea for mercy.) A short film of 1902 entitled *Terrible Teddy, the Grizzly King* reinforced the popular image of a feral Nimrod. The president-elect appears on the screen in the company of two flunkeys, one carrying a sign reading "My Press Agent," the other "My Photographer." Teddy shoots his gun in the air and down falls a dead cat which he proceeds to stab with a knife. But it took a much publicized incident, in which Roosevelt allegedly spared a bear cub, to fuse the hunter irrevocably with his totem. Teddy's act of clemency, according to one account, inspired a Russian immigrant toymaker to create and market, with historic consequences, a stuffed bear modeled on the fortunate cub. A few years later, Teddy bears were selling by the thousands, and "The Teddy Bear March" had become a popular song.

Another film, *The "Teddy Bears,"* made in 1907 at the height of Roosevelt's popularity, introduced a sinister tone into what was ostensibly a comedy. Based on the tale of Goldilocks and the Three

Bears, the film ends suddenly and equivocally with the appearance of Teddy the Hunter. Teddy kills Momma and Papa Bear as they are chasing Goldilocks across snow-covered fields; then he leads Baby Bear off on a leash. *The "Teddy Bears"* underscored what I think was always latent in the newspaper cartoons and in the parodies about the man with the big scary teeth, glinting eyeglasses, and death-dealing gun—that for Roosevelt hunting was serious business. A photograph he had taken of himself in hunting gear, rifle and knife prominently displayed, his expression cold and judgmental, strengthens this supposition.

Clearly, as the thousands of words he devoted to the subject might suggest, he regarded hunting less as a leisure-class diversion than as a rite fraught with moral and social meaning. The accolade "Mr. President, you are no tenderfoot," bestowed upon him by one of his guides, was a public testimonial to his manhood. Roosevelt equated the hunterly virtues—courage, honor, tenacity, a willingness to take risks and accept pain without whimpering—with civic virtues. He upheld the virile outdoor man, tested by exposure to wilderness conditions, as a salutary corrective to what he called the "unadulterated huckster or pawn-broker type" that flourished in the immigrant-infested urban east. Roosevelt's conservation measures, in the opinion of many his most lasting contribution, preserved for the nation vast areas of unspoiled nature, but he had more in mind than recreation for urban vacationers. He was giving unborn generations a taste of the character-building frontier experience that had toughened and tempered him. Conservation was tantamount to social regeneration, a hedge against creeping decadence.

For Roosevelt, hunterly and military virtues smoothly blended. "Only those are fit to live who do not fear to die and none are fit to die who have shrunk from the joy of life and the duty of life," reads one of his pronunciamentos inscribed on the walls of the Theodore Roosevelt Memorial in New York's American Museum of Natural History. "Aggressive fighting for the right is the noblest sport the world affords" is another. "If I must choose between righteousness and peace," it continues, "I choose righteousness."

The image of Roosevelt the Soldier for a brief time dominated the media no less compellingly than Roosevelt the Hunter. Between the early spring of 1898, when he formed his volunteer regiment of Rough Riders to fight the Spanish "dagoes" in Cuba, and the demobilization of his military "cowboys" in the late summer of that year, he became a national celebrity.

He resigned his position as assistant secretary of the navy and sought military combat, he assured his friends, not because he dreamed of glory. After all, he had "consistently advocated a warlike policy." Now it was time to practice what he preached if he expected to go anywhere in politics. "I have a horror," he said, "of the people who bark but don't bite." Moreover, he thought the war would speed American expansion in the Pacific and Caribbean and give the nation a much needed "moral lift." Privately he excoriated both "the timid and scholarly men in whom refinement and culture have been developed at the expense of all virile qualities" and "the big moneyed men in whose minds money and material prosperity have finally dwarfed everything else."

Roosevelt's confidences, private or public, must be studied with caution, for he wasn't one to examine his inmost feelings, much less to reveal them. "Father has depths of insincerity not even he has plumbed," Roosevelt's daughter, Alice, remarks in Gore Vidal's *Empire*. At least this reader of Theodore Roosevelt's letters feels the force of the fictional Alice's observation. He wasn't two-faced, and he didn't speak with a forked tongue, but he was hard to pin down. The pupil of Admiral Mahan had a grasp of international power politics and was a sophisticated player of the diplomatic game. The evangelical nationalist read history romantically. He studied it for personal edification and faulted and praised mighty captains and men of power from the Romans until his own times. His judgments on Cromwell, Hamilton, Gouverneur Morris, Thomas Hart Benton, Andrew Jackson, Abraham Lincoln, and the military leaders of the Civil War are clues to his character and ambitions.

Nothing in Roosevelt's correspondence suggests a calculated policy to make political capital out of his military adventures. Still, the examples of Washington, Jackson, and Grant would hardly have escaped the amateur historian, and his negotiations with magazine publishers, even before he sailed for Cuba, to write up his experiences look as if he didn't intend to hide his light under a bushel. From the start, "nineteenth-century America's greatest master of press relations," as Edmund Morris calls him, scarcely missed a chance to use the correspondents (most notably Richard Harding Davis, whom he particularly favored) and the photographers. Newspapers churned out human interest stories about the First U.S. Volunteer Cavalry, three-quarters of them recruited from the Rocky Mountain states, the rest made up of Eastern polo-playing "bluebloods," Southern gentlemen, and a sprinkling of Mexicans and Indians. Needless to say, their leader, the lieutenant-colonel of this motley regiment, got more than his share of space. Whether he planned it or not, he was freighted for the White House at the conclusion of the "splendid little war."

For almost a decade thereafter, Roosevelt exhorted, educated, and entertained a national audience from what he called his "bully pulpit." Simply being president kept him on center stage, but the periodic spectacles he arranged—the signing of the Russian-Japanese peace treaty at Portsmouth, New Hampshire, the neat surgical operation without congressional assistance that separated Panama from Colombia, the dispatching of the "Great White Fleet" on its intimidating goodwill voyage around the world—guaranteed the president star billing. His transparently motivated rupture with Taft (whose nomination he had dictated) and his abortive presidential campaign on the Progressive Party ticket against the incumbent President Taft and Woodrow Wilson, the Democratic candidate, marked the beginning of his political decline.

Until then he had made his self-image the public's. He had spoken for this public and in its name blistered any interest group or party he considered "Wrong," that is to say, any faction that in his view threatened to upset the national equilibrium by challenging his policy of balance and compromise. These included "swinish" corporations; "mushy," "Bedlamite," and "foolish" reformers; "vicious" trade unionists, socialists, and anarchists, and all such "vermin." He was most in tune with the old-stock citizenry of the lower and upper middle class whose traditional values were like his own. And he had a special affection for "ordinary citizens," by which he meant not the industrial working class, not the newer immigrants with whom he had only gingerly ties, but soldiers, policemen, boxers, and cowboys. He called them "splendid fellows" and treated them as his grown-up children.

When he left the White House, Roosevelt was generally respected as a capable chief executive and a responsible custodian of the nation. Once out of office, he thirsted for his old prerogatives. Defeated in his bid for the Republican nomination, he aligned himself with party malcontents and independents, the same political types he had castigated for almost thirty years as mollycoddles, pussyfooters, milk-and-water philanthropists, and "nice little men." He had stuck with the Grand Old Party, notwithstanding his quarrels with some of its managers, because it stood in theory for the conservative principles he favored. But now, to the dismay of Republican loyalists, he zoomed off on an eccentric tangent to collaborate with men whose support would have embarrassed him only a few years earlier. He had moved from the political consensus into the "lunatic fringe" (his term), and although he remained a celebrity, a hero to the Teddyites, he had good reason to believe before the end of his life that the American people had grown a little tired of him.

If Roosevelt was out of touch with the country after 1912, the world war made him obsolete. I have concentrated on the Teddy Roosevelt whose bravura performances, dash, and style endeared him to a national claque. That figure has ossified into a period piece.

But there is a Theodore Roosevelt at odds with the artifact, a troubled and un-Teddyish personality. He shows lapses of self-confidence, and he is more vulnerable to the barbs of the satirists than he lets on. His antipathies and rages hint of unacknowledged guilt. He subjects himself to endless tests; he registers aesthetic vibrations, feeds on plaudits, and is addicted to reading. This bookish Roosevelt gets his due in the press, but some deeper political instinct tells him to subordinate the cap and gown to the lariat and the rifle. So he neither parades his cultural preoccupations before the rank and file nor condescends to them. Nor does he hint of the gulf separating Theodore Roosevelt of Oyster Bay and Harvard's Porcellian from the worthy people he conscientiously serves.

Theodore Roosevelt was a latter-day representative of the old Federalist elite first dispossessed by Andrew Jackson and his sweaty Democrats and later denied power by the major parties. Hopes that the Civil War would burn out the national rot and restore a civic-minded, gentlemanly minority to positions of influence were briefly entertained and quickly flattened. The good-government people ("Goo-Goos" or "Mugwumps," as stalwart Republicans contemptuously referred to them) carried little weight in party councils. High-minded aspirants to political office faced cheerless options. They could organize campaigns to elect honest candidates in state and local contests, knowing that the rascals would be back after the flurry of reform; or, like the sardonic Henry Adams, they could withdraw from the action and watch—and document—the downfall of the republic. They could concede their political impotence and take up some other vocation; or (and this was the most atypical of strategies) they could work with the party bosses who determined the outcome of elections and bide their time. Roosevelt wanted to rule instead of being ruled by his inferiors. That meant taking the plunge into machine politics and braving the warnings of his social peers that politics was a dirty game, one no gentleman ought to play.

He proved them wrong. He bearded the bruisers. And thanks to his unquenchable ego and boldness, well-placed allies, a widely publicized act of derring-do in a brisk war, and a fortuitous assassination, he found himself president of the United States. Brooks Adams, Henry's brother and the brother-in-law of Henry Cabot Lodge, Roosevelt's closest friend, hailed him as the new Caesar. " 'Thou hast it now: King, Cawdor, Glamis, all—' " he wrote him. "The world can give no more. You hold a place greater than Trajan's, for you are the embodiment of a power not only vaster than the power of the empire, but vaster than men have ever known." Roosevelt listened more attentively to Adams's historical scenarios than he would admit, but he also considered him a little cracked. Having already pondered Macbeth and rebuked Cromwell (while half forgiving him) for his dictatorial acts, he wasn't about to upset any applecarts. If the business tycoons and professional politicians questioned his soundness, informed conservatives claimed him rightly as one of their own. He might verbally whip the Trusts and "the malefactors of great wealth," shake his finger at them, appeal to their patriotism, but he followed an expedient course.

Even when he appeared to have broken out of the traces between 1912 and 1916, consorting with ideologues and nostrum-mongers and sounding very radical indeed, his political philosophy hadn't significantly changed. He still believed in order at all costs, in an idealism sensibly constrained; and though he was exasperated by the greed, stupidity, and arrogance of the big capitalists, he continued to worry more about a surly and knavish working class and the possibility of class war.

A book published in Roosevelt's heyday inadvertently abstracted him into a social type. This was Thorstein Veblen's 1899 *The Theory of the Leisure Class*, a study in the customs, attitudes, and styles of behavior of America's leisured elite, its would-be patriciate. Veblen presented this well-heeled tribe as the preservers of "archaic traits" and "devout observances." Their barbarian rituals obviously served no useful purpose in modern industrial society, but paradoxically their very obsolescence made them reputable in American cultural and institutional life. Veblen noted in particular how the leisure class prolonged the "puerile phase" in its children's development by encouraging their "proclivity for exploits" and truculent athleticism.

Similarly, a great deal of make-believe, he observed, pervaded leisure-class sporting pastimes. The mildest of men who went out shooting were "apt to carry an excess of arms and accoutrements in order to impress upon their own imagination the seriousness of their undertaking." They were also prone "to a histrionic prancing gait and to an elaborate exaggeration of the motions, whether of stealth or of onslaught, involved in their deeds of exploit." Football as well was imbued with "a colourable make-believe of purpose." Just as hunters systematically slaughtered their prey in the name of wholesome outdoor recreation and nature worship, so college football purportedly built strong bodies and fostered "a manly spirit." In reality, Veblen dryly asserted, that popular sport bore the same relation to physical culture "as the bull-fight to agriculture," and far from inculcating good fellowship and self-sacrifice, it encouraged a ferocity and predatory cunning that were readily adaptable to business or military enterprise.

Reading Veblen's deadpan sociological satire with Theodore Roosevelt in mind, one is reminded time and again of his sentiments and tastes, of his letters to Harvard football captains, for example, or his celebration of the fighting instincts, his eagerness for battle, and his frequent recourse in speaking and writing to the metaphors of war. Again, Roosevelt's pleasure in bloody Icelandic sagas and his wish that "The Battle Hymn of the Republic" (in which God is the "Him" of Battle) would become the national anthem are consistent with Veblen's profile of the martial socialite chieftain presiding over the sanguinary rites of his class.

In a discerning review of Veblen's book, William Dean Howells noted the insatiable appetite of ordinary Americans "for everything that relates to the life removed from work, from the simple Republican idea." The Roosevelt who in exalted moments conflated peaceful habits with besotted materialism and whose most cherished memories were of war and the chase became for them a figure of absorbing fascination. He lived their daydreams and touched their hearts and minds so long as he stayed in the limelight toward which he was tropistically drawn. Not long after his ouster from "the corridors of power," he dwindled in the public eye, and although never without champions while he lived, or thereafter for that matter, he never again assumed Mt. Rushmore proportions in the popular imagination.

Today his labors seem less herculean than his dazzled supporters perceived them to be. No public policy of lasting importance is attached to his name, save perhaps his conservation legislation, which in our environment-conscious age seems more important than it did in his. Roosevelt the expansionist sent the fleet around the world and engineered the securing of the Panamanian isthmus and the construction of the canal ("by far the most important action I took in foreign affairs," he wrote); but (and to his deep regret) no major domestic crisis or foreign war tested him to the extreme. He wrote no outstanding state paper or literary work. To be sure, the same could be said of all but a few American presidents, but then not many of them were reputedly blessed with such splendid and diverse talents or shared his Icarian aspirations.

What's still arresting about him has less to do with the artifact, the posturing Teddy Roosevelt of the cartoons, than with his tenderer double who occasionally emerges in his letters and books, one who could drop the remark that the Dakota Badlands looked the way Poe sounded, or compare the extinction of the passenger pigeon to the destruction "of all the works of some great writer." "Charming" was the word often applied to him, a curious term for the thickset, hand-crushing monologuist but understandable to a reader of his correspondence. His tough carapace, like Hemingway's, protected a sensibility evidenced in moments of passivity, very rare with him, when nature (bird songs, plains, mountains, forests, and the like) imposed on him rather than the other way around. Walt Whitman detected such moments in Roosevelt's western reminiscences. They showed "a little touch of the dude," Whitman told Horace Traubel, but when Roosevelt looked and listened, he "realized" the alluring contours and spirit "of that wild Western life" and got "pretty near the truth."

During Theodore Roosevelt's incumbency, the White House acquired an imperial tone, but it wasn't dull or parochial or vulgar. It became a place where civilized company gathered at the behest of an energetic and cultivated host. Driven by an ungovernable curiosity, his range of interests and concerns exceeded those of all other presidents, Jefferson excepted. He reached out to men and women who wrote and said things that appealed to him, and he strained to stay abreast of the world's work. Can the same be said (and I include the second Roosevelt and John F. Kennedy) of the previous or subsequent occupants of the White House?

When Theodore Roosevelt died, according to one of his contemporaries, "it was as though the wind had fallen, a light had gone out, a military band had stopped playing." He had been on display for almost forty years, a public-spirited man ablaze with good intentions, self-absorbed if not introspective, and totally devoid of skepticism. He remained attractively and unattractively boyish until the end. In the Wilson years, his behavior was mischievous and vindictive. He withheld his sympathies from anything alien to his ancestral pieties, whether it was the muck raked up by reformers or the import of Tolstoy's "decadent" *Kreutzer Sonata.* He was broad, not deep. He liked happy endings, and he closed his ears to reports from the pit. He doesn't really belong on the granite mountain top with the titans.

How to Read Don DeLillo

He sits on a stair in a hallway and gazes unsmiling into the camera, his expression severe and suspicious. He looks alert and intense and unrelaxed, almost prim. Coatless, open-collared, sleeves rolled, he might be an intellectual apartment house super with a hidden past (some refugee from graduate school? a lapsed priest?) wary of interrogators.

Who is Don DeLillo? He's rather skimpy with his interviews, shuns the milieu and company of literary gossip-mongers (privacy is a theme in *Great Jones Street*), and doesn't say much about himself or his social origins or family upbringing. No one character in any of his nine novels can confidently be said to speak for him. He is in all of them and none of them, diffused in the eddies of his inventions.

DeLillo is the son of Italian immigrants and a graduate of Fordham University. I think it's worth noting that nothing in his novels suggests a suppressed "Italian foundation"; hardly a vibration betrays an ethnic consciousness. His name could just as well be Don Smith or Don Brown. His ethnic past doesn't serve for him as an "intoxicant of the imagination" (Allen Tate's phrase) in the way New England Puritanism did for Hawthorne and Emily Dickinson or the experience of being Jewish did for several generations of Jewish writers. DeLillo can be very funny, but unlike black and Jewish writ-

Originally published in the *South Atlantic Quarterly*, 89, no. 2 (Spring 1990), 305–319. Copyright © 1990 by Duke University Press.

ers who have sucked humor from their humiliations, there's nothing particularly "ethnic" about his dark comedy unless we imagine that traces of the uneasy alien or of ethnic marginality are discernible in his brand of grotesque parody, his resistance to the American consensus, and his sympathy and respect for the maimed, the disfigured, and the excluded people in his novels.

DeLillo's presumably Roman Catholic upbringing rarely surfaces in his books although his accounts of the spiritual and carnal excesses of his seekers, prodigies, terrorists, spies, academicians, gangsters, entrepreneurs can be read as the musings of a crypto-Christian and profane moralist who finds his most rewarding subject matter in the precincts of a fallen world. The sexual episodes in his novels, of which there are a good many, are at once "explicit" and lust-chilling. He charts the curves, angles, declivities of entangled bodies with a topographical exactness, but the lovemaking itself is usually a joyless and unrevelatory business.

He promises but holds back. The signs, sounds, signals his characters think they see or hear or feel defy reason and intuition. These unexplained phenomena, whether presented in the language of scientists or cranks, seem to hint of a religious disposition or at least a hankering for transcendent answers, but DeLillo never takes the reader into his confidence, leaves few if any clues to point to his philosophy, social views, habits, and tastes. He is a withholder, a mystifier, a man without a handle and, like the trickster mushroom of Emily Dickinson's poem—surreptitious, circumspect, and supple—he keeps popping up in unexpected places.

Impressions of DeLillo: I see him as an Ear, an Eye, a Nose, a Camera, a Tape Recorder, a Sound Track; as a Fact-and-Word Collector; as a restless and speculative artist utilizing ideas to counterpoint the action of his narratives; as a popular culture specialist and possessor of a considerable stock of disparate information, some of it pretty esoteric stuff acquired very likely by purposeful reading, a lot of it simply the by-product of astute observation and whimsical interest in what goes on about him. His vocabulary is large and rich, and he names things exactly.

I see something of him in his own creation, Dr. Pepper, the "awthentic genius" in *Great Jones Street,* authority on "crisis sociology," dope-master and brain mechanic, wheeler-dealer of the illicit, changeable as Proteus, blending into his surroundings so completely that he can become anonymous, given to a "tightfisted humor," and blessed with the "gift of putting distance between himself and his applauders." In his fictive world, DeLillo, like Dr. Pepper, has "lived among dangerous men, worked in hazardous circumstances."

Here are a few key topics that keep erupting in the thoughts and conversations of his characters and in the mini-essays interspersed throughout his novels.

Catastrophe: (Under this rubric I include destruction in all its varied manifestations—plain murder and assassination, the Holocaust, nuclear explosions, toxic pollution, etcetera.)

Gary Harkness, of *End Zone,* playing lethal football for Logos College in West Texas, is both "seriously depressed" and fascinated by the prospect of nuclear war. He is addicted to doomsday statistics and impressed by "the rationality of irrationality," by the verbal magic that can impersonalize killing on a cosmic scale through the employment of "words and phrases like thermal hurricanes, overkill, circular error probability, post-attack environment, stark deterrence, dose-rate contours, kill-ration, spasm war." (To paraphrase a remark in *Ratner's Star,* the more extreme the danger, the more abstract the vocabulary to describe it: euphemism is tantamount to terror.) The pleasure Gary takes in reading the beautiful language of destruction is "almost sensual," he unhappily concludes. Is he mad? Do others share his feelings?

Yes they do. Heinrich Gladney in *White Noise,* one of DeLillo's formidably informed adolescents, also savors with "some kind of out-of-the-world elation" the mechanisms and logistics of disaster. And so does his father, Jack Gladney, DeLillo's narrator and founder of the department of Hitler studies at College-on-the-Hill. Friday evenings find the Gladney family riveted to the TV set silently watching "floods, earthquakes, mud slides, erupting volcanoes." Their appetite for lava and burning villages is insatiable; every cataclysm makes them "wish for something bigger, grander, more sweeping." This yearning, Jack's knowing friends tell him, is perfectly natural and normal. Disasters focus our attention. We need them and depend upon them so long as they occur elsewhere.

DeLillo's presentation of his catastrophists' eerie tastes is witty and unsolemn, and it's not always easy to tell when (like one of his pop-cult experts) he is being playful "in a pulverizing way" and when he's being seriously apocalyptic. For me he is most himself as the sociologist of crisis, pondering the ways in which the raw facts of natural and man-made disasters are processed into theory and insinuated in the public mind.

Conspiracy: "This is the age of conspiracy," says Moll Robbins (*Running Dog*), the age of "connections, links, secret relationships." The magazine she writes for fans popular belief in international conspiracies and "fantastic assassination schemes." In the era of Watergate and Dallas when "every stark fact" is layered in ambiguity, faith in conspiracy theory can be very comforting: a stay against chaos and a support for an "ordering instinct."

DeLillo has thought a lot about conspiracies and kindred operations (military and industrial espionage, secret plans and schemes, covert criminal and terrorist activities) that flourish in a technological climate. His archetypal plot is a mystery whose generally inconclusive solution depends on the deciphering of clues—a name, word, number, code. The protagonists are usually troubled intelligent persons already poised to kick over the traces and susceptible to intrigue. He sets them tunneling deeper and deeper toward some unreachable solution or explanation, then shows them to be players in a game manipulated by unknowable forces. As they press beyond confining boundaries in quest of spiritual independence and self-recognition, they are likely to fall into the chaos they had hoped to shape and correlate. At bottom they are only integers in a vast information network created and controlled by "banks, insurance companies, credit organizations, tax examiners, passport offices, reporting services, police agencies, intelligence gatherers." Only the real men of power in finance, government, and the military speak and comprehend "the true underground idiom," and they are the beneficiaries of a technology they can't control, shadowy figures doubly dangerous because they are ignorant of their ignorance.

More palpable are their technicians and agents who gather and condense multifarious data for the masters. Such a person is Rowser (*The Names*), specialist on "money, politics, and force" and fact-gatherer for a subsidiary of "the point," a $2 billion conglomerate. Rowser's "Group" sells risk insurance to multinationals whose executives have become ransom targets for kidnappers and terrorists in the Middle East. Calamities per se—"meltdowns, runaway viruses," and the like—have for him only an actuarial significance, yet if oblivious of "deep and unseen" things, he is physically affected by the atmosphere of fear so pervasive in DeLillo's downward- and deathward-pointing novels.

Landscape: DeLillo's fictional landscape isn't confined to the United States. Greece is the setting for *The Names,* a novel which besides its many other virtues is a remarkable piece of travel writing. *Ratner's Star* takes place at a dreamlike superscience complex in some distant nameless territory. Mostly, however, he favors American cities (New York, Dallas, Washington, among others), terminals of fear whose "casual savagery" and "fatal beauty" seem to energize his imagination. From these centers of infection, urban sickness filters into the hinterlands. A good deal goes on in office buildings, warehouses, dingy flats, and bars, but his camera eye ranges as well over suburbia and small towns and stretches of highway. He is never supercilious or smart-alecky about places and regions (his social satire when he indulges it is muted, sly) and he is particularly sensitive to supermarkets and to motels situated beyond the limits of "large and reduplicating" cities.

His supermarket is a magical and sexy place. Inside the "great omniscient door," sliding and closing unbidden, are aisles of plenty, a lotusland, a temple of fecundity where fruits are always in season. David Bell, the narrator of *Americana,* observes the checkout girls moving "their hips against the cash registers." In *White Noise,* Murray Jay Siskind likens the supermarket to a Tibetan heaven, "well-lighted . . . sealed off . . . self-contained." To Siskind, who has spent his life "in small steamy delicatessens with slanted display cabinets full of trays that hold soft wet lumpy matter in pale colors," the "large and clean and modern" cornucopia is a revelation full of "psychic data" ready for analysis. But his friend Jack Gladney hears a disturbing undercurrent: "The toneless systems, the jangle and skid of carts, the loudspeaker and coffee-making machines, the cries of children. And over it all, or under it all, a dull and unlocatable roar, as of some form of swarming life just outside the range of human apprehension."

Motels provoke in DeLillo an even more complex and discordant response. No one, with the possible exception of Nabokov, has written so eloquently and penetratingly about them. For DeLillo the motel is "a powerfully abstract" invention—hermetic, temporary, and bland. As in these descriptions from *Americana,* he wonderfully catches motelness: chill damp sheets, the "steady and almost unendurable whispering of ventilation," the "too many hangers in the closet, as if the management were trying to compensate for a secret insufficiency too grievous to be imagined." And yet the motel room is "in the heart of every man," an idea of deliverance from chaos, a kind of depersonalization chamber in which the sojourner can achieve "mathematical integrity" and merge with other transients who occupy similar cells all over the world. Such a state would be unattainable in the "all too personal" borrowed apartment or fleabag. Only in the motel "flows the dream of the confluence of travel and sex."

America: After the publication of *Libra,* one prominent reviewer called DeLillo a literary vandal and a bad citizen, another declared him to be a self-proclaimed outsider who holds an "ostentatiously gloomy view of American life and culture" and loathes American society. Had he confined his "paranoid" visions and "lurid imaginings" to science fiction, say, and eschewed "real people and important events," his tediously predictable "politics" wouldn't matter much. But in serving up suppositions and half-truths about a momentous national tragedy, he has committed a mischievous act.

Such charges are similar to those made several years ago against Gore Vidal's *Abraham Lincoln, A Novel* and revive old questions that touch on the legitimacy of certain kinds of historical fiction, the social responsibilities of writers, and definitions of literary transgression. Historical truth, Vidal insisted, is "what is best imagined," particularly when it's based on "the disagreed as well as agreed-upon facts." Literature (I quote a remark attributed to Carlos Fuentes) is "what history conceals, forgets, or mutilates." I think this comes close to DeLillo's view of the matter. *Libra* draws "from the historical record," he advises his readers, while making "no claim to literal truth," but he affirms the novelist's privilege to alter and embellish.

This isn't the occasion to debate the charge that he has traduced "an ethic of literature" by taking liberties with historical facts and flouting "the judicious weighing of possibilities." The accusation, however, does have a bearing on the depiction of him as a "leftist" suffering from "ideological virulence," a flag burner whose vision of America is unmitigatedly bleak and sinister. The simplest reply to such an allegation would be to say that how writers see and describe their country is their own business and that nay-saying isn't unconstitutional. Then one might want to add that the conception of DeLillo as a surly revolutionary is based on a partial or superficial reading of his books and misrepresents his position.

Given his diffidence toward his readers, and the games and puzzles he confronts them with, and given his inclination to dress his ideas in masquerade, it's no wonder that he has been misjudged. "The writer is working against the age," he told an interviewer in 1983, "and so he feels some satisfaction in not being widely read. He is diminished by an audience." Furthermore, DeLillo has taken pains to separate himself from his characters. He neither likes nor dislikes them, he says; he recognizes them and reports their attitudes, leaving it up to the reader to decide the degree to which he shares or rejects their sentiments. (I think he does care about their ideas, although he is professedly indifferent to them as "persons," and he isn't always so detached as he claims to be.)

Yet it so happens that a good many speakers in his novels from *Americana* to *Libra* roundly and eloquently savage American society and culture. In brief, their collective indictment might be summed up as follows: the country is "totally engulfed by all the so-called worst elements of our national life and character." It is populated with lonely, bored, empty, fearful people inured to abominations and complicit, whether they realize it or not, in the destruction of what they ostensibly revere—including the treasured beliefs and artifacts of the past. Perceived from abroad, America signifies ignorant, blind, and contemptuous corporate power, "the whole enormous rot and glut and glare" of its popular culture spreading across the world like a cancer. It is "big business, big army and big government all visiting each other in company planes for the sole purpose of playing golf and talking money."

This hyperbolical indictment is usually voiced by wacky or disintegrating personalities launched on obsessional quests. They may serve as vents for DeLillo's own vagrant meditations, but there's no reason to assume that in unequivocally rejecting an "Amerika" devoid of "beauty, dignity, order, proportion," they are invariably speaking for him. DeLillo is no ideological Jeremiah. He thrives on "blaring" social imperfections and is fascinated by the one-dimensional, ruthless half-men, the single-minded system planners and management consultants and nuclear strategists who exhibit "distinctly modern" characteristics. The blackened America in which they flourish is less a historical place, a people with a history, than it is a premonition, a clue to the puzzle of what's to come, and a target of a universal grievance. America in DeLillo's fiction is object-ified in the accents and tones of American language. It's a real place with its own colors and textures, not like the allegorical or ab-stracted settings of Kafka and Beckett. "Fiction without a sense of real place," he tells an interviewer, "is automatically a fiction of es-trangement." Contrary to the accusations of his detractors, he is no more estranged from America than the best of his predecessors and contemporaries. (American literature, politicians need constantly to be reminded, abounds with marginal men and women, savage mis-anthropes, avid experimenters, all dissatisfied and restless.)

Essays and Set Pieces: DeLillo's characters might be likened to actors in a traveling theatrical company, ready at any moment to harangue, comment, speculate, and improvise, yet they stick to their scripts and seem to have no real autonomy, no continuing presence or independent life once they have delivered their lines, spoken their monologues, and disappeared into the wings. Whoever or wherever they are, they speak in the voice of the author, if not necessarily for him, and tend to be smart as well as fluent. While not exactly playing interchangeable roles, a number of them could easily blend into any one of DeLillo's nine novels, for they are more than mere fictional inventions: they are emanations of Don DeLillo.

Some readers may find his novels too talky and become fatigued by the plethora of opinions his speakers all too willingly offer and by the recondite lore that wells up in their talk. (David Bell, in *Americana,* concedes that one of his "main faults was a tendency to get blinded by the neon of an idea, never reaching truly inside of it.") Others, like me, will be charmed and instructed by their com-ico-serious chatter. DeLillo can be boring at times, and occasionally he overwrites, strains too hard; but how quick his speakers are to spot the extraordinary in the commonplace, how sensitive to shades and nuances, sounds and colors, and how perceptively they read the language of movement and gesture:

A woman spied on by a lustful adolescent through half-closed blinds, "ironing with the smooth movements of a lionness caressing her cubs."

Another woman observed cutting a hedge, "her arms beating somewhat like a bird discovering flight."

A rock musician "strait-jacketed in crushed velvet" who somehow "managed to invest the simple act of sniffling with an element of the gravest accusation."

A hospital scene: "People crossed the hall like wandering souls, holding their urine aloft in pale beakers."

A sound heard in an old house: "the indolent sermon of a saw on wood."

A detail: "He opened the trailer door and watched them get out, two men showing the stiff weighted movements of long-distance drivers."

An observation: "Collings had the spare build, the leanness and fitness of an older man who wants you to know he is determined to outlive you."

"I have reached the point," one of DeLillo's characters in *Americana* announces, "where the coining of aphorism seems a very worthy substitute for good company or madness." Whether or not De-Lillo is speaking for himself here, his novels are studded with aphoristic comment on such matters as living defensively ("the central theme of our age"); on death ("an unknotting of consciousness in a space of n dimensions"); on digital clocks (they tell time "too bluntly" and are hard to connect with homely quotidian events); on the "solitary trance of power" released in the act of sighting down the barrel of a gun; on growing old quietly after the shock of reaching forty; on sunsets ("A sunset is the story of the world's day"); on self-deprecation as a form of ego and aggression ("a wanting to be noticed even for one's flaws").

Concise observations of this sort can lengthen into little essays. In *Great Jones Street*, Bucky Wunderlick reflects for a paragraph on how a disconnected telephone,

> deprived of its sources, becomes in time an intriguing piece of sculpture. The business transacted is more than numbed within the phone's limp ganglia; it is made eternally irrelevant. Beyond the reach of shrill necessities the dead phone disinters another source of power. The fact that it will not speak (although made to speak, made for no other reason) enables us to see it in a new way, as an object rather than an instrument, an object possessing a kind of historical mystery. The phone has made a descent to total dumbness, and so becomes beautiful.

The narrator in *The Names* soliloquizes on the tourist as an escapist from accountability:

> Tourism is the march of stupidity. You're expected to be stupid. The entire mechanism of the host country is geared to the travelers acting stupidly. You walk around dazed, squinting into fold-out maps. You don't know how to talk to people, how to get anywhere, what the money means, what time it is, what to eat or how to eat. . . . Together with thousands, you are granted immunities and broad freedoms. You are an army of fools, wearing bright polyesters, riding camels, taking pictures of each other, haggard, dysenteric, thirsty. There is nothing to think about but the next shapeless event.

DeLillo's set pieces are longer than his essayettes and more studiedly keyed to the novels' moods and themes. They might be described as strategic pauses in the action, as literary arias. Some examples:

In *Americana*, an artfully composed recollection of deadly summers in a small town. The lyricism of the narrator's language oddly contrasts with his intimations of impending terror ("The menace of the history of quiet lives") especially strong on Sundays when the "neat white churches stand in groves of sunlight," and it seems to him "as though the torpor of Christianity itself is spread over the land."

In *Great Jones Street*, a failed pornographer, happy to be free from his mechanical labors ("Every pornographic work brings us closer to Fascism") describes his "terminal fantasy." During the day he writes, sustained by tomato juice, saltines, and Budweiser beer, but at night he prowls the building in which he lives, armed with a magic shotgun and a "giant machete" and escorted by two vicious German shepherds. The fantasy culminates with the slaughter of eight invaders, a scene of "choreographed movie violence," and making bonfires of the bodies in the street. But a new fantasy has supplanted the old: writing "terminal fiction" after the financial system goes kaput, not for money or fame but to let survivors know what they've survived. (That might be a DeLillo fantasy too.)

The ramblings and inspired messages of the possessed heard over the airways: like the rant of Tom Thumb Goodloe (*Americana*), "the midnight evangelist": "If you can't pronounce a man's name, that man is a stranger. . . . Keeryst Jesus was not a stranger in his own land. He spoke the lingo. He ate the grub. He felt right at home." Like the voice of the announcer Doo-Wop "churning with gastric power." Like the pleased and excited expostulations of Dr. Pepper (*Great Jones Street*), friend of all the legendary nuts and con-persons and a legend in his own right, who wants "to tap untapped fields of energy" and control "biorhythms from the basic frequencies of the universe." (He isn't all that far removed from the Nobel Prize scientists in *Ratner's Star* or from sundry of DeLillo's listeners who hear messages in glossolalia.)

The crazies move comfortably and confidently in their grooves, unlike, for example, Sherwood Anderson's sad grotesques. Their obsessions, far from bottling them up, have liberated them, made them coherent, shaved their lives down to a point, eliminated doubt. Whether they know it or not, they have joined the company of the twice-born and are en route to some ultimate epiphany. The coach in *End Zone* finds his zone of tranquility in the center of a football scrimmage. His career is the parody of a saint's: renunciation of self, spiritual preparation "in an inner world of determination and silence," and finally the blessed conviction that "pain is part of the harmony of the nervous system." Earl Mudger, professional American soldier and organizer of a rogue intelligence apparatus in *Running Dog*, is a variation of the type of terrible simplifier, "honed" (to use one of DeLillo's favorite words) to the sharpness of the knives he makes in his workshop for the good of his soul, a model of controlled violence and a sensitive monster.

Writers, monsters of another sort, are interested in obsession, DeLillo is quoted as saying, "because it involves a centering and a narrowing down, an intense convergence." "Convergence" he often associates with a historical event, "the angle at which realities meet." (Compare with Emerson's "veracity of angles.") The obsessed are intense. They have a special integrity for him, are "already on the page," so to speak. Thus DeLillo sees obsession as a state "close to the natural condition of a novelist at work" and an obsessed person as "an automatic piece of fiction."

Pure mathematics is also an obsession, at least as it is defined by Billy Twillig, the young math genius in *Ratner's Star,* and akin in its aims and discipline to DeLillo's literary aesthetic. That is to say, it is simple, severe, and intense, balances "inevitability" with surprise, disdains the "slack" and the "trivial," strives for "precision as a language," pursues "connective patterns and significant form," and offers "manifold freedom in the very strictness it persistently upholds." The narrative line in DeLillo's novels is not consecutive, and logical connections aren't heavily underscored, but his books have their story forms, their own musical structures. They can be read as fables of the artist's breakthrough, after attendant tortures, into a realm of order in which all hitherto discordant things fall into place as past and present conflate.

Plots: Detective DeLillo sifts the clues, tries to make sense out of the babble. "Plot" in his novels is the imposition of a design. Plots, like mathematics, make sense. The fiction writer's impulse to "restructure reality" becomes more urgent the messier the world is or seems to be. His tools are words; he uses them to reorder disorder and "to know himself through language." Words are open sesames to secret caves.

The most recent DeLillo novel, *Libra,* one way or another subsumes most of the themes, topics, mannerisms, slants, attitudes, and styles of the previous eight, but it differs from them in several interesting respects. *Libra* makes greater concessions to reader expectations: its principal characters are less flattened; it moves by a logic that is more inexorable than the logic in the early works, although the order and continuity may only be a consequence of DeLillo's choosing to harness the action of the novel to historical persons and events. But if *Libra* is more sequential than his earlier novels and moves more relentlessly toward an inevitable resolution, hedged by the "facts" of history, it reflects like them his preoccupation with the meaning of chaos and order, conspiracy and buried revelation.

The kinship between the cast of *Libra* and DeLillo's other free-floating actors isn't hard to detect. No borderline divides their personal worlds from "the world in general." Hitler, Trotsky, Dallas, New Orleans, the Mafia, the CIA, Lee Harvey Oswald—the mix of "players" who inhabit "a world within a world" and form "a daisy chain of terror, suspicion and secret wish"—all these are in DeLillo's pre-*Libra* books. It's as though, unbeknownst to himself, he was always nosing toward the most dramatic of his historical scenarios. Subways figure in the educations of both Billy Twillig and Oswald. The creepy David Ferrie finds thoughts of bombs heart-lifting (as do, to their dismay, Gary Harkness and Jack Gladney), and he dreams of living in a hole—as one of the scientists in *Ratner's Star* actually does.

And *Libra* in a masterly and assured fashion recapitulates other familiar DeLillo themes:

Technology and human values: the human cost of exposure to vast spy systems, the literal and symbolic transgressions of U-2 planes, electronic devices, "orbiting sensors" and the like that, as an ex-CIA operative puts it, drain conviction out of us, "make us vague and pliant." Clandestine intelligence gathering by government agencies and the selecting and processing by corporations of "all the secret knowledge of the world" acquire "an almost dreamy sense of connection to each other."

Language and secrecy: *Libra* further explores the metaphysics of codes and cryptonyms, the power of secrecy. DeLillo's nest of plotters acts on the principle espoused by the cultist leader in *The Names:* "When the name is itself secret, the power and influence are magnified. The secret name is a way of escaping the world." Secrecy engenders "a special language," the key to which lies in a locked safe or in the bowels of a buried computer.

The aesthetics of conspiracy: "A conspiracy is the perfect working of a scheme . . . everything that ordinary life is not. It's the inside game, cold, sure, undistracted, forever closed off to us. We are the flawed ones, the innocents, trying to make some rough sense of the daily jostle. Conspiracies have a logic and a daring beyond our reach. All conspiracies are the same taut story of men who find coherence in some criminal act."

The analogy between the conspirator and the writer is instructive. A perfect conspiracy matches Poe's formula for a short story in which each part and word must fit into "one pre-established design." Henry James's artist-conspirator cuts through the "inclusion and confusion" of "clumsy Life" (what DeLillo calls the "daily jostle"), selects and discriminates "in search of the hard latent *value.*" *Libra,* among other things, is a literary exercise on the subject of conspiracy, and the conspirators themselves are characters in a larger plot whose involutions they are unaware of.

Win Everett, the initiator of the original plot plan, thinks of himself as a kind of supernovelist. After all, he has really invented Lee Oswald before the drifter comes into the plotters' focus. Oswald is the incarnation of a hypothetical construct, an idea materialized into "a name, a face, a bodily frame," or, to use a writer's phrase, into "plain text." The next stage in Everett's procedure is to "show the secret symmetries in a nondescript life," but he's troubled by the possibility that the plot he has concocted, and Oswald's destined part in it, may follow a logic of its own and go awry. In his version, the president is to be spared. All the same, he knows "that the idea of death is woven into the nature of every plot," and that "a narrative plot" is "no less than a conspiracy of armed men" prepared to disregard the author's injunctions. Everett is thrust aside by the forces he had fondly hoped to direct as precisely as a surgeon uses a laser beam in a tricky operation.

Nicholas Branch is assigned the task of piecing together the fragments left in the wake of the Kennedy assassination. This would seem to be an easier task than Everett's, since Everett is ignorant of the counterplot at work inside his own, and is unable to anticipate accident and chance. Branch has only to organize and assess the evidence of a finished episode. Yet the historian finds himself bogged down in the "fact-rubble of the investigations" that increases in volume as the event itself recedes in time. It is premature, he decides, to turn his "notes into coherent history," and it will remain premature so long as new data and new theories keep altering the slippery story. He must perforce turn artist, think imaginatively, and arbitrarily impose a design on the muddle.

Don DeLillo is a writer of fiction, not a historian, but like Nicholas Branch his mind's eye fixes on the shadowy connections professional historians usually fail to see or dismiss as baseless supposition. All of his novels breathe a kind of historical essence. They catch what he has described as the "movements or feelings in the air and the culture around us" and (I should add) the reverberations from below. I like to read him for many reasons: for his intelligence and wit, his range of reference, vocabulary, energy, and inventiveness, and not the least for the varieties of styles in which he couches his portentous bulletins to the world.

Epilogue

The Etiquette of Grief: A Literary Generation's Response to Death

In October 1854, a Georgia clergyman wrote to his son a circumstantial account of a death in the family. The deceased, a younger brother of the clergyman's wife, had contracted yellow fever and died in his twenty-ninth year. The letter writer reports every detail he can remember:

> We found your uncle in the shed room off the parlor *pulseless*, his hands blackened, the blood settling under the nails, perfectly calm and conscious when roused, then falling into sleep. He turned over and gave me his hand, saying, "What do you think of my case?" He had taken much quinine, and was then taking brandy at intervals; his hands and feet rubbed with brandy and pepper, and blisters applied on legs, thighs, stomach, breast, and arms and back of neck. Every effort made to bring on reaction. Your dear mother rubbed his hands and arms incessantly, others his feet.

Friends and relatives gathered around the bed of the dying man. He continued to sink. Asked if he would like his brother to pray with him, he replied he would be glad to have him do so. He repeated audibly two verses from the 103rd Psalm. It was comforting to know that shortly before his illness, he had professed his "firm reli-

A version of this essay was delivered as the Kenneth B. Murdock Memorial Lecture at Leverett House, Harvard University, March 8, 1978. It was published in *Prospects*, 4 (1979), 197–213.

ance upon the Lord Jesus Christ . . . and his resignation to the divine will." His last conscious act, the letter writer continues, was to turn to the face of his wife bending over him, *"My own dear Sallie."* The letter concludes with an emotional paragraph on family sorrow, an explanation of how and when the dead man caught the disease, a description of the burial, a reflection on the transitoriness of life, and an appeal from the father to his son to see this sad death as a warning and to accept Christ.[1]

Comparable letters were being written everywhere in the United States at this time when medicine was still primitive and when the American population—a good part of it in transit from one place to another—was exposed to all manner of natural and man-made hazards from yellow fever and cholera epidemics to exploding steamboats.[2] Death was not yet the shameful and unmentionable topic it became in twentieth-century America, nor was it Whitman's "strong and delicious word." If the extant letters and diaries can be trusted, it was a palpable reality, an everyday presence, a possibility not to be blinked away, however it came to be depicted in lachrymose Victorian verse and fiction.[3]

What may seem striking, and even morbid, to modern sensibilities (members of that "conspiracy of silence" in regard to death) is the unsparing realism and detail in the reports of deaths—reports written without circumlocution or prettification. A good many Americans living today have never been present at a natural death or even seen a corpse. Deaths usually occur in hospitals.[4] Coffins are increasingly being covered in churches and funeral homes. But not so long ago the deathbed watch (during which the demeanor of the dying was closely scrutinized), the laying out and "shrouding" of the corpse, the burial, the period of mourning that followed constituted a communal ritual supposedly of great social and psychic value.[5] It disciplined the survivors. It brought home to them the meaning of life's transience. It dignified the "distinguished thing" (a phrase Henry James allegedly uttered at his last moment), and provided a formula for the readjustment of the living.

This paper, however, will not focus on ordinary Americans confronted with the fact of death and its consequences, but rather on the styles of grief and mourning discernible in a particular group: a generation of American intellectuals and writers who flourished shortly before and during the last half of the nineteenth century.

They formed a community of sorts, linked by common attitudes toward culture and by their adherence to a number of acknowledged and unacknowledged assumptions. Old-stock Americans brought up in the Protestant faiths, some of them were later attracted to high Anglicanism and Roman Catholicism, but the majority found no refuge in a strong religious faith and had no expectations of an afterlife.

I conceive of this literary fellowship as living in a sort of intellectual and cultural suburbia quite detached from the society of the less-lettered majority whom they ostensibly were entertaining and instructing. At moments of personal desolation, they had only themselves and their intimate circle to fall back upon. They felt little inclination to avail themselves of the broader range of sympathies offered to the bereaved in simpler and less socially differentiated communities. It was no "privilege" for them to attend a deathbed drama, nor were they comforted by promises of reunions in heaven with dead relatives and friends.

Roughly at mid-point in the nineteenth century, the patterns and styles of funerals and mourning were beginning to become more mechanical, more stiff, than they had been earlier in the century and before. Older traditions lasted longer in rural communities, where the death of one touched all,[6] but in urban America the rites of death grew increasingly formal. The habit of covering up or privatizing death and mourning hadn't yet approached the stage it did in the twentieth century, but at least among the urban middle class the style or etiquette of mourning had already been prescribed in books on manners and correct behavior. Those uncertain about how to dress, the proper length of mourning periods, the appropriate way to treat the bereaved, or the approved style and content of the condolence letter found the answers in these manuals.

My select company, of course, wasn't bound by the do's and don'ts set down for the sort of people who required such advice.[7] All the same, they exhibited their own style of grieving and consoling, a style seemingly spontaneous but taking on a ritual character of its own. Sufferer and consoler acted out their roles in predictable ways, almost as if they had been rehearsed. This is not to suggest any insincerity or want of feeling on the part of the dispensers and receivers. I am suggesting only that both mourner and consoler appeared to be following undefined but recognizable conventions.

Since the men and the one woman writer I shall be talking about were used to addressing one another through the medium of letters, I have concentrated on letters of condolence and the replies to these letters as one approach to a literary generation's response to death. My method will be descriptive rather than analytical, yet I think the letters themselves often reveal more than they say. The very writing of a condolence letter or the reply to it can be a positive act, the first step, one might say, in distancing the sufferer from the source of his anguish. And this is probably especially true of writers who are more adept than ordinary people in sheathing their emotions in words and, through words and tropes, in controlling and perhaps dissipating their grief. The classical Victorian expression of this kind of self-therapy is contained in a few lines from Tennyson's *In Memoriam*:

> But, for the unquiet heart and brain
> A use in measured language lies;
> The sad mechanic exercise
> Like dull narcotics, numbing pain.

Ernest Samuels, in his biography of Henry Adams, remarks on how the "ritual of grief" sometimes went "to extremes," and he cites as one example Queen Victoria's practice of memorializing her dead consort by ordering his evening clothes to be laid out each night. The conspicuous omission of any reference to his wife's suicide in *The Education of Henry Adams* is seem by Samuels to be Adams's "contribution" to this ritual. None of the other literary sufferers I'm concerned with internalized his agony quite so ostentatiously; none was more insistent that the name of the lost one never be mentioned in his presence. But Adams's declaration that his life was smashed, that he belonged to the living dead, was very much in the manner of his age.[8]

After Longfellow's wife died in 1861 from burns suffered when her dress caught fire, he announced to friends that he had no future. Thenceforth, "utterly wretched and overwhelmed," he could only look to the past. To the world, he explained, he might appear calm, but inwardly he was "bleeding to death." He was still "speechless and bewildered," he wrote a month later, but doing his best "to bear sorrow patiently and silently."[9]

The deaths of two small daughters and an infant son shortly before his first wife died in 1853 temporarily darkened the life of the ebullient James Russell Lowell. "No matter how self-sustained the soul may be," he discovered, "there are bodily horrors and shocks connected with Death which leave a deep mark."[10]

William James's death left Henry James (so he wrote to a boyhood friend) sitting "heavily stricken and in darkness."[11] He used the same histrionic phrase a week later in a letter to Edith Wharton.

William Dean Howells confided to William James his terrible distress after the death of his grown daughter, Winifred: it "fell like a blow on the heart." To another he professed to feel "quite beaten into the dust, from which I do not know how to lift myself." Winifred's death, he wrote to William James's sister, Alice, "has changed the whole import of death and life; they seem at times almost convertible."[12]

Mark Twain's grief, when his twenty-four-year-old daughter, Susy, died of spinal meningitis while the Clemenses were abroad, was violent and unrestrained. "To me," he wrote to Howells, "our loss is bitter, bitter, bitter." His wife's grief "would bankrupt the vocabularies of all the languages." He saw in Susy's martyrdom a "ghastly tragedy," cruelly and precisely plotted by a remorseless nature. "It is my quarrel," again to Howells two years later, "that traps like that are set. Susy and Winnie given us in miserable sport, & then taken away." He likened Susy's death to a house burned to the ground, and almost two years after he could find it "one of the mysteries of nature that a man, all unprepared can receive a thunder-stroke and live."[13]

All of these thunder-stricken casualties—after reeling from the shock—continued to live and to write. Even the shattered Adams, as he played to the hilt his role of the abandoned husband, aloof and secret, took comfort in the thought that any future blow, no matter how devastating, would seem anticlimactic by comparison.[14] As for the others, with the possible exception of the guilt-ridden Mark Twain, who blamed himself for Susy's death, they resumed their former living patterns after participating in the drama of mourning. The process of healing and restoration was aided by consoling friends, a number of whom had "passed through the shadows," as the saying went, and become experts in dispensing the balm of sympathy. Some wrote tender and tactful messages. Others commiserated, as I shall show, in a bleaker vein.

Bear in mind an important fact: the correspondents were friends—often close friends—and could address each other with a tacit understanding denied to outsiders. This association freed them from some of the constraints that usually inhibit those whose letters of condolence are prompted by merely social considerations, but it also made the task of consolation a delicate one. Outsiders beyond the magic circle might blunder with impunity. An intimate was expected to know which remarks would lacerate and which would soothe—when to be concessive and when to be firm. It's worth noting in this connection that persons seeking guidance from etiquette books on how to write condolence letters were advised to say nothing likely to reopen recent wounds and to convey a warm but unspecific sympathy—nothing more.

Not infrequently the letter writer well acquainted with grief recommended to his correspondent a dignified stoicism and dismissed almost impatiently the platitudes of consolation as ineffective. Lowell, while still untouched by death, had once resorted to such clichés. In a letter to a fellow writer who had lost a child, Lowell called Death God's emissary. His friend must trust Providence, lean on God. Now was the time for him to test the truths of the poets—Chaucer, Spenser, Shakespeare, Milton, among others. But after death had laid low his own family, Lowell found no surcease in these remedies.[15] Writing to the mother of Colonel Robert G. Shaw, the Civil War hero who fell with his black troops at Fort Wagner, he declared: "There is nothing for such a blow as that but to bow the head and bear it. We may think of many things that in some measure make up for such a loss, but we can think of nothing that will give us back what we have lost." Experience had taught him that the unhappy must be left alone, that time was "clearly the only lenitive."[16]

Lowell's friend, the Olympian Charles Eliot Norton, was if anything more detached and philosophical in his ministrations to the bereft. A nonbeliever writing in most cases to other nonbelievers, he felt obliged to reassure with no resorting to what he considered the delusive "consolations of religion" and to "stand really upon firmer ground for the meeting of sorrow." As he expressed it to Leslie Stephen: "To accept the irremediable for what it really is, not trying to deceive oneself about it, or elude it, or to put it into a fancy dress, is to secure simple relations with life, and tends to strengthen the character without, I trust, any hardening of heart or narrowing of sympathies."[17] The death of Stephen's wife in 1895 recalled to Norton the death of his own wife more than twenty years before. He had never been the same, he told Stephen; in fact his own children had never really seen the vital part of him since their early childhood, for the natural springs of life had ceased to flow after she died. But he had learned, he said, "to live without joy, and without hope of it." Stephen would find that "the hardest time" was "yet to come, when the excitement or immediate sorrow and the need of strenuous effort is past; when the dreary routine of the joyless day begins, and when the sense of diminished personality weighs heavier and heavier."[18]

The man who harped most insistently on this sense of diminishment, Henry Adams, also had "died"—figuratively speaking—in 1885, the same year his wife did, although his body continued to function for another thirty years. Fifteen years earlier, he had watched his sister die very painfully, an experience he described in brutal detail to a correspondent.[19] "Sooner or later," he wrote subsequently, in what turned out to be a self-fulfilling prophecy, "fate commonly gets bored by the restless man who requires Paradise, and sets its foot on him with so much energy that he curls up and never wriggles again."[20] After his wife took her own life, he was incapable of either receiving or giving consolation. Death left nothing to be said. One might take comfort in the knowledge that others had suffered comparable woes, but "as for me," he wrote to a close female friend, "waste no sympathy. My capacity for suffering is gone."[21]

His letters written thereafter to friends in mourning hardly justify, it seems to me, his biographer's claim that "he became a master of the condolence letter." Samuels is more accurate when he describes the typical Adams letter of condolence as "a sad accolade of initiation"—which is something else.[22] A characteristic specimen of his condoling style is the letter he sent to Sir Robert Cunliffe (a favorite English friend), from Smyrna in 1898:

On arriving here this morning, I saw, in a chance newspaper, the announcement of Lady Cunliffe's death. I need hardly tell you how it weighs on my mind, and the thought of you continually recurs to remind me how I have had to tread that path before you, and how infinitely useless all attempt at consolation was, and still is. Yet the one slight relief which I then felt, was in the expressions of sympathy which made me a little less terribly conscious of total solitude. It was something to know that others had suffered like me. It was almost a relief to think that others had still got to suffer. More than twelve years have passed since then, and I have seen, one after another, almost all my friends require in their turn the sympathy they gave me. All my experience did not help me to give them more. It is heartrending to sit, year after year, and think of life past, interests lost, and pleasures extinct. The effort for distractions becomes ferocious and careless of consequences. You are older than I was when the life was knocked out of me, and perhaps you can bear it better for the years that you have had more than I. Anyway I will hope so. I am sorry not to be near enough to have at least a chance of showing sympathy.[23]

Never having found any way to expunge his own sorrow, Adams thought himself incapable of saying anything to relieve another's except to extend dumb sympathy or to say "that the army of sufferers had a common watchword which helped them to help each other without other expression." His friends must take his sympathy for granted. For years he had marched in the vanguard; he was "tired of the march, I can only whisper the word to you, and pass on."[24]

But Adams, the old veteran and memorializer, kept on living to his professed chagrin while the "goodly company" diminished. His cry of being abandoned can also be heard throughout the letters of other bereaved and bereaving writers, especially as the list of deaths lengthened. Lowell had once thought that "as we grow older we get used to death," but even if that were in a measure true, it made us "no less sensible to deaths which made us older and lonelier by widening the gap between our past and present selves. Our own lives seem to lose their continuity, and those who died long ago seem more wholly dead when some one who was associated with them and linked our memory more indissolubly with them goes out into endless silence and separation."[25] Mark Twain, calling Howells and himself a couple of "old derelicts," dictated an autobiographical entry in which he complained of literary friends dropping off before they were entitled to: "Howells and I have been postponed, and postponed, and postponed, until the injustice of it is becoming offensive."[26] The intellectual and literary fellowship consisted of something more than a collection of individual persons; it was an entity. The death of one diminished the totality, for they had invested a good deal of their personal and intellectual substance in each other's lives and work. Hence everyone died a little with the death of a member. As one after another fell out of what Mark Twain called "the great procession,"[27] the dwindling remnant stood out like drumlins on a rocky coast. At this stage in their lives, the condolence letter seemed less an expression of sympathy than a mournful meditation on the pain of living.

All the letters I have been quoting were written by men haunted by the memories of a Civil War whose violence and terror they had experienced only through the histories of soldier friends and relatives. None could be described as martial or heroic (Henry James referred to himself as a "poor worm of peace"), and some, it appears, felt guilty about their inglorious activities while their contemporaries were risking and losing their lives.[28] It may not be too farfetched, then, to read into their rather hyperbolical expressions of despair at the loss of friends and family, in their violent descriptions of the savage blows and wounds and mutilations which these deaths inflicted upon them, an attempt to equate their emotional wounds and spiritual deaths with what Whitman called "the real article." Were they not, too, "veterans" of grief? Was there not something heroic as well as pathetic in their postures of pain?

Every condolence letter of any consequence can be taken as an excerpt from an unpublished autobiography. The condoler, with the ostensible purpose of raising the spirits of the bereaved, tells of his own time of despair; and if, as in the case of Adams, the death of another simply seems to provide an excuse to draw attention to his own flickering grief, the theme of "I am the man, I suffer'd, I was there" is not uncommon in the letters of others.

The condoler has other acceptable gambits of which to avail himself. He might remind the mourner that death is a blessed relief, or that the deceased died young enough to escape the sting of envious Time. The mourner might be congratulated for having had the good fortune to know and enjoy the dead, to have loved and been loved. But what really distinguishes the effective from the perfunctory letter lies less in its substance than in its tone. Whether the writer is adjuring the recipient to be up and doing or simply compassionating, his genuineness of concern and his awareness of the feelings of the person addressed are immediately discernible.

A good example of what I mean is the letter William James sent to Howells on the death of Mrs. Howells. It has nothing of the lugubriousness or Spartan restraint of Adams's or Norton's letters. It is warm, almost cheerful, in its reference to "gallant little Mrs. Howells's taking off." How sad, James writes, that Howells is to be "left alone in this strange, growing world" after "so many years of unbroken companionship." Still, he has his children to cling to. And James concludes with a robust matter-of-fact message of affection and congratulation similar in spirit to the famous letters he wrote to his dying father, Henry James, Sr., and to his sister, Alice: a kind of *bon voyage* on the eve of a trip to eternity:

> Well, dearest Howells, it's the beginning of the end which all of us must look to—it is strange how near it seems to one after certain crises have been past and one is a septuagenarian! Whatever is ahead, your retrospect is fine. Your work stands as that of a man who used his opportunity to the full, and made the world happier and better while he wrote there. Also it seems pretty certain that the work will grow in importance year by year and stand as the great chronicle of the manners and morals of people as they really were during the 50 years we have lived through.[29]

William James may have been a better psychologist than a literary prophet in this instance, but an unfeigned tenderness and warmth are communicated in the letter to Howells and in his other letters of condolence.

The same can be said of the letters of his brother Henry, perhaps (with Emily Dickinson) the most consummate letter writer of all, or at least the writer who developed the condolence letter into an artistic form. In his letters of condolence, Henry James remains within the traditional mode insofar as "themes" or "strategies" are concerned, for his laments and encouragements are not very dissimilar to those of his contemporaries. They reveal, however, an uncommon mastery of expression, a sensitivity combined with a power of feeling. James was not a Christian in the technical sense. He could not, as he told his brother William, accept their father's theological premises or "throw myself into conceptions of heavens and hells."[30] He made no bones about his dislike of certain funeral customs, graves buried under mountains of flowers, in fact "the act of *burial*" itself, which seemed to him "inacceptably horrible, a hideous old imposition of the church."[31] Yet he possessed to a high degree the power of identification. His probing sympathy was implicit in the words and images, the prose rhythms, the allusions he employed to evoke it. The degree of intensity of a given letter, its frankness or guardedness, of course, depended on how well he knew the mourner and the mourned, but he unerringly divined the appropriate measure of intimacy and addressed himself to his or her personality and condition. To Mrs. John Hay, with whose eminent husband he had had a long but never a particularly close association, he was eloquent but formally gracious; to Charles Eliot Norton's sisters and other confidants he could be urgent, sententious, elegiac.

The sadness of an old friend, made desolate by the death of his wife, draws from James an analysis and a solution. After one has lived so long and unbrokenly with one person, separation, James tells him, "is like a violent and unnatural mutilation." (Few ever equaled James in use of what might be called solicitous hyperbole.) To one accustomed to the "roaring, rushing world," there are "props and crutches when the great thing falls." The case of his friend is "rare and wonderful" and desperate as well, because he has hitherto escaped the "brutal and vulgar racket." Yet though cut off from his protected past as he now is, he will discover that the dead will not fail him, that their "making us ache" is their way of "being with us."

> But I talk, my dear George, for mere tenderness—and so I say vain words—with only the *fact* of my tenderness a small thing to touch you. I have known you from so far back—and your image is vivid and charming to me through everything—through everything. Things abide—*good things*—for that time: and we hold together even across the grey wintry sea, near which perhaps both of us are tonight.[32]

The poignancy of this letter and other elegiac letters he wrote lies in James's ability to recover the past in the act of recollecting it. He will remember with affection times and places in which, by what he calls "a sort of providential charm," the dead resume their living forms and attain a kind of fictive solidity. For James this restoration becomes both a privilege and a duty. By performing a priestly function—tending the altars of the dead, so to speak, in the act of memorializing them—he is practicing what he preaches elsewhere: that the dead can only be rescued from oblivion by "independent, intelligent zeal," that the "sense of the state of the dead is but the part of the sense of the state of the living," that it is not being morbid to live with the memories of the dead housed within our consciousness.[33]

James's condolence letters perform many services, but one of them is to preserve important moments for the survivors. For the daughter of Fanny Kemble, he describes her mother's funeral, "all bright, somehow, and public and slightly pompous." In order to "bring everything a little nearer," he mentions "the soft, kind, balmy day," the people attending, the look of Fanny Kemble after death, "the very touching" infirmity of her last months—and yet "her wonderful air of smoldering under ashes."[34] Writing to the widow of Robert Louis Stevenson, in one of his most impressive letters, he converts her husband's death into high drama. The "hideous news," about which there was at first some doubt, is confirmed by her telegram. He pictures her desolation "in the presence of such an abysmal void." And then he bursts out: "To have lived in the light of that splendid life, that beautiful, bountiful being—only to see it, from one moment to the other, converted into a fable as strange and romantic as one of his own, a thing that *has* been and has ended, is an anguish into which no one can drain the cup for you." The death of an artist who "lighted up one whole side of the globe, and was himself a whole province of one's imagination" can only have a glory about it. James must add, at the risk of "a certain indelicacy," that few deaths have been "more remarkably right," for Stevenson "had the best of it—the thick of the fray, the loudest music, the freshest and finest of himself." The letter closes on a note of pity: "More than I can say I hope your first prostration and the bewilderment are over, and that you are feeling your way in feeling all sorts of encompassing arms—all sorts of outstretched hands of friendship. Don't, my dear Fanny Stevenson, be unconscious of *mine,* and believe me more than ever faithfully your, Henry James."[35]

This reads like a literary composition (and a rather melodramatic one) as well as a condolence letter, I suppose, but for me it is no less felt or personal. Certain deaths seem to have affected James in multiple ways. The loss of a friend, a parent, a brother, a sister cast him into darkness, but it might at the same time quicken his imagination and become a writer's "subject" to be studied, even savored. No better example comes to mind than his response to the death in 1870 of his cousin Minny Temple, whom he almost immediately translated into an ideal of womanhood or girlhood and youth. His affection for her, he protested, was "as deep as the foundations of my being"; yet he felt "vulgarly eager" for any fact about her last hours, saw a "dramatic fitness" in her "early death," found something "immensely moving in the sudden and complete extinction of a vitality so exquisite." Death freed her from her long suffering and elevated her "from this changing realm of fact to the steady realm of Thought," where she lived "as a steady unfaltering luminary in the mind," a "pure eloquent vision." Such fancies, James conceded to his brother, arose in part as a defense against "too direct a sense of death," but in these early letters as well as in his later ones, he was doing more than trying to "transmute" death "from a hard fact into a soft idea."[36] He was appointing himself defender of the defenseless dead and announcing his belief in the power of the artistic consciousness to immortalize. His letters of condolence, in distinction to those best described as "graceful social gestures,"[37] were expressions of that belief. For, as he said to Henry Adams in a famous letter, "I am that queer monster, the artist, an obstinate finality, an inexhaustible sensibility,"[38] and for James the artist carried "the field of consciousness" to the point where it lost "itself in the ineffable."[39]

By this definition, Emily Dickinson was an artist and the only letter writer I have discussed thus far who tended the altars of the dead even more assiduously than Henry James. Like James, too, her letters of condolence carry additional burdens of implication; they hint of unannounced anxieties and startle and shock as well as minister to pain. To Emily Dickinson as well as to Henry James, Death was the "distinguished Thing."

Nothing could be more unlike the correspondence of the literary men I've been quoting from than the idiosyncratic and metaphysically witty messages she dispatched to friends and relatives. Both the letters she wrote to the bereaved and her replies to the condolences from others suggest that for her the act of dying was only a high point in an extended and complex drama begun long before and continuing long after the event itself. Death brought "great pain" but it also provided flashes of illumination. "These sudden intimacies with Immortality," she wrote to her alleged "Master," Thomas Wentworth Higginson, then mourning a dead child, "are expanse—not Peace—as Lightning at our feet, instills a foreign Landscape." Such cryptic consolations were characteristic of a half-believer or would-be believer in immortality, for whom Death was the "Detriment divine" and who asked to sing for the suffering "because she cannot pray." In another letter to Higginson, in which she reported the death of her father, Emily Dickinson wrote, "I am glad there is Immortality—but would have tested it myself—before entrusting him," and to Higginson's wife she wrote, "Hamlet wavered for all of us."[40]

She had a firsthand knowledge of deathbeds and the bustle of funerals, as we know from her poems, and a strong curiosity about the deaths of loved ones who died beyond her surveillance. In her letters she requests a detailed account of their last hours. Did he or she have premonitions of death? Did her letter arrive in time? Did the dying aunt wear the bouquet sent by her solicitous niece? "You must tell me all you can think about her." "Dare I ask if he suffered?" she writes to the widow of the editor Josiah G. Holland. Such questions were not prompted by morbid curiosity. They show the concern of the pioneer explorer seeking information about the "Wilderness"—one of her references for the unmapped territory—that may enable her to guide those less familiar with its mysteries. The dead who slip away narrow the small circle of friends upon whom she depends as well as removing a part of herself. "A friend is a solemnity," she observes, "and after the great intrusion of Death, each one that remains has a spectral pricelessness besides the moral worth." She mourns them not merely as a loving friend or family intimate might but as the actual mother, father, widow, widower. In some of her letters she seems to be virtually tiptoeing into the rooms of grief, depositing verses in place of "noisy words" or bringing flowers that serve "without a sound" and whose "intrusiveness is brooked by even troubled hearts."[41]

Only one who lacked the strength to endure the suffering of others with equanimity could have consoled so tactfully and delicately and inventively. Often she describes the dead in her letters as clever fugitives who escaped, stole off, absconded, or were lifted up or blown away "like a flake gathered by the wind." She compares them to a bird who "adopts a better latitude" when the frost arrives. Her injunctions to the living—perhaps her own whistlings in the dark— are sturdy as well as tender. "To have lived is a Bliss so powerful— we must die—to adjust it—but when you have strength to remember that Dying dispells nothing which was firm before, you have avenged sorrow." Or again, she begs them to trust the human Jesus, not the divine: "When he shows us his Home, we turn away, but when he confides to us that he is 'acquainted with Grief,' we listen, for that also is an Acquaintance of our own." She understands "that bleeding beginning that every mourning knows" and recalls the sensations she felt when her own mother died: "like many kinds of cold—at times Electric, at times benumbing—then a trackless waste, Love has never trod." At such moments, "sorrow almost resents love, it is so inflamed," but she knows from experience that the "broken words" of letters from loving friends can be more soothing than messages from a "Saviour" on high. She also knows the letter writer is seeking as well as offering condolence and that in consoling she consoles herself.[42]

One letter written to the mother of her favorite nephew, who died of typhoid fever in his eighth year, is a passionate and poetic expression of a loss neither she nor her brother ever got over: "I see him in the Star, and meet his sweet velocity in everything that flies—His life was like a Bugle, which winds itself away, his Elegy an echo—his Requiem—ecstasy—"; and she closes with his versified epitaph:

> Pass to thy Rendezvous of Light
> Pangless except for us—
>   Who slowly ford the Mystery
>   Which Thou has leaped across![43]

These letters of Emily Dickinson and James are unaffectedly gentle and intuitive, but, as I've suggested earlier, they are more than spontaneous expressions of sympathy; they are "literary" as well. To Howells, cast down by the death of his daughter, James's consoling message revealed his friend's magical power of putting into words the sorrowing family's "mute despair." In his own letters, Howells told James, "I was breaking my heavy heart into mere rhetoric," and the same could be said with even greater justice of some of the other writers I have mentioned.[44]

Lowell, for example, is self-consciously "literary" in the letter already alluded to in which he describes his feelings after the death of his first wife. One feels that he is shedding his grief in the process of anatomizing it and mentally closing one chapter of his life as he prepares for the next. Curiously enough, he seems to be half aware of what he is doing. The past, he says, is "alien." He is "exiled" from it. And although he can contemplate it dimly through his tears, and although he prays that the "sweet influences" of thirteen years of marriage "may be seen and felt in my daily life henceforth," he fears his recollections will blur as he becomes absorbed in humdrum affairs. "I do abhor sentimentality from the bottom of my soul, and cannot wear grief upon my sleeves, but yet I look forward with agony to the time when she may become a memory instead of a constant presence." One is hardly surprised to find him two months later sending a jolly poem to Charles Eliot Norton thanking him for "certain cigars, of which I am now smoking the third and find it excellent."[45]

These condolence letters might be seen, then, as a release for articulate mourners who found insufficient satisfaction in the conventional outlets of grief—religion, confidence in the afterlife, the ceremonials of death. And just as "Adonais" and In Memoriam turned out to be more than rhymed regrets for dead friends, so occasional letters of great writers like Emily Dickinson and Henry James sometimes took on dimensions transcending the events that evoked them. The death of someone dear served as a text for the celebration of memory and love or for the affirmation of human endurance.

Other literary forms offered themselves as devices to preserve the dead from oblivion. The memorial poems and biographies so plentiful in the nineteenth century would seem to be more enduring testimonials than condolence letters, and so indeed they often were. But in the poetry, personal sentiment too frequently hardened into public rhetoric, and the biography—as Lowell and Adams and James felt very keenly—could turn into a murderous implement. The subject lay at the mercy of the biographer, most dangerous of all when he was clever and truthful, because, as Lowell warned, "Truth is not enough, for in biography, as in law, the greater the truth sometimes the greater the libel."[46] The biographer's "devilish art," Henry James declared, "is somehow practically *thinning*. It simplifies even while seeking to enrich—and even the Immortal are so helpless and passive in death."[47]

The writers of condolence letters felt no obligation to be critical; rather, they followed the injunction to say only good things about the dead. Although their eulogies-cum-elegies usually revealed more about the authors than about the persons they were addressing or who were being mourned, at one fixed moment before the onset of forgetfulness, these letters joined the dead and the living.

As might be expected, the etiquette of grief practiced by my select group was already anachronistic according to the standards codified in the manuals composed by professional arbiters of "good form." After the Civil War, the rites of death had been "rationalized" in the current spirit of American business enterprise and bore no resemblance to the grisly jollifications Hawthorne had noted in seventeenth-century obsequies or to the robust and matter-of-fact attitudes of antebellum America when death was a familiar visitor and no elaborate precautions were taken to shield the bereaved from its realities or reverberations.[48] Under the new dispensation, as readers of *The Bazar Book of Decorum* (1870) were reminded, the human body was "the object of a punctilious observance of ceremony. The mourning relatives are usually spared many of the painful details of funereal civility by the convenient officiousness of the undertaker, upon whom devolve the chief arrangements of the burial and its attendant formalities."[49] Correspondingly, condolence letters were not only supposed to express authentic and uncalculated sympathy but also to do so in such a way as not to aggravate wounded sensibilities. The arbiters advised the writer of condolences to keep his letter short and to the point. No morbid dwelling on sickness and death was permissible, no admonitions instructing the husband, wife, and parent to bear their afflictions or warning them of greater ones to come. "It is the wine mixed with gall which they gave our Lord to drink," declared one authority on social usage, "and as He refused it, so may we."[50] In fact, words like "die," "death," "killed"— even "sadness"—ought not to be used.[51]

By this time, death was no longer a public sacrament but one of those inevitable and harrowing interruptions to be coped with as decently and efficiently and as swiftly as possible. And from then until comparatively recently, the subject of death was relegated pretty much to religious ceremonies, sociological and psychiatric discourse, the deliberations of lawyers and insurance people, and the anthologies providing useful quotations for the sad occasions when the forbidden theme necessarily intruded. Eventually, Emily Post would declare that condolence letters might be "abrupt, badly constructed, ungrammatical," so long as they were sincere.[52]

The literary generation I have been considering would probably have been bewildered by Emily Post's implication that content bore no relation to form. Any condolence letter which conveyed a sense of spontaneous sympathy transcended the mere dictates of etiquette, but a skillful writer could turn it into a great deal more: a way to handle Death with the glove of words, to convert its raw components into ineffable spirit and thereby to diffuse its terrors. This was no task for the clumsy. In its finest and most poetic form, the condolence letter was an answer to death itself, at once a statement of faith in the power of words to soothe and fortify and an act by which the disbelievers in immortality, confronting their own extinction, might immortalize themselves in the process of comforting or memorializing another.

Notes

1. Robert M. Myers, *The Children of Pride: A True Story of Georgia and the Civil War* (New Haven: Yale University Press, 1972), 98–100.

2. L. O. Saum, "Death in the Popular Mind of Pre–Civil War America," *American Quarterly,* 26 (December 1974), 477–495.

3. Ann Douglas, "Heaven Our Home: Consolation Literature in the Northeastern United States, 1830–1880," ibid., 496–515.

4. Philippe Ariès, *Western Attitudes Toward Death: From the Middle Ages to the Present* (Baltimore and London: Johns Hopkins University Press, 1974), 87–90.

5. Geoffrey Gorer, *Death, Grief, and Mourning in Contemporary Britain* (London: Cresset Press, 1965), 110–116.

6. Laurel Shackelford and Bill Weinberg, *Our Appalachia: An Oral History* (New York: Hill and Wang, 1977), 21–22, 71–72, 89–90.

7. See, for example, W. D. Howells's comment on the "vulgar tone" in behavior books in the *Atlantic Monthly,* 26 (July 1870), 122.

8. Ernest Samuels, *Henry Adams: The Middle Years* (Cambridge, Mass.: Harvard University Press, 1958), 286.

9. Andrew Hilen, *The Letters of Henry Wadsworth Longfellow* (Cambridge, Mass.: Harvard University Press, 1972), IV, 242–245.

10. Charles Eliot Norton, ed., *Letters of James Russell Lowell* (New York, 1894), I, 176.

11. Percy Lubbock, ed., *The Letters of Henry James* (New York: Charles Scribner's Sons, 1920), II, 167.

12. Mildred Howells, ed., *Life and Letters of William Dean Howells* (Garden City, N.Y.: Doubleday, Doran, 1928), I, 424–426.

13. H. N. Smith and W. M. Gibson, eds., *Mark Twain–Howells Letters* (Cambridge, Mass.: Belknap Press of Harvard University Press, 1960), II, 663, 669; Justin Kaplan, *Mr. Clemens and Mark Twain* (New York: Simon and Schuster, 1966), 335, 337.

14. Samuels, *Henry Adams*, 284.

15. Norton, ed., *Letters*, I, 78.

16. Ibid., 176.

17. M. A. Dewolfe Howe, ed., *The Letters of Charles Eliot Norton* (Boston and New York: Houghton Mifflin, 1913), II, 211.

18. Ibid., 228.

19. Worthington Ford, ed., *Letters of Henry Adams, 1858–1891* (Boston and New York: Houghton Mifflin, 1930), I, 189.

20. Ibid., 400.

21. Ibid.

22. Samuels, *Henry Adams*, 286.

23. Ford, ed., *Letters*, II, 161.

24. Ibid., 517.

25. Norton, ed., *Letters*, II, 126.

26. Smith and Gibson, eds., *Mark Twain–Howells Letters*, II, 8.

27. Ibid.

28. For a more detailed discussion of this theme, see Daniel Aaron, *The Unwritten War: American Writers and the Civil War* (New York: Alfred A. Knopf, 1973), 91–145.

29. William James to W. D. Howells, May 26, 1910, Houghton Library, Harvard University, Cambridge, Mass.

30. Lubbock, ed., *Letters*, I, 111–112.

31. Leon Edel, ed., *Henry James Letters* [1875–1883] Cambridge, Mass.: Belknap Press of Harvard University Press, 1975), II, 184.

32. Lubbock, ed., *Letters*, II, 113–114.

33. R. P. Blackmur, ed., *The Art of the Novel: Critical Prefaces of Henry James* (New York: Charles Scribner's Sons, 1934), 244–245.

34. Leon Edel, ed., *The Selected Letters of Henry James* (New York: Farrar, Straus & Cudahy, 1955), 183–184.

35. Ibid., 189–191.

36. Edel, ed., *Henry James Letters* [1843–1875] (Cambridge, Mass.: Belknap Press of Harvard University Press, 1974), I, 221–223.

37. F. O. Matthiessen, *The James Family* (New York: Alfred A. Knopf, 1947), 593.

38. Lubbock, ed., *Letters,* II, 361.

39. Matthiessen, *The James Family,* 611.

40. Thomas Johnson and Theodora Ward, eds., *The Letters of Emily Dickinson* (Cambridge, Mass.: Harvard University Press, 1958), III, 660–661; II, 420–421, 528, 587.

41. Ibid., II, 362, 713, 469, 603, 800.

42. Ibid., 750, 594–595, 678, 752, 601.

43. Ibid., 799.

44. W. D. Howells to Henry James, June 7, 1889, Houghton Library, Harvard University, Cambridge, Mass.

45. Norton, ed., *Letters,* I, 206–207.

46. Ibid., II, 316.

47. Lubbock, ed., *Letters,* II, 431–432.

48. R. W. Habenstein and W. M. Lamers, *The History of American Funeral Directing,* rev. ed. (Milwaukee: Bulfin Printers, 1962), 211 ff.

49. W. D. Howells, *Atlantic Monthly,* 26 (July 1870), 122.

50. Mrs. John Sherwood, *Manners and Social Usages* (New York: Harper & Brothers, 1884), 188.

51. Amy Vanderbilt, *Amy Vanderbilt's Complete Book of Etiquette* (Garden City, N.Y.: Doubleday, 1952), 136.

52. Emily Post, *Etiquette in Society, in Business, in Politics and at Home* [Replica Edition] (New York: Funk and Wagnalls, 1922), 484.

ACKNOWLEDGMENTS

My special thanks to Susanne Klingenstein, Neil Jumonville, and Louis Masur, who encouraged me to prepare this volume and helped me to select and arrange its contents. I am also indebted to the following friends for their counsel and caveats: Sacvan Bercovitch, Warner Berthoff, Philip Fisher, Eugene Goodheart, Justin Kaplan, R. W. B. Lewis, Joel Porte, John Tobin, Helen Vendler, and Robert Walker.

CHRONOLOGICAL LIST OF PUBLICATIONS

◈

1930s

"Melville and the Missionaries." *New England Quarterly*, 8 (1935), 404–408.

"An English Enemy of Melville." *New England Quarterly*, 8 (1935), 561–567.

"A Postscript to *The Last Puritan*." *New England Quarterly*, 9 (1936), 683–686.

Rev. of *Puritans in the South Seas*, by L. B. Wright and M. I. Fry. *New England Quarterly*, 9 (1936), 536–538.

H. M. Jones and Daniel Aaron. "Notes on the Napoleonic Legend in America." *Franco-American Review*, 2 (1937), 10–26.

Rev. of *The Anatomy of Revolution*, by Crane Brinton. *Boston Evening Transcript*, October 22, 1938.

Rev. of *Adventures in America, 1857–1900: A Pictorial Record from Harper's Weekly,* by John Kouwenhoven. *Boston Evening Transcript*, December 31, 1938.

Rev. of *A History of American Graphic Humor, 1865–1938*, by William Murrell. *Boston Evening Transcript*, January 14, 1939.

Daniel Aaron and Henry Nash Smith. "Recent Works on the Social History of the United States, 1935–1939." *International Review for Social History*, 4 (1939), 499–509.

1940s

Rev. of *Three Centuries of American Hymnody*, by Henry Wilder Foote. *New England Quarterly* 14 (1941), 172–174.

Rev. of *American Renaissance*, by F. O. Matthiessen. *Kenyon Review*, 4 (1942), 102–106.

"The Case for the Liberal Arts. A Symposium." *Smith College Monthly* (May 1943), 5.

Rev. of *The Shock of Recognition: The Development of Literature in the United States by the Men Who Made It*, by Edmund Wilson. *New England Quarterly*, 16 (1943), 523–524.

"Letter to Moscow." *Smith College Spectator* (March 1944), 8.

"Southern Stereotype." Rev. of *J. C. Calhoun, Nationalist: 1782–1828*, by C. M. Wiltse. *George Fitzhugh: Propagandist of the Old South*, by Harvey Wish. *Ranger Mosby*, by V. C. Jones. *"First With the Most" Forrest*, by R. S. Henry. *Pitchfork Ben Tillman, South Carolinian*, by F. B. Simkins. *The Wil-*

son Era, Years of Peace: 1910–1917, by Josephus Daniels. *New Republic* (March 5, 1945), 338–340.

Rev. of *Big Business in a Democracy,* by James Truslow Adams. *New Republic* (September 24, 1945), 379–381.

Rev. of *Piety and Intellect at Amherst College, 1865–1912,* by Thomas Le Duc. *Remembrance of Amherst: An Undergraduate Diary by William Gardiner Hammond,* ed. George F. Whicher. *New England Quarterly,* 19 (1946), 418–420.

"A Note on the Businessman and the Historian," *Antioch Review,* 6 (1946–47), 575–581.

"The Truly Monstrous: A Note on Nathanael West." *Partisan Review,* 14 (1947), 98–106.

"Remarks on a Best Seller" [*The Fountainhead,* by Ayn Rand]. *Partisan Review,* 14 (1947), 442–445.

"Thorstein Veblen, Moralist and Rhetorician." *Antioch Review,* 7 (Fall 1947), 381–390.

"The Unusable Man: An Essay on the Mind of Brooks Adams." *New England Quarterly,* 21 (1948), 3–33.

Rev. of *America's Economic Supremacy,* by Brooks Adams. *New England Quarterly,* 21 (1948), 281–282.

Rev. of *The American Political Tradition and the Men Who Made It,* by Richard Hofstadter. *American Quarterly,* 1 (1949), 94–96.

Rev. of *The Literary History of the United States,* vol. 1, ed. Robert E. Spiller et al. *American Quarterly,* 1 (1949), 169–173.

"Melville's Descent into Tartarus." Rev. of *The Complete Stories of Herman Melville,* ed. Jay Leyda. *Tomorrow* (October 1949), 53–56.

Rev. of *Henry David Thoreau,* by Joseph Wood Krutch. *Kenyon Review,* 11 (1949), 145–148.

Rev. of *Foundations of Democracy,* ed. F. Ernest Johnson. *Unity and Difference in American Life,* ed. R. M. MacIver. *American Literature,* 21 (1949), 127–129.

1950s

"A Bluestocking in the American Wilderness." *Tomorrow* (March 1950), 54–56.

Rev. of *Two Friends of Man,* by Ralph Korngold. *Young America: 1830–1840,* by R. E. Riegel. *Backwoods Utopias,* by Arthur E. Bestor, Jr. *New England Quarterly,* 24 (1951), 104–106.

"Winslow Homer's America, 1860–1874." In *Winslow Homer: Illustrator.* Catalogue of the Exhibition With a Checklist of Wood Engravings and a List of Illustrated Books Prepared by Mary Bartlett Cowdry. Northampton, Mass.: Smith College Museum of Art, 1951, pp. 8–10.

Men of Good Hope: A Story of American Progressives. New York: Oxford University Press, 1951.

Rev. of *The Day of the Locust*, by Nathanael West. *Hudson Review*, 3 (1951), 634–636.

"Directives for Salvation." Rev. of *The Age of Longing*, by Arthur Koestler. *The Burned Bramble*, by Manes Sperber. *The Case of Comrade Tulayev*, by Victor Serge. *From Here to Eternity*, by James Jones. *The Place of the Lion*, by Charles Williams. *Darkness and Day*, by Ivy Compton-Burnett. *Conjugal Love*, by Alberto Moravia. *Hudson Review*, 4 (1951), 314–320.

Rev. of *Stephen Crane*, by John Berryman. *Hudson Review*, 4 (1951), 471–473.

Intro. *America in Crisis: Fourteen Crucial Episodes in American History*, ed. Daniel Aaron. New York: Alfred A. Knopf, 1952.

"The Helsinki the Athletes Didn't See." *The Reporter* (September 2, 1952), 24–27.

Rev. of *The Life of Ralph Waldo Emerson*, by R. D. Rusk. *Emerson's Angle of Vision*, by Sherman Paul. *Spires of Form: A Study of Emerson's Aesthetic Vision*, by Vivian Hopkins. *New Leader* (March 18, 1953), 18–22.

"The American Professor and the Soviet Cookie Pusher." *The Reporter* (March 31, 1953), 24–27.

"The Proud Prejudices of Sinclair Lewis." *The Reporter* (August 4, 1953), 37–39.

Rev. of *Runaway Star: An Appreciation of Henry Adams*, by R. A. Hume. *Henry Adams: Scientific Historian*, by William Jordy. *Democracy: An American Novel*, by Henry Adams. *The Selected Letters of Henry Adams*, ed. Newton Arvin. *Hudson Review*, 5 (1953), 608–614.

"Jonathan Edwards." In *The Northampton Book: Chapters from 300 Years in the Life of a New England Town, 1654–1954*, ed. L. E. Wikander et al. Northampton, Mass.: The City of Northampton, 1954, pp. 15–21.

"Conservatism, Old and New." *American Quarterly*, 6 (1954), 99–110.

"Parables of Disaster." Rev. of *The Cobweb*, by William Gibson. *The Wars of Love*, by Mark Schorer. *The End of an Old Song*, by J. D. Scott. *Scotland's Burning*, by Nathaniel Burt. *The Prospect Before Us*, by Herbert Gold. *Born in Captivity*, by John Wain. *The Joker*, by Jean Malaquais. *Hudson Review*, 7 (1954), 315–320.

Rev. of *Howells and the Age of Realism*, by Everett Carter. *New Leader* (December 20, 1954), 17–18.

Rev. of *The New American Right*, by Daniel Bell. *Political Science Quarterly*, 71 (1956), 128–130.

Rev. of *The Raven and the Whale: The War of Words and Wits in the Era of Poe and Melville*, by Perry Miller. *New England Quarterly*, 29 (1956), 538–541.

Rev. of *Brooks Adams: A Biography*, by A. F. Beringause. *New England Quarterly*, 29 (1956), 106–108.

"Seven Novels." Rev. of *A Walk on the Wild Side*, by Nelson Algren. *Night*, by Erico Verissimo. *The Flight from the Enchanter*, by Iris Murdoch. *The Lonely Passion of Judith Hearne*, by Brian Moore. *The Fall of a Sparrow*, by

Nigel Balchin. *A Certain Smile,* by Françoise Sagan. *The Unfaithful Wife,* by Jules Roy. *Hudson Review,* 9 (1956–57), 622–632.

Rev. of *Politics and the Novel,* by Irving Howe. *The Reporter* (May 2, 1957), 216.

Richard Hofstadter, William Miller, and Daniel Aaron. *The United States: The History of a Republic.* Englewood Cliffs, N.J.: Prentice-Hall, 1957.

"Fiction Chronicle." Review of *Two Women,* by Alberto Moravia. *I'm Not Stiller,* by Max Frisch. *The Affair,* by Hans Koningsberger. *The Italian Wife,* by Emyr Humphreys. *The Rainbow Has Seven Colors,* by Nadia LeGrand. *Strangers When We Meet,* by Evan Hunter. *The Ginger Man,* by J. P. Donleavy. *Portrait of a Man Unknown,* by Nathalie Sarraute. *Hudson Review,* 11 (1958), 461–467.

Alfred Kazin and Daniel Aaron, eds. *Emerson: A Modern Anthology.* Boston: Houghton Mifflin, 1958.

Rev. of *The Great Days,* by John Dos Passos. *New Leader* (June 2, 1958), 24.

Rev. of *Henry George in the British Isles,* by E. P. Lawrence. *Victorian Studies* (1958), 277–278.

"The Epic Is Yet to Be Written." *American Heritage,* 9 (October 1958), 112–116.

1960s

Writers on the Left. Episodes in American Literary Communism. New York: Harcourt, Brace & World, 1961.

Rev. of *The Cultural Life of the New Nation, 1776–1930,* by Russell B. Nye. *American Literature,* 33 (1961), 393–394.

"A Decade of Convictions: The Appeal of Communism in the 1930s." *Massachusetts Review,* 2 (1961), 736–747.

Rev. of *Cannibals All or Slaves Without Masters,* by George Fitzhugh. *American Sociological Review,* 26 (1961), 159.

Rev. of *The Muckrakers,* ed. Arthur and Linda Weinberg. *Nation* (December 9, 1961), 477–478.

Rev. of *The Novels of Henry James,* by Oscar Cargill. *New Leader* (December 25, 1961), 19–20.

"The Riddle of John Dos Passos." *Harper's* (March 1962), 55–60.

"American Writers in Russia: The Three Faces of Lenin." *Survey,* no. 41 (April 1962), 43–57.

Rev. of *Sad Heart at the Supermarket,* by Randall Jarrell. *New Leader* (November 12, 1962), 28–29.

Rev. of *Patriotic Gore,* by Edmund Wilson. *Massachusetts Review,* 3 (1962), 555–570.

Intro. *The Disinherited,* by Jack Conroy. New York: Hill and Wang, 1963.

The Memoirs of an American Citizen, ed. with Intro. (pp. vii–xxxii). Cambridge, Mass.: Harvard University Press, 1963.

Rev. of *President Harding,* by Francis Russell. *The Listener* (December 18, 1963), 863.

Shelbourne Essays on American Literature, by Paul Elmer More. Ed. with Intro. New York: Harcourt, Brace & World, 1963.

"The Hyphenate Writer and American Letters." *Smith College Alumnae Quarterly* (July 1964), 213–217.

Rev. of *Soviet Attitudes Toward American Writing,* by Deming Brown. *American Sociological Review,* 29 (1964), 436–437.

Rev. of *Because I Was Flesh: The Autobiography of Edward Dahlberg,* by Edward Dahlberg. *Hudson Review,* 17 (1964), 312–315.

Rev. of *William Faulkner, The Yoknapatawpha Country,* by Cleanth Brooks. *My Brother Bill,* by John Faulkner. *Faulkner's People,* by R. W. Kirk and Marvin Klotz. *New Statesman* (July 3, 1964), 25.

Rev. of *The Naked Society,* by Vance Packard. *New Statesman* (October 16, 1964), 584.

"Some Reflections on Communism and the Jewish Writer." *Salmagundi,* 1 (1965), 23–36. (Rpt. in *The Ghetto and Beyond: Essays in Jewish Life in America,* ed. Peter Rose. New York: Random House, 1969, pp. 253–269.)

"Self or Society?" *New York Times Book Review,* February 14, 1965, pp. 37–38.

"The Treachery of Recollection: The Inner and the Outer History." *Carleton Miscellany,* 6 (1965), 3–19. (Rpt. in *Essays in History and Literature,* ed. R. H. Bremner. Columbus: Ohio State University Press, 1966, pp. 3–27.)

"Howells's 'Maggie.' " *New England Quarterly,* 38 (1965), 85–90.

Rev. of *Dreiser,* by W. A. Swanberg. *The Reporter* (June 3, 1965), 37–39

Rev. of *The New Radicalism in America, 1889–1963,* by Christopher Lasch. *New York Times Book Review,* June 13, 1965, pp. 6, 37–38.

"Late Thoughts on Nathanael West." *Massachusetts Review,* 6, no. 2 (1965), 307–317.

Rev. of *The Seeds of Liberation,* by Paul Goodman. *Sunday Herald-Tribune,* July 5, 1965, pp. 5, 12.

Rev. of *Part of the Truth: An Autobiography,* by Granville Hicks. *Sunday Herald-Tribune,* August 8, 1965, pp. 5, 12.

The Hales and the "Great Rebellion": Letters: 1861–1865. Northampton, Mass: The Sophia Smith Collection. Smith College, May 1966.

Rev. of *Manchild in the Promised Land,* by Claude Brown. *New Statesman* (August 5, 1966), 204.

Rev. of *Radicalism in America,* by Sidney Lens. *Progressive,* 85 (August 1966), 30–31.

"Norman Thomas and the Thirties." *Claremont Journal of Political Economy,* 2 (1966), 33–34.

"The American Left: Some Ruins and Monuments." *Denver Quarterly,* 1, no. 2 (1966), 5–23.

"The Thirties—Now and Then." *American Scholar,* 35 (Summer 1966), 490–494.

Panelist in "Thirty Years Later: Memories of the First American Writers' Congress." *American Scholar*, 35 (Summer 1966), 495–516.

Intro. *American Pantheon*, by Newton Arvin, ed. Daniel Aaron and Sylvan Schendler. New York: Delacorte Press, 1966.

"The Salzburg Seminar: A Retrospective View." *International Educational and Cultural Exchange* (Winter 1966), 20–24.

Rev. of *The Social Novel at the End of an Era*, by Warren French. *American Literature*, 38 (1966), 414–416.

Rev. of *The Life of the Mind in America*, by Perry Miller. *The Problem of Boston*, by Martin Green. *New Statesman* (January 20, 1967), 84–85.

Rev. of *James Russell Lowell*, by Martin Duberman. *Partisan Review*, 34 (1967), 479–483.

Rev. of *Nothing More to Declare*, by John Clellon Holmes. *Commonweal* (May 5, 1967), 211–212.

Rev. of *The Intellectuals and McCarthy*, by Michael Paul Rogin. *Commonweal* (September 8, 1967), 556–557.

"Confrontation: The Old Left and the New" [Tom Hayden, Ivanhoe Donaldson, Richard Rovere, Dwight Macdonald]. *American Scholar*, 36 (Autumn 1967), 567–588.

"Youth and Revolt in Contemporary North America: A Backward Glance." *American Studies in Scandinavia*, no. 1 (1968), 6–18.

"Edward O'Connor Remembered." *America* (May 4, 1968), 604.

Rev. of *Stephen Crane: A Biography*, by R. W. Stallman. *New Republic* (September 7, 1968), 33–34.

"The Radical Humanism of John Steinbeck." *Saturday Review* (September 26, 1968), 26–27, 55–56.

"Bellamy—Utopian Conservative." In *Edward Bellamy, Novelist and Reformer*. Union Worthies no. 23. Schenectady: Union College, 1968, pp. 7–15.

"Sinclair Lewis. *Main Street*." In *The American Novel from James Fenimore Cooper to William Faulkner*, ed. Wallace Stegner. New York: Basic Books, 1968, pp. 166–179.

Rev. of *The Crisis of the Negro Intellectual*, by Harold Cruse. *The Listener* (March 20, 1969), 394–395.

" 'Good Morning' and 'Art' Young: An Introduction and an Appraisal." *Labor History*, 10 (1969), 100–104.

Rev. of *Henry James: The Treacherous Years, 1895–1901*, by Leon Edal. *New Republic* (June 14, 1969), 33–34.

"The Trial of John Brown." In *Six Trials*, ed. R. S. Brumbaugh. New York: Crowell, 1969, pp. 42–59.

1970s

Daniel Aaron and Robert Bendiner, eds. *The Strenuous Decade: A Social and Intellectual Record of the 1930s*. Garden City, N.Y.: Anchor Books, 1970.

Rev. of *Kate Chopin: A Critical Biography*, by Per Seyersted. *The Complete*

Works of Kate Chopin, ed. Per Seyersted. *New York Times Book Review*, February 8, 1970, pp. 5, 30.

Rev. of *Robert E. Lee*, by Clifford Dowdey. *The Listener* (April 16, 1970), 518–519.

Rev. of *The Americans: A Social History of the United States, 1587–1914*, by J. C. Furnas. *New Statesman* (October 9, 1970), 463–464.

"Richard Wright and the Communist Party." *New Letters*, 38 (1971), 170–181.

Rev. of *McClure's Magazine and the Muckrakers*, by Harold S. Wilson. *American Literature*, 43 (1971), 496–497.

"Per Seyersted: Kate Chopin. A Critical Biography." *Edda-Hefte*, 6 (1971), 341–343.

Rev. of *The University of Virginia Edition of the Works of Stephen Crane*, vol. 9, ed. Fredson Bowers, Intro. J. B. Colvert. *American Literature*, 44 (1972), 332–333.

Rev. of *Run-Through: A Memoir*, by John Houseman. *The New Deal Arts Projects: An Anthology of Memoirs*, ed. F. V. O'Connor. *Partisan Review*, 39 (1972), 615–620.

Rev. of *American History and American Thought: Christopher Columbus to Henry Adams*, by Bert J. Loewenberg. *Journal of American History*, 59 (1972), 672–673.

Rev. of *Poe, Poe, Poe, Poe, Poe, Poe, Poe*, by Daniel Hoffman. *Commentary*, 53 (May 1972), 98–100.

The Unwritten War: American Writers and the Civil War. New York: Alfred A. Knopf, 1973.

Rev. of *The Dream and the Deal: The Federal Writers' Project, 1935–1943*, by Jere Mangione. *Reviews in American History*, 1 (1973), 277–286.

Richard Hofstadter, William Miller, and Daniel Aaron. *The Structure of American History*. Englewood Cliffs, N.J.: Prentice-Hall, 1973.

Rev. of *The Emergence of Richard Wright: A Study in Literature and Society*, by Kenneth Kinnamon. *American Literature*, 45 (1973), 474–475.

" 'Writers on the Left' Assessed." *Indian Journal of American Studies*, 3 (June 1973), 1–7.

Rev. of *Regeneration Through Violence*, by Richard Slotkin. *Commonweal* (December 18, 1973), 346–347.

Rev. of *Humboldt's Gift*, by Saul Bellow. *New Republic* (September 20, 1975), 28–30.

" 'The Man Without a Country' as a Civil War Document." In *Geschichte und Gesellschaft in der Amerikanischen Literatur*, ed. Karl Schubert and Ursula Müller-Richter. Heidelberg: Quelle & Meyer, 1975, pp. 55–62.

"Reflections on Growth and Literature in America." In *Growth in America*, ed. C. L. Cooper. Westport, Conn.: Greenwood Press, 1976, pp. 143–153.

"The New York Draft Riot of 1863." In *Conflict in America: A History of Domestic Confrontation*. Voice of America, Forum Series, 1976, pp. 91–103.

"Reuben Arthur Brower." Memorial Minute Adopted by the Faculty of Arts and Sciences. *Harvard University Gazette*, January 28, 1977, p. 9.

"The Occasional Novel: American Fiction and the Man of Letters." In *American Fiction: Historical and Critical Essays*, ed. James Nagel. Boston: Northeastern University Press, 1977, pp. 127–141.

"The Pursuit of Health and Beauty." *Harvard Magazine* (March–April 1977), 72–78.

Rev. of *Fact and Fiction: The New Journalism and the Non-Fiction Novel*, by John Hallowell. *Columbia Journalism Review* (July–August 1977), 61.

Intro. *Edmund Wilson: Letters on Literature and Politics, 1912–1972*, ed. Elena Wilson. New York: Farrar, Straus and Giroux, 1977, pp. xv–xxix.

Intro. *On the Line*, by Harvey Swados. New York: Dell, 1977, pp. 11–21.

Rev. of *The Culture Watch: Essays on Theater and Society, 1969–1974*, by Robert Brustein. *Partisan Review*, 44 (1977), 628–632.

Rev. of *The Superfluous Men: Conservative Critics of American Culture, 1900–1945*, by Robert M. Crunden. *Commonweal* (October 14, 1977), 28–29.

"An Approach to the Thirties." In *The Study of American Culture: Contemporary Conflicts*, ed. Luther Leudke. DeLand, Fla.: Everett/Edwards, 1977, pp. 1–17.

Rev. of *The Literary Politicians*, by Mitchell S. Ross. *New York Times Book Review*, January 15, 1978, pp. 9, 26.

Rev. of *The Federal Writers' Project: A Study in Governmental Patronage of the Arts*, by Monte N. Penkower. *Times Literary Supplement*, January 28, 1978, p. 837.

Rev. of *Above the Battle: War-Making in America from Appomattox to Versailles*, by T. C. Leonard. *Chronicle of Higher Education*, March 13, 1978, p. 19.

Rev. of *Mencken: A Study of His Thought*, by C. A. Fecher. *Commonweal* (October 13, 1978), 666–668.

Rev. of *The New Humanism: A Critique of Modern America, 1900–1940*, by J. D. Hoeveler, Jr. *American Literature*, 49 (1978), 646–647.

Studies in Biography, Intro. and ed. Harvard English Studies 8. Cambridge, Mass.: Harvard University Press, 1978.

Rev. of *Radical Will: Randolph Bourne, Selected Writings, 1911–1918*, ed. Olaf Hansen. *New York Review of Books*, November 23, 1978, pp. 36–40.

"The South in American History." In *The South and Faulkner's Yoknapatawpha: The Actual and the Apocryphal*, ed. Evans Harrington and Ann J. Abadie. Jackson: University Press of Mississippi, 1979, pp. 3–21.

Rev. of *The Wages of Expectation: A Biography of Edward Dahlberg*, by Charles DiFanti. *American Literature*, 51 (1979), 437–438.

"The Etiquette of Grief: A Literary Generation's Response to Death." *Prospects*, 4 (1979), 197–213.

"James T. Farrell (1904–1979)." *New Republic* (October 6, 1979), 38.

Rev. of *Thornton Wilder: His World*, by Linda Simon. *American Character-*

istics and Other Essays, by Thornton Wilder, ed. Donald Gallup. *New York Times Book Review*, December 30, 1979, pp. 8, 9, 18.

1980s

"Howells at Harvard." *Harvard Library Bulletin*, 28 (1980), 438–442.

"Fictionalizing the Past." *Partisan Review*, 47 (1980), 231–241.

Rev. of *The Dream of the Golden Mountain*, by Malcolm Cowley. *Washington Post Book World*, March 16, 1980, pp. 1–2.

Rev. of *John Dos Passos: Twentieth-Century Odyssey*, by Townsend Luddington. *New Republic* (November 8, 1980), 34–36.

Rev. of *Naming Names*, by Victor S. Navasky. *New York Review of Books*, December 4, 1980, pp. 6, 8.

Rev. of *Failure and Success in America: A Literary Debate*, by Martha Banta. *Yearbook of English Studies*, 11 (1981), 280–281.

"Morley Callaghan and the Great Depression." In *The Callaghan Symposium*, ed. David Staines. Ottawa: University of Ottawa, 1981, pp. 23–35.

Foreword. *The Letters of H. L. Mencken*, ed. Guy J. Forgue. Boston: Northeastern University Press, 1981, pp. v–x.

"The Extra: A Letter." *American Literature*, 52 (1981), 628–632.

"Edmund Wilson's Political Decade." In *Literature at the Barricades: The American Writer in the 1930s*, ed. R. E. Bogardus and Fred Hobson. Tuscaloosa: University of Alabama Press, 1982, pp. 175–186.

"The Man of Letters in American Culture." In *The American Future and the Humane Tradition: The Role of the Humanities in Higher Education*, ed. Robert E. Heidemann. Associated Faculty Press, 1982, pp. 60–76.

"The Idea of Boston: Some Literary Responses to the Sacco-Vanzetti Case." In *Sacco-Vanzetti: Developments and Reconsiderations—1979*. Conference Proceedings. Boston: Trustees of the Public Library of the City of Boston, 1982, pp. 21–25.

Rev. of *Voices of Discord: Canadian Short Stories from the 1930s. Labor History*, 23 (1982), 284–286.

Rev. of *The Letters of Archibald MacLeish, 1907–1982*, ed. R. H. Winnick. *New Republic* (January 24, 1983), 28–31.

Rev. of *The War Within: From Victorian to Modernist Thought in the South, 1919–1945*, by D. J. Singal. *Virginia Magazine of History and Biography*, 91 (1983), pp. 236–237.

"The 'Inky Curse': Miscegenation in the White American Literary Imagination." *Social Science Information*, 22, no. 2 (1983), 169–190.

"An Informal Letter to the Editor." *Daedalus*, 112 (1983), 27–33.

"Trash, Classics and the Common Reader." *Texas Humanist*, 6 (1984), 41–43.

"Letter to a Chinese Friend." *Yale Review*, (1984), 32–46.

"Cambridge, 1936–39." *Partisan Review*, 50/51 (1984–85), 833–836.

"The Hyphenate American Writers." *Rivisti di Studi Anglo-Americani*, 3 (1984–85), 11–28.

Rev. of *The Optimist's Daughter*, by Eudora Welty. *One Writer's Beginnings*, by Eudora Welty. *The Collected Stories of Eudora Welty. Conversations with Eudora Welty*, ed. Peggy W. Prenshaw. *London Review of Books*, May 2, 1985, pp. 15–16.

Rev. of *Irving Babbitt: An Intellectual Study*, by Thomas Nevin. *New Republic* (July 17, 1985), 36–38.

Rev. of *Letters to Bab: Sherwood Anderson to Marrietta D. Finley, 1916–1933*, ed. W. A. Sutton and Walter Rideout. *New York Times Book Review*, September 8, 1985, p. 41.

Rev. of *The Journals of Thornton Wilder, 1934–1968*, ed. Donald Gallup. *New Republic* (November 11, 1985), 33–36.

Foreword. *The Shores of Light: A Literary Chronicle of the 1920s and 1930s*, by Edmund Wilson. Boston: Northeastern University Press, 1985, pp. ix–xviii.

Editor. *The Inman Diary: A Public and Private Confession*, by Arthur Crew Inman. 2 vols. Cambridge, Mass.: Harvard University Press, 1985.

Rev. of *The Republic of Letters in America: The Correspondence of John Peale Bishop and Allen Tate*, ed. T. D. Young and J. J. Hindle. *Yearbook of English Studies*, 16 (1986), 350–352.

"*Stoner* and the 'College Novel.' " *Denver Quarterly*, 20 (1986), 107–113.

"Homage to Benjamin Franklin." *Bulletin of the American Academy of Sciences*, 49 (1986), 28–46.

Rev. of *Persons and Places: Fragments of an Autobiography*, by George Santayana. *George Santayana: A Biography*, by John McCormick. *New Republic* (May 18, 1987), 28–32.

"The Unholy City: A Sketch." In *American Letters and the Historical Consciousness: Essays in Honor of Lewis P. Simpson*, ed. J. G. Kennedy and D. M. Fogel. Baton Rouge: Louisiana State University Press, 1987, pp. 177–190.

Preface. *The Unwritten War: American Writers and the Civil War*. Rpt. Madison: University of Wisconsin Press, 1987, pp. xiii–xvi.

"The Great Diarist" [George Templeton Strong]. *American Heritage*, 39 (March 1988), 94–101.

Rev. of *The Life of Langston Hughes*, by Arnold Rampersad. *New Republic* (October 10, 1988), 34–38.

"The Legacy of Henry Wadsworth Longfellow." *Maine Historical Quarterly*, 27 (1988), 42–66.

"Whitman and the Founding Fathers." *Mickle Street Review*, 10 (1988), 5–12.

"Literary Scenes and Literary Movements." In *Columbia Literary History of the United States*, ed. Emory Elliott. New York: Columbia University Press, 1988, pp. 733–757.

"An Interview with Daniel Aaron on The Library of America." *South Central Review*, 5 (1988), 60–71.

Rev. of *Tobacco Culture: The Mentality of the Great Planters on the Eve of the Revolution*, by T. H. Breen. *London Review of Books*, January 19, 1989, p. 20.

Rev. of *The Selected Correspondence of Kenneth Burke and Malcolm Cowley, 1915–1989*, ed. Paul Jay. *New Republic* (March 13, 1989), 34–37.

Rev. of *All the Right Enemies: The Life and Murder of Carlo Tresca*, by Dorothy Gallagher. *New York Review of Books*, March 13, 1989, pp. 43–45.

Rev. of *Unseasonable Truths: The Life of Robert Maynard Hutchins*, by Harry S. Ashmore. *New Republic* (October 9, 1989), 32–36.

"A Memorial Gathering for Malcolm Cowley." *Horns of Plenty*, 2 (1989), 12–14.

"With a Light Brush." *American Heritage*, 40 (December 1989), 76.

1990s

"Another Immodest Proposal." In *America Seen from the Outside—Topics, Models, and Achievements of American Studies in the Federal Republic of Germany*, ed. Brigitte Georgi-Findlay and Heinz Ickstadt. Berlin: John F. Kennedy Institut für Nordamerikastudien Frei Universität Berlin, 1990, pp. 136–147.

Rev. of *Henry Adams*, by Ernest Samuels. *The Letters of Henry Adams*, ed. J. C. Levenson et al., 6 vols. *London Review of Books*, January 25, 1990, pp. 13–14.

" 'Strongly-Flavored Imitation': Henry Adams's *Education* Reviewed by John Jay Chapman." *New England Quarterly*, 63 (1990), 288–293.

"How to Read Don DeLillo." *South Atlantic Quarterly*, 89, no. 2 (Spring 1990), 305–319.

"American Studies and the Chinese State." *China Exchange News* (September 18, 1990), 4–17.

Rev. of *Theodore Dreiser: An American Journey, 1908–1945*, vol. 2, by Richard Lingeman. *New Republic* (November 12, 1990), pp. 34, 37, 40.

"Theodore Roosevelt as Cultural Artifact." *Raritan*, 9 (1990), 109–126.

"Two Boston Fugitives: Dana and Parkman." In *American Literature, Culture and Ideology: Essays in Memory of Henry Nash Smith*, ed. Beverly R. Valoshin. New York: Peter Lang, 1990, pp. 115–132.

Rev. of *Carl Sandburg: A Biography*, by Penelope Niven. *New Republic* (September 23, 1991), 46–49.

Rev. of *The Journals of John Cheever*, intro. Benjamin H. Cheever. *Boston Globe*, September 29, 1991, pp. 15, 18.

"George Santayana and the Genteel Tradition." In *Critical Essays on George Santayana*, ed. K. M. Price and R. C. Leitz, III. Boston: G. K. Hall, 1991, pp. 223–231.

Foreword. *1915, The Cultural Moment: The New Politics, the New Woman, the New Psychology, the New Art, and the New Theatre in America*, ed. Adele Heller and Lois Rudnick. New Brunswick, N.J.: Rutgers University Press, 1991.

Foreword. *Time and the Town: The Provincetown Chronicle*, by Mary Heaton Vorse, ed. Adele Heller. New Brunswick, N.J.: Rutgers University Press, 1991.

"On Ross Lockridge Jr.'s *Raintree County*." In *Classics of Civil War Fiction*, ed. David Madden and Peggy Bach. Jackson: University Press of Mississippi, 1991, pp. 204–214.

Rev. of *The Making of Middlebrow Culture*, by Joan Shelley Rubin. *New Republic* (July 6, 1992), 34–36.

"What Can You Learn from a Historical Novel?" *American Heritage*, 43 (October 1992), 55–66.

Rev. of *The American Religion: The Emergence of a Post-Christian Nation*, by Harold Bloom. *Raritan*, 12 (1992), 133–146.

Cincinnati, Queen City of the West, 1819–1838. Columbus: Ohio State University Press, 1992.

Intro. *The Song of Hiawatha*, by Henry Wadsworth Longfellow. Everyman's Library. London: J. M. Dent, 1992, pp. vii–xvii.

"Disturbers of the Peace: Radicals in Greenwich Village, 1920–1930." In *Greenwich Village: Culture and Counterculture*, ed. Rick Beard and Leslie Berlowitz. New Brunswick, N.J.: Rutgers University Press, 1993, pp. 229–242.

Rev. of *My Life as Author and Editor*, by H. L. Mencken, ed. Jonathan Yardley. *Washington Post Book World*, January 17, 1993.

INDEX

American Communist Party, 31;
Lenin's tomb, 35–36; on treason trials, 36; in the USSR, 30–36
Wilson, Woodrow, 21, 264, 273, 278
Wister, Owen, 266

Wolfe, Thomas, 125–126, 127
Wright, Richard, 73, 75, 80, 91–101
Writers on the Left (1961), xxv–xxvi, 1–2, 177–178